PENGUIN BOOKS

COLOUR BAR

Susan Williams is an historian and author of many books, most recently *Spies in the Congo: the Race for the Ore that Built the Atomic Bomb* (2016) and *Who Killed Hammarskjöld? The UN, the Cold War and White Supremacy in Africa* (2011), which triggered a new UN investigation in 2015 into the death of the Secretary General. She grew up in Zambia and has worked in Britain, Zimbabwe and Canada. She is a Senior Research Fellow at the Institute of Commonwealth Studies, School of Advanced Study, University of London.

SUSAN WILLIAMS

Colour Bar

*The Triumph of Seretse Khama
and his Nation*

PENGUIN BOOKS

PENGUIN BOOKS

UK | USA | Canada | Ireland | Australia
India | New Zealand | South Africa

Penguin Books is part of the Penguin Random House group of companies
whose addresses can be found at global.penguinrandomhouse.com

First published by Allen Lane 2006
Published in Penguin Books 2007
This edition published in 2016
009

Copyright © Susan Williams, 2006
Artwork © Pathé Productions Ltd, 2016
All rights reserved.

ISBN: 978-0-141-98570-1

www.greenpenguin.co.uk

For Gervase

Contents

III

Lies and Denials From Whitehall

IV

Exile

V

Colonial Freedom
'The Big Issue of This Century'

CONTENTS

List of Illustrations

Every effort has been made to contact all copyright holders. The publishers will be happy to make good in future editions any errors or omissions brought to their attention.

Acknowledgements

This book is based on a mass of evidence, in a number of countries. I could not possibly have carried out such extensive research without the assistance of many people and institutions.

First and foremost, I should like to thank the family of Sir Seretse and Lady Ruth Khama for their support and help. Before starting work, I went to Botswana to seek the approval of Sir Seretse and Lady Ruth's children: Vice-President Lt General Seretse Khama Ian Khama, Jacqueline Khama, Tshekedi Khama and Anthony Khama. They were kind enough to give me their approval. They have also given me valuable help with my research and allowed me privileged access to private family papers and photographs. Vice-President Ian Khama set up key meetings for me with important witnesses in different parts of Botswana. Former President Sir Ketumile Masire was kind enough to spare some of his valuable time to discuss the legacy of Sir Seretse Khama.

I am indebted beyond measure to Jackie Khama. She has taken an active role in the research, giving me vital information. She also read every draft of every chapter, with care and insight, offering comments and suggestions that have been indispensable.

Naledi Khama, Sir Seretse Khama's sister, granted me long interviews. She also took my husband and me on a tour of Serowe and I shall never forget my excitement as we drove up to the gate of the house in which Seretse and Ruth made their first home in Africa. Muriel Sanderson, Lady Khama's sister, was very welcoming and was generous with her time and her memories. Goareng Mosinyi enriched my understanding of the situation in Botswana in the 1950s.

Vice-President Khama put me in touch with Charles Njonjo in

Kenya, Seretse's close friend from their years at school, who gave me several fascinating interviews and also allowed me to telephone him in Nairobi with queries. Vice-President Khama also enabled me to speak to family relatives and friends in the UK, including Ruth's cousin John Goode and his wife Esme, with whom I spent a delightful afternoon. Another wonderful contact and a new friend was Betty Thornton, Ruth's friend at the start of her marriage.

I am grateful to Tony Benn not only for his recollections of many years of friendship with Seretse and Ruth, but also for his kindness. For most of this book, the writing went ahead smoothly. But I had one horrible block – when I was totally confused by the different strands of attitudes on the Left to British colonialism in the 1950s. I explained this to Tony Benn, who carefully and clearly unpicked it all for me until I understood.

Clement Freud, another friend of the Khama family, was kind enough to share his memories of Seretse and Ruth in the 1950s. The Hon. Gerard Noel recalled his friendship with Seretse Khama in the late 1940s at the Inns of Court.

Several members of the UK Botswana Society have shared their recollections. Alan and Juni Tilbury helped me to understand the difficulties faced by Botswana's new government in 1966, which are analysed in *Botswana: The Road to Independence* (2000), by Peter Fawcus and Alan Tilbury. I am also grateful to George Winstanley for kindly sending me *Under Two Flags in Africa. Recollections of a British Administrator in Bechuanaland and Botswana* (2000).

For a study of this nature, I was dependent on archives and libraries. I am grateful to the government of Botswana for granting me a Research Permit and I should like to acknowledge the assistance of archive repositories in Botswana, South Africa, the UK, the USA, and Canada.

In Botswana, I was given valuable assistance by the Botswana National Archives and Records Services in Gaborone and should like to thank the director, Kelebogile Kgabi, Rre Gilbert Mpolokeng, and Kebafentse Modise. I am grateful to Maria Tali at the SADC Secretariat Library in Gaborone, who went out of her way to help me with an important document.

At the Khama III Memorial Museum in Serowe, I was given expert

assistance with the archive collection by Scobie Lekhutile, the curator, and by Gase Kediseng and Kelly Golekwang. Scobie was kind enough to share with me his reflections on Botswana's history and his memories of Nelson Mandela's visit to Serowe in 1995. The Phuthadikobo Museum in Mochudi enriched my understanding of Botswana's history. I am grateful to Sandy and Elinah Grant for taking me round the exhibitions and for helping me with my research.

The staff at the National Archives of South Africa in Pretoria were most helpful and I was able to benefit from the opening of many relevant files since the ending of apartheid in 1994. Where I was unable to complete my research in South Africa itself, Zabeth Botha followed up my inquiries with great efficiency. At the University of the Witwatersrand in Johannesburg, I am indebted to two archivists in particular: Michele Pickover at the William Cullen Library; and Marius Coetzee at the Central Records Office.

I am deeply indebted to Verne Harris and Anthea Josias at the Nelson Mandela Centre of Memory and Commemoration Project in Johannesburg. Verne and Anthea responded to my endless inquiries with a high level of expertise, as well as genuine interest. They helped me to find a number of key documents in different repositories in South Africa, including one that had eluded me for two years. The Centre of Memory was launched in September 2004 to document Mandela's life and promote his legacy. It seems to me to represent all that is best in an archive repository and its approach is wholly original. Because materials documenting Mr Mandela's life and work are fragmentary and scattered, both geographically and institutionally, the Centre is pulling them together in different ways to create a priceless resource for the world. It is also finding new and exciting ways to take the archive out to the people of South Africa and beyond, not restricting it to academics and to people who are able to visit the institution. The Centre's materials – and the Centre itself – tell the story of a continuing walk to freedom, in the context of the broader struggles for justice in South Africa.

In the UK, the Royal Archives at Windsor Castle enabled me to see relevant pages of Queen Victoria's Journal. I am grateful to Her Majesty Queen Elizabeth II for permission to make use of these papers.

I have examined well over 1,000 files at The National Archives in the UK. Studying them took many long months of hard work and I was fortunate to have the expert help of Mandy Banton. Many key files were still closed or retained when I started my research, but Penny Prior at the Foreign and Commonwealth Office facilitated the opening of these files with prompt efficiency.

Lucy McCann, at Rhodes House Library, University of Oxford, was unstinting in her assistance and I always enjoyed the restful space of Rhodes House. Anna Sander of Balliol College unearthed valuable information about Seretse Khama's student days at Oxford. I was also helped in Oxford by Janet McMullin of Christ Church College, and by the staff in the Modern Papers and John Johnson Reading Room at the Bodleian Library.

At the University of London, I am indebted to the archives and library of the Institute of Commonwealth Studies, especially to Ian Cooke, and to the staff of the library and archives at the School of Oriental and African Studies. Clare Rider, the archivist at the Inner Temple, gave me valuable time and information.

Darren Treadwell of the Labour History Archive and Study Centre, at the John Rylands University Library of Manchester, discovered some important documents. I am also indebted to the staff at the University of Sussex Special Collections; to Pearl Romans at the University of Southampton; to Ieuan Hopkins and Ruth Hammond at the Churchill Archives Centre at Churchill College, Cambridge; to the staff at Durham University Library; to John McAleer at the British Empire and Commonwealth Museum in Bristol; and to Jim Davies at the British Airways Archive and Museum.

The staff of the British Library in London are efficient and courteous and I am indebted in particular to the staff of Humanities 2 and of the newspaper collection at Colindale. I am also grateful to the London Library for its excellent collection and its forbearing attitude towards long-term borrowing.

In the USA, staff at the National Archives and Records Administration in Washington DC were very helpful, notably Michael Hussey. I am grateful to Greg Murphy for follow-up research at NARA and also to Cliff Callahan for his work at the Library of Congress. Many archivists in the USA assisted me well beyond the call of duty: Joan R. Duffy at Yale Divinity School Library; Michael Roudette at the

Schomburg Center for Research in Black Culture, New York Public Library; and Nicolette A. Schneider at the Special Collections Research Center, Syracuse University Library, New York.

At the National Archives of Canada in Ottawa, Peter Stockdale followed up my inquiries with care and genuine interest.

I should like to acknowledge a debt to key books, especially *Seretse Khama*, by Thomas Tlou, Neil Parsons and Willie Henderson (1995), which is the definitive biography. Two other invaluable books for my research were Gasebalwe Seretse's *Tshekedi Khama: The Master Whose Dogs Barked At. (A Critical Look at Ngwato Politics)* (2004) and Michael Dutfield's *A Marriage of Inconvenience. The Persecution of Seretse and Ruth Khama* (1990).

Newsreels have been a unique source of information and I have been given expert help by Luke McKernan, Head of Information at the British Universities Film and Video Council.

I am fortunate to have an academic 'home' at the Institute of Commonwealth Studies in the School of Advanced Study, University of London. Tim Shaw, the director, has created a stimulating and supportive environment in which scholars thrive, and which has been ideal for writing this book. Robert Holland has helped in various ways and I enjoyed presenting a paper relating to this book in his Commonwealth History seminar series, which generated valuable feedback.

At the University of Botswana, I should like to thank Peter Sebina, who has been a source of invaluable and inestimable advice and information. Neil Parsons has been generous and helpful with his vast fund of knowledge.

It has been an immense pleasure, and very stimulating, to discuss aspects of this book with Pam Ditchburn, Lesley Hall, Mungai Lenneiye, Gugu Mahlangu and Myfanwy Williams.

Margaret Hood, Ann Oakley, James Sanders and James Thomas contributed in various ways. Michelle Millar carried out some difficult research for me with flair, imagination and persistence. Vivien Burgess did some last-minute research with great efficiency. Janet Tyrrell is a thorough and thoughtful copy-editor, who is unruffled under pressure. Many other people helped me with their constructive interest: Richard Aldrich, Melissa Cinque, Dennis Dean, Theresa Hallgarten, Raymond Harris, Roger Hewitt, Jackie Lee, Tina Perry, Kate Philbrick, Clea

Relly, Desna Roberts, Robert Smith, Sandra Stone, David Thomas, James Williams, Joan Williams, and Margaret Wynn.

Reading a book in draft is a time-consuming and arduous task and I am more than grateful to the people who did this for me. Jackie Khama and Gervase Hood read several drafts of the book, including the first – and very long – one, offering important suggestions. Richard Aldrich, Dennis Dean, Jackie Lee, Mungai Lenneiye, Peter Sebina, and Myfanwy Williams read the penultimate draft and gave me invaluable criticism and comments.

This book is the outcome of a genuine collaboration with my editor, Margaret Bluman, which transformed the proposal and the various drafts into the final product. Margaret has the remarkable gift of seeing what a book is – and what it is about – before I know myself. It is a privilege for me to write with her.

I have had unfailing support from my lovely aunt, Monica Ede. Benedict Wiseman has shown real interest and assisted me with the baffling cricket terms which were so favoured by colonial officials. My daughter Tendayi Bloom has given me many original and lively insights in our wonderful conversations, as well as loyal encouragement. Gervase Hood, my husband and my partner in everything, has been at my side at every stage of writing the book and has made important contributions. For that reason, the book is dedicated to him.

Note on Language

Any book about a British colony in Africa in the days of Empire needs to engage with problems of language. The British favoured the words 'tribe' and 'chief', which have pejorative overtones and seldom convey the right meaning. The narrative of this book uses the word 'nation' or 'people' rather than 'tribe', and the Setswana word 'kgosi' (plural 'dikgosi') or the English word 'king' rather than 'chief'. To refer to Seretse Khama's people in the Bechuanaland Protectorate, the British used the form 'Bamangwato'. This book uses the more correct 'Bangwato'. It also uses Lobatse and Mafikeng, which are the current names for these towns (different spellings – 'Lobatsi' and 'Mafeking' – were used by the British Administration in the colonial era).

However, all quotations from primary documents retain their original form and the colonial language is employed in the narrative where this is appropriate to the discussion.

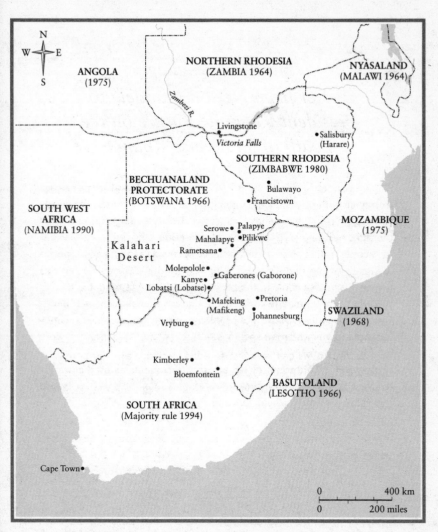

Bechuanaland Protectorate and neighbouring countries in the 1950s
(showing dates of independence and post-independence names)

Prologue
Letter from Nelson Mandela to President Ketumile Masire on the death of Sir Seretse Khama

Robben Island.

My President,
  The African National Congress of South Africa
must have sent you a message of condolence on the
death of Sir Seretse Khama, a message which
expressed the sympathies of all our members
inside and outside prison. Nevertheless I
consider it proper to add a personal message
because of the fine rapport he and I struck in
our days at Wits, and the admiration and esteem
in which I have always held him since then. Due
to my current circumstances, however, this
message could not reach you earlier than now.
  Sir Seretse was an able and widely respected
leader and his death was not only a loss to his
family and people, but to Africa as a whole. As
the first President of the independent Republic
of Botswana his memory will long be illumined by
the devotion and skill with which he served his
country and people and by the statesmanship he
evinced in world affairs. Under his leadership
the contribution of Botswana to the Organisation
of African Unity and the Front Line States has
been invaluable. Without that contribution the
major problems of Southern Africa would have been
far more difficult to solve.

To the people of South Africa independent Botswana has become another home which provides a haven for those who flee from political persecution. Its tragedies are our tragedies. It is for this reason that Sir Seretse's death has affected us in a special way, and it is because of this that we miss him so much. It is also in this spirit that we send our condolences to Lady Khama and family, and to the Government and people of Botswana.

Fortunately, Botswana is rich in men of talent and vision who are capable of closing the gap Sir Seretse left behind, and his mantle has now fallen on the shoulders of an equally able and respected man. In giving you my warmest congratulations on your honour, I would like to add that you enjoy our good wishes for the best of health and success in assuring continually rising living standards among the people.

It is remarkable to find that in Africa, as in other colonies on this continent, men who had no previous experience whatsoever in government as it functions today should be able to run modern states with such success and to curb, and even eliminate altogether, some of the evils of Colonialism so soon after gaining independence. The data that is available to us in our circumstances indicates that inspiring progress in Africa is being made. I am happy to note that this trend is particularly evident in your country, and that you can now look forward to a future of prosperity and happiness.

In conclusion I wish to repeat the statement I have made above that Botswana is to us another home. Long before the political conflicts that have rocked South Africa since the early sixties, and before the exodus of persecuted people from

our country began, the Batswana and the oppressed
majority at home were already bound together by
strong historical ties. These conflicts have
considerably strengthened those ties, and the
knowledge that we enjoy the solid support and
good will of the people of Botswana is a source
of tremendous inspiration in our struggle to
remove the evils of minority rule. My fondest
regards to your government and your people and
family. Pula!!!

Nelson Mandela
[July 1980]

Reproduced by kind permission of the Office of Mr Nelson Mandela
and of the University of Fort Hare Library (Source: Oliver Tambo
Papers, African National Congress Archives, University of Fort Hare
Library).

I

The House of Khama

I

From Africa to wartorn Britain

In September 1945, a 24-year-old student called Seretse Khama arrived in England from his home in British colonial Africa. Victory in Japan had been celebrated the month before and Britain was at last emerging from the trauma of the Second World War. But the aftermath of the conflict was visible everywhere, in the pinched faces of the people and the rubble of bombed-out buildings. Everything looked grey and drab. It was a very different country from his own: the British Protectorate of Bechuanaland, 6,000 miles away in southern Africa. At home, dry scrubland stretched out far into the distance and the sun blazed hot in a blue sky.

Seretse had come to study law at Oxford University. Tall and long-legged, with a strong build and genial good looks, he was the heir to the kingship of the Bangwato, the largest nation in Bechuanaland. His uncle, Tshekedi Khama, who was ruling the Bangwato as Regent, was grooming him carefully for his future role as Kgosi and had long been interested in the idea of Seretse studying law in Britain; European law, he thought, would help him to deal from a position of strength with the colonial administration.[1] He also wanted to remove Seretse from the racial segregation and inequalities of southern Africa, which had made his nephew bitter. 'I had adopted certain attitudes towards a certain race, if I may put it that way, and that is the white race,' said Seretse years later. 'I disliked them intensely because I thought that they disliked me. I suppose some of them did.' All whites seemed to him cruel and unjust and he had 'just no trust at all for any white man,' he told his uncle. 'Well,' replied Tshekedi, 'that is all the more reason why you should go to the United Kingdom to continue your studies.'[2]

3

Seretse was already extremely well educated. He had attended the premier schools for Africans in South Africa: Adams College, a mission school near Durban; the missionary-run Lovedale College in Alice, in the Eastern Cape; and Tiger Kloof in Vryburg, which was not very far from the Bechuanaland border and was run by the London Missionary Society. At all these schools he distinguished himself as a scholar and an individual. After secondary school he went to Fort Hare Native University, near Lovedale in Alice, which was the only black university in South Africa. Here he took courses in Native Law, Native Administration, Roman-Dutch Law, History, English and Setswana, and obtained his BA degree in 1944. These years at Fort Hare were inspiring ones. The University was the focus for the intellectual elite of black South Africans and was 'a beacon for African scholars all over Southern, Central and Eastern Africa,' wrote Nelson Mandela, who also studied at Fort Hare. It educated many of the future leaders on the African continent – not just Seretse and Mandela, but also Oliver Tambo, Julius Nyerere, Kenneth Kaunda, Herbert Chitepo, Desmond Tutu, Robert Mugabe and many others.[3] Debates about social injustice and the future of the region were recurrent and urgent.

After Fort Hare, Seretse registered for a law degree at the University of Witwatersrand in Johannesburg.[4] Here he grew to know Mandela, who was also studying law, who later referred to 'the fine rapport he and I struck in our days at Wits, and the admiration and esteem in which I have always held him since then'.[5] Seretse also became a very good friend of Joshua Nkomo, who was not a student at Wits but was staying at one of the university hostels.[6] Seretse, Mandela and Nkomo frequented the Blue Lagoon restaurant in Johannesburg, where they mixed with other Fort Hare graduates, including Oliver Tambo.[7]

Being a student at Wits was difficult and unpleasant in many ways. There was only a handful of black students, who were not allowed to use the sports field, tennis courts or swimming pool, and were treated with contempt by some of the white lecturers. Mandela recorded many humiliations – when he sat at a table in the law library, a white student moved away; and when he went to a café with some white students, they were kept out because a 'kaffir' was among them.[8] But, added Mandela, he also met students such as Joe Slovo and Ruth First and was introduced to stimulating new ideas about the future of southern Africa:

Wits opened a new world to me, a world of ideas and political beliefs and debates, a world where people were passionate about politics. I was among white and Indian intellectuals of my own generation, young men who would form the vanguard of the most important political movements of the next few years. I discovered for the first time people of my own age firmly aligned with the liberation struggle, who were prepared, despite their relative privilege, to sacrifice themselves for the cause of the oppressed.[9]

But whereas Mandela stayed at Wits to complete his course, Seretse left Africa for Britain after less than a year. In the chill of the British autumn, he went up to Oxford for the start of the Michaelmas term and became a student at Balliol College. His initial plan of study included both Law and a combined course of Politics and Economics: he would take examinations in both, which would add up to an Oxford BA.[10] He made an excellent first impression on his academic adviser, Sir Reginald Coupland, the Beit Professor of Colonial History. 'I have seen Seretse Khama,' wrote Coupland soon after the young student's arrival. 'What a very good sort he is!'[11]

But Seretse had trouble settling in. The British students showed no interest in getting to know him and there were hardly any students from Africa. In 1945 there were about 750 students from Africa in the UK, but most of them were at the Universities of Edinburgh (where Julius Nyerere was a student of history), Aberdeen and London, or at the Inns of Court in London.[12] 'I was miserable the first term,' recalled Seretse later. 'I thought I was intensely disliked because nobody talked to me or showed any interest in me and I thought it was just another way of showing me that I did not belong.'[13] This isolation was especially painful because he had always been popular with his peers – at Fort Hare, he had been regarded as likeable and unassuming, even though he was one of the most prominent royals. 'He was not posing himself as if he was going to be king,' commented one student. 'He was just part of the student body; that is one of the things I liked about him. He never put his personality above anybody else.'[14]

Seretse felt, too, that in Britain he was always identified by his colour: that people did not see him as a student from Bechuanaland, but as a 'coloured' man or 'negro'.[15] It was usually assumed by the British public that he was American or West Indian. But he had very little in common with American GIs or with West Indians who had come to the UK to find work, apart from the colour of his skin. His family background and his experience were those of a crown prince, who had been marked out for privilege since the day of his birth.

The number of black people in Britain in the early postwar years was tiny – less than 0.02 per cent of the population, who mostly lived in London or the major port cities of Liverpool, Bristol and Cardiff.[16] There was no official colour bar, but black people in Britain were routinely refused employment and accommodation. They also encountered colour prejudice in their everyday contacts with the general public, on public transport, and in restaurants. One Nigerian student noticed that

in trains, if I enter a coach first, very few people will enter the coach if they can find room in another. In cafes very few like to sit beside a coloured person unless personally known to them. In picture houses some people asked what I was doing there as they were sure I should not understand the picture.

Colonial students from Asian and Mediterranean backgrounds also suffered from the colour bar. One Indian student from Kenya complained that when he was travelling on the underground with an English girl, two men shouted, 'These bloody foreigners, they come here and spoil our girls.' Another Indian from East Africa observed the way in which colour prejudice was learned –

It is taught to children, it is bred in them, but it is not natural to them. I was in hospital to have my tonsils removed, and there were no beds, so I was put in the children's ward; one of them said to me: 'Tell me mister, have you been out in the sunshine long?'[17]

'Yes, there are penalties if one has a coloured skin, and hardly a day goes by without one being reminded of them,' observed Learie Constantine, the legendary cricketer from Trinidad, who had moved to Britain in 1929 and who had been employed as a welfare officer to care for West Indians arriving for work. In 1944, Constantine had sued Imperial Hotels in London for refusing him accommodation, and successfully established a case of discrimination.[18] 'Is there a Colour Bar?' asked the illustrated British weekly, *Picture Post*. The answer to this question, it argued, was a resounding *yes*. It reported the case of a man in Liverpool who had lived in five European countries and had been a British prisoner-of-war in Germany, but who knew of no European country where the 'coloured' man was treated with more unofficial contempt than in Britain, from restaurant-keepers and landladies, employers and employees, even from the man in the street.[19]

The issue of the colour bar had been spotlighted by the arrival in Britain of American servicemen. By the end of 1942 there were about 170,000 American men, of whom about 12,000 were black and rigidly segregated. White American troops became angry if they found black soldiers in places of entertainment, especially if they were with white women. Under pressure from American command, the British Secretary of State for War asked the Cabinet to approve a policy of educating the army to adopt the attitude of the US authorities towards black American troops. But some members of the Cabinet strongly resisted this plan. It was agreed that personnel should respect the American attitude, but not adopt it – that there could be no question of segregation in Britain.[20]

Within the British services, the colour bar became less oppressive during the years of war. The army changed its rules so that men who were 'not of pure European descent' were allowed to hold commissions as officers.[21] There was also a sense that everyone was fighting the same enemy, which created a feeling of camaraderie between blacks and whites. But this did not transfer to civilian life once peace had been restored.[22]

Men had come from every part of the Empire to fight for the Allies in Europe and the Far East. Among them were 10,000 men from Seretse's own country, the Bechuanaland Protectorate, who had served in the African Auxiliary Pioneer Corps.[23] Seretse watched the victory parade in London in 1946, when some of the Bechuanaland veterans marched down the city streets.[24] They were loudly cheered by the British spectators, but instantly forgotten. Seretse thought it was odd that British people, who were so proud of their Empire, appeared never to have heard of Bechuanaland and were unaware of its contribution to the war.[25] He was angry that men who had been seen as equal in war and death, were no longer seen as equal in the postwar political and economic life of the colonies. This feeling was shared in British colonies across Africa and was a contributing factor in the outbreak of the riots that rocked the cities of the Gold Coast in February 1948 and in the Mau Mau uprising in Kenya in the early 1950s.[26]

One of the Protectorate veterans who spoke to Seretse at the victory parade noticed that he 'did not seem taken up with the English. He said to me: "The English like to show you their nice side but they hide their poverty and slums." '[27] What could not be hidden, though, was the austerity of daily life and the rationing of food and clothes – even bread rationing was introduced for the first time by the Ministry of Food in July 1946.[28] 'I am still feeling awfully homesick,' wrote Seretse to his uncle. 'Perhaps that is one reason beside [the] food shortage that I am losing weight so rapidly.'[29] Some people in England tried to be friendly, including members of the London Missionary Society, the Congregationalist organization which dominated the religious life of the Bangwato Reserve. Dr Roger Pilkington, one of the LMS directors, who had a doctorate in genetics from Magdalene College, Cambridge, took a special interest in Seretse and invited him on several occasions to stay with himself and his wife. But Seretse was lonely.

In his second term at Balliol, Seretse started to feel happier. He struck up a friendship with John Zimmerman, another Balliol student who, like Seretse, was an outsider, because he was Jewish.[30] Seretse also found acceptance on the sports field. He was an outstanding sportsman and a strong team player, characteristics which had distinguished his school and university career in South Africa and earned him such nicknames on the soccer field as 'Small Hops', 'Machine Gun', 'Flexible Six Forty-Five' and 'C to C' (Cape to Cairo).[31] Now these gifts made him an asset to his Oxford College. 'For some reason,' he wrote years later, 'somebody asked me if I played rugby in South Africa, and I said yes. I was picked to practise. I then played for my college; then I boxed for my college.'[32] He was 'an unstoppable wing three quarter' for the college rugby XV, commented a rugby enthusiast at Balliol.[33] Seretse was now starting to fit into College life. 'We liked him as a person,' observed the Master of the College – 'he was a very acceptable member of the College, and he worked well.'[34]

While studying at Oxford, Seretse enrolled in the Inner Temple in London, as part of his plan to study for the Bar.[35] He was determined to become a barrister – Bechuanaland did not have a single law professional and badly needed lawyers. His uncle Tshekedi relied on a white advocate in Cape Town, Douglas Buchanan. Tshekedi himself had been studying law at Fort Hare when he was recalled to Bechuanaland in 1926 to take up the role of Regent. But Seretse's plans came up against an unexpected obstacle in the spring of 1946. Just before the end of his first year at Oxford, he was informed that he was not eligible to sit the law examinations, because he had not qualified in Latin. Before coming to Oxford, he had been assured that a course he had taken at Wits in Roman-Dutch Law was an adequate substitute. But now he was told that the exemption was only valid if he had done military service. He was compelled to give up Law, which meant that he could only be examined in Politics and Economics. He now attached more importance to his studies for the Bar. 'I know that Oxford has got a very big name,' he acknowledged to his uncle. But this name would not help him, he objected with some vigour, 'if I cannot do what I have come here for – to study adequately'.[36]

Seretse spent the summer of 1946 in Northumberland, working as a volunteer on a dairy farm. This healed some of his homesickness: land and animals were at the centre of Bechuanaland life. Seretse was the heir to many thousands of cattle and he was keen to learn about different methods of farming. 'He is getting up at five and works hard,' noted Pilkington with approval.[37]

After the summer, Seretse went back to Balliol. But by the spring of 1947 he was feeling frustrated by the obstacles put in his way by the university. He decided to leave Oxford and to focus his energies instead on the Bar exams at the Inner Temple. Pressure was put on him to stay by members of the University. 'There are social and intellectual advantages in college life at Oxford,' maintained Sir Reginald Coupland, 'which cannot be obtained in the scattered world of London.'[38] But he had come to England to study law, argued Seretse, not simply for the adventure of being an Oxford undergraduate. By now, he had now completed five terms at Oxford – nearly two years.[39] It was time to go to London.

*

Seretse's new home in London was Nutford House, a hostel for colonial students run by the Colonial Office, not far from Marble Arch in the West End.[40] A squat grey brick building, it had none of the splendour of his Oxford College – its little urban garden was the size of a handkerchief in comparison with the Balliol gardens. But after Oxford, Nutford House was a haven. As soon as he crossed the threshold, he met other young men from Africa and from colonies all over the Empire. These included Abubakar Tafawa Balewa, later the first Prime Minister of the Federation of Nigeria; Veerasamy Ringadoo, the first President of Mauritius; Forbes Burnham, later the President of Guyana; and Milton Cato, the first Prime Minister of St Vincent.[41]

One of the residents of Nutford House was his old friend Charles Njonjo, a Kenyan who had been with him at Fort Hare and who was now enrolled as a student at the Middle Temple. The two young men had rooms next to each other and spent their spare time together. Twice a week they cooked for themselves, with two young men from India, which gave Seretse a lifelong taste for curry. Tshekedi was not very generous with Seretse's allowance, but when money did arrive from Bechuanaland, the four men promptly went out to an Indian restaurant.[42] Seretse and Charles were often invited to the north London home of John Zimmerman, Seretse's friend from Balliol. John's mother cooked hearty meals for them and her motherly warmth was a welcome contrast with the cold stares of people on the street.[43]

Another close friend at Nutford House was Harry Nkumbula from Northern Rhodesia (Zambia), a 'thickset, very forceful'[44] man who was studying Economics at the London School of Economics and was later to play an important role in his country's politics. Seretse also got to know people from the colonies who were not students, such as Dr Hastings Banda from Nyasaland (Malawi), who was practising medicine in Willesden in London and was later to become the first President of his country.[45] Banda and Nkumbula worked together in 1949 to produce an important document criticizing the plan of the Attlee government to create a Federation of Southern Rhodesia, Northern Rhodesia and Nyasaland. This plan was bitterly opposed by the African populations because it would extend the inequalities and colour bar of Southern Rhodesia throughout the region.[46]

The Inner Temple was an elite institution reminiscent of Oxford, but it was in the heart of London and just moments from the lively, metropolitan atmosphere of Fleet Street. Seretse often relaxed with fellow students at a pub called 'The Feathers' and was popular with everyone.[47] He felt less of an alien here than at Oxford: a quarter of the African students in the UK were studying Law and many were at the Inns of Court in London.[48] A number of them would take a leading role in the politics of their own countries in future years, including Charles Njonjo, who would later become the first Attorney General in independent Kenya. Joe Appiah, who was a student at the Middle Temple, was a member of a family of Ashanti Kings from the Gold Coast (Ghana) and had already begun a long career as a political activist. A short, slight man with thick spectacles, he had a sharp legal mind and a gregarious personality[49] and he and Seretse very quickly struck up a friendship.

Appiah had been offered a place at Cambridge University, but he chose not to go because he felt 'magnetized' by the excitement of African political activities in London.[50] As far back as the mid-1930s, noted the Trinidadian writer C. L. R. James, there had been a collection of notable black people in London – Paul Robeson, the American actor and singer; Jomo Kenyatta, the Kenyan activist who spent sixteen years in Britain and was to become the first President of independent Kenya; George Padmore, a Trinidadian who was a key figure in the African nationalist movement; and Amy Garvey, an African American activist who was the widow of Marcus Garvey. 'Some of us,' wrote C. L. R. James, 'were becoming active politically, but not on the question of race – on the question of independence for the colonies.'[51] There were a number of students from West Africa in the UK between the wars, who in 1925 set up the West African Students Union at Camden Square in North London. In 1935, the patron of WASU was Paul Robeson. WASU provided hostel amenities for students and was a lively centre for discussions about the future of Africa.[52] In 1942, WASU demanded immediate internal self-government for Britain's West African colonies and complete independence in five years.[53] Joe Appiah was an active member, becoming Vice-President and then President in the late 1940s.[54]

The issue of self-government seemed even more pressing after the Second World War. 'We have fought against fascism, the enemy of mankind,' wrote a soldier from the Gold Coast who had fought in Burma, 'so that all people, white or black, civilised or uncivilised, free or in bondage, may have the right to enjoy the privileges and bounties of nature.'[55] There was widespread faith in the Atlantic Charter signed by Roosevelt and Churchill in 1941, which had referred to the right of all peoples to choose the form of government under which they would live. The independence of India and Pakistan in 1947 seemed to be consistent with these developments. For the generation that had fought the war – in Britain and her Empire – there was a sense of hope that it really was possible to make the world a better place.

Britain after the war was directly responsible for fourteen African states, with a total population of 56 million. For African students in London, at the political heart of the Empire, the idea that it was now time for change was reinforced by the election of the Labour Party in July 1945. Key members of the Fabian Colonial Bureau, who had made clear their sympathy with colonial aspirations, were now in power.[56] But WASU and other organizations of African students were quickly disappointed by the failure of the Labour government to deliver on its promises. 'I am not prepared to sacrifice the British Empire,' announced Aneurin Bevan to the House of Commons in February 1946, 'because I know that if the British Empire fell it would mean the standard of life of our own constituents would fall considerably.'[57]

Just months before Seretse's arrival in the UK, Kwame Nkrumah – later the first President of Ghana – registered for a PhD at London University and was admitted as a student by Gray's Inn. Now in his mid-thirties, he had studied for many years in the USA, where he had been heavily involved in African-American politics. Once in London, he joined WASU and, along with Amy Garvey and W. E. B. Du Bois, the African-American political activist, worked to organize the Fifth Pan-African Congress in Manchester in October 1945. This Congress passed resolutions demanding the end of the colour bar in Britain and independence for colonial nations: 'We affirm the right of all colonial peoples to control their own destiny. All colonies must be free from foreign imperialist control, whether political or economic.'[58]

At a meeting of the Congress addressed by the Lord Mayor of Manchester, the hall was decorated with the flags of Haiti, Liberia and Ethiopia and a map of Africa.[59] Among the delegates at the Congress were Hastings Banda and Jomo Kenyatta. 'One thing we must do,' asserted Kenyatta at the end of his speech,

is to get political independence. If we achieve that we shall be free to achieve other things we want. We feel that racial discrimination must go, and then people can perhaps enjoy the right of citizenship, which is the desire of every East African. Self-government must be our aim.[60]

Nkrumah later commented that the Pan-African Congress marked the turning point in Pan-Africanism from a passive to an active stage and 'brought about the awakening of African political consciousness. It became, in fact, a mass movement of Africa for the Africans.'[61]

Although Seretse Khama was in Oxford during the Pan-African Congress, it is likely that he knew of its existence and, indeed, of its importance. But even if the Congress in Manchester in 1945 *had* passed him by, he would have been exposed to its aims and ideas when he moved to London, through his friendships with African students at Nutford House and the Inns of Court, and with men like Dr Banda. 'By this time,' wrote Nkrumah in his autobiography, 'the political conscience of African students was aroused, particularly in London, and whenever they met they talked of little else but nationalist politics and the colonial liberation movements.'[62] Seretse belonged to a unique generation of young Africans, who were destined to lead their countries to freedom from imperialism and the prejudice of race. Some of these future leaders had been his fellow students and friends at Fort Hare and Wits – and some of them were his new friends in London.

2

Love match

One evening in June 1947, after a dinner dance at Nutford House in London, Seretse rushed off to find Charles Njonjo. In great excitement, he announced to his friend that he had fallen in love – 'I met a girl, and I think you should meet her!' Then he added, 'Somebody I should like to be my wife.' Charles was astonished. As he recalled years later, it was not like Seretse to make dramatic remarks for the sake of effect: clearly, this was serious.[1]

The young woman Seretse had met was called Ruth Williams. She had been a guest at an event arranged for the students – a reception by the warden, followed by a formal dinner and then a dance. She had been brought by her elder sister Muriel, who was a Congregationalist associated with the London Missionary Society, which helped to organize social activities for African students. Muriel had been looking forward to introducing Ruth to Seretse, because she expected them to have a lot in common: they both had a lively sense of humour and liked listening to jazz.[2] However, Ruth did not take any particular notice of Seretse. 'I saw a tall, well-built, smiling African with wonderful teeth, broad shoulders, and perfect manners,' she said later. 'I must confess that at this first meeting he seemed as alike to me as half a dozen other African students my sister introduced me to that night.'[3]

But Seretse was immediately attracted to Ruth.[4] Twenty-three years old, Ruth Williams was not so much beautiful, as attractive and elegant: when she walked down the street, heads turned. Slim and fit, she had a slight, almost bony, frame. Her strawberry-blonde hair highlighted her clear complexion, which was pale and freckled. Her eyes were unusual: although both eyes looked green at first glance, one of them was half green and half brown. Brought up in London, she worked as a confidential clerk in the City, in the foreign claims department of a big firm of Lloyd's underwriters. Although she came from an ordinary middle-class family, she belonged to a new generation of capable young women, who had seen active service during the war and had modern, fresh ideas.

Some days later, Ruth returned to Nutford House with Muriel. Seretse had been longing to see her again and he was delighted when she stopped to chat with him. Then she started to visit on a regular basis. There were very strict rules at Nutford House about women visitors, who were only allowed to enter a few of the public rooms, much to the annoyance of some students.[5] But Seretse and Ruth were perfectly happy sitting together in the lounge or garden, getting to know each other better. It was at least three months, recalled Seretse later, 'before I dared ask Ruth for a date, but even then I did not know how she would react to my suggestion'. He had bought two tickets for a concert in London's West End, to see the Ink Spots, a jazz and blues group of black Americans.[6] But he felt very nervous about asking her out. One day in August 1947, said Ruth,

> Seretse phoned me in my office. 'Would you do me a great honour tonight?' he asked.
>
> 'Certainly if I can,' I replied gaily – by this time I had really got to like him – 'and what is this great honour, sir?'
>
> Seretse answered quickly – 'I have two tickets for the Inkspots . . . I'll . . . I'll get three if you'd like your sister to come along with us.'
>
> 'I'd love to come – without my sister,' I said.
>
> So we went to the Inkspots. That was our first outing.[7]

After this first date, Seretse and Ruth found themselves spending more and more time together. He told her about life in Bechuanaland and she talked about the years of war. Gradually, their friendship blossomed and they became a couple. Ruth watched Seretse play football, but drew the line at boxing matches, which she thought were brutal; he came with her to the ice-rink, though found it impossible to like skating. They soon had their own favourite coffee shop, and when Seretse passed an exam he immediately called Ruth to tell her.[8] He was working hard at his studies for the Bar and she was proud of his success: by the end of 1947, he had passed the Law of Torts, the

Law of Contracts, Roman-Dutch Law and Roman Law and was planning to take his final examinations the following year in Constitutional Law and Criminal Law.[9]

But their growing pleasure in each other was marred by anxiety, because Ruth was concealing from her parents the fact that she was going out with an African. Her father, she knew, took a dim view of black and white people mixing together; when Muriel had started her work with African students, he said he would not object, but only so long as she didn't bring any of them home with her.[10] When Ruth did finally tell her parents about Seretse, it was a disaster: her father told her to stop seeing him or to get out of the house.[11] The atmosphere of the home became tense and her mother, 'always lively, anxious and affectionate, was uneasy whenever she knew I was going out with Seretse – though she was not as antagonistic as my father'.[12]

By now, Seretse had no doubts at all that Ruth was the woman with whom he wanted to spend the rest of his life. He decided that he must tell Ruth how he felt – that he loved her and wanted her to be his wife.[13] One evening, when they were sitting together in the lounge at Nutford House, he turned to her and asked, 'Ruth, do you think you could love me?' – but she didn't answer. 'She didn't have to,' said Seretse later. 'The light in her sky-blue eyes and the smile on her face told me what I wanted to know.' He asked her to marry him and she said yes. They went out to celebrate in a little Soho restaurant and then Seretse kissed Ruth for the first time – 'We had reached an understanding at last, after nearly a year of secret meetings and outings.'[14]

But a mixed-race couple, they quickly discovered, were faced with enormous obstacles. One of these was looking for a flat to live in once they were married. In war-damaged London, it was hard for any couple to find accommodation to rent. But if one of them was black, it was almost impossible:

We were plagued by landlords and landladies who, though they had flats to let, slammed the door in our faces when we asked to see them. We'd write down a list of flats advertised vacant in the morning, jump into a taxi, and do the rounds. In every case, the places had 'just been let' a few minutes before we came along.

But if they telephoned the landlord immediately afterwards, pretending to be somebody else, they were told that the accommodation was still available.[15] They had been turned down simply because of Seretse's colour. Eventually, they found a tiny flat in Notting Hill Gate: a room with an alcove kitchen at 10 Campden Hill Gardens, on the top floor of a tall grey Victorian building. Seretse moved in straightaway.

Just a few minutes' walk away was the Anglican Church of St George's, Campden Hill. Seretse went to see the elderly vicar, the Reverend Leonard Patterson. He asked him to marry them and the wedding day was set for Saturday 2 October. But when Ruth told her parents the news, they were appalled and her father said he wanted nothing more to do with her.[16] Her mother, in great distress, implored her daughter to think again, but Ruth had no intention of giving up Seretse. Now, though, she had to keep out of her father's way. When she finished work, she went to the flat in Notting Hill Gate; then, at 11 o'clock at night, she went to her parents' flat, to sleep.[17] At work, too, news of her imminent marriage was met with hostility. The head of her department said he was transferring her to the firm's New York office: if she didn't accept this transfer, she would be sacked. She refused, announcing that she would leave her job at the end of the week.[18] 'It began to look as though we wouldn't have a friend in the world on our wedding day,' said Ruth, unhappily.[19]

Hanging over Seretse was the need to tell his uncle, the Regent Tshekedi, about his plan to marry Ruth. Seretse was aware that according to Bangwato law and custom, the wife of the Kgosi should be selected by his people; usually, the wife would be from a royal family. He was afraid, too, that his uncle would not like the idea of him marrying a white woman. Forty-three years of age, Tshekedi had been Regent of the Bangwato for twenty-three years and was a formidable man. Seretse wrote Tshekedi a long letter. Addressing him as 'Father', he announced his plan to marry Ruth on 2 October and asked him to accept her as his wife:

I assure you, father, that there has been nothing improper between the girl and myself. I have known her now for a year and two months. She knows very well what she is doing and we are aware of the difficulties that await us. These difficulties have already begun.

'I am not marrying her out of pity,' he added. 'I love her, moreover she is a suitable person father. You will agree that this is so when you meet her.' He asked Tshekedi to send some money:

I cannot do this without financial assistance from you father. Therefore Sir no matter how you feel please send me the necessary funds as soon as possible to enable us to start at least without financial worries.

He concluded:

Please do not try to stop me father, I want to go through with it. I hope you will appreciate the urgency of my request. I do need help.
  Ke le ngwana wa-gago ['I am your son']
  Seretse.[20]

But when the blue airmail letter arrived in Africa, it provoked a crisis. It was 'so unexpected', observed a friend of Tshekedi, 'that it had the effect of going off like a bomb . . . The news of the marriage almost made Tshekedi mad.'[21] The Resident Commissioner described the Regent's reaction in his memoirs. 'Tshekedi came to me with a face like a fiddle,' he recorded. 'That Seretse should marry at all without going through the usual forms of consultation was bad enough. That he should marry a European was the end.' The Resident Commissioner argued that such a development was hardly surprising. After all, it was Tshekedi who had insisted that Seretse go to England – 'and then raised the roof at the not unpredictable consequences'.[22]

Tshekedi was used to having his own way and now he resolved to stop Seretse's marriage. He sent a cable to his lawyer, Douglas Buchanan, in Cape Town:

Have just received most disturbing letter from Seretse. He is engaged to English girl banns published intends marry second October. Please take immediate possible steps possibly assisted by your brother Jack, Professor Coupland and others to stop this marriage by arranging immediate air transport for Seretse return South Africa.

'Please contact Sir Evelyn Baring immediately,' he added, 'and ask for his immediate support to get London office [to] arrange departure of Seretse.'[23]

Sir Evelyn Baring, who was the High Commissioner of Bechuanaland, was horrified by the news. Tall and patrician – some said cold and aloof – Baring was in his mid-40s, two years older than Tshekedi. He was a graduate of Winchester School and New College, Oxford, where he had gained a First in History; now he was following in the footsteps of his father, Lord Cromer, who had been consul-general in Egypt, as an imperial mandarin. He immediately cabled the permanent secretary at the Commonwealth Relations Office in London. 'Most grateful,' he urged, 'for any help you can give since marriage would be disastrous for Bamangwato Tribe and Seretse personally.'[24]

Buchanan sent a cable to his brother John, a London solicitor. 'Chief authorises me,' he wired, 'to urge you to take every possible step to prevent Seretse . . . marrying English girl.' He asked him to caution the parson who had called the banns – 'If Congregational contact LMS. If Church [of] England contact Archbishop.' Once he had done this, he should inform Ruth's parents of the 'ostracism and misery awaiting her. Such marriage possibly cause Seretse's deposition.'[25] Next day, Buchanan cabled Ronald Orchard, the Africa Secretary of the LMS, and asked him to act immediately to prevent the marriage.[26]

Meanwhile, Tshekedi sought to deal with Seretse directly. First he stopped his allowance. Then, on Friday 24 September, he cabled a blunt warning:

Your proposal [is] more serious and difficult than you realise. It is [the] surest way of disrupting [the] Bamangwato Tribe. You seem to have forgotten your home is [in] south[ern] Africa not England. Have made immediate arrangements for your immediate return.[27]

But this telegram had the opposite effect from the one that was intended. Seretse's and Ruth's determination to marry stiffened into defiance and they decided to bring the wedding-day forward. They went to see Dr Patterson, who agreed to change the date of their wedding to the next day, a Saturday, at 1.30 p.m.[28]

But at 10 o'clock on the Friday evening, the vicar was astonished to receive a telephone call from Dr Roger Pilkington – a man he had never heard of before – asking if he might come and talk to him about the wedding plans of Mr Seretse Khama. Pilkington had been surprised to find in his morning post a note from Seretse, inviting him to his wedding. But surprise turned into horror, when he realized that Seretse's future wife was a white woman. He immediately telephoned Seretse, urging him to reconsider. Seretse was bitterly hurt: he could hardly believe that the man he had called his friend disapproved of his plan to marry Ruth, clearly on racial grounds. Pilkington quickly sought out Ruth, advising her against the marriage, but she politely and firmly refused to discuss the matter with him. Then he went to see Ruth's parents, but her father said they had washed their hands of the whole affair.

'I realised that something must be done,' explained Pilkington to Tshekedi, 'in view of the very serious situation which would be created in Africa if the marriage was to go through against the wishes of Seretse's people.'[29] In fact, Pilkington knew nothing about the 'wishes of Seretse's people' and he had never been to Africa, let alone Bechuanaland. But his antipathy was so strong that he felt he *must* act. He was very shortly to become a member of the British Eugenics Society, which in the 1930s had articulated a clear opposition to marriage across racial lines. By the mid-1940s the eugenics movement had been discredited in many people's eyes by Hitler and Nazism, but it continued to exist, presenting its theories in weaker and more neutral terms. In 1944, the British Eugenics Society set out its aims in the name of 'racial hygiene' – to 'improve the inborn qualities of mankind' through the marriage of 'best-endowed couples'.[30] Pilkington worked as a marriage guidance counsellor, to help couples make eugenically healthy decisions about whether or not to marry.

He went to see Dr Patterson in the late evening and energetically tried to dissuade him from marrying Seretse and Ruth. But the vicar was uncomfortable: so far as he could see, the two young people were perfectly within their legal rights to marry and he was pleased they wanted a Christian marriage. By now, Pilkington had spent the whole day rushing about, trying to stop the marriage, but he still had one last person to speak to – Seretse himself. At half past midnight, he and his wife appeared on Seretse's doorstep. They insisted on coming in and proceeded to argue with him for three and a half hours; they told him he was 'behaving disgracefully'.[31]

In the meantime, John Buchanan had contacted John Keith, who was the head of the overseas student department at the Colonial Office.

Tall and scholarly, Keith was a bachelor who had twenty years of colonial service in Northern Rhodesia behind him when he joined the Colonial Office. He believed that 'race relations in this country should be on a sensible and what one might call a Christian basis', and had robustly resisted moves within the British forces during the war to follow the colour bar of the Americans.[32] Keith was well liked by the students at Nutford House and often invited them to his own home, which he shared with his mother; when they ran out of money, he did what he could to help.[33] But this warmth did not extend to approval of Seretse's plan to marry Ruth. He went to see Charles Njonjo and Harry Nkumbula, asking them to reason with their friend. They said they would, hoping that this would buy time for their friends.[34]

The alleged reason for stopping the marriage was that Seretse had not consulted his uncle or his people. But both Seretse and Ruth were British citizens and under British law there was no requirement for such a consultation. They were adults – Seretse was now 27 and Ruth was 24 – and they were fully entitled to marry. 'You will appreciate,' explained Sir Cecil Syers, Deputy Under-Secretary of State for Commonwealth Relations, in a telegram to Baring, 'that it would be difficult for us to intervene officially unless of course the marriage would not be valid in the Bech[uanaland] Prot[ectorate] but I assume that this point does not arise.' The real reason for the opposition was a conviction that it simply would not do for Seretse to marry an Englishwoman. 'I fully appreciate the undesirability of the marriage,' wrote Sir Reginald Coupland in Oxford to Sir Cecil. 'If I could do anything to help to prevent it,' he added, 'I should feel obliged to do so, unpleasant though it would be.'[35]

But it was not as if Seretse was the first African student to marry a white woman in Britain. In 1942, Jomo Kenyatta had married a white woman called Edna Grace Clarke, who became the second of his four wives. According to the *West African Review* in September 1949, 'In the Gold Coast today more Africans are married to English girls than ever in its chequered matrimonial history, and every other student brings out . . . a white bride.[36] There was also a rumour at the Colonial Office that Kwame Nkrumah was considering marriage to an Englishwoman with whom he may have been 'on terms of intimacy', according to a British mandarin, when he was in the UK in 1947.[37]

In the late 1940s, the issue of colour was moving up the British agenda. In June 1948, the *Empire Windrush* arrived in Southampton from Jamaica, bringing about 450 people – a number of them with war service records – who were hoping to find work in Britain. This was the start of a wave of migration to the UK from the British colonies of the West Indies. Under the British Nationality Act of 1948, all crown colonial subjects were British citizens and were entitled to unrestricted entry into Great Britain, as the 'mother' of the empire. But many people in Britain were horrified. Within two days of the docking of the *Empire Windrush*, a group of eleven Labour MPs wrote to the Prime Minister, calling for controls on black immigration. In his reply, Attlee defended the admission of British subjects to Britain. But he took a different line in the Cabinet, where he censored Arthur Creech-Jones, the Colonial Secretary, for not 'having kept the lid on things' in the colonies. As a way of getting rid of the new problem, he asked whether there was a way of sending the *Windrush* migrants to East Africa to work on a project known as the Tanganyikan Groundnuts Scheme (which turned out to be a complete failure).[38]

The British population had been grateful to colonial men for their contribution to the war effort. But now their attitude had changed. A Jamaican man who had served in the RAF commented:

I suppose you could say racism crept up on me – although some other people may have seen it straight away. But it is something that crept up on me very slowly ... Just after the war was over, I was on a bus and there were two service people in front of me, one a woman. And she was saying, 'Isn't it about time they went back to their homes?' and it was the first time that it hit me that, you know, that people were putting up with us, that they didn't really want us, but we were a necessary evil.

'People were more aggressive to you,' said another Jamaican who had served in the RAF. 'In short, they are trying to say that you shouldn't be here.' Not everyone he met felt like this:

I would say a third of the people in Britain still had imperialist ideas. People from the colonies should be planting bananas and chocolate and whatever it is. Another third, I would say, [thought it] did not really matter [so long] as

Arsenal win on Saturday. The other third, they were just nice, ordinary people.

But the third who were hostile made his life very difficult.[39]

Sometimes, when Seretse and Ruth were out together, people shouted abuse at Ruth, calling her a tart. This was not an uncommon experience for a white woman who went out with a black man. 'If I am with a European girl,' said a Nigerian student at London University, 'other English people look the girl up and down with the implication that she cannot be a respectable girl.'[40] On one occasion, a friend of the Williams family deliberately crossed the street to avoid greeting Ruth.[41] 'No colour bar in London!' exclaimed Ruth bitterly. 'Might as well say no sand in the Sahara. Of course there's a deep-rooted colour bar in London, and all Britain.'[42]

Seretse and Ruth got ready for their wedding on the morning of Saturday, 25 September. Ruth had chosen a wedding dress of turquoise wool, with a pillbox hat; Seretse was dressed in his one dark suit.[43] Muriel was going to be their bridesmaid and John Zimmerman best man. Both Seretse and Ruth had wanted Njonjo to share in their special day, but he had warned them against this: two black men in the company of two white women might draw unwelcome attention to the occasion.[44]

That same morning, the leading men of the London Missionary Society met together in London at Mission House – Orchard, John Buchanan, Pilkington and also the Reverend A. J. Haile, who was the LMS representative in southern Africa. Their first tactic was to send a message to Ruth by taxi – but there was no reply. Then, at 1.00 p.m., with just half an hour to go before the wedding, Pilkington called the vicar, instructing him to telephone Seretse and tell him that he was not willing to perform the ceremony. Patterson hesitated, then made the call.

But Seretse and Ruth refused to accept that their wedding was off. They rushed down to the vicarage and entreated with Patterson to marry them. Sympathetic, he tried hard to think of a solution – and decided to consult his Bishop. He knew that Dr Wand, the Bishop of London, was coming that day to officiate at an ordination service at

St Mary Abbots Church, not far away. He suggested that they all make their way there, straightaway, and ask the Bishop to sort out the difficulty. The vicar and his wife took Seretse and Ruth to St Mary Abbots, where they sat anxiously together in a pew, waiting for the Bishop to complete his service. They assumed that he would be bound to approve of their wish for a Christian marriage, in the house of God.

In the meantime, Pilkington had set off with Orchard and Haile for St George's Church. They were absolutely determined to prevent the marriage and had developed a new strategy. If the vicar were to start proceedings, they would simply raise an objection to the marriage and it could not possibly go ahead. But although they waited and waited, no one came to the church. Again they rang the vicarage – and were told about the plan to consult the Bishop. In angry frustration, they hurried out to the street and hailed a taxi to St Mary Abbots, where they rushed in and wrote a note for the Bishop, with instructions that it should be given to him as soon as the service was over. The note advised him not to consent to the marriage.

The verdict of the Bishop went against Seretse and Ruth. He did not even bother to speak to them himself, but sent the Archdeacon of Middlesex with a message. 'Get in touch with the Colonial Office,' he advised. 'When they agree to the wedding, I will.'[45] Stunned, the little party returned to St George's Church and Ruth broke down in tears.[46] 'Does the Church want to force me to live in sin?' she asked in despair. She had left her parents' home that morning expecting to be a married woman by the evening. She could hardly return home, but nor – since she was not married – could she now spend the night in the flat with Seretse. In despair, she took a room in a hotel in Bayswater, nearby.[47]

Pilkington realized that Seretse and Ruth were very angry – 'in an emotional condition which rendered it useless to try to approach them in any way'.[48] But he was not worried about this, he explained to Tshekedi, because he believed that Seretse's 'whole future and to a certain extent even that of his country depended upon our inter-vention, though I cannot expect that he will easily realise the good turn that was done to him when the affair was held up on Saturday'.[49] He suspected that Ruth had 'started this business out of a kind of emotional reaction to the colour bar in Africa', and believed that she was 'not altogether a bad kind of girl'.[50] John Buchanan took the same view. But if this was true, he worried, she 'will possibly be more difficult to deal with than if it had been a case of a chorus girl or suchlike, when money would have talked possibly'. Should the marriage go ahead, he predicted, it would be a tragedy. 'How long,' he wondered, 'could such a marriage last in this country (where just as I know so well in Northern Rhodesia) there is in theory no Colour Bar but in practice!! Looking further ahead what possible hope have any children of such a marriage?'[51]

Just four days after the fiasco at St George's Church – on Wednesday 29 September 1948 – Seretse and Ruth were married in a civil ceremony at Kensington Registry Office. Early that morning, Seretse collected Ruth from her little hotel in Bayswater. She was wearing a black suit with a white blouse; the jacket was fitted, flaring slightly at the back, and she wore a black hat. It was a severe outfit and not very bridal, but it reflected their determination.[52] They walked swiftly to the Registry Office, looking over their shoulders to check whether anybody was following them.[53] They were waiting outside the Office when it opened, with their three witnesses – 'my sister Muriel, loyal to the last',[54] John Zimmerman and one of Ruth's cousins.

Shortly after nine o'clock, Seretse and Ruth were husband and wife.[55] Despite the combined efforts of the Regent Tshekedi, the British High Commissioner in South Africa, the Colonial Office, the Church of England and the London Missionary Society, as well as lawyers in South Africa and Britain, they had started their lives together. They walked from the Registry Office to the hotel where Ruth had stayed the previous few nights, to collect her things and move them into her new home with her husband – the little flat in Campden Hill Gardens. Seretse sent John Keith a telegram. 'Have married Ruth,' he told him, adding playfully, 'Do you still want to see me?'[56] I *am* sorry,' wrote Coupland to the Commonwealth Relations Office, when he heard the news. 'It will be a miracle,' he added, 'if the marriage turns out happily in the end for either of them or for their children. It's a real tragedy or so it seems.'[57]

In the evening after the wedding, a cable arrived for Seretse from Tshekedi, who was unaware that they were now man and wife. 'I wish you [to] pay attention to what Commonwealth Office advises you,' he warned. 'Your obstinacy can only result [in] serious consequences [to] yourself. On no condition can we agree to your marrying an English girl.'[58] Next day, Seretse wired Tshekedi with the news that he was too late – that the wedding had already taken place.[59] His uncle was outraged. 'Formal signing of document in England does not constitute your marriage,' he thundered back in reply, ordering him to come home, and adding:

As far as we are concerned no marriage exists. Apparently you took my strong advice for a threat. We accept nothing short of dissolution of that marriage. Our decision firm. Welfare of tribe paramount in this case.[60]

Seretse tried to reason with his uncle: 'Tribe and you important to me. Suspension of allowance being felt.' Then he made it clear that his commitment to Ruth was absolute: 'Suggest passage for two. Dissolution unacceptable.'[61]

3

The Bechuanaland Protectorate

The country of Seretse Khama was the Bechuanaland Protectorate – a vast expanse of sand dunes and scrub, with more animals than people. Herds of cattle wandered across the wide plains, together with sheep, goats and wild donkeys. In the more remote areas there was every sort of wild animal – lions, snakes, cheetahs, elephants, hippos, rhinos, zebra, crocodiles, hyenas and leopards. When Mandela sought refuge in Bechuanaland from apartheid in the 1960s, he fell in love with the country at first sight: it was a wilder Africa, he said, than the one he knew in South Africa and he was astonished when he saw a lioness crossing the road. After the jungle of Johannesburg, he reflected, he was in a place 'where the survival of the fittest was the supreme law and where the tangled vegetation concealed all kinds of danger'.[1]

The Protectorate was a landlocked country, bordering South Africa to the south and the south-east, Southern Rhodesia (later Zimbabwe) to the north-east, Northern Rhodesia (Zambia) on the other side of the Zambezi River in the north, and South West Africa (Namibia) to the west. Much of Bechuanaland was parched and inhospitable – about three-quarters of the western part of the country lay buried under the scrub and dust of the Kalahari, a semi-desert. Green grass would grow after good rains; but for much of the time, the soil was ravaged by drought. Water was so scarce that *pula*, the Setswana word for 'rain', was one of the most important and frequently used words. It was used to offer greetings and '*Pula!*' was a shared cry of approbation at formal and informal gatherings. Thorn bushes were the chief source of shade from the blazing sun. Few of the roads in Bechuanaland were gravelled, and transport was limited to ox-drawn carts and wagons, although there were a few cars belonging to wealthy cattle-owners; the British officials drove around in lorries.[2]

There were eight principal nations in the territory – the Bakgatla, the Bakwena, the Bangwaketse, the Balete, the Bangwato, the Baralong, the Batawana, and the Batlokwa.[3] The largest of these was the Bangwato, to which Seretse belonged. The other inhabitants of the Protectorate included sub-clans and also the Basarwa, also known as the San or Bushmen, hunter-gatherers with very limited rights, who were widely used as servants.[4]

Under British rule, the affairs of each nation were controlled by their own Kgosi, who was known as the Native Authority; he and his office were responsible for land tenure, educational arrangements, licensing, collection of taxes, administering justice within certain limits, and various other duties. He was subject to the overriding authority of the British Administration, which was represented in each reserve by a District Commissioner. But the Kgosi not only shouldered the secular leadership of his people: he was also responsible for his people spiritually and was at the centre of everything in their lives.[5] There was a saying that the Kgosi 'is a demigod, no evil must be spoken of him' – *Kgosi modingwana, ga a sejwe.*[6]

Bechuanaland had far fewer white inhabitants than any of its neighbouring countries in which white settlers had taken most, if not all, of the fertile land away from the indigenous populations and had developed their own communities. But in Bechuanaland in 1946, out of a total population of nearly 300,000 people, fewer than 1 per cent – just over 2,000 – were white.[7] Most of these were farmers or traders, who were allowed to own land only in a few demarcated areas. Generally, white people were concentrated in or around Francistown, in the north of the Protectorate, which resembled a small Rhodesian or South African town in appearance and where Africans had to live in the 'location', an area demarcated for occupation by people who were not white. But elsewhere in the Protectorate, 'Europeans' were not allowed to purchase land. They had no title to the land upon which their houses and shops were built and held them at the discretion of the diKgosi.

The Bangwato lived a hard, but peaceful, existence, depending on their cattle for survival; crops were of secondary importance, because of the lack of good soil and rain. The capital of the Bangwato Reserve was Serowe, where about 30,000 people lived in neat clusters of family groups, in mud huts thatched with straw. It was one of the largest villages in Africa, sprawling for five miles through shallow, parched valleys. The village was clean and tidy, but it was also rocky and dusty, with huge red ant-hills everywhere. Most people had three homes: one in their village; one at their lands; and one at the cattle-post where they kept their cattle. It was customary for boys to spend their childhoods at the cattle-post. Families lived in their village from about June to October or November, when the rainy season started and they moved to the lands to start ploughing. Women carried pots of water and grain on their heads, with their babies on their backs.

The royal family lived in the centre of Serowe in cool brick houses, near the tribal offices and the Kgotla ground – the place where a Kgotla, or Tribal Assembly, was held. It was a large open space, semi-circular in shape, and surrounded by tall camel-thorn trees. Overlooking the Kgotla place was a rocky hill, at the top of which was the sacred burial ground of the Bangwato royal family. There were a few stores scattered around the town – tin-roofed buildings, which were mostly owned by the few 'Europeans' and so-called 'coloureds', the South African term for people of mixed race. All traders had to construct their buildings out of corrugated iron and wood, so that if they had to be expelled for any reason, they could simply dismantle them and leave.[8] The British officials lived on a hill-top in the south-west of the town, in brick houses. The largest building in Serowe was the LMS Church, which had been opened in 1912.

Serowe was a quiet, peaceful world, into which Seretse Goitsebeng Khama was born on 1 July 1921. He was the grandson of Khama III, who was also known as Khama the Great. Khama had been converted by missionaries to Christianity when he was a young man, and when he became Kgosi he gave a monopoly on religion in the Bangwato country to the London Missionary Society, which had had strong roots there ever since Robert Moffatt and David Livingstone had been sent on missions to Bechuanaland in the nineteenth century. No other religious sect or society was allowed to operate under Khama and in effect the LMS became a state church. But Khama kept the missionaries firmly in their place and when he disagreed with any of them – which happened quite frequently – he sent them away.[9]

Under Khama's influence, Christianity spread through the land. He banned polygamy and rainmaking ceremonies and outlawed the custom of the bride price. He also published an edict that there should be no cruelty towards 'subordinate peoples'. But he did not simply ban traditional customs; rather, he changed and modified them, as in the case of the initiation of young men. From time to time, a new group of young men – known as an 'age regiment' – was created and all those who had become adult since the previous regiment were enrolled in it. In the past, the young men had been taken into the bush, where they were circumcised and challenged with endurance tests which sometimes, it was maintained, led to the death of an initiate. Khama abolished these practices, but he did not abolish the age regiments themselves: instead, the initiation was transformed into a ceremony with prayers and lectures. The regiments were then given community projects to carry out, such as building a school, church or house. There were also age regiments of girls, who were given projects such as gardening and sewing. Under Khama's reforming zeal, a new order was created, which emphasized self-help, compassion and the needs of the community.

The drinking of liquor was strictly prohibited under Khama's laws. 'Drink puts devils into men,' Khama told a British official, 'and destroys both their souls and their bodies for ever.' When some European traders got drunk in his territory one weekend, he summoned them before him and told them to leave:

Well, I am black, but if I am black, I am chief in my own country at present. When you white men rule in the country, then you will do as you like; at present I rule, and I shall maintain my laws which you insult and despise . . .[10]

Khama III died in 1923, leaving his son Sekgoma as Kgosi of the Bangwato. But after only two years, Sekgoma II died, which meant that Seretse – who was Sekgoma's son, by his fourth and last wife, Tebogo – was now officially Kgosi. But he was just a small child, so the tribal elders decided in 1926 to recall Tshekedi from Fort Hare, where he was studying, to act as Regent until Seretse was old enough to take on the role of Kgosi; as the son of Khama and Khama's fourth wife, Semane, Tshekedi was second in the line of succession. He was installed as Regent at an elaborate ceremony, which was attended by

4-year-old Seretse, dressed in the clothes that had been brought by the Scottish missionaries – a kilt, sporran, plaid and silver-buckle shoes. Tshekedi's mother Semane, in a dress of black silk and a long shawl, rested her hand gently on Seretse's shoulder.[11]

Tshekedi, like Khama III, was a devout Christian and a man of austere discipline who loathed alcohol. He was also highly charismatic. His manner was 'always quiet and fatherly', said a woman school-teacher, but 'there was something else indescribable about him that was very magnetic, like a force. I'd say one felt towards him what one felt about God.'[12] Growing up under Tshekedi's rule, observed a school-teacher, 'we were encouraged to learn and education often went beyond book learning – there was a great stress on character building'. After school and family chores, the children were sent off in the evenings to Bible classes:

We were given simple Bible stories, the singing of psalms and hymns and yearly there'd be a competition for all the [Bible study] groups in the village. This way of life affected us all – it created a people who were keen to learn, responsible.

'No other man,' she added, speaking of Tshekedi, 'cared for us as much as he did.'[13]

Tshekedi had great plans for his nephew. At first Seretse's childhood was managed by his mother Tebogo. But gradually his care was taken over by Tshekedi, who called him 'Sonny'; Seretse, in turn, addressed Tshekedi as 'Father'. They rode together round the cattle-posts, inspecting the vast herds owned by the Khama family. The British Administration had wanted Seretse to go to Dombashawa, a vocational school in Southern Rhodesia, but Tshekedi vigorously resisted this: he was adamant that his nephew should receive a rigorous academic education in South Africa.[14]

When he was 15, Seretse – dressed in wing collar and black tie – was best man at Tshekedi's wedding. This marriage ended in divorce and, three years later, Seretse was once again best man at his uncle's wedding. Tshekedi's second bride was Ella Moshoela, who had been a teacher and was a trained nurse; her father was a Methodist minister. This was a happy marriage, producing five children.

Tshekedi was utterly committed to the needs of his people and wanted to better their lives, especially through the building of schools and the improvement of the water supply. But his methods were not always appreciated. He had numerous work projects going on at the same time, for which the labour provided by the age regiments was his only resource.[15] This led to widespread resentment, especially in connection with his pet project, the building of Moeng College. Tshekedi had no money to pay for the College and had to rely completely on tributary labour and on cattle donations which were supposed to be voluntary, but were often enforced.[16] Seretse's age regiment, which was called the Malekantwa, had been compelled by Tshekedi to take part in this work. Lenyeletse Seretse, a cousin and close friend of Seretse, belonged to this regiment and described 'the suffering we went through':

It was 1948. It was a year of drought. It was hot, as only drought years can be and we worked all day outdoors. Each man had to bring along his own rations, paid for out of his own pocket, but it didn't really work out. Those of us who had more means were forced to share with those who had less. Soon, we were all starving. Some members of the regiment had brought their horses. They died. We ate them. We ate wild rabbits or anything we could catch in the bush.[17]

Most of the men wanted to leave but dared not, because men who left a work regiment were put on trial and punished.

Tshekedi's methods were harsh. But, on the other hand, his projects were often admirable – such as building the only secondary boarding school in the whole of Bechuanaland. Tshekedi had radical, progressive ideas for the College: for example, he wanted black and white teachers to live together in the same hostel as equals.[18] Tshekedi also wanted to protect the freedom of people in other parts of the region: when Jan Smuts sought to incorporate mandated South West Africa into South Africa, he vigorously opposed the merger.

All over British colonial Africa, people had to pay a hut tax; in Bechuanaland, the hut tax had been introduced in 1899 for every man of 18 years or more. Since traditionally most families' wealth lay in cattle and grain, which would not pay taxes, men were forced into wage labour. Most of the able-bodied men of the Protectorate went to South Africa to find work: some of them were employed on farms or in domestic service, but most worked in the gold mines of Johannesburg and the diamond mines of Kimberley.[19] The working conditions of miners in South Africa were brutal. Margaret Bourke-White, an American journalist from *Life*, went on a fact-finding journey to South Africa in the 1940s and was appalled by what she saw. Although a miner worked an eight-hour day, he was often underground for as many as eleven hours:

The white-skinned foremen must come up first, before the elevators take up the blacks. On each landing stage, as I made the ascent, I saw the black gold-miners clustered in large groups, awaiting their release to the outside air and open sky. They would see little of this sky.

The miners had to endure harsh living conditions: 'They would sleep in concrete barracks, without windows, rolled up like sausages on the floor, forty to a room, crowded into compounds surrounded with barbed wire.'[20] Only once a year were the miners allowed to return home for a visit. For the women left behind in Bechuanaland, life was very hard.

Bechuanaland was a Protectorate. This meant that African traditional leaders kept some of their powers but were subject to British rule; the British Government was regarded as a sort of trustee for the population. This was a very different situation from Southern Rhodesia and Kenya, which were self-governing colonies with almost Dominion status; their governments were controlled by large white settler communities, entirely excluding the black majority of the population.

There were a number of Protectorates in the British Empire, including Nyasaland and Northern Rhodesia. But the designation of 'protectorate' had a very particular meaning for the people of Bechuanaland – that of protection, in the most literal sense, from a threat of incorporation by South Africa. Bechuanaland had always been vulnerable to South Africa, because it was directly on its border. In the 1880s it had come under attack from the Transvaal Boers, which led the diKgosi to appeal for British protection. This was backed by Cecil Rhodes, for his own purposes, and in 1885 Bechuanaland was proclaimed to be under the protection of Queen Victoria.

Then, in 1894, people were horrified to hear that Rhodes had asked Britain to transfer the Protectorate to the British South Africa

Company. To prevent this happening, the three leading diKgosi – Khama III of the Bangwato, Bathoen II of the Bangwaketse and Sebele of the Bakwena – went to Britain in 1895 to appeal for help. They emphasized that they wished to remain under the protection of Queen Victoria, who received them at Windsor Castle. She wrote in her diary:

After luncheon I went to the White Drawing-room to receive 3 Chiefs from Bechuana Land, who are Christians . . . The Chiefs are very tall & very black, but their hair is not woolly. One of the Chiefs is said to be a very remarkable & intelligent man [presumably Khama]. One of their chief objects in coming was to obtain a permit from the Govt. to suppress strong drink, which demoralises & kills the poor natives. Alas! everywhere this terrible evil, which has such a fatal effect on the population, seems to follow civilisation!

She was given skins of leopards and jackals by the diKgosi and to them she gave New Testaments and framed photographs of herself, as well as Indian shawls for their wives.[21]

As they toured the country, the three diKgosi were explicit about their fears for their land. At a chapel meeting in Leicester, Khama explained that:

We think that the Chartered Company will take our lands, that they might enslave us to work in their mines. We black people work on the land; we live on the farms. We get our food from the land, and we are afraid that if the British South Africa Company begin in our country we will not get these things and that it will be a great loss to us.

Why, he asked, should the British Government 'hand us over to the other people without asking us?'

They hand us over like an ox, but even the owner of the ox looks to where the ox will get grass, and water, land, that sort of thing. I think they ought to have asked us, and found out what we think about it. Although we are black people we have tribes that we rule over, [and] if a chief wants to make a new law or anything he must speak with his people.

'We were progressing very [well] under the Imperial Government,' he said, 'but now you are teaching us the word of war, and I think these things ought to cease.'[22]

It looked at first as if the visit of the diKgosi w
because Joseph Chamberlain, the Colonial Secretary, simpl
to negotiate terms with Rhodes. But then the Jameson Raid took
in December 1895, when Jameson invaded the Transvaal from inside
Bechuanaland, on Rhodes's orders. It failed within three days and
Britain was widely criticized for allowing its Protectorate to be used
as a springboard for an attack on another country. Not wishing to be
further discredited and aware, too, of the widespread support for the
diKgosi from the British public, especially among Nonconformists
and teetotallers, the Government refused to transfer the Protectorate
to the British South Africa Company.

Bechuanaland was still not safe from South Africa, however. For in
1908–9 the leaders of the Boers and of the British met to develop
proposals for the unification of South Africa. Under this plan, the
Cape, Natal, the Transvaal and the Orange River Colony would unite
to form the Union of South Africa. It was assumed that Bechuanaland,
along with Swaziland and Basutoland (later Lesotho) would also form
part of the Union. Once again, however, the people of Bechuanaland
protested strongly and pleaded with Britain to protect them from
South Africa and, in the event, neither Bechuanaland, Swaziland, nor
Basutoland were included in the Union. But the Union of South Africa
Act of 1909 empowered the King to 'transfer' to the Union the government of any of these territories at any time, so long as their inhabitants
had been consulted, their wishes had been considered, and the British
parliament had approved. This left a prevailing feeling of vulner-
ability. On the one hand, many people had faith in the protecting
power of Britain – in 1947, when George VI and his family visited
Bechuanaland, Tshekedi greeted them in the full-dress uniform of the
Royal Horse Guards, presented to Khama III by Victoria. But, on the
other hand, there was a nagging fear that the transfer might take place
some day.

This fear was felt even more keenly after May 1948 – just months
before Seretse's marriage to Ruth – when the Afrikaner National
Party, under Dr Daniel Malan, was voted into power by South
Africa's white minority, defeating the United Party led by General Jan
Smuts. It was a victory that was described by Malan as 'a miracle
of God'. The Nationalists came to power on an election platform

the separate development of the races.
apidly prepared in order to maintain and
ion of the majority by the few – of 8,500,000
ian 2,500,000 whites, who owned nine-tenths
ea of apartheid was hardly new. It was built on
le racist policies of the colonial-settler state, above
1936 Land Acts that had placed the legal limit on
Afri   and at 13.7 per cent of South Africa's total area. In
1948, sho   before the Nationalists came to power, Alan Paton
published *Cry the Beloved Country: A Story of Comfort in Desolation*
– much admired by Seretse Khama[23] – which painted a picture of a
society that was riddled with racial injustice.

The people of Bechuanaland continually opposed the idea of transfer to the Union, on any terms. But they could not avoid living under its shadow. The postal services were administered by South Africa, so the stamps were South African. The currency was the South African rand and customs, too, remained under South African control; Roman-Dutch law was in force. The only railway was a single-track system, operated by South African Railways, running inside the eastern border of Bechuanaland from Cape Town in South Africa to Bulawayo in Southern Rhodesia. Economically, the Protectorate was dependent on the Union. Even the administrative capital, Mafikeng, was located in South Africa – sixteen miles south of the southern boundary of Bechuanaland. It was the only capital in the world to lie outside the country it governed. This was a historical anomaly, but was consistent with the way in which Bechuanaland lay in the shadow of its southern neighbour. The houses and offices of the Protectorate Administration were on the edge of Mafikeng, on a square mile of land grandly called the Imperial Reserve.

The overall authority in Africa for Bechuanaland was the British High Commissioner, who was based in South Africa. As he was also responsible for the British territories of Basutoland and Swaziland, the three countries were described collectively as the High Commission Territories – or, for the sake of convenience, as the HCTs. They were different countries in many ways, especially geographically. Whereas Bechuanaland was the size of Kenya or France, the other two were tiny by comparison. Moreover, Basutoland was entirely enclosed by

South African territory; Swaziland, too, was dominated by South Africa, except where it shared a border with Mozambique.

Bechuanaland was managed by the British on a shoestring and little was provided in the way of formal education and health care. What services *did* exist were segregated along racial lines, with hugely preferential facilities for whites. At most of the few African and 'coloured' schools, classes were often held under a tree, and the children used slates, not paper. Nor were there any secondary schools for Africans until Tshekedi decided to build Moeng College. Few places had electricity or running water. Serowe did have piped water, but it had to be collected in buckets. Many of the children and adults in Bechuanaland were malnourished and suffered from preventable diseases; malaria and yellow fever were endemic and diphtheria widespread.[24] Throughout the period of British administration, at least a third of all children did not live to the age of 5.[25]

There was no official colour bar in Bechuanaland but the practice of segregation was firmly rooted in daily life. The small white community – or 'Europeans', as they called themselves, although most of them came from South Africa – regarded black people as inferior.[26] If a black person went to the home of a white, he or she was expected to go to the back door. In the shops and post-offices, black and white people were served separately, with blacks receiving summary service.[27] One young colonial official, Michael Fairlie, was appalled by the level of separation between the lives of blacks and the lives of whites when he first arrived in Bechuanaland in the late 1940s. He found that 'there was no social contact at all with the local Africans' and even Tshekedi, who was widely respected by the Administration, 'was never invited into a European's house for a cup of tea, let alone a meal'.[28] Fairlie wanted to invite some of the people who lived near him to his home, but white public opinion 'would have been scandalized at this breach of the racial code'. He was already the subject of gossip for playing tennis on the government court with his African staff.[29]

On the trains, segregation did not stop once the train had crossed the border from South Africa into the Protectorate. Some trains were wholly reserved for whites. But even on the 'mixed' trains, the rule of *net blankes* – 'whites only' – applied to the first- and second-class coaches. Black people had to make do with third and fourth class, which were far less comfortable. Nor were they allowed into the dining cars. At the stations, there were separate waiting rooms and facilities for whites and blacks.[30] The nearest train station to Serowe was at Palapye, thirty miles away. Facing the station was the Palapye Hotel, which had a front entrance for whites, surrounded by pink bougainvillea bushes and tall palm trees, providing shade. It had a dingy back entrance for blacks, who were not allowed inside unless they were servants.

In the early days of his Regency, when he was only 28, Tshekedi Khama was briefly deposed by the British Administration. A number of cases of European men seducing Bangwato girls had come to his attention and he made repeated complaints about this to the Resident Magistrate, but nothing was done. Then, in August 1933, a young white man called Phineas McIntosh, who was a wagon-builder and had been a frequent offender, struck a black youth during a quarrel over a young Bangwato woman. Tshekedi summoned McIntosh and did the unthinkable – he sentenced him to a flogging, even though he was white. The Resident Commissioner, Charles Rey, who didn't like Tshekedi anyway, took this opportunity to have him removed from office. He asked the Acting High Commissioner, Admiral Evans, who was Commander of the British fleet in South Africa, to depose the Regent. Evans immediately sent armed marines from his Simonstown naval base all the way to Bechuanaland, which was a journey of some 1,000 miles.

A trial was held. Douglas Buchanan came up from Cape Town and did his best to defend Tshekedi; McIntosh, in any case, said he had no complaint against him. But it was announced that Tshekedi was not fit to be Regent, because he had unlawfully inflicted corporal punishment on a white man. A formal ceremony was held to sentence him, at which Tshekedi was made to stand on the ground in front of a wooden dais that had been specially constructed, bearing the Union Jack. Powerful guns were trained on him and on the 15,000 Bangwato people who had come to show solidarity with their Regent.[31] On the dais stood Admiral Evans, Percivale Liesching, who was the Deputy Commissioner for the United Kingdom and was dressed in full ceremonial regalia, including a sword and feathered hat, and Colonel

Rey, who wore khaki uniform, pith helmet and knee-high boots. Tshekedi was told he was suspended. He was then marched to his car and banished to Francistown, in the north of Bechuanaland.[32]

Tshekedi immediately sought to reverse this injustice by following the model set by his father, Khama III, and appealed to supporters in Britain. This led to heavy criticism of Evans and Rey in the press and in the House of Commons. A Movietone newsreel interviewed Tshekedi, who reminded viewers of the kindness of the British people towards Khama III in 1896.[33] Meanwhile, the Bangwato resisted Rey's attempts to replace Tshekedi and no one would agree to act in his place as Native Authority. This created an impossible predicament for Evans and Rey, who needed a way out. This was offered by Tshekedi himself, who declared that he had never assumed it was his right as Native Authority to sentence a white man – a statement they seized on, announcing that he had 'apologized'. Within weeks of deposing Tshekedi, a humiliated Evans had to return to Serowe to reinstate him.[34]

The episode generated a great deal of sympathy for Tshekedi in the Protectorate and in liberal circles in Britain. For, as Learie Constantine drily observed, 'though a white man may flog or kill a black one, no black man may flog a white one on a Court order or under any circumstances'.[35] But it also led to support for Tshekedi from an unexpected quarter: from many of the whites in Britain, South Africa and Southern Rhodesia who were opposed to sexual contact between the races. Tshekedi's action against McIntosh, they argued, demonstrated that he felt as strongly about this as they did. Fifteen years later, his hostility to the marriage of Seretse and Ruth suggested that perhaps they were right.

4

The decision of the Bangwato Assembly

Seretse returned to Bechuanaland just three weeks after his marriage. It was not a good time to go: he longed to stay with Ruth and he was planning to take the second part of his Bar exam in December. But he felt obliged to explain himself to his family and his people. After a long and tiring journey, he finally arrived home in Serowe. The sun was harsh and very bright, because this was the beginning of summer, when temperatures could reach a blistering 44°C. Seasons here were the opposite of Britain – Ruth in London would have been dressing up warmly against the cold and damp of autumn.

Almost as soon as Seretse returned home, his uncles reprimanded him on his failure to consult them on his marriage. Tshekedi told him that he must give Ruth up, suggesting that some kind of financial compensation could be offered to her.[1] But Seretse adamantly refused. Since neither side would back down, it was decided to hold a Kgotla in Serowe to discuss the issue. The Kgotla ground was the centre of the moral and political life of the Bangwato people, where every important issue was discussed. Every adult man was entitled to attend and sometimes many thousands of men would arrive from all over the Bangwato territory. Everyone who wished to speak was encouraged to give his view and assemblies lasted until it was clear that nothing new was being said. Only then could the Kgosi sum up the discussion and the overall consensus. There were many small Kgotlas in the small wards of the village and elsewhere throughout the Reserve, but the Kgotla in Serowe was paramount.

The Kgotla to discuss Seretse's marriage started on 15 November 1948 and lasted four days. Between 2,000 and 3,000 men travelled to Serowe on foot, on horseback, on donkeys, and in trucks, some of them bringing stools or chairs to sit on. As was customary, it was opened with a prayer; people sat in a semi-circle, facing the Regent and his senior advisers. Tshekedi, who was an eloquent speaker in both Setswana and English, explained his objections to Seretse's marriage. Then Seretse apologized for not marrying according to custom, but added that he was very much in love with his wife. In the discussion that followed, only seven men spoke in favour of the marriage, while seventy-eight opposed it.[2] However, this was not necessarily the consensus of Bangwato society. For one thing, women were prohibited from attending Kgotla meetings. For another, Tshekedi had banned men under 40 years of age from speaking, on the grounds that the issue was beyond their understanding.[3]

Seretse made preparations to leave the village. But before going, he asked for another Kgotla to be held; he believed that many of the younger men did not object to his marriage and he was still hopeful that it would be accepted. On 28 December 1948, over a month after the first Kgotla, a second Assembly took place. This time, between 3,000 and 4,000 men made their way to the kgotla ground and the discussions lasted two days. Seretse stated emphatically that if his wife was not acceptable to his people, he would not come back.[4] The Nationalist South African newspapers *Die Burger* and *Transvaler* were quick to report that this second Kgotla demonstrated that Africans wanted 'racial purity' as much as the white Nationalists.[5] But the Kgotla showed no such thing. In fact, it was inconclusive and men spoke for each side. One visiting Kgosi from another region of Bechuanaland, who was watching the faces of the men, noticed that many favoured Seretse but were afraid to speak.[6] It was apparent that there had been a shift of opinion since the Kgotla of November. Doubts had grown that Tshekedi was trying to keep the kingship for himself and there were fears of losing Seretse for ever, even though he was the rightful Kgosi.

'Tshekedi's stock is low,' reported the LMS to London.[7] According to Lenyeletse Seretse, Seretse's cousin, there was a section of the community that believed in magic, who were 'absolutely convinced' that Tshekedi wanted the kingship for himself and had stumbled upon a particularly potent potion which had made Seretse marry a foreign woman, so that he would remain Kgosi.[8]

No consensus was reached. This meant that the matter would have to be discussed again, at a further Kgotla. Gerald Nettelton, the Government Secretary of Bechuanaland, suggested to Seretse that he go to England for now, complete his examinations, and then come back in June. By now, believed Alan Seager, the LMS missionary in Serowe, Tshekedi was close to a nervous breakdown.[9]

Seretse left for London. On his way to Johannesburg airport, he stopped off in Mafikeng to speak to the Resident Commissioner, Anthony Sillery. After the visit, Sillery sent a report to the British High Commission; Sir Evelyn Baring was on leave, so it went to Sir Walter Harragin, the Chief Justice for the HCTs, who was Acting High Commissioner. 'There is no opposition to Seretse's claims to be Chief,' reported Sillery. 'These are completely accepted by all including Tshekedi. Opposition is concentrated on his European wife.' But, he added, 'Seretse was unwaveringly loyal to his wife, and his attitude remains what it has always been: that the Tribe, if it wants him as Chief, must accept his wife.'[10] Harragin praised Sillery for his impartiality. 'I am extremely pleased that you seem to have been able to preserve an attitude of strict neutrality in the whole matter,' he wrote, 'so that it can never be said in the future that Government had influenced the decisions in any way whatsoever.' He could not help feeling, he added uneasily, 'that there are some who would like to consider Seretse as a young man who has committed some wrong, whereas in fact all he has done is to make an honest woman of his wife.'[11]

On 7 January 1949, Seretse was met at the Heath Row aerodrome by his wife. The joy of their reunion was captured by the press in photographs: Ruth, sparkling with happiness, in a dark suit and hat, and a beaming Seretse, swinging a walking cane.[12] Ruth took him to their new home in north London – a garden flat in a cheerful house at 34 Adolphus Road. Knowing how much Seretse disliked cramped quarters, she had managed to find a larger flat before his return.[13]

They settled into a happy routine, where she kept house and he returned to his law studies. Ruth did what she could to encourage him with his preparation for the Equity exam: he loved reading detective stories but whenever he picked one up, she firmly took it away and put a textbook in his hands.[14] As the evenings grew warmer, friends would fill their little garden and the velvet voice of Leslie – 'Hutch' – Hutchinson, singing Gershwin and Porter, rang out from their gramophone player.[15]

Five months after his return from Bechuanaland, Seretse had to return for the third Kgotla, as he had promised. 'Once more my spirits fell,' sighed Ruth. 'Yet another separation!'[16]

When he arrived in Serowe on 15 June 1949, he quickly found that people's attitudes had grown in his favour. 'The people [had become] just as adamant that Tshekedi was trying to steal the chieftainship from Seretse,' recalled one of Tshekedi's friends, years later. 'I remember standing up in kgotla one day,' he said, 'and trying to set the facts straight on this point, but I was shouted at from all sides.' By June, he added, life had become impossible for Tshekedi or anyone who supported him in Serowe.[17]

People had split into two camps: for Seretse and against him. One of Seretse's royal uncles, Peto Sekgoma, had completely uprooted his life to support him. A gentle and soft-spoken man, two years older than Tshekedi, Peto had left the north of Bechuanaland, where he owned a store, and moved to Serowe, so that he could use his resources and influence to help his nephew.[18]

The Administration was largely on Tshekedi's side. Nettelton said he was surprised at all the fuss. 'We all know,' he said, 'who will always run the Ngwato – Tshekedi of course.'[19] But Sillery felt uncomfortable at the pressure from Tshekedi to take his side. He wrote to the Regent to say that he had been directed by Harragin to tell him that the Bechuanaland Protectorate Administration 'has endeavoured to maintain an attitude of strict impartiality in the matter of Seretse Khama's marriage to Miss Ruth Williams, which primarily concerns the tribe and Seretse'.[20]

As the day of the third Kgotla approached, Tshekedi became nervous and prickly. Sillery had suggested a guard of honour to mark the importance of the occasion, but the Regent was adamant that Seretse's arrival should not be 'heralded with undue pomp'.[21] He was hurt by Seretse – the young man who used to call him 'Father'. Seretse was driving around in one of Peto's cars, instead of his own.[22] And although Seretse was staying at Tshekedi's house, he was not eating there; noticing this, a British official wondered if he was afraid of being poisoned.[23]

Tshekedi furnished the Police Commissioner with a list of people who, he alleged, were plotting against him and holding secret meetings. By secret meetings, he meant meetings that were held without the knowledge of himself, as Native Authority. As a precaution, the Commissioner obtained additional Bren light machine-guns, tear-gas bulbs and canisters.[24] Tensions grew higher when it was announced that meetings were forbidden and Peto Sekgoma and another man disguised themselves as women, by wearing women's shawls, in order to meet one of Seretse's supporters off a train without being stopped.[25] This was Serogola Seretse, one of Seretse's cousins, who was an enemy of Tshekedi.

The atmosphere was electric when the third Kgotla started on Tuesday 20 June. At least 8,000 men had come from all over the reserve, many of them wearing their greatcoats and uniforms from World War II.[26] Tshekedi had invited three diKgosi from neighbouring nations: Kgosi Kgari of the Bakwena, Kgosi Mokgosi of the Balete, and Bathoen II, Kgosi of the Bangwaketse. Kgosi Kgari was a man of about 40, who had been a sergeant-major in the army during the war.[27] Bathoen II, also in his forties, was small and slight, with spectacles, and always seemed to be frowning.[28] He was a close friend and a political ally of Tshekedi. Like him, he was rigid and austere: a teetotaller who did not even drink tea or coffee, as he thought them too stimulating.[29] Kgosi Mokgosi belonged to Seretse's generation. The diKgosi had been invited as witnesses and, if necessary, to offer guidance on Tswana procedures and customs; it was normal among Batswana people for one nation to act as a 'guardian' of another, if it was in trouble.[30]

Vivien Ellenberger, First Assistant Secretary in Mafikeng, was in attendance as the Government Representative; he was fluent in Setswana and it was his job to write a record of the proceedings. A quiet and reserved man, Ellenberger came of Swiss missionary stock and his father had been Resident Commissioner of the Protectorate in the 1920s. 'All the VIPs are accommodated on a platform with roof,' reported Ellenberger to the resident commissioner with satisfaction – 'Quite pleasant and certainly better than sitting in the sun!'[31]

Tshekedi opened the Kgotla and Alan Seager said a prayer. Then the business of the Assembly began: the Regent stated that Seretse had married a woman who was unacceptable as the wife of the Kgosi and the mother of the future Kgosi. Seretse quietly, and with dignity, pointed out that Khama III had also married against the wishes of his people, as had his father and even Tshekedi himself; he stated firmly that he would not divorce his wife.

On the second day, attendance increased. 'From the dais above the ground level of the kgotla,' reported the South African Press Association, 'there is a good view of the crowd of 9,000 men seated below on stools and chairs beneath the camelthorn trees. The crowd is about 1,000 more than yesterday . . .' First there was a prayer. Then Manyaphiri Ikitseng spoke. He was a senior member of the Royal House, who was now in his fifties and lived at Mahalapye village. He described a meeting of the elders on 13 November, when they had tried to persuade Seretse that his marriage was a mistake. But they had had no intention, he said, of depriving him of his right to be Kgosi – and if Seretse would not divorce his wife, then he would accept her. 'Today,' he affirmed, 'I say that I want that woman even though at first I objected to the marriage.' Manyaphiri was followed by another senior man, who was blind. In a long speech he rebuked Seretse for his marriage. If he wanted to marry and light the family fire, he said, it must be done according to custom – 'but Seretse has broken the family water pot'.[32]

In the afternoon, Seretse put forward a request regarding procedure. Tshekedi had started the Kgotla with the instruction that a few people on each side should speak, to be answered by the same number of people on the other side. He defended this method on the grounds that it would avoid a string of speakers, all addressing the same point. But some people objected. 'Chief Tshekedi has stopped us from speaking,' complained one man, 'because he has noticed that Seretse's followers would outnumber his.' Seretse shared this concern. 'I request that the usual procedure should be adopted when people speak at random,' he said. 'I ask that *anybody* be allowed to speak, according to our usual custom. The Government Representative is here to obtain your views, whether you are poor or rich, clean or dirty.' His request was granted: it was agreed that no limit should be put on the number of speakers.

Seretse told the Assembly that he wished to stay in Serowe, but that he would not abandon his wife. If they wanted him to stay, they would have to accept Ruth too. He argued that the discussion was not really about his marriage, but about who was to be Kgosi. 'We have finished talking about the wedding,' he said. 'The question is, "Am I to be your Chief or not?"'[33]

'The town is on fire,' commented an elder in dismay, 'and I look to the representatives of other tribes here.' Turning to the visiting diKgosi, he said,

We cannot put it out, we look to you. Seretse has taken himself a wife and we were united that every effort must be made to undo the marriage. I do not want the woman. I asked the Government to separate Seretse and his wife.

But, he added,

Now I have changed my attitude, I am no longer concerned with the woman, I am concerned with the question of the Chieftainship . . . Seretse has taken a wife, but that cannot spoil his birthright. He is the heir. Let discussion of his wife be put aside.

The next speaker thought this was the right approach. 'The woman is an excuse only,' he said. 'I agree to the woman. Seretse can be installed by the Tribe and the Government.' It was time to be reasonable, argued the nobleman Goareng Mosinyi:

We refused the woman, but he refused to part from her, although he asked forgiveness for failing to consult us. He still refuses to part from her. Now I see that we cannot part him from the woman, so I think it better to let her come.

By the end of the second day, Ellenberger judged that Seretse was far more popular than Tshekedi. 'It begins to look fairly certain that Seretse will have a *per capita* majority,' he reported, 'but that the "gents" of the tribe who are the large property owners and heads of large sections will stick to Tshekedi.'[34]

On the third day, Oabona Nthobatsang made a plea on Seretse's behalf. He pointed out that his own people had sought asylum from Khama III, who took them into his care, so that they were all now

Bangwato – 'What would happen if we Makalaka said we do not want a Mongwato?' Oabona then asked, 'What is the opinion of the Government?' and was told that it was neutral. 'Have we any power,' he went on, 'to annul the marriage which has been solemnised by the white people?' – a question that was answered by a roar of 'No'. He concluded: 'I want that European woman to come here. We have nothing bad against her except her colour. I entirely support Seretse.'[35]

At noon, Serogola Seretse argued strongly in Seretse's defence. 'The talk is no longer about the wife but about the Chieftainship,' he said. 'Sekgoma's son, not Khama's, is the Kgosi. Seretse is the Kgosi. I say, let the woman come and their child shall succeed.' In that heated moment, Serogola threw his hat on the ground.[36] Tshekedi, he argued, had shown that he wanted to keep the kingship for himself. In two private meetings, he had said nothing. But, he went on, whereas there was an English proverb which said silence gives consent, among the Bangwato silence meant dissent. He said he was suspicious about Tshekedi's motives, wondering if the Regent was trying to usurp his nephew's right to the Khama inheritance. Then he ended his speech by saying:

Tshekedi said that he will not give Seretse the inheritance unless he gives up the woman. Had he not said that, I should have still persisted in opposition to the marriage; as it is I am changed, I now say let her come. His child by her shall be our Kgosi.[37]

Serogola's speech was heard in attentive silence.

On the fourth day of the Kgotla, after a prayer, Ellenberger was aware of a change in the atmosphere – 'emotions rising and some exhibitions of excitement'. He warned the Assembly not to lose self-control, or he would have the meeting closed.[38] Tshekedi made a 'long and impassioned' reply to Serogola. Then, looking directly at Seretse, he said, 'These people want to destroy the House of Khama by separating me from you. The House of Khama is Seretse's, but I want him to have a black child, not a white one.'[39] But this appeal on the grounds of colour was unsuccessful. One man pointed out that the members of the British Administration were a different colour. 'By saying we object to colour,' he said, 'we are objecting to the Protectorate. Our protectors are of a different colour, we cannot disregard them; they are here.' Little interest was shown in the issue of colour, beyond a concern about the way many whites behaved towards black people – 'I cannot accept a woman who will probably send dogs after me when I attempt to go to her home.'[40]

Then Tshekedi spoke at great length. He concluded with a comment on Khama's property, which he claimed had been left to him and not to his nephew. He had been planning to hand it on to Seretse, he said, but now he had decided not to do so. 'Seretse disregards our customs,' he said, 'and therefore we must go all the way. I shall not give Khama's property to him. This action will be hurtful to you and to him but you have hurt me more.'

His next move was to turn to his natural supporters – the 'gents' of the tribe, as Ellenberger had described them, who were men of influence and substance. He called them up to the dais – nine senior men, including Rasebolai Kgamane, who was third in line of succession to the kingship. 'The people you see standing here,' said the Regent to the Assembly, 'are my successors if I should die.' Each one of the men gave their view that Ruth was not a suitable wife for Seretse. This dramatic moment was followed by tea. 'I have spoken at great length,' said Tshekedi, wearily, 'and I feel I cannot concentrate. We shall therefore have a little break.'

After this interval, Seretse launched into a gentle speech that responded to the points made by his uncle. Then he asked the members of the Royal Family who agreed with him to stand. Thirteen men stood up – including Keaboka Kgamane, Peto Sekgoma, Manyaphiri Ikitseng, and Serogola Seretse – and he called them to the dais. These men of the Royal Family outnumbered the royals who had stood up for the Regent, although Tshekedi later suggested they were not as senior as the people who supported him – 'Of all the people I presented to Government, I did not show the number, but the quality.'[41]

But then Seretse made a bold move. He turned to the many thousands of men in front of him – the commoners – and said:

I want the Acting Deputy Resident Commissioner [Ellenberger] to know that I have supporters. I would like all the [royal headmen] standing inside and outside the kgotla to sit down so that those who want me and my wife should show me by standing.

This brought nearly every man to his feet – the whole Assembly, in a cloud of brown dust – thousands of men shouting '*Pula, Pula, Pula!*'[42] Then Seretse asked those who did *not* want his wife, to stand up – and not more than forty did so. The consensus of the Kgotla was visible for all to see – Seretse had been acclaimed as Kgosi and Ruth had been accepted as his wife. 'It was a stirring spectacle, a magnificent expression of public sentiment,' reported Ellenberger, evidently moved. According to Noel Monks of the *Daily Mail*, who was watching, the Assembly applauded thunderously for ten minutes.[43]

'I am not bringing this discussion to an end,' said Seretse. 'I was merely following a suggestion made that a vote should be taken.' But the discussion *was* at an end, because the majority had given their view. Ellenberger sent an urgent telegram to Sir Evelyn Baring in Pretoria: 'Assemblage has demonstrated in unmistakeable terms that it desires Seretse as Kgosi and accepts wife. Meeting will conclude tomorrow.'[44] Seretse, though a novice in kgotla practice, had triumphed over Tshekedi, the veteran. But this popular show of opinion was not part of the kgotla tradition. It was a new way of doing things – and an early sign that Seretse believed community affairs could be run in a different way, if this was appropriate and necessary.[45]

But in any case, Seretse could not have succeeded if he had not had a genuine interest in the views of the commoners and the poor. This was a concern that was entirely in the spirit of the tradition of the Kgotla: that commoners had as much right to air their views as members of the Royal Family. Under Tshekedi, this spirit had often been lost.[46] But it was an important influence on Seretse: when at Lovedale College, he had been critical of royals who had insisted on others addressing them as 'Kgosi'. On one occasion, when Seretse trod on the foot of another student, the boy complained, 'You act just like a chief!' Seretse responded firmly: 'At school there are no chiefs. We are all *equal*.'[47]

On the day after Seretse's triumph at the Kgotla, diKgosi Bathoen, Kgari and Mokgosi gave addresses in turn. Bathoen showed his support for Tshekedi in a bitter attack on Seretse. But Kgosi Kgari was strictly impartial. 'Although we seem to differ in certain respects,' he argued, 'we should work together and forget all the minor differences, let alone what transpired in this dispute. Whether you have lost or not, there should be peace.' Kgosi Mokgosi mentioned the possibility that Tshekedi's chief aim was to stay in power. 'I don't say Tshekedi may wish to retain the Chieftainship,' he observed, 'but he *may* be using this as an excuse to do so.'[48]

'I have heard your decision,' Ellenberger told the thousands of Bangwato men in front of him, 'and I shall report it to the Resident Commissioner, and it will also be intimated to the High Commissioner and the Secretary of State.'[49] To demonstrate his neutrality on the issue, he paid an equal measure of respect to Seretse and to Tshekedi: 'To you Seretse I wish to assure you of my good wishes. To Chief Tshekedi, I tender an expression of my esteemed regard.'

Saturday 25 June was the sixth and final day of the Kgotla. After a prayer, Tshekedi told the people assembled that he now wished to give them leave to return to their homes – *Go naya tsela*. Then he expressed his sorrow at what had transpired. 'I am grieved by all your accusations but I do not propose to reply,' he said, sadly. 'I take asylum in the Sechuana expression, "Dogs always bark at their Master."'' He then announced his intention to leave the Bangwato Reserve.

I bid you farewell. I have fled from you. I said I will go alone, I will not contest the land with Seretse, but will go to Mokwena [the Bakwena Reserve], or to Mongwaketse [the Bangwaketse Reserve], or to Mokgatla [the Bakgatla Reserve]. I shall have to hand over the work and the buildings to your child. All this will take time, but then I shall go.[50]

Then, choked with emotion, he cried, *'Phatalalang!'* – 'Disperse!'[51] He was completely overwrought. But he had no choice but to accept the will of the Kgotla. 'A Chief with the Tribe against him,' explained Seretse later to government officials, 'cannot carry on as Chief unless he accepts the Tribe's will. If he is adamant and will not bow to it, he must flee or be killed. This has always been the custom and, except for the killing, is still the custom.'[52]

Tshekedi was still formally Regent but his authority had been overthrown, and in any case he was making plans to leave the Reserve.[53] And although Seretse had been acclaimed as Kgosi, he had not yet been installed. This left a vacuum in the leadership of the Bangwato, which worried the new District Commissioner of Serowe, Richard Sullivan. On his very first day, he received a letter from Peto Sekgoma:

The Tribe gave its verdict on Thursday last week, who by a majority which could only be estimated they declared their willingness to accept Seretse with his English wife as their Kgosi and Mohumagadi [Mother of the Nation]. It is our strong desire, Sir, that this matter should be brought to a speedy conclusion and in this connection we pray the Government to have Seretse given his birthright and installed Kgosi of the Bamangwato with the least possible delay.[54]

On 13 July, Sullivan was given a petition signed by nine senior headmen. It pointed out that they had spent eight months thinking over the question of whether or not to accept Seretse and his wife. But now they had given their opinion: 'Let Government authorise Seretse to start duties of his heart-broken tribe.'[55]

The same message was sent to London, to the Secretary of State for Commonwealth Relations, by some of the many thousands of Bangwato working in the mines of South Africa. Grant Kgosi, who was a member of the Kimberley General Workers' Union, sent a letter on behalf of 'the Bangwato-Bakwena and Barotsi Brothers'. He stated that 'The Crown Prince of the Ma-Mmangwato Seretse Khama, has done a very very good job by marrying an English Lady.' This would be one way, he argued, of frustrating 'the existing "Colour bar namely the South African Discrimination"'. As blacks working in South Africa, he and his friends knew at first hand the suffering caused by apartheid. For this reason, he said, 'we *welcome* our *Ruth* as and/or to be our *Queen*'. They would like, he added, to see their Queen at Serowe.[56]

5

Ruth

Waiting in London for the outcome of the kgotla, Ruth was missing Seretse badly. One consolation, at least, was a reconciliation with her mother. 'She had never been as strongly opposed to my marriage as my father,' wrote Ruth, 'and she quickly realized my loneliness after Seretse's departure and he being six thousand miles away. So she came to see me, sometimes in the mornings, which enabled us to have lunch or tea together.'[1] Ruth had also made a new friend – Betty Thornton, another newly married woman, who lived in a bed-sitter at the top of the house. They had bumped into each other early one morning, while rushing to the front step to collect their precious bottles of rationed milk.[2]

Ruth was continually hounded by the press. Scarcely two weeks after their marriage the newspapers took it up. Early one Saturday morning, a young ex-serviceman in London was woken up by his mother frantically waving a newspaper in front of his face. He could hardly believe what he saw as he looked up from the pillow – banner headlines, proclaiming that his cousin, Ruth Williams, had married an African man called Seretse Khama.[3] 'Ruler-to-be Weds Office Girl', announced the *Daily Mirror*. 'Marriage that Rocks Africa' was the headline of the *Daily Mail*.[4] The press 'began to make headlines of everything we did,' said Ruth, 'prodding, mocking, seizing almost every opportunity to make our marriage a public curiosity. People stared at us in the streets.'[5] The newspapers insisted on calling her 'a London typist'; they knew that she had had an office job in the City, but it never crossed their mind that she might be a confidential clerk, with her own typist.[6]

The *Mirror* and the *Express* were the worst offenders, watching the house all the time while Seretse was away. The *Mirror* reporter spent long hours standing outside Ruth's bathroom window, trying to catch sight of her; he reported that she painted her nails with red varnish, in a way that was designed to raise questions about her reputation. He was so insidious that Ruth started to refer to him as 'Creeping Paralysis'. To help Ruth get out of the house without being followed, Betty would act as a decoy: she dressed up in her friend's coat, with a headscarf over her hair, and walked out of the front door. Ruth watched out of the window and as soon as she saw the posse of reporters chase after Betty, she slipped out of the house in the opposite direction. But she did not always manage to give 'Creeping Paralysis' the slip. On several occasions, when she had taken a seat on a bus, her heart sank as she heard him ask from the seat behind her, 'So what are you doing today, Mrs Khama?'[7] When the *Mirror* offered Ruth £100 for an interview, she turned it down in fury.[8] The South African press also watched Ruth. They reported that she was seen leaving her home 'with a native escort'.[9]

Ruth was thrilled when she received a telegram from Seretse about the decision of the Bangwato: 'Have been accepted by tribe. Will be recognized in three weeks. Delay passage till then.'[10] She immediately made her final preparations. Her mother and Muriel had managed to collect enough clothing coupons to buy some cool cotton dresses for hot weather. After a day of shopping in London's West End, Ruth came back to Adolphus Road and excitedly showed three new dresses to Betty. She was particularly delighted with one of them, because of its pattern on the skirt – a springbok leaping up. How appropriate, they thought, for her new life in southern Africa.[11]

But she had no romantic illusions about what life in Bechuanaland would be like. Seretse had made certain that she knew exactly what she would find there:

I did not try to romanticise the picture. I reminded her of the problems that might confront us, of the things we would have to face as two people of different races, reared on different continents.[12]

In any case, as Ruth was quick to point out, the automatic assumption that Britain was preferable to Africa was misplaced. London, with its severe rationing and the lingering effects of war, 'wasn't exactly the bright lights'.[13]

Gerald Nettelton, the Government Secretary of Bechuanaland, was on leave in the UK and heard the news about Seretse's acclamation from the Commonwealth Relations Office. He and his wife went to see Ruth, wondering what kind of Chief's wife she would turn out to be. 'Ruth Khama is a nice looking girl,' he wrote in surprise to Ellenberger:

much nicer looking than she appears to be from her photos – pretty golden hair – tallish – I should say 5 ft 6ins. She speaks and behaves nicely and is quite presentable – in fact, in Serowe, she can hold her own in the European social circle such as it is without trepidation. She was nicely and simply dressed and conversed freely and intelligently.

Ruth had told Nettelton and his wife how difficult the past year had been. 'She says she has been so worried,' he told Ellenberger, that 'she lost 14 lbs when Seretse first went out and has lost 9 lbs since he left this time. She looks rather thin but not bad.' But clearly, he thought, she would be a handful: 'In fact, she is a tougher proposition than we had hoped she might be – she will *never* be bought off. Our impression is a good one.'[14] Nettelton sent a similar account of Ruth to a friend at the CRO:

My wife and I had Mrs Khama, as she styles herself, to tea more out of curiosity than anything else. She will be *no* cipher and undoubtedly she will influence Seretse greatly. She is a young woman of her own ideas – better bred than we expected and with a special mission in life.[15]

John Keith, despite his initial reservations, was coming round to the same view. He had been asked by the CRO to visit Ruth and was surprised by what he found: that Ruth was 'quite reasonable and more intelligent than he had previously supposed'.[16] He was disgusted by the fact that the opponents of the marriage, even some members of the London Missionary Society, were advocating a divorce and a plan of 'paying Ruth off'. The Khamas, he believed, 'are decent Christian people who were deeply offended by this suggestion and by the fact that the Bishop of London prevented their marriage in a Church of the Ch[urch] of England'.[17]

Ruth Williams had been born on 9 December 1923. She and her sister, Muriel, who was one year older, grew up in Blackheath, a comfortable suburb in south London, where they attended Eltham Hill School for Girls. Leggy and athletic, Ruth loved games – lacrosse, netball, tennis and hockey. George Williams, their father, was a big and kindly man, who had been an officer in the British army in India in the First World War and was now working as a commercial traveller. Their mother Dorothy – 'Dot' – ran a happy and efficient home. She and Ruth were alike and shared a strong sense of humour.[18] They were also similar in appearance and were both of average height. Muriel was tall, like her six-foot father. She looked rather forbidding, because she wore severe spectacles and her hair was scraped back from her face, whereas Ruth loved stylish clothes and had an eye for fashion.

Ruth left school to start a two-year course in hotel and restaurant cookery. But then war arrived, disrupting family life. On 1 September 1939, she and Muriel – along with one and a half million other children in London – were evacuated to the countryside.[19] Ruth went by train to Sussex, where she was billeted in a cottage on a country estate; she was treated kindly but, like many evacuees, suffered badly from homesickness and begged her mother to let her come home. By January 1940, more than half of the evacuees had returned to the city.[20] Muriel, though, who had been sent to Folkestone and then to Wales, was content to stay there. She had been billeted with chapel people and although the Williams family was Anglican, she decided to become a Congregationalist.

By the time the Luftwaffe began their raids on London, Ruth was back in London. One night in September 1940, when she was 16, her road in Blackheath was bombed. Several people living in the road were killed and her own house – like two out of every seven homes in Britain during the war – was rendered unfit for habitation.[21] The family searched for several weeks for another home and finally found a ground-floor flat in Belmont Hall Court, an apartment building in Lewisham, not far away.[22] Ruth, who had a strong sense of duty,[23] now started to take turns with fire-watching. In 1942, as soon as she was old enough, she joined the Women's Auxiliary Air Force, becoming one of the half million British women serving with the forces.[24] In the powder-blue uniform of the WAAF, she began a routine of drilling and discipline. 'There is nothing like the Service to knock the ego out of a girl,' she observed. She volunteered as a driver and was very proud when she learned that she had passed her training courses – it was, she thought, 'the first major achievement' of her life. 'Some poor girls,' she realized with sympathy, 'just could not make the grade.'

Her first posting was to a section of the Royal Air Force Battle of Britain Group: 'nice people to drive about, unassuming fighter pilot heroes,' thought Ruth. But it was at her next posting, a satellite airfield at RAF Friston, near the south coast, that she came 'face to face', as she put it later, 'with the stark reality of war'. To this airfield flew the crippled planes of bomber command which had been hit by the enemy over Berlin, the Ruhr or the Channel. It was Ruth's job to stand by with a crash ambulance and to rush out whenever a plane landed. The crashes were frequent: 'One minute you would hear the cheery voices of pilots over RT [radio telephone]: "Coming in now. Not sure whether the old kite will hang together, but will have a go. Cheerio."' Next moment, a tongue of flame would shoot along the runway. 'One of our fighters,' said Ruth, 'had returned to base only to perish. I would rush my crash ambulance over, but little could be done.' Sometimes, though, the damaged aircraft would survive the landing: 'I would dash over to be greeted by grinning pilots, who would say: "Not this time, chum." They would pile in and I would drive them back to the canteen.' The runway and station buildings were frequently bombed and she risked her life on many occasions. Twenty months of this work, said Ruth wearily, 'took all the glamour out of war for me'.[25]

Ruth stayed in the WAAF for a year after the end of the war. Then, in 1946, she went on her last parade. 'The first thing I bought when I went home after being demobbed,' she remembered later, 'was a pair of nylons. They had just come back in the shops again. A friend of mine had a tip where I could get them.' She had saved up her clothing coupons and was eager to get back into civilian dress. 'Girls,' she thought, 'were never really meant to live in uniforms.'[26] Now, she wanted some fun. 'I had come out of the war completely heart-whole, believe it or not,' she said, 'and all I wanted were days of sleep, some home life, and pretty clothes again, in that order.' Like many other ex-servicemen and women, she and her cousin 'went mad' some evenings.[27] She found a good job and enjoyed the freedom of peacetime – ice-skating, listening to music, and ballroom-dancing.

The years of war – and especially her four years in the WAAF – had toughened Ruth into an independent and determined young woman. But in any case, she was by nature very capable: ready to roll up her sleeves and get on with things. She also had a strong sense of justice and was forthright, never hesitating before speaking her mind. She became very angry if any of the other servicemen or women made jokes at the expense of Jews or black people – pointing out that this kind of prejudice was exactly what they were supposed to be fighting.[28]

Seretse admired Ruth's spirit. He also believed, reported Lawrenson, the District Commissioner, that 'it might be an advantage as far as the women of the tribe are concerned for him to have an enlightened wife'.[29] Bangwato society was strongly patriarchal and women were excluded from the kgotla; they also did most of the hard work necessary to keep their families alive, such as carrying water and ploughing the land. For the large number of women whose husbands were away working in South Africa, life was especially tough and many women felt they had suffered additional burdens under Tshekedi's regime. Women in the village of Mahalapye were especially angry at Tshekedi because he opposed prostitution and beer-brewing, which were some of the few ways in which they had been able to make a living.[30]

But many more women than men in Bechuanaland had received some kind of education. Boys spent much of their childhood at the family's cattle-post, which meant that they were unable to attend their village school – so that the number of girls at school far exceeded the number of boys. At one school in this period, there were sixty-six girls and only one boy.[31] Moreover, the Bangwato Royal Family often sent their daughters to South Africa to be educated, as well as their sons. Seretse's younger sister Naledi, who was his half-sister by his mother Tebogo and to whom he was devoted, was sent to Lovedale and then went on to train as a nurse in Durban.

There had been a long line of powerful women in the Royal Family. Three of Khama III's daughters – Baboni, Mmakgama and Milly – had challenged their brother Tshekedi's authority in the 1920s, arguing that he was authoritarian and cruel. In a letter of complaint to the High Commissioner, they objected that he had revived 'ridiculous native laws and customs, which as you know Khama had abolished'.[32] Seretse's other half-sister, Oratile, the eldest daughter of the late Kgosi Sekgoma, joined in this protest. Twenty years older than Seretse and a widow, she lived in Francistown, her husband Simon Ratshosa having been banished there by Tshekedi many years earlier. She wrote a further letter to the Resident Magistrate in 1929, in which she argued that Tshekedi had none of the qualities which had distinguished Khama – and that the Government ought 'to teach him to learn to think in the new ways of new things, to perform his duties as Kgosi'.[33]

Sekgoma II had shown an enlightened attitude towards his daughter Oratile: when he died, he had left cattle, small stock and money not only to Seretse, but to Oratile as well. She and her aunts argued in a letter to the high commissioner that 'Khama's law was equal to both sexes, women had the same right as men. Estates were always proportionally divided to the deceased family, sons and daughters.'[34] But when Oratile claimed her inheritance, Tshekedi withheld it from her – just as he had done in the case of her aunts. She wrote a letter of protest to the administration:

Tshekedi has confiscated every one of my cattle without saying a word to me. I am shocked that he has burnt down my houses when I have done him no wrong, and that he has gone further and confiscated my cattle that my father gave me.[35]

As Ruth waited for permission to travel to Africa in 1949, she was looking forward to meeting her sisters-in-law, Oratile and Naledi, for the first time. When the British High Commissioner, Sir Evelyn Baring, gave instructions that she might travel to Bechuanaland after 23 July 1949, she quickly bought a ticket for the BOAC flying-boat.[36] This would take her to the Victoria Falls on the Zambezi River, between Southern and Northern Rhodesia. From there she would fly to Bechuanaland in a two-seater plane. John Keith had gently warned her not to fly to Johannesburg, where her notoriety as the white wife of Seretse Khama might lead to some unpleasant incidents. This was good advice. John Redfern, a reporter working for the *Daily Express*, who stopped in Johannesburg on his way to Serowe, was astonished by the invective triggered by even a mention of Seretse's name:

I had flown into Palmiefontein, Johannesburg's main airport, from London, and had unwittingly raised a crop of scowls by asking how I could get on to Seretse Khama's country. 'God, man!' whispered an airport official. 'Don't mention that name here!' ... Seretse was a menace. At the mention of his name jaws jutted, eyes glared, and hatred joined the company.[37]

But even going to the Victoria Falls was problematic, because the flying-boat usually landed on the Southern Rhodesian side. Sir Godfrey Huggins, the Prime Minister of Southern Rhodesia, knew that if Ruth were to disembark there, it would provoke an outcry from the whites of his country. He had been sent a letter from a particularly hostile man, insisting that she be forbidden from landing in Southern Rhodesia:

I submit that this is one of those occasions in which those who understand Africa should protect the Continent against silly women and politicians, who, in their ignorance, have a tendency to lower the prestige of the European races. I am confident that pucka Rhodesians will be glad to hear that our Government will prevent 'Ruth' from using our soil to fulfil her desire.[38]

Huggins took this seriously. He decided to get in touch with Baring, who was a good friend – Baring had been the Governor of Southern Rhodesia from 1942 to 1944, when they had struck up a rapport. He asked Baring to make sure that Ruth would land on the other side of the Falls, in Northern Rhodesia, at a town called Livingstone. From there, he added, she should fly to Bechuanaland, to avoid having to drive through Southern Rhodesia. 'It would help me (in the event of the lady coming by air)', he wrote to Baring, 'if she stayed at Livingstone and flew direct from there to her palace in Bechuanaland. I think you know the background here well enough to make it unnecessary for me to elaborate.'[39]

'The lady will arrive at the Falls by British Overseas Air Corporation flying boat on the 19th August,' wrote Sillery to the Provincial Commissioner in Livingstone, 'and in order to save further publicity, and possible embarrassment, it has been decided to fly her from

Livingstone to Francistown, where Seretse will meet her. May I once more invoke your good offices?'[40] The pilot was given instructions to fly along the edge of the Kalahari Desert, in order to keep as far away as possible from Southern Rhodesia.[41]

Ruth left London on 15 August 1949. The press were still hanging around her flat, at all hours, but she managed to give them the slip. She and Muriel borrowed their father's car and went late at night to Adolphus Road. Here they parked the car at the end of the road and then collected Ruth's suitcases – in darkness, because they didn't dare to use a torch – and put them in the car, which they drove back to Lewisham. Next morning, Ruth went to Waterloo to catch a train for Southampton; she took an ordinary train, not a fast boat train, in case this attracted attention.[42]

With a reservation under the name of Mrs S. Jones, Ruth finally embarked on the BOAC flying-boat for Africa.[43] All the crew knew who she was but kept her secret; not one of her forty fellow passengers discovered her identity. It was a far more leisurely way of travelling to Africa than an aeroplane. The flying-boat took four days to reach its final destination of Johannesburg and offered luxury travel: four-course meals and Pullman-style upholstery, with ample space to walk about and chat and enjoy refreshments. Ruth had expected the journey to be boring and tedious. But she loved it – 'I could go on and on just taking off and landing on water, as one's vision becomes completely screened by the water,' she wrote to Betty. The first night stop was at Augusta in Sicily, the second at Luxor in Egypt, 'where we looked over an old temple. It took 45 minutes, and was not worth missing, because the work was beautiful.' The next night stop was Kampala, in Uganda, from where they flew to the Victoria Falls. This took her breath away. The original name for the Victoria Falls was *Mosioathu-nya* – 'the smoke that thunders'. The spray, flung so far into the air as the Zambezi plunges into the gorge, looks like smoke – and as the sheer mass of water pours over the top, it makes a deafening roar. The falls 'are indescribable', Ruth told Betty in delight, 'they are such a picture'.[44]

When Ruth landed at the Falls on 19 August, she was taken to Livingstone. Here she was met by a portly British official, in khaki shorts and long socks. She looked slim and smart, in a dark coat and light scarf, with low heels. She was radiant with the anticipation of seeing her husband the following day.[45]

II

A Conspiracy of Nations

6

The dark shadow of apartheid

Three days after the June Kgotla in Serowe, the British High Commission in South Africa cabled London to confirm the decision of the Bangwato.[1] All that remained was to install Seretse as Kgosi. But the next day, there was an intervention from an unexpected quarter – from Dr Daniel Malan, the South African Prime Minister, a stout Afrikaner with a bald head, whose eyes peered out through thick glasses. He was a Doctor of Divinity and a Minister in the Dutch Reformed Church, the dominant religion of Afrikaners and the Nationalist Party, which believed in the superiority of whites over blacks. Now, in response to Seretse Khama's marriage, Dr Malan told his Secretary for External Affairs, Douglas Forsyth, to send a top-secret telegram to Leif Egeland, the South African High Commissioner in London. Egeland was instructed to speak to the British Government and advise them to withhold recognition of Seretse's Chieftainship.[2] This issue – a local matter that should have been of no concern to anybody but the Bangwato – was now starting to assume international proportions.

As soon as Egeland had read this cable, he went to see Philip Noel-Baker, the Secretary of State for Commonwealth Relations, and asked him to refuse to recognize Seretse as Chief. The Union Government was certain, he added, that it was within the power of the United Kingdom to do this. Egeland dressed his request in terms of concern about the Bangwato and the risk of losing Tshekedi – a 'most serious loss not only to Bechuanaland, but to Africans in general, for Tshekedi was almost the only African leader who had shown real vision and statesmanship'. He elaborated, too, on the problems ahead for Ruth. 'Coming from an English home,' he argued, 'she would find it extremely difficult to settle down to the kind of accommodation and living conditions which Seretse could offer her.'[3] This comment betrayed Egeland's prejudice: for the Bangwato royal family lived in brick houses that were far more spacious and comfortable than the flat in which the Williams family lived in London.

Noel-Baker promised to consider the matter carefully. Then Egeland got up to go.

Egeland was not at all reassured by his talk with Noel-Baker, a man now in his sixties who was well known as an idealist. Though the Commonwealth Secretary was 'understandably non-committal', he reported in an urgent telegram to Forsyth, 'I did not, repeat not, get [the] impression that there was much prospect that recognition of Seretse's chieftainship would be withheld.' The best strategy, he believed, would be to concentrate on Sir Evelyn Baring, the British High Commissioner in South Africa. 'I feel [the] United Kingdom Government will be largely guided by advice which will be received from Baring,' he urged, 'to whom no doubt strong representations will have been made at your end.'[4]

As Forsyth had predicted, Noel-Baker immediately got in touch with Baring. 'You will no doubt,' he said, 'be sending me shortly your recommendation on the whole question, and in particular as to confirmation of Seretse's succession.'[5] But Baring asked for a delay, because he was waiting for a report from Anthony Sillery, the Resident Commissioner. This report arrived on 5 July: Seretse's election by acclamation, said Sillery, was so overwhelming that there was 'really little more to say', and the Kgotla had been 'as representative as one could have hoped or as African meetings generally are'. In any case, he added, 'The Batswana are fanatically attached to the principle of hereditary chieftainship.' He concluded his report with a formal recognition of Seretse as chief:

It only remains for me, in accordance with Section 3 of the Native Administration Proclamation . . . to recommend that Seretse Khama be recognised by you as Chief of the Bamangwato and that the Secretary of State's confirmation be sought.[6]

In this first week of July 1949, Baring shared Sillery's assumption that Seretse should – and would – be installed as Kgosi. He had misgivings about Seretse's marriage and, indeed, had said that he regarded the possibility of Seretse becoming Chief as the 'worst development [that] might occur'.[7] But he did not question the decision of the June Kgotla. He had already met with Seretse in South Africa and told him that he expected his confirmation as Chief to come through in a few weeks. The High Commissioner, noted Sillery,

saw Seretse on Monday 4.7.49. HC is going to press for an early confirmation of Seretse's appointment by S/S [Commonwealth Secretary of State]. And a telegraphic reply. I should say that if all goes well we shall hear by the end of the month . . . When that decision is made we must proceed to the installation as soon as we decently can.[8]

But at this point, Sir Percivale Liesching intervened in the affair. Liesching was the Permanent Under-Secretary to Noel-Baker and therefore the official head of the Commonwealth Relations Office. On 8 July, he sent Baring a carefully worded telegram. 'While outcome of tribal discussion on the Seretse affair appears to be clear,' he argued, 'the difficulties in our path are obvious.' These difficulties, he said, were the objections of South Africa and Southern Rhodesia. Then Liesching introduced the idea of a new strategy: he asked whether there was any interim measure, in accordance with tribal custom, which could be used to produce a 'cooling off' period in the Seretse affair.[9]

As it turned out, there *was* an interim measure that could be used to produce a delay. For on the day before Liesching's cable arrived, Sir Evelyn had been handed a document signed by Tshekedi and about forty headmen who supported him, demanding a judicial inquiry into the question of whether or not Seretse should be Kgosi.[10] He was given the document by Tshekedi's lawyer, Douglas Buchanan, who had devised the plan. At first, Baring dismissed it out of hand. 'I have given the High Commissioner a way out,' complained Buchanan, 'but he seems antagonistic thereto and I really do not think he grasps or understands the seriousness of the situation.'[11] But Liesching's suggestion prompted Baring to reconsider – an inquiry might be useful after all, as a way of holding things up. He badly needed time to think, and warned Noel-Baker that there would be a further delay before he could send a report, in view of 'representations made to me by Tshekedi and of other developments'.[12]

These 'other developments' included top-level talks with the South African Government. On 7 July, Baring had had his 'first opportunity of seeking Forsyth's help', as he explained later to Sir Percivale. Forsyth, he told him, had discussed the whole matter in Cape Town with Dr Malan, who was 'greatly worried and distressed'. Two key points had emerged. The first was that the prospect of the official recognition of Seretse greatly offended Malan's government and probably most white South Africans. The second was more of a threat – that the installation of Seretse as Chief would give ammunition to those groups seeking the transfer of the High Commission Territories to South Africa. Even more seriously, J. G. Strydom, who led an extreme faction of the Nationalists, would be strengthened against Dr Malan. These extremists, Forsyth had argued, would exploit the recognition of Seretse to appeal to the country for the establishment of South Africa as a republic – outside the Commonwealth.[13]

Forsyth had also told Baring that the installation of Seretse would endanger the prospects of reaching an agreement on defence measures; the same point had been made to Baring by General Beyers, Chief of the South African General Staff.[14] A number of defence issues were currently being negotiated between South Africa and the UK. That very month, the South African Defence Minister had gone with General Beyers to London for discussions: South Africa wanted to extract promises of arms supplies, while Attlee was anxious to secure a commitment by South Africa to the defence of the Middle East.[15] There were other defence issues, too. One of these was uranium, which had been discovered in South Africa just a few years before and was regarded as vital for the British atomic weapons programme.[16] These defence issues assumed particular importance in the context of the developing Cold War between East and West. It was seen as particularly necessary for the West to secure atomic superiority, because of Russia's successful testing of an atomic bomb the year before.

As well as having discussions with Forsyth and receiving advice from Sir Percivale, Baring was under pressure from Sir Godfrey Huggins, the Prime Minister of Southern Rhodesia. 'I am writing to you re your White chieftainess-to-be (?) in Bechuanaland,' wrote

Huggins to his old friend Baring, in a jocular fashion. Then he became deadly serious: 'As you can imagine, I am being bombarded to interfere in a matter of no direct concern of ours, but which has the possibility of repercussions here.' He did not know, he said, what Baring and the Secretary of State were going to do about it,

but I do want you to know (if you do not know already) that we consider an official Native–European union in Bechuanaland would increase our difficulties here, and also add a little fuel to the flames of the fire kept burning by our, fortunately diminishing, band of anti-Native Europeans.

You will appreciate why I have to write this letter re a domestic problem of another state.[17]

After writing this letter, Huggins drove to the colonial-style Parliament building in the centre of Salisbury (now Harare). Here the all-white Legislative Assembly presented him with a resolution – agreed by all the political parties – protesting against Seretse's marriage and his installation as Chief; it demanded that Huggins officially inform the British Government of this view. 'If we allow the principle of mixed marriages to expand in Southern Rhodesia,' argued the leader of the Opposition, 'those of us who have been brought up in the country know that it will lead to nothing but misery, confusion and degradation.' What would be the position, he asked, 'with regard to the offspring of such a marriage? What will be their status in society, in this country, whether native or European? . . .' It was necessary to think 'not only of ourselves,' he argued with false concern, 'but of the masses of natives throughout Africa'–

If we are proud of our purity, so is the native. Charity of course begins at home. First of all we think of ourselves and of our own natives, but I feel confident that by this motion we are doing the Bamangwato tribe a great and invaluable service . . .

Huggins replied that the Government's view was very largely the same. 'There is no doubt,' he assured the House, 'that the tribesmen's decision is a disastrous one. First, it shows lack of racial pride in Bechuanaland; secondly, it is disastrous from the effect it will have on neighbouring territories.' He said that he had already written to the

British High Commissioner but promised to follow this up with a further communication, 'informing him of the opinion of this House and how disastrous it would be if this fellow is allowed to become Chief of Khama's people'.[18]

Huggins's statement to the Legislative Assembly in Salisbury was widely reported in Southern Africa. His dismissive description of Seretse as 'this fellow', which was standard language by white South Africans to refer to black men, led to a complaint to the British High Commissioner from the African Tribal Affairs Committee at Retreat, a town in the far south of South Africa. 'We strongly object,' they wrote, 'to that term they used, *fellow*.' The Committee demanded respect for Seretse – 'all our Africans observe him as our Prince, we would not like anyone to call him by funny names. The Man we want is an able man, we are not concerned about his Wife, who she is, or how she is.'[19]

'Fellow' was used by whites in central and southern Africa to refer to black men who had been educated. Less well-educated black men, especially servants, were routinely referred to as 'boy', regardless of their age. Kenneth Kaunda, who became president of Zambia (formerly Northern Rhodesia) in 1964, described this offensive usage in his autobiography. In one incident in 1957, when he was visiting a town called Kitwe in Northern Rhodesia with Harry Nkumbula, they found themselves in a white area of town and went to a café which, according to their driver, would sell them food so long as they did not ask to take their meal there. They went inside the café and Kaunda asked for some sandwiches, to which a young white girl of about 17 replied that 'boys' were not served at the counter. When he told her that he was not a 'boy' and only wanted some sandwiches, she consulted an elderly white woman, who repeated that 'boys' were not served at that counter. At this point, recalled Kaunda,

I was dragged out of the café by my clothes by a European man who had already dragged Harry Nkumbula outside the café. This white man hit Harry and called him a cheap, spoiled nigger. Five other white men joined him in attacking us and we defended ourselves. White men and black men passing joined in the fight, and an apartheid type of brawl took place.

Kaunda and Nkumbula were taken to the charge office, where Nkumbula began by saying that the girl at the counter had refused to serve them. But before he could finish his sentence, the white superintendent of police said, 'You cannot call a white lady a "girl" or a "woman".' Harry ignored this and went on speaking, describing the behaviour of the elderly woman. But again,

before he could finish his sentence, the superintendent said, 'I say, you cheeky nigger, you cannot call a European lady a woman.'

Then this police officer called Harry to a room and closed the door and beat him up. Harry told this officer that he was lucky he was wearing Her Majesty the Queen's uniform, or one or other of them would have been killed.[20]

The whites of Northern Rhodesia were as bitterly opposed to the idea of Seretse being Chief as were their white neighbours in Southern Rhodesia. In their Legislative Council in Lusaka, the capital, one Member of Parliament received rapturous applause on 8 July 1949 when he said that he hoped mixed unions would not be permitted in Northern Rhodesia. He was also opposed, he said, to the practice of European men cohabiting with native women.[21]

Baring reflected on the arguments that had been put to him by Forsyth and Huggins. He *could* have dismissed them and backed the decision of the Serowe Kgotla. But he did not. Instead, he decided to go ahead with Tshekedi's request for an inquiry. On 11 July, he finally sent Noel-Baker the report he had promised. Ordinarily, said Baring, Seretse would be installed as a matter of course – but the situation bristled with complications. He drew attention to the possibility of 'external repercussions which I cannot ignore':

Adverse reactions in the local press are widespread and forceful. The Prime Minister of Southern Rhodesia has stated in the Legislative Assembly that his Government too is addressing to me official protests. I need not, I am sure, emphasise how repugnant mixed marriage of this nature is to the great majority of people in Southern Africa. It is apparently the possibility of immediate official recognition of Seretse and his wife which arouses most criticism.

He therefore proposed holding a judicial inquiry into whether or not Seretse should be chief. This would put the whole problem on hold for a period, during which time any number of developments could occur, such as the disillusionment of Ruth with life in Serowe.[22]

This shift in opinion had been swift. In the space of just one week – between telling Seretse on 4 July that he would be confirmed as Kgosi, and his despatch to Noel-Baker on 11 July – Baring had changed his mind about the recognition of Seretse. 'Baring told Stimson [Robert Stimson, a BBC journalist] after June Kgotla', noted the US Embassy in South Africa, 'that HMG would have to see Seretse through and not knuckle to Malan, but a week after strong statements by Malan and Huggins he had completely about-faced.'[23]

Baring sent a long letter to Liesching. He believed, he said, that they were faced with a 'choice of evils'. On the one hand, refusal to recognize Seretse as Chief 'would open us to accusations of having surrendered to representations made by the Union Government and of having flouted the views of the tribe'. But on the other hand, the recognition of Seretse during the next months – rejecting the representations made by Dr Malan – 'would lead to a head-on collision with the Union' at the worst possible time and for the worst possible reason. 'We must play for time,' he urged. 'At any rate,' he added, getting to the point, 'we should avoid a snub to the Union Government. We would show that we realised the seriousness of the position.'[24] Only one day after sending this long letter, Baring followed it up with a cable. He was grateful, he said, for Liesching's suggestion of a measure to produce a 'cooling off' period. 'It was a great relief,' he went on, 'to find that our minds were working along the same lines.'[25]

Liesching wrote a minute for Noel-Baker, backing Baring's plan for an inquiry. The day before, he said, he had been told by General Beyers that if Seretse were allowed to be Chief with his white wife, it would not simply be a matter between the UK Government, Bechuanaland and South Africa,

but would light a fire through the British Colonial Territories in Africa which would not soon be quenched. He said that the very existence of white settlement in these territories depended, in view of the numerical inferiority and defencelessness of the white population, upon the principle that the native mind regarded the white woman as inviolable.

Then he set out his own feelings about the colour question:

I do not wish here to discuss at length the question of our attitude towards the colour bar, on which, I dare say, I am as doctrinally correct as yourself, the Colonial Secretary and all those in this country who most strongly disapprove of discrimination based on racial colour.

Nevertheless, he had never been able to reconcile himself to the 'ultimate logical consequences of this principle of non-discrimination when it takes practical forms affecting oneself or one's family in terms of miscegenation'. Nor, he said, did he

believe that many who hold their antipathy to the colour bar would, if confronted with this matter in personal terms, view with equanimity, or indeed without revulsion, the prospect of their son or daughter marrying a member of the Negro race.

Liesching then turned to the risk that South Africa might 'whip up' feeling among white settlers in Southern Rhodesia, in Kenya, and in the Tanganyika territory:

I have little doubt that Southern Rhodesia will react violently. There has always been a rather unholy alliance between the South Africans and the Kenya settlers over native policy and the colour bar. Tanganyika can be easily infected. In short there may be a very bitter harvest here.[26]

Patrick Gordon Walker, who was Noel-Baker's Parliamentary Secretary, saw Liesching's minute and commented on it with one of his own. 'This is an extremely grave matter,' he argued, 'and can involve us in historic calamities if we are not careful – I would wholly support Baring's proposal for an enquiry.' He himself was ready to take an even stronger position against Seretse, on racial grounds. 'I would not put out of court the possibility of declaring that a chief cannot have a white wife,' he said. 'There is a lot to be said for this argument and we should consider facing that uproar that would result. We must all think about this carefully.'[27]

Clearly, Liesching's and Gordon Walker's desire to carry out South

Africa's wishes regarding Seretse were generated from deeply felt racism. A related factor was their commitment to the Dominions for which they, as the Commonwealth Relations Office, were responsible – Australia, Canada, New Zealand, Ireland and South Africa. These 'white' Dominions were seen as vital to the continuation of Britain's world role, and part of Baring's job as British High Commissioner in South Africa was to maintain this relationship. In comparison with South Africa, the needs of Bechuanaland – a Protectorate with very few white people and no role in the international community – were seen by the CRO as irrelevant.

Liesching's and Gordon Walker's minutes were read by Noel-Baker. He may have been surprised to read Sir Percivale's uncompromising statement of his racist beliefs and Gordon Walker's recommendation. In any case, he had misgivings about Baring's strategy.

On 16 July he wrote to Arthur Creech Jones, to let him know what Baring had suggested.[28] Creech Jones was the Secretary of State for the Colonial Office, which held responsibility for most of the British colonies in Africa. It was not responsible for Bechuanaland because of the Protectorate's close relationship with South Africa, which was a Dominion and therefore associated with the Common-wealth Relations Office. The CRO, which had been formed in 1947 by a merger of the Dominions Office and India Office, following the independence of India and Pakistan, had a deeply conservative approach to policy. In this respect it differed from the Colonial Office, which had attracted some recruits with a genuine sense of mission about the future of the colonies and concerns about racial exclusion. Creech Jones was a member of the Fabian Colonial Bureau and had clearly articulated his sympathy with the aspirations of African colonies for self-government.

But Creech Jones did not back the decision of the Bangwato. Instead, he favoured the plan for an inquiry, to buy time. He took the view that it would be necessary in due course to refuse recognition of Seretse, but that to do so just then would be to place the whole emphasis on the racial issue and would look like what it was – a concession to South African opinion.[29]

The Commonwealth Secretary was uncertain and worried. 'I am not sure that Mr Egeland's arguments are conclusive,' he had written in a note to Liesching, 'and I hope Sir E. Baring won't think that we think they are.'[30] He and his Permanent Under-Secretary were not of like mind. When Liesching had taken over the post in January that year, Noel-Baker had at first been pleased. Liesching had considerable experience of Africa and had been Deputy Commissioner in the High Commission Territories at the time of Tshekedi's deposition after the flogging affair. But as the months had passed, their differences became increasingly apparent. A lean man in his mid-fifties, with a sharp-featured and aquiline face, Sir Percivale – an Oxford Blue and President of the Civil Service rugby club – was a tough realist, to the point of ruthlessness.[31] In the view of a colleague:

Temperamentally, they were poles apart – Noel-Baker regarded Liesching as a racialist and thought he was disloyal. Liesching considered Noel-Baker an ineffective busybody and relished repeating a comment that he was an 'intellectual mosquito'.[32]

The junior staff of the CRO were busy studying photographs of Ruth Khama in newspapers to see if she looked pregnant; a photograph in the *Star*, which showed a pencil-thin Ruth out shopping, convinced them she was not.[33] Then Noel-Baker came up with a plan of his own. He prepared a memorandum for Cabinet members, in which he proposed that Seretse be invited to the UK for talks:

I feel that there is some hope that if we can have a frank discussion with Seretse and his wife, they may both decide that it would be undesirable that Seretse should take up the chieftainship of the Tribe.[34]

In a draft telegram to Baring, which he circulated to the Cabinet, he argued that there was a 'certain chance' that Seretse might be prepared to withdraw his claim to the chieftainship, if he appreciated the difficulties felt by the United Kingdom Government.[35]

But there was no support from the Cabinet for Noel-Baker's plan. It was decided instead to give the green light to a judicial inquiry. Creech Jones argued particularly vigorously for this strategy.[36] Shortly after the meeting, Liesching wrote to Baring. He was about to go on leave, he said, but he wanted to thank him for his reports 'on this terribly difficult Seretse problem. I can well imagine the very anxious time you are having over it.' He wanted to know that among Ministers here there has now developed a complete unanimity against recognition of Seretse with Ruth as his wife. It was very difficult to estimate how Ministerial opinion would go on this and Creech Jones has come out entirely on the right side.

Then he offered him a fulsome compliment: that Baring's judgement was 'trusted to an extent which has never been exceeded in the case of any High Commissioner I have known'.[37]

These discussions took place against a background of increased racial inequality and segregation in South Africa. On 1 July 1949 the Prohibition of Mixed Marriages Act was passed, which made marriage between a 'European' and a 'non-European' illegal. Many white South Africans argued that the marriage of Seretse Khama was conclusive proof of the need for the Act. The day after it had been passed, the *Natal Witness* condemned Seretse and Ruth in a leading article entitled 'A Marriage We Must Condemn'. Miscegenation, it argued,

is contrary to our fundamental beliefs and legislation has recently been introduced for its prohibition . . . The mixed marriage strikes at the root of White supremacy; even if it were limited to exceptional cases, it tends to breed ideas which are antipathetic to our conviction that the colour bar in Africa must be maintained.

It made a particular dig at the fact that Seretse had been allowed to study at Oxford:

Whitehall may pet and pamper its colonial Native populations as much as it likes, sending them to Oxford and Cambridge and giving them false ideas of their importance, but the Colonial Secretary should exercise a modicum of circumspection in his attitude to Natives whose territories adjoin that of the Union.

The veld farmer, it maintained, had a 'much more realistic appreciation of the Native question' than the colonial administrator, who governs 'from a chair in a London office'.[38]

The Dutch Reformed Church took a public position on the Khama marriage. A week after the new legislation, a resolution was unanimously passed by the DRC Conference in Johannesburg, opposing the recognition of Seretse as chief.[39] 'Two million white people,' it stated, 'were the spearhead of Christendom and civilisation in a land containing eight million Natives, of whom at least half were still semi-civilised ... and living in barbarism.' Anything calculated to reduce the influence of the white man as the standard-bearer of civilization, it insisted, would harm the best interests of all people living in South Africa.[40] This resolution caused great offence to a senior member of the Bangwato. 'We are not surprised in that the Afrikaner people disagree with Africans,' he complained to the British Administration. But he asked the British to ignore the interference of South Africa:

We speak freely in that our Protectorate Government does care for us in all respects. The administration is ours as the Bamangwato, it has no connection with other countries outside the Protectorate that are without justice. We ask that the Government enquire into this matter accordingly while considering the wish of the Bamangwato. We want our Chief and his wife.[41]

On Friday 29 June 1949, Noel-Baker sent a top-secret note to the South African High Commissioner in London, enclosing the text of an announcement to be made by Sir Evelyn Baring the next day – that a judicial inquiry would be held into the designation of Seretse Khama as chief.[42] On the same day, Baring cabled the news to Godfrey Huggins. 'What a good thing you have some machinery to put in action,' replied Huggins, gratefully, 'but what a case for a judge unless he has no views of any sort on the subject. I am assuming Seretse would be a suitable person if he had made a suitable marriage.'[43]

Not until the next day was news of the inquiry finally given to the people who would be most closely affected by it.[44] At a Kgotla in Serowe, Seretse and about 2,000 men listened to the announcement with disbelief. Even Tshekedi was surprised.[45] In just over a month since the Kgotla at which Seretse had been acclaimed as Kgosi, the decision of the majority of the Bangwato people had been called into question by the British Government. Feelings of hope for the future gave way to mistrust and dismay.

7

Our Mother – *Mohumagadi*

Just over six weeks after the public announcement of the judicial inquiry, Ruth arrived at the Victoria Falls on 19 August 1949.[1] She spent the night in Livingstone and on the following morning she flew to Francistown, in the north of Bechuanaland. The heat was baking: although it was still the winter season, the clear and cloudless skies meant that the sun blazed down. When at last the little aircraft touched down at the grass airstrip, she clambered out of the cabin and saw a large, pale green Chevrolet glinting in the sunlight, which Seretse had bought in preparation for her arrival; American cars were preferable to British ones in Bechuanaland, because they were sturdy enough to withstand the rough roads. Beside the car stood Seretse, a broad smile on his face, waiting for her. 'Nothing mattered now,' she wrote later. 'At last I had come home to my husband. I was once more in Seretse's arms, believing that this time we were together for good.'[2]

The Khamas drove to the African township on the edge of Francistown, where Ruth met Seretse's sister, Oratile; there they spent the night. Next day they went on to Palapye, a three-hour drive away, where they spent two happy days with Minnie Shaw, a trader's wife, who was the local midwife. When Seretse had asked if he and Ruth might stay a few days in her home, she knew that their presence with her would upset many in her own, local white community. Unsure what to do for the best, she fell on her knees and asked for God's guidance. She was then in no doubt – she warmly opened her door to welcome the Khamas.[3]

From Palapye, Seretse and Ruth drove to Serowe, a distance of thirty miles, arriving before lunch. As they drove, said John Redfern, 'a small aeroplane prowled over the brick-red track, and a cameraman hung out vertiginously, eager for pictures of the most talked-of couple in the world'.[4] The culprit was Noel Monks, the *Daily Mail* correspondent. Monks, an Australian in his early forties, had been a war correspondent – and now he had come to southern Africa to report on the marriage of Seretse and Ruth. Journalists were flocking into Serowe from all over the world. Some of them were 'straight out of *Scoop*, and nearly all pretty grisly', complained Sillery in a reference to Evelyn Waugh's savage portrayal in the 1930s of British newspapermen in Africa.[5] In the middle of Seretse's and Ruth's first night in Palapye, in Minnie Shaw's house, her adult son had been woken by a noise and a beam of light shining through his bedroom window. It was the press, hoping to get a photograph of Ruth and Seretse in bed together. They quickly ran away when a gun was levelled at their heads.[6]

All along the road from Palapye to Serowe, remembered Seretse later, 'there were crowds cheering us, and it was good to know that the Bangwato, my people, had accepted her as my wife as well as me as their chief'.[7] Several times, Seretse had to stop the car so that people could shake her hand and welcome her.[8] When at last they arrived in the capital, said Ruth, 'a dense throng of African men, women and children pressed round us, the women making the sound of ululation, a kind of trilling with the tongue – the traditional Bangwato greeting'.[9] For a moment, Ruth felt a little frightened, but Seretse put his hand on her arm to reassure her. Seeing Serowe for the first time was 'love at first sight'.[10] But it was not a surprise – 'Seretse had explained in great detail what it would be like. He didn't want me to be under any illusions, so it was exactly as I'd expected.'[11]

In Serowe they stayed for six days in the Mission, with Seager and his family. This was not successful, as Seager reported in a letter to LMS headquarters in London:

My own impression is one of disappointment. I had tried to convince myself that perhaps I was prejudiced against it and that it might look better when I saw them together. On the contrary, it looked worse, not merely from the point of view of colour but from their attitudes to each other and to the tribe. They seem very much in love but completely unconcerned as to the effect of their actions on the tribe.[12]

The 'point of view of colour' may have bothered Seager, but it was of little matter to the Bangwato who supported Seretse. 'We accepted his wife with love,' said one of his uncles.[13] 'Strange as it may sound to some,' remarked Seretse later, 'my people despite their lack of education are far more tolerant and intelligent than many so-called civilized people whom I have met. They are not nearly as blinded by colour prejudice.'[14] *Naledi ya Batswana*, a newspaper that was published in Johannesburg but directed at readers in the Protectorate, received numerous letters supporting Seretse's decision to marry Ruth. According to the editor, 'All the letters have to a lesser or greater degree supported the stand taken by Seretse . . . There seems to be a fairly wide view that it was nothing more nor less than a love match.'[15]

Sillery, the Resident Commissioner, was struck by the happiness of the Bangwato at Ruth's arrival. 'One gets the impression that Seretse's cause is growing in strength and that the unpopularity of Tshekedi is increasing,' he reported to the High Commissioner. 'Prior to Ruth's arrival,' he added, 'we received a petition from 58 women of Mahalapye asking that Seretse be Kgosi and signifying their acceptance of Ruth.'[16] A Kgosi is 'for us all,' insisted the petition, 'and not for men only who speak in Kgotla; Seretse Khama is our only Kgosi'. Sillery was surprised by this intervention by women because, traditionally, Bangwato women did not become involved in political issues.

Within a week of their arrival in Serowe, on Monday 29 August 1949, the Khamas moved into their own home – a large bungalow, built for a British official – in a district of Serowe called Newtown. It was the only modern brick house in the area and was surrounded far into the distance by huts. There was a large garden in the front and the back, with a prickly pear tree at the entrance and thick thorn bushes around the perimeter. Ruth described the house in a letter to Betty:

It is far from being finished, but we couldn't care less. We are on our own, and as you know, it is pretty grim living with someone else. However the house is liveable, and in time will be completed no doubt. It has three bedrooms, lounge and dining room, kitchen, bathroom, and lavatory. Two of the bedrooms have yet to be furnished.[17]

There were shelves over the fireplace, where they put their books: mostly law books, as well as a few volumes on African and world affairs – and Paton's *Cry the Beloved Country*.[18] Outside, there was a veranda with a red floor, where they played table tennis; part of the veranda had a roof, for use as a sleeping porch on hot nights. There was no electricity, no running water, no plumbing and no telephone, but the house was much grander than their garden flat on Adolphus Road in North London. There were five servants to do the housework.

As soon as they had moved in, headmen and their families came from all over the Bangwato Reserve, to welcome Seretse's wife and to offer gifts. They waited patiently outside the house for their turn to enter.[19] Church choirs and school choirs sang songs of greeting, and across the main road there was a huge banner welcoming the young couple. Women were especially keen to show their friendship to Ruth. 'When Ruth Khama stepped out of a Serowe store here today,' reported a correspondent for the *News Chronicle*, the British Nonconformist newspaper, 'a group of women set up a welcoming chant. Soon thousands of natives were milling around the London-born wife of the chief-designate.'[20]

After Ruth's arrival, a delegation of elders asked Mrs Page-Wood, the proprietress of Serowe's largest store, to teach her something about traditional customs. Mrs Page-Wood was fluent in Setswana and knew more about the life of the Bangwato than most other whites. But she felt she could not help: 'You are asking more of me than I can do,' she told the elders, but she sent Ruth a set of flowered dinner plates to show willing. Mrs Page-Wood had definite ideas of what the queen should do – she would have to

lead the women with water on her head. She must choose the songs at harvest time. She must be first to smear the floor with cow dung – not much, but a little as a symbol of cleanliness. The people may appeal to her in any trouble, and she must intercede with the chief on their behalf. She is her husband's menial, part of his job.[21]

Mrs Page-Wood believed that Ruth's life as the wife of the Chief looked pretty hopeless.

Seretse wanted to improve the lives of his people and to bring improvements in the form of education and health care – the *Cape Times* had described him just before the third kgotla in June 1949 as 'a modern young man with progressive ideas'.[22] Very quickly, Ruth, too, was joining in discussions about what needed to be done. 'Ruth and I,' said Seretse to Margaret Bourke-White, who had come to Serowe to write an article on the Khamas for *Life*, 'think alike about these things.'[23] A rector of the Bangwaketse had great hopes for the work that Ruth could do. In a letter to *Naledi ya Batswana*, he argued that life in Bechuanaland was no better than in South Africa:

The good Tswana customs have gone with the forefathers. I think Seretse's white wife would do much to help right the wrongs of our territory and her appeals for better conditions would be listened to better. The wages paid the workers here are lamentably low.[24]

'It would take me years to introduce all the reforms I want,' said Ruth sadly. 'The Bangwato may have had Queen Victoria's protection all these years,' she argued, 'but precious little care.' She was especially concerned about the hard lives of the women, who fetched water and wood, cooked, ploughed and looked after the children and the old people. 'I am more convinced than ever that I, as the chief's wife, could do so much for the women,' said Ruth. 'There's no social life for them. The men have their kgotlas, but the women have nothing. They are just chattels. They must have a status.' She went on to describe the conditions endured on the reserve:

There are few, if any, organised sports. No radios or gramophones. There is no compulsory education. Hygiene and health are practically unknown subjects. There are no welfare centres or clinics worth mentioning. There is a terrific need of these things among the Bamangwatos.

She contrasted these deprivations with the comforts of the British officials: 'At the Residency there is a magnificent flower garden – but there are no proper roads in Serowe.' The stores, too, she thought, were an affront to the community. The white traders did a good trade with the Africans and were able to send their children to expensive boarding schools in the Union and to drive smart cars; and their homes, though not elegant, were comfortable.[25] But the 'shacks that go for stores' were a disgrace. 'When I think of all the money that passes over the counters, year in, year out,' she said, 'I fume every time I have to enter the mouldy old places.'[26] This tendency to 'fume' was a difference between Seretse and Ruth: for he rarely became angry, whereas Ruth lost her temper. 'Perhaps that is why we have got on so well together,' reflected Ruth years later. 'Seretse is patient, peace-loving and slow to anger; I am hot-tempered.'[27]

'We are extremely happy,' wrote Ruth to Betty. But they found the ambiguity of Seretse's position difficult to manage. 'Although the Gvt. don't recognise Seretse as chief,' Ruth told Betty, 'the tribe do, so he has all his work cut out for him.' Duty was always calling him, she added proudly.[28] Noel Monks accused the Commonwealth Secretary of hypocrisy. The Administration was relying on Seretse to support their work, he objected, as if he had been installed:

Your representatives . . . told Seretse: 'You're not chief yet' – but every day they went to him for help in running things.

Seretse could have turned them down flat, and even greater chaos than there is now in this country could have resulted.

'But he sportingly played along,' said Monks, 'and used his influence for good.'[29]

Meanwhile, Ruth had settled into a daily routine as a Serowe house-wife. 'Groceries and greengroceries, and bread, here,' she informed Betty, 'is much more expensive than in England, but meat and eggs are very plentiful, and very cheap. Eggs are a penny each.' She enjoyed cooking their meals, which Seretse put on the table. She was making plans for ecru lace curtains to go with a rug she was having made of twenty lion skins; Seretse had given out the skins to the villagers, who were softening them up with fat and cattle brains.[30] 'The countryside here is very pretty and lovely,' she exclaimed in pleasure. 'We have been horse riding a few times.'[31] She had planted a little English flower garden but was finding it hard to keep the seedlings alive, because of the shortage of rain.[32]

'I'd have been a dumb blonde indeed,' said Ruth, 'if I failed to sense the great love the majority of the tribe, particularly the younger generation, have for Seretse.'[33] Wherever Seretse and Ruth went in the reserve, people rushed to greet them. 'I have seen old Bamangwato women fall on one bony knee, clutch at the hem of her flowered frock and kiss it,' wrote Redfern, 'as she was striding from her car to the stores or the Post Office.' When husband and wife appeared together in their car – the apple-green Chevrolet – 'Bamangwato would jump up in front of the radiator as though they had been concealed underneath trapdoors.' The women danced and ululated.[34] In the UK, Learie Constantine commented on the easy way in which Ruth had settled into Serowe. 'These Africans would still have raised objections if they had found in Ruth anything to disapprove,' he pointed out. 'They did not. They liked her.'[35] She was accepted as the Kgosi's wife and as the mother of the people – *Mohumagadi*.

But the European community did *not* like her. John Redfern witnessed their hostility at a film show in the Palapye hotel. Once a week at the Palapye hotel, where many of the whites' social events took place, wrote Redfern,

they put on 'the bioscope'. The old-fashioned word is current in Southern Africa. Like many things in that region the word is forty years behind the times.

It was 'the bioscope' on my second night. The film, a shockingly old number with Lon Chaney in the leading role, was shown in the lounge of the small hotel. Outside, young Africans pressed their noses against the meshed windows and strained to get a view of the marvels of the screen.

Africans were not allowed inside, though an exception was made for Seretse – the white community assumed he would be Kgosi and they needed his consent to trade in the Bangwato reserve.

Inside, Redfern listened to the conversation of the white men who were drinking at the bar:

A young Afrikaner railway clerk wearing the same shape of beard as the Voortrekkers wore 100 years before, was boasting heavily of what he would do should Seretse turn up with 'his woman'. Seretse had been an occasional visitor to the movies. But it would be another thing if he came along this time with the woman.

The beefy Afrikaner and his friends fumed over their beer and cheap brandy, and began to rant about white civilisation. Their language was vigorous, and occasionally disgusting. Although they normally spoke in Afri-

l was watching events in Serowe. For many months, the
d been flooded with reporters, who were sending regular
Britain, the USA, and other countries. 'The little wooden
,' said Noel Monks, 'where an ex-Royal Navy signaller did
postmaster and telegraph operator – and yeoman service it
ame the hub of the sprawling mud-hut capital.' There was
raffic over the single telegraph line to the outside world,
operators had to be sent down from Salisbury, 500 miles
he north. 'I always felt that the thirty or so Europeans in
sented our intrusion on their back-bush privacy,' added
'hey certainly resented *both* sides of the Seretse Affair being
the world, having been used to one side only, the Adminis-
7

uite true that some of the journalists who came to Serowe
ext few months gave the Khamas' side of the Seretse Affair.
ks was sympathetic, especially towards Ruth. 'You can't
ring her,' he said. 'She's not a tart, she's a respectable girl
.'48 But this was not true of all the journalists, and certainly
e Robertson, who came to Serowe to write a feature for the
gazine *Picture Post*. Robertson, tall and thin in his khaki
it, was uncomfortable about the Khama marriage. 'One of
est taboos, particularly to a girl of Ruth's class,' he told his
the marriage of a white girl and a black man.' He disliked

saw of her at Serowe the less I liked her . . . She is of medium
hair between corn and red, the very fair complexion that often
his . . . She often uses, when speaking, an appealing and beautiful
lips, and her voice is good but monotonous.

ple', he said – referring to the small numbers of Europeans
– 'thought her laugh affected. She appears to take quick
nd to nurse them tenderly. Her humour takes the form of
imed at friend or foe, and she goes embarrassingly out of
be cutting to people she dislikes.' But he had some grudging
ough she can be peremptory with them, I liked the way she
her servants,' he said. And he could not help but admire
courage: 'Few women would bear up as she did under her

kaans, they switched to English this night because there were English people
in listening range.

Then, just as the film began, the screen was momentarily blotted out
by two shadows: Ruth and Seretse, quietly taking their places in a
couple of chairs reserved for them by Mrs Shaw. 'They sat there,'
observed Redfern, 'holding hands just like a couple in a cinema in
Purley. At the interval, one of Mrs Shaw's party fetched soft drinks
from the bar round the corner.' The boasting men at the bar, however,
did nothing. They knew that 'Seretse and his woman' had arrived,
'but they were content to stick to their boasting. They had a final
round and then they too took their places to watch Mr Chaney's
exploits. It must have cost them a great effort.'36

To Seretse, the white traders were respectful. They spoke no ill of
him – at least, when their servants were in earshot. But some of them,
observed Redfern, were predicting that within three months the tribe
would 'put something' in Ruth's tea or that within six months Seretse
would tire of her and seek consolation in his own tribe. Red fern also
noticed that many of them, who had known Seretse from when he
was a small boy, liked him as a person. But his wife was a different
matter – she had let down her race and had broken the unwritten
rules of their community. They were polite to her, out of deference to
Seretse, but they smouldered with resentment. One day, when Ruth
was driving through Serowe, she felt faint in the heat and asked a
passer-by to fetch her a glass of water from one of the stores. He went
to get her one and then, feeling better, Ruth went on her way. Later,
when the incident was recounted to Redfern, a white woman nastily
said to him, 'If she thought she was going to get invited inside by a
trick like that, she was dead wrong.'37

But Ruth did have some white friends, including Phineas McIntosh,
the man who had been flogged by Tshekedi in 1933 for fighting over
native women. As much as anything else, he had been punished for
not respecting the colour bar against miscegenation, so they had
something in common. Doris Bradshaw and her husband Alan, who
worked for the Native Recruiting Corporation in Johannesburg,
which recruited local labour to work in the gold mines of South

Africa, became special friends.[38] 'When we knew Seretse had married a white girl,' wrote Alan to Doris's sister,

we knew she was going to face many difficulties in a strange and foreign country ... We made a point of doing all we could for her. Seretse I have known for years and he is a good lad. I like many of his ideas for the future of his people. Our home was always open to them and they came to us very often.[39]

But the Bradshaws lived in Palapye. 'The Serowe Europeans,' said Doris, 'just about ignored her, only Stan Woodford and his wife and Phil McIntosh and his wife would even speak to her.'[40]

Sillery laid the blame for this on Ruth herself. 'A good many stories are current about Mrs Khama,' he reported to Baring, 'which, if true, indicate that she is not managing her racial relations as delicately as one would have wished.' He was also troubled by Seretse's wish for 'European' alcohol, which Africans were not allowed to buy or drink. For unlike Khama III and Tshekedi, Seretse was not teetotal. It was a 'minor but tiresome matter',[41] complained Sillery, who argued that

it is not only against the law but it is also strictly against Khama's most stringent edict against liquor of any kind ... While admittedly Khama's law is now more honoured in the breach than in the observance, since the Bamangwato tipple as freely as anyone else, at the same time Government cannot abet an offence against tribal tradition any more than it can break its own law.[42]

On the day that Ruth arrived in Serowe, Seretse's uncle Tshekedi went into voluntary exile – 'for as long,' he announced, 'as the white woman Seretse has married stays here'.[43] Tshekedi and the headmen who were leaving made a public declaration about the crisis before they left. They were compelled to take this 'drastic step', they said, not because they did not love their country, but because of their concern for the future of the Protectorate. Nor did they challenge the position of Seretse as heir-apparent, but they questioned the legality of the steps that had been taken by his supporters. The administration, worried that violence between the two camps would break out, were maintaining a high level of police in Serowe: 'three Europeans and 37 African ranks'.[44]

About forty senior men of the Bangwa their families and their cattle. They w in the Bakwena Reserve, about 200 m and two miles outside the Bangwato Re: was the domain of Kgosi Kgari. Rame *Observer*, lay on the 'unfriendly fringe everywhere sand lies ankle-deep like 'inaccessible as it is friendless ... sprawl thorn trees'. In this wilderness, almost 'thirstland given over almost entirely to ostriches and lions'.[45]

'If we had stayed,' recalled one of the m years later,

there would have been bloodshed ... This has a Whenever it was felt that tensions had built u remove himself from the main body of the tri quently and is so much a part of our history, th

But it was very hard to go into exile:

I was among those two hundred and what at whole life upside down. My father had died, mother and family. Tshekedi bought four r children were transported on them, while th cattle on foot.

'Those of us who left,' he added, 'had all administration – senior treasurers, tax col and so forth – and we'd all been in a pos Tshekedi's character.' Rametsana was inf to come right inside the village and kill ou to shoot a lion there!' They had to sta school. 'It was not a question of loving all had,' he said. 'It was a question of mo not do without. It takes a man years to see what it cost us. That is our history an always turned out. It broke our lives.'[46]

*

The wor village h reports t post offic service a was! – b so much that extr away to Serowe Monks. sent out tration's

It was over the Noel M help adm with ide: not of Fy British n safari ou our stro readers, Ruth:

the more height, w goes with turn of th

'Most pe in Serow dislikes, sarcasm, her way praise. ' addresse her for h

difficulties.' He was sure, too, that 'Ruth is very much in love with Seretse'. His personality, he thought, 'was much more pleasing' than Ruth's:

He will be a big man, for already he is thickening about the hips. His complexion is surprisingly light, and his face is Negro rather than Negroid – he has not the finer features, showing Nilotic influence, found among many Africans. His lips, over fine teeth, are thick, the lower one rather pendulous. His upper lip is long, his nose short, broad, flat. He has wit, a quick intelligence, wide knowledge and a sense of humour, proof against misfortune. He never breaks a promise.

'He is obviously,' he added, 'deeply in love with Ruth.'[49]

Margaret Bourke-White was very sympathetic to Seretse and Ruth, although she had difficulty persuading Ruth to be formally interviewed or to have her photograph taken. 'I hate to disappoint you,' wrote Ruth politely in a note, 'but I just don't want to have my picture taken. Please understand that this is not personal, but drop in on us any-time to sample my coffee.'[50] Finally, after long weeks of argument, Margaret told Ruth that getting a story in *Life* would help her husband. Ruth went to ask Seretse if he thought so and when he said that he did, she finally agreed.[51] Margaret thought that Seretse had been on her side all the time: during one of their conversations, he had wandered in from time to time and said with great amusement, 'Haven't you girls come to a decision yet?'[52]

Ruth and Margaret became great friends. They both liked cats and Margaret decided to find some kittens as a present for Ruth. She could not find a single pet cat in Bechuanaland, so looked for some in Johannesburg. 'At last,' she wrote to her editor, 'I found a pair of tiny kittens which I took back in a car to Serowe':

For most of the way, the only shade was under the car, and I stopped at intervals to give the kittens saucers of milk and a brief respite from the heat in the shadow of the car. They soon lost interest in the fast-souring milk; they were panting like thirsty puppies with their tongues hanging out.

When she arrived in Serowe it was nearly midnight. But the lights were still on in the Khamas' bungalow and the kittens, miraculously, were still alive, so she decided to take them to their new home. Ruth was enchanted with the kittens and Seretse immediately named them Pride and Prejudice.[53]

Ruth explained to Margaret the inaccuracies that had caused her to become embittered against the press. One of these was the claim that Seretse couldn't cope with his studies because of Ruth. But in actual fact, Margaret wrote to her editor in New York, 'she's deeply interested in his career and keeps him at his studies'.[54] Another false claim

was that she met Seretse in a dance hall. Another was that she was a typist. Also that Serowe is a place of baboons, hyenas and marauding lions – Ruth commented that the only baboons she had seen were the reporters. Finally, that 'all Seretse's wives' would 'have to bathe me and brush my hair – that's so ridiculous, so silly,' said Ruth.

In many ways, thought Margaret, Ruth 'is a remarkable person who has overcome the difficulties of her fantastic situation to a creditable degree'. She had been boycotted 'mercilessly' by the European women – yet she had built up 'a pretty complete life of her own':

They 'pity' her loneliness. Yet in many ways her life is fuller than theirs, with a much closer degree of companionship with her husband, identification of herself with his interests, and intelligent understanding of the broader problems he has to face.[55]

'When it comes to inequalities between blacks and whites,' Margaret continued in her letter to New York, 'she is fierce in her stand against such inequality':

For example, she learned that the native nurses in the local Serowe hospital had recently had their pay slashed four pounds a month so as to raise the salaries of the white nurses. She is passionate in her denunciation of this injustice. When Seretse is given full powers as chief he hopes to change it, and she is fully airing her views.

Margaret thought that Ruth was a good influence on her husband:

She kept urging Seretse to decide things himself, act for himself, not pay any attention to what Government told him. She turned to me and talked about how the British Empire 'doesn't really try to help the people. That's why they're losing colonies right, left and center.' Then she added, 'I hate hypocrisy.'[56]

Margaret observed the treatment of the Khamas by the whites with distaste. Sunday was a big day in Bechuanaland, she observed, 'and the small colony made the most of it'. She went along to a Sunday cricket match, 'the weekly event of dusty Serowe', on a day that was 'a scorcher':

On reaching the tiny cricket club, I saw that servants had erected a gay little striped awning and placed a couple of long, narrow picnic tables under its welcome shade. A handful of shopkeepers' wives were engaged in that womanly task which English wives do so well the world over, preparing iced tea, lemonade, mounds of fresh-baked cookies and tiny flaked pastries.

The match had already started when the Khamas' car drove into sight. It parked on the far side of the field, from where they could watch the game. There was an audible buzz from the feminine contingent under the striped awning: 'Poor thing! She must be *so* lonely . . .' 'No one of her own kind to talk with . . .' 'Oh, I feel so sorry for her!' But despite these protestations, noted Margaret, not one woman – or man – walked across the field to say hello or offer a glass of cold tea.[57]

From South Africa, millions of whites were watching in horror as Ruth settled down in Serowe. 'Our colour problem,' argued the Nationalist newspaper *Die Burger*, 'will be detrimentally influenced if Seretse Khama and his white wife are permitted to assume the chieftainship'.[58] Many whites felt sorry for Ruth's European neighbours. 'Please think of the little band of Europeans who have their homes in Serowe,' pleaded a woman in Johannesburg in a letter to the Commonwealth Relations Office – how 'degrading' it was for them.[59]

Baring was sent a letter by the Dutch Reformed Church of Natal just days after Ruth's arrival in southern Africa. It argued that:

This marriage (native and European) is a contradiction to age-long tradition and racial custom and a cause of internal hatred and splitting of the Bamang-wato race. Acknowledgement of this marriage will mean social equalisation of black and white, and if this example of the King be followed – which certainly will be done – racial purity will gradually be wiped out. This will mean that European Christendom in South Africa has a dark future.

In all earnestness, the Church wishes to request his Excellency the British High Commissioner to advise the British Government that this marriage not only be denounced but also that Seretse Khama will not be admitted to succeed to the throne of the Bamangwato people.[60]

Ruth was happy and content in Serowe. But one day, at lunch, the room started to swim and she slipped to the floor.[61] She recalled later:

Unfortunately I was not to have long to settle in my new life. I had barely become used to being called 'Mother' by the tribal women when I was taken ill . . .

Seretse brought Dr Don Moikangoa, the junior government doctor at Serowe Hospital, to see me. He sent me to bed for six weeks.

No doubt the heat had triggered the collapse, as well as nervous exhaustion from an accumulation of difficulties in the first year of her marriage – rejection by her parents, separation from Seretse by thousands of miles, harassment by the press, contempt from so many people in her own home country, and vilification by the whites of Serowe, South Africa and Southern Rhodesia. But there was another reason, too: she and Seretse discovered, to their great joy, that they were going to have a baby.[62]

Ruth arranged for Dr Moikangoa, a South African who had trained at the University of Witwatersrand, to look after her pregnancy. She also booked a room for the confinement at Serowe's hilltop hospital on the edge of the village – the Sekgoma II Memorial Hospital, named after Seretse's father, which had been a personal gift from Edward, Prince of Wales, on a visit to Serowe in 1925.[63]

Then she got busy knitting.[64] 'At last I've got my baby things together,' she told Margaret Bourke-White. She had made eight coats, six jackets, and four pairs of bootees. 'This is all I'm going to do until I see whether it's a girl or a boy,' she said, holding up yards of white silk and white muslin and lace edging. 'Then I'll make dresses if it's a girl and rompers if it's a boy.' Then Margaret said:

Ruth, I shouldn't ask you this. You don't have to answer it if you don't want to. But everybody wonders about it. How about the colour of your child? Do you do any thinking about that? How do you feel about it?

Ruth looked at her before answering the question and her eyes were very serious. 'I couldn't care less,' she replied.[65] 'And you could tell from her manner,' wrote Margaret to her editor in New York, 'that she couldn't.'[66]

8

The Harragin Inquiry

When Ruth was up and about, Dr Moikangoa gave her strict instructions to take things easy. But this was out of the question. For in just ten days time, on 1 November 1949, the Judicial Inquiry was due to start, to determine whether Seretse was 'a fit and proper person to discharge the functions of Chief'.[1] The Inquiry was to be presided over by Sir Walter Harragin, Chief Justice of the High Commission Territories, who was based in Pretoria. Harragin was a tall, handsome man in his late fifties who – according to Noel Monks – was 'the lion of the many society cocktail parties that are a never ending part of the diplomatic life of Pretoria, where he had his headquarters'. He was also, said Monks, a good, humane judge.[2] His background was unusual for a senior member of the colonial service. Born in British Guiana, he had been sent to school in Britain, but had not gone to Oxford or Cambridge. He was best known for his role as Attorney General in Kenya during the sensational trial in 1941 following the murder of Lord Errol, one of the Happy Valley set.

Harragin had few illusions about the motives of the British Government, but he insisted on correct procedure. 'I fully realise that [the] Secretary of State does not wish to be embarrassed by a definite finding of [the] Enquiry contrary to his views,' he wrote drily to Baring's chief secretary, 'but in that case he cannot pretend to appoint Enquiry under proviso to Section 3(1)'.[3] He had directed that Tshekedi should be regarded as plaintiff and Seretse as defendant, to facilitate procedure. He changed the wording, though, when Seretse's supporters complained that it put Seretse in the role of someone who had been accused of a crime.[4] But Seretse *was* being put in the dock and he understood this perfectly well. He engaged the services of a lawyer –

Percy Fraenkel, a clever and principled man of middle age, from the offices of Fraenkel and Herricke, in Mafikeng.[5] Fraenkel came up to Serowe to help Seretse prepare for the proceedings. Tshekedi, meanwhile, had gone to Cape Town for consultations with his own lawyer, Douglas Buchanan.

Gerald Nettelton was selected as a member of the Inquiry, as was R. S. Hudson, who was in charge of the African Studies Branch at the Colonial Office. His invitation had followed hard upon a report he had sent to Creech Jones, outlining Seretse's unsuitability to be Kgosi.[6] The British Government was to be represented by A. C. Thompson, the Attorney General of the High Commission Territories – 'the most unliked man in all the Protectorates', according to Monks.[7]

Early on in the preparations, Baring set about marshalling his staff to deliver the result required by the CRO. His approach was cold and ruthless. 'The indications are,' he wrote to Sillery, 'that the Commonwealth Relations Office already contemplates reaching a position where we might not want to recognise Seretse and where Tshekedi's continued Regency would also be out of the question.' It would be a great mistake, added Baring, if any member of the Inquiry insisted on putting views opposed to such a solution.[8] Baring was ably assisted by his Chief Secretary, W. A. W. Clark. Some people thought of Clark as 'Baring's *éminence grise*', said Sillery – or, as Harragin put it, 'the Rasputin'.[9] The local administration, wrote Clark to Nettelton, were mistakenly assuming they must adopt an impartial attitude. But this was precisely what they should *not* do:

Whatever may be the viewpoint of individual local officers it is clear that the Administration per se must exert every effort to ensure that the weight of the evidence placed before the enquiry is *against Seretse*. I am doubtful whether in the absence of specific instructions to this effect the local administration will fully appreciate this important point.

The Inquiry was turning into something more than a means of buying time: it was being set up as an expedient to achieve a particular result.[10]

'Quite clearly,' wrote Baring to Sillery, 'having appointed a judicial enquiry, we cannot *lead* direct evidence about the Government view on the decision at issue.' But, he insisted, 'we must ensure that the relevant facts and considerations, important from our point of view, are brought forcibly to the notice of the enquiry.' Tshekedi and Buchanan would give useful evidence, he thought, but might omit some key points. Ellenberger, who had attended the third Kgotla as the Government Representative, would be a key witness, so Baring arranged for him to come to Pretoria to be briefed. He also asked Sillery to arrange for any Chiefs who supported Tshekedi against Seretse to give 'their opinions about the undesirability of a white wife. Perhaps Bathoen could be very discreetly inspired to speak about the real interests of the tribe and of the Protectorate.' The important thing was

to ensure that a position does not develop in which the enquiry has to listen to a mass of evidence from Seretse's followers supporting his appointment and hears little or nothing from Tshekedi on the other side. This is what we must avoid at all costs.[11]

For Sillery in Mafikeng, it was a far less straightforward business than Baring seemed to imagine. 'It is by no means easy for this Administration to inspire African witnesses to give evidence of the kind required,' he told the High Commissioner. 'First, because all African notables in this Protectorate who would be willing to give evidence are committed to one side or the other and secondly, because they are extremely suspicious of Government's aims and objects.' He sent a list of 'independent' people giving evidence, either called by Tshekedi or 'inspired by Government'. Tshekedi fully understood the importance of 'non-party evidence', he added, and had gone to Johannesburg to get some.[12]

New instructions arrived daily on Sillery's desk from the High Commissioner's Office. 'I hope you will take all possible steps to make sure that Chief Kgari gives evidence, and evidence which will be useful to us,' wrote Baring. 'Have you been able to do anything to prevent Mrs Moremi and Kgosi Molefi from giving evidence in favour of the marriage?' he asked, referring to the Regent of the Batawana and the Kgosi of the Bakgatla. 'What about Haile? Do you think he should be called?' It would be advantageous, he thought, 'if both a Catholic and a London Missionary Society missionary witness spoke generally against the marriage'.[13]

By the last weekend of October, all the members of the Inquiry had arrived in Serowe and everything was ready. Then, on the very eve of the Inquiry – on the evening of 31 October – South Africa delivered a carefully timed reminder of its antagonism towards Seretse and Ruth Khama. The Union Government declared that they were prohibited immigrants: it had taken this step, it said, to prevent the Khamas from emigrating to South Africa in the event that Seretse was found unfit to serve as Chief.[14] But this was not the reason, since the Khamas would almost certainly not live in apartheid South Africa. The real reason was to stack the argument against Seretse – for if he was unable to cross the border into Mafikeng, the capital of Bechuanaland, it would be difficult for him to perform adequately the duties of Kgosi.

Speaking in Bloemfontein a few days earlier, on 25 October, Dr Malan had announced that he had already taken every possible precaution to prevent Seretse being acclaimed as Chief, and that he had sent a telegram to the British authorities to this effect. The great danger of the marriage, he argued, was that 'natives' might take it as a sign that a new path had been opened for all of them.[15] This repeated an earlier statement by Malan about a month before, in a speech to the Nationalist Party Congress. On this occasion, too, he had stated that his Government had despatched a telegram to the British Government, and that Southern Rhodesia had done the same.[16] In fact, South Africa had not sent any telegram, preferring to speak 'off the record' to individuals at the highest level of the British Government. But Malan needed to reassure his party that he was dealing with the problem.

South Africa was working hard to maintain pressure on the British Government. Douglas Forsyth used a conversation in the middle of October with Gordon Walker, Noel-Baker's Parliamentary Secretary, to emphasize the 'Union's continuing anxiety that at [the] earliest moment after [the] judicial commission has reported [a] satisfactory solution should be found'.[17] Then, on the second day of the Inquiry, Malan gave notice to Attlee, through Sir Evelyn Baring, of his intention to make formal representations for the transfer to the Union of the High Commission Territories. Attlee replied that it was not an opportune time to raise the matter, as any proposal for transfer would be unlikely to receive support from Parliament or from public opinion in the UK. All it would achieve, he argued, would be to strain the good relations between the UK and the Union.[18]

Under the shadow of these threats from South Africa, the Commission commenced its sittings in a large brown marquee, which had been specially erected in Serowe. Inside, reported the *Daily Mirror*, it was 'steaming'.[19] Outside, without any protection from the blazing sun, more than 3,000 Bangwato men were sitting in a semi-circle. At this time of year, if there was no rain, the temperature during the day could climb to over 30 degrees, even in the shade.

The chairman read aloud the document submitted by Tshekedi to Baring, which argued that the decision of the Kgotla to accept Ruth had been a mob decision and was politically motivated.[20] This document was Baring's pretext for the Inquiry, although it did not raise the issue of whether or not Seretse was 'a fit and proper person to be Chief'. But it successfully deflected responsibility away from the British Government, setting up the Regent as a target for all the anger and frustration of Seretse's supporters.

After Harragin had opened the Inquiry, Buchanan introduced an unexpected difficulty. He read a petition from Tshekedi, which asked the Inquiry to take his evidence at Lobatse – a small town 250 miles away in the south of the Protectorate, which housed the judicial court. Tshekedi was making this request, he said, because he felt unsafe in the Bangwato Reserve. Harragin was cross: he argued that the former Regent had been moving about freely in the Reserve, so could not have been all that worried. Harragin was also aware that many of the Bangwato had travelled long distances to Serowe, in order to be at the Inquiry: for them to travel on to Lobatse would have been impossible. But he grudgingly agreed to Tshekedi's request. As a result, only A. J. Haile and Ellenberger were heard on the first day. Haile gave an account of the efforts by the LMS in London to stop the marriage. Afterwards, Haile reported to London. Seretse 'can't be allowed to get away with it altogether,' he insisted. 'The present mood of the tribe is to forgive him everything, but I feel pretty sure the Judicial Commission will come down heavily on the side of stricter Gov[ernment] control – I certainly hope so.'[21]

Next day, a letter of protest about the move to Lobatse was handed in for delivery to the High Commissioner; it was signed by 136 senior men, who gave their names and their village. 'We the undersigned heads of the Bamangwato tribe,' they stated firmly, 'wish to draw His Excellency's attention' to

our astonishment and alarm whence our protest at the step decided upon and dropped like a bombshell in our midst yesterday by His Majesty's honourable Commissioners of the Judicial Enquiry as arising from the latest petition of Ex-Regent Tshekedi Khama read to us yesterday morning.

'From time immemorial,' they continued, 'our Kgotla has been invested with authority in the determination of our affairs equivalent to that of Parliament to the British people' – and for the first time in their history, a decision taken in the Kgotla was being treated with contempt. They were being sacrificed to the Government's wish to appease South Africa and Southern Rhodesia 'in their detestable and oppressive Native Policy'.[22]

But the letter had no effect on proceedings. Everyone packed up and went to Lobatse, where the Inquiry reassembled in the baking tin-roofed court house on 4 November. Tshekedi's evidence began. He fully accepted that Seretse was the heir to the chieftaincy, stated Buchanan, but he challenged the procedure of the June Kgotla: appealing to people to vote was contrary to custom. Tshekedi had nothing against Ruth as a European, but was opposed to marriage without the consent of the Kgosi and the elders. Ten witnesses who supported Tshekedi's case were then examined. One of these was from South Africa: Selope Thema, who had been the editor of *Bantu World* since it was established in 1932, and who had been a founder member of the African National Congress. Thema said that although he was not against inter-marriage as such, he objected to Seretse marrying a white woman, because he was Kgosi and their children would be 'coloured'. He was also concerned about the status of Ruth's family:

the woman who is going to be the mother of the future Kgosi must come from a Kgosi, or if she comes from a family, that family must be of standing. In this way I am not suggesting that Mrs Khama does not come from a family of standing, but I am only telling the law as it pertains amongst us. We would know that if there had been negotiations between the Tribe and the family of Mrs Khama.

Despite Thema's prominence in South African black politics, his position there was a vexed one. He was one of the old guard of the ANC – one of those people described years later by Nelson Mandela as an 'impediment' to the struggle against apartheid. Shortly after the Harragin Inquiry, when J. B. Marks was elected president of the Transvaal ANC, Thema led a breakaway ANC group called the Nationalist Minded Bloc. In *Bantu World*, he fiercely criticized the new direction being taken by the ANC: he claimed that communists had taken over and that Indians were exploiting the Africans.[23] He was expelled from the ANC in 1951.[24]

The Inquiry finished sitting in Lobatse on 10 November and reassembled at Serowe four days later. 'The day came when Seretse had to give his evidence at the enquiry,' recalled Ruth later. 'I did not go down with him because I was still not really fit. He was in the witness-box for a day and a half.'[25] But she brought tea and sandwiches for him during adjournments, when they sat quietly together outside the marquee, in the shade.[26]

Dressed in a dark suit, Seretse stood up to give evidence. Outside the marquee, many of the assembled Bangwato people chanted his name.[27] 'I acted as a good Christian,' he stated, adding that he and Ruth had 'true affection for each other, and I did not marry to spite anyone.' At the June Kgotla, he pointed out, practically everybody had stood up in his support:

the Tribe, almost to a man, is with me . . . The Government said: 'The Tribe could decide,' and it has done so. The Tribe expects its decision to be honoured.

I claim the Chieftainship as it is due to me.

He argued that the Kgosi's wife had no official standing and that, in any case, his uncles' wives would help Ruth. Seretse spoke well and easily: he was dignified and courteous, but also forthright and often amusing. He was comfortable on the stand and showed to advantage his years of training for the Bar. As the days of the Inquiry passed, Harragin showed increasing respect for Seretse, as well as pleasure in their shared sense of humour.

But Thompson, the Attorney General, disliked Seretse intensely and tried to humiliate him. When Seretse mentioned Smuts, he barked,

'Who is Smuts?' Then, when Seretse replied politely, 'General Smuts', he sneered, 'Do you mind referring to him as General Smuts?' Seretse, with his usual good nature, simply replied, 'I am sorry.' But when Thompson started to interrogate him about his drinking habits, Seretse became playful in his answers:

ATTORNEY GENERAL: When did Mrs Khama arrive here in Serowe?

SERETSE: About 20 August.

ATTORNEY GENERAL: I find that there was only one permit issued to her to purchase liquor. Do you know about that?

SERETSE: Yes, I went to Mr Sullivan [the District Commissioner] for it.

ATTORNEY GENERAL: And the permit was for one dozen bottles of beer, two bottles of some sort of liquor, three bottles of brandy and three bottles of gin. Do you remember getting that permit from Mr Sullivan?

SERETSE: Yes.

ATTORNEY GENERAL: Was the liquor obtained?

SERETSE: Yes, Sir.

ATTORNEY GENERAL: The beer as well? My information is that the beer may not have been supplied. Do you remember whether you got the beer or not?

SERETSE: I am trying to think. I don't know whether I got it or not.

ATTORNEY GENERAL: The suggestion is that you got brandy instead of beer?

SERETSE: Twelve brandies?

ATTORNEY GENERAL: No, five brandies instead of twelve quarts of beer.

SERETSE: No, I don't think I got more brandy.

ATTORNEY GENERAL: Two bottles of liqueurs, three bottles of brandy and three bottles of gin. What was that liquor intended for?

SERETSE: It was intended for my consumption.

ATTORNEY GENERAL: Your personal consumption? Have you still got some of it left?

SERETSE: Unfortunately, no . . .

ATTORNEY GENERAL: This liquor was intended for yourself and your wife?

SERETSE: She hardly drinks.

ATTORNEY GENERAL: And your visitors?

SERETSE: I have not offered them any.

ATTORNEY GENERAL: There is none left?

SERETSE: I am afraid not.

At this point, Harragin interjected with a general remark; he was clearly embarrassed by Thompson's rude battery of questions and wanted to close it down.

Then, with a dry irony that he knew Seretse would appreciate, Harragin turned to his marriage:

You then did something – which we now know was getting married – which in effect the Regent or your guardian was suggesting was so serious that you could not, or should not, be designated as Chief, much in the same way as if you had committed murder or something.

At the June Kgotla, Harragin went on, the tribe 'rose as a man and said, "We will have Seretse and his wife" – whether she is a white or a green one.' It was clear that Harragin sided with Seretse – not only in his clash with the Attorney General, but in his confrontation with the British Government.

Thompson raised the issue of South Africa. Given that the Protectorate's capital, Mafikeng, was in the Union, he asked, how could Seretse – as a prohibited immigrant – function as chief? But it ought to be possible to set up alternative arrangements, countered Seretse. Being a prohibited immigrant, he added, meant that he was not very different from practically every black South African – 'because even in the Union itself African people are practically prohibited immigrants; they cannot move from one part of the Union to another without some sort of permission from the Native Commissioner'. In any case, he shrewdly pointed out, South Africa was irrelevant to the Inquiry – the Secretary of State had said so.

When Ellenberger, who had been carefully briefed by the High Commissioner's Office, was called as a witness, he returned to the issue of South Africa. He argued that the Bangwato required 'very strong' leadership and the 'closest contact' with the Administration, so their Chief would need to be able to go to Mafikeng. He added that the Protectorate needed to import food from the Union and was dependent upon the export of cattle; in addition, families were dependent on funds from men working in the Union. He was asked about the political views of the Union and of Southern Rhodesia and at this point the Attorney General handed in – as evidence – the statement of the Union Prime Minister to the Nationalist Party Conference on 26 October 1949. A copy of the debate in the Legislative Assembly of Southern Rhodesia, when there had been unanimous agreement that Seretse should not be installed as chief, was also included as evidence.

Fraenkel tackled Ellenberger on the issue of South Africa. He argued that, in actual fact, the Union was dependent upon the Protectorate for labour in the mines. On the matter of the export of cattle, he added, the market for beef was expanding in the north.

Walter Stanford Pela had come to Serowe from South Africa to express the views of the Bangwato men working in the mines on the Rand and in Pretoria. Pela had been Seretse's boarding master at Tiger Kloof and had a degree in Native Law and Administration. He had already made public his support for Seretse's marriage in June that year, in a South African magazine called *Common Sense*.[28] Now he contended that under Sotho-Tswana customary law, the Kgotla occupied the same position as Parliament according to Western concepts. 'Tswana customary law,' he argued, 'recognises no colour distinction, and an objection based on this ground is untenable for lack of precedent.' He accused Tshekedi of wanting his children to succeed to the chieftainship after Seretse's death. He pleaded with the Commission not to be influenced by the recent statements of the Prime Ministers of the Union and of Southern Rhodesia.

Kgosi Mokgosi of the Balete also disputed Tshekedi's position, arguing that he was motivated by political ambition. 'I and my Tribe agree to Seretse's marriage,' he said. 'I may say that Seretse's marriage really did not cause any offence.'

A memorandum from Kanye, the capital of the Bangwaketse Reserve, was read aloud. Dated 20 October 1949, it was signed by fifteen people who could not attend, including teachers, clerks, administrators, sanitary inspectors and policemen. They took a very different view from their Kgosi, Bathoen II. They praised Seretse's leadership qualities – pointing out that he was chief prefect at Tiger Kloof and Lovedale – and argued that his education was good for the people. While he was in England, they said, Seretse had worked on a farm to gain knowledge of farming methods there. But the chief argument of the memorandum was that

Seretse's unquestionable royal birth has never been a hindrance to his free association with persons of all classes. He 'walked with kings but never lost the common touch'. This is evidenced by the way he was always ready to serve others even if it was a matter of fetching water for somebody both of lower rank and younger than he. Such seemingly small deeds go a long way in the hearts of men.

Then it added, by way of example:

Once, in a social gathering, a number of people asked to hear 'the voice of the Kgosi'. He was bound to say one or two things, and inter alia he said something very significant of his character: 'Well, you have heard my voice, it is no different from yours . . .'

'Such interest in the common man, so rare among many of our leaders,' argued the authors of the memorandum, 'augurs well for a successful leader who will not remain at the topmost stratum but will go down in order to uplift the masses up the ladder of progress fully understanding their shortcomings.' He was not the first Kgosi to marry the woman of his choice – and a 'woman of one's choice refers equally to all colours, whether white, black, green or yellow in this respect'. The matter had only cropped up 'because of the dislike for the unlike, which the more democratic and liberal peoples of the world are trying to fight against everyday'.

A memorandum had also been submitted by Monametsi Chiepe, from Vryburg in South Africa. Chiepe was an intellectual who had been a Tribal Secretary under Tshekedi but had resigned after a mis-understanding.[29] In the memorandum he challenged Tshekedi's claim that the decision at the June Kgotla was a mob decision, arguing that it was the product of careful consideration by the Bangwato. It was true, he acknowledged, that initially the Bangwato had wanted Seretse to marry someone from his own people. But by refusing to pander to the wishes of those who wanted to separate him from his wife, Seretse had persuaded them to change their view.

Sir Walter Harragin brought the Inquiry to a close on 18 November. 'We would like to thank the Bamangwato people who have assembled in their thousands round this tent, sitting silently through sun and rain, always orderly and courteous under any circumstances,' he said to the crowd outside the marquee. He was concerned that after all their efforts and loyalty, they would not discover the result of the Inquiry for a long time. Many people, he knew, would expect the Inquiry to operate like a kgotla meeting, where a consensus would be reached by the end, or like a law court trial, where a judgement would be given:

I am afraid many [people] are going to be disappointed today because I feel sure that they imagine that this is a case and that the Judge will immediately give judgement, but that is far from the fact. No judgement is given by us.

In due course, he explained, certain recommendations would be made to the British High Commissioner in Pretoria, who would in turn forward them to the Secretary of State in London. 'It may be several months,' he warned, 'before you hear the result.'

Harragin finished his speech by entreating the crowd to go to their fields and start ploughing – for this was the time of year when people left their homes in the village and went to their lands. 'We have, I am told,' he said, apologetically,

been to some extent responsible for keeping you away from ploughing your fields, and as I understand that some of you are waiting for the word to be given – I believe it is called *Letsema* – insofar as I have any authority, may I say that it is my pious hope that you will now proceed to your fields and proceed with your ploughing and that in due course more rain will come.

Despite the cynical decisions behind the Inquiry, it had been thoroughly and conscientiously conducted by Sir Walter and had produced a mass of material. When a final record of the evidence was collected together, it amounted to many thousands of pages, in fourteen thick volumes. Everyone was exhausted. The clerk who had taken shorthand returned to her home in Durban, where she started to type up her notes. 'I am really feeling dead beat now,' she complained. 'It is eight weeks of solid hard graft without a single week-end or public holiday, and only stopping for meals and bed late at night, and how I stuck it I just don't know.'[30]

A few days after the inquiry closed, there was a prayer service in the Serowe Kgotla. It was an annual event, when the Kgosi spoke to the people and told them they might start ploughing when they wish

– the formal *Letsema*. Now, in November 1949, it was expected that Seretse would give this service. It was the first time that he had taken on this formal role, and beforehand, said Ruth, he was nervous – 'but once he started to speak everything was all right'. He was given a huge reception and as they left the meeting, 'a way for us had to be forced through the crowd'.[31]

9

'A fit and proper person to be Chief'

The report of the Harragin Inquiry was ready in the first week of December. It gave the 'right' answer – that Seretse should not be recognized as Chief. But it gave the 'wrong' reason – the hostility of South Africa and Southern Rhodesia. The Commission had found overwhelmingly that Seretse was 'a fit and proper person to be Chief' and accepted that the Kgotla of June 1949 had adequately expressed the views of the tribe:

Though a typical African in build and features, he has assimilated, to a great extent, the manners and thoughts of an Oxford undergraduate. He speaks English well and is obviously quick to appreciate, even if he may not agree with, the European point of view. Thus he was an easy witness to examine, he immediately understood the questions and answered them without hesitation, clearly and fairly.

'We have no hesitation,' the report went on, in finding that

his prospects of success as a Chief are as bright as those of any native in Africa ... He is admittedly the lawful and legitimate heir and, save for his unfortunate marriage, would be in our opinion, a fit and proper person to assume the chieftainship.

Seretse had won the battle for himself and his wife 'not by force of arms, but by force of votes'.[1]

Baring was pleased with the result. He wrote to Huggins, telling him in confidence of Harragin's recommendation. If it was accepted by the Commonwealth Secretary, he said, then he would try to induce Seretse and Ruth 'to go and take their medicine in England'. If they cooperated, an announcement could be made in Serowe in early January. It would be necessary to make an announcement to the tribe and there might be some trouble – 'They are a pretty feeble lot of natives but on this particular occasion it would, I think, be wiser to take no chances.' He therefore asked his old friend to lend sixty native ranks of the British South Africa Police, the police force of Southern Rhodesia.[2] Huggins was happy to help but said he would prefer 'to send unarmed guards under six or seven good Europeans'.[3]

Additional reinforcements were brought in from Basutoland and Swaziland.[4] Baring thought the police should have riot equipment. This was not available in the Protectorate, so Sillery arranged to borrow 100 steel helmets and three wireless sets from the Union Defence Force in South Africa. But there was a difficulty, reported a brigadier from the British army, because the UDF would not tolerate the idea of whites wearing hats that had been worn by black police:

Unfortunately as they no longer have any native soldiers in the UDF they are not prepared to hire tin hats for native police, and then issue them later to European troops. The tin hats, therefore, will have to be purchased outright at a cost of 9/10d each. I asked Clark whether we could purchase them if necessary and he agreed. As I understand that the native head is usually smaller than the European, I have asked for 45 small, 45 medium and 10 large.[5]

It was announced in the Serowe Kgotla that the District Commissioner had been appointed Native Authority, to fill the vacuum created by the lack of a Kgosi. This was heard with angry resentment by the Bangwato and Fraenkel sent a letter of complaint to Nettelton:

We are instructed to protest very strongly against the step taken by the Government of appointing a DC as Native Authority without first consulting the people . . . Our clients resent the appointment of a Native Authority other than the rightful heir, Seretse Khama, and feel that they cannot cooperate with the DC in the administration of the Tribe.

He was further instructed, he went on, to point out

that the Tribe made its decision in June 1949. The Government's Representative at that Kgotla meeting accepted the decision and had Tshekedi not applied for the appointment of the Commission, the Government would have immediately installed Seretse as chief.

The Inquiry was a farce, he added darkly, 'unless use was being made by the Government of this Commission to placate Dr Malan or the Rhodesian Government'.[6]

For Baring, the Harragin Report had been a good result, because he was only concerned about its conclusion. But when it arrived at the CRO, it was read with dismay. The mandarins in London, too, were gratified with the conclusion. But they were conscious that 'public opinion, if the Report is published, will surely find the reasons for the finding rather inadequate':

The first is that, being prohibited from entry into the Union, he cannot visit the Resident Commissioner's headquarters at Mafikeng and therefore cannot discharge adequately the functions of a chief; secondly we should forfeit the 'beaux yeux' of the Union and S. Rhodesia if we let him succeed; and thirdly, approval of his succession would cause disruption in the tribe.

These reasons seemed in fact to contradict the conclusion of the report – 'it seems from the report that greater disruption will follow if he is *not* allowed to succeed . . . In fact, the Enquiry does find Seretse to be a very fit and proper person to be Chief if it were not for his wife . . .'[7]

Baring was recalled to London for urgent consultations and as soon as he arrived on 16 December, he hurried to the CRO for a meeting with Noel-Baker, Liesching, the colonial secretary, and other senior officials. Creech Jones opened the discussion by complaining that the Harragin Commission 'seemed to have arrived at the right conclusions by the use of wrong arguments'. Noel-Baker agreed. He objected, as well, to the finding that Seretse's prospects of success as a chief were 'bright', since Seretse was breaking tribal custom by drinking alcohol. The idea that Seretse could not adequately perform his duties as Chief, because he was a prohibited immigrant in South Africa and could not go to Mafikeng, struck Creech Jones as absurd. Noel-Baker thought they should consider at once transferring the capital to somewhere inside the territory of the Protectorate. But Sir Evelyn quickly intervened. He had discussed this idea with General Smuts, he said, who strongly opposed it. He argued that repercussions in South Africa would be highly unfavourable – it would be understood as a move to draw Bechuanaland and the High Commission Territories further away from the Union.[8]

No solution to the dilemma of the Harragin Report could be found. Then, after much discussion, the meeting agreed on a strategy to be presented to Cabinet – that Seretse and Ruth should be summoned to London. This had been advocated by Noel-Baker at the very start of the crisis, but had been rejected in favour of the Judicial Inquiry. Now it was seen to have some advantage: for it would introduce some further delay and would also avoid the need for any kind of announcement while the Khamas were still in Serowe. It was agreed that a paper setting out this strategy should be presented to the Cabinet, for discussion.

It fell to Noel-Baker, as Commonwealth Secretary, to tell the Prime Minister about the report of the Judicial Inquiry. Harragin had come down against recognition, he wrote in a minute for Attlee, and this was probably the right conclusion. But the reasons given – although admittedly the real ones – were the very reasons which the British government were trying to conceal. The report would not, he thought, be an easy document to defend. He had recalled Baring to London and had been discussing the matter with him for some days. They had sent for the full evidence and in the meantime he did not think there was any need to trouble the Prime Minister or the Cabinet with the report. He warned that it was

an inflammable document and I am afraid that, if any hint of its contents got out before we are ready to publish it and announce our considered decision, a position which is already difficult enough would be made even more difficult.[9]

Along with this minute for the Prime Minister, Noel-Baker sent a detailed assessment of the report, which emphasized the risk of giving any impression that the British Government's policy had been dictated by the Union of South Africa.[10]

Attlee responded immediately. 'I do not think we should be precipitate in this matter,' he ruled, saying that he would look at the report before deciding what to do about circulation.[11] This was a most inopportune time to be presented with such a difficult crisis. Not only was it just days before Christmas, but also – and far more importantly – a general election had been set for 23 February 1950, just two months away.

The details set out in Noel-Baker's memorandum to Attlee had been drawn from information provided by Baring, which he had gathered before leaving Africa. He had gone to the office of the Bantu Press in Johannesburg, where he had spoken to B. G. Paver, the general manager, to Selope Thema, the editor of the *Bantu World*, and to Dr Alfred Xuma, the president of the ANC (who would shortly be defeated in his efforts to be re-elected, because of his opposition to the mass campaign of passive resistance to apartheid that had been advocated by Walter Sisulu, Oliver Tambo, and Nelson Mandela).[12] Thema had repeated the views that he had offered at the Judicial Inquiry and Dr Xuma had agreed with them.[13] Baring had also gone to Swaziland to consult Sobhuza, the Paramount Chief. Sobhuza had said he was keenly alive to the great dangers from South Africa of recognizing Seretse – dangers which would affect Swaziland as well as Bechuanaland, because they were both High Commission Territories. But, added Sobhuza, he 'disliked the idea of Government overriding the decision of a customary meeting in a matter usually decided by custom'.[14]

To discover the views of white liberals, Baring had consulted Quintin Whyte, the Director of the South African Institute of Race Relations. Although the Institute opposed the South African Mixed Marriages Act on principle, said Whyte, the executive did not approve of mixed marriages; support among liberals, he added, would go to Tshekedi. But he also made the point – which did not appear in Baring's notes for the Commonwealth Secretary – that it was a mistake to assume that a concession to South Africa on the issue of Seretse would help to avoid the consolidation of the Nationalists. On the contrary, he said, the Union Government 'will go on as it intends to go on, its nationalism growing on what it feeds on. In this case a concession from UK.'[15]

On instructions from Baring in London, following the meeting of 16 December 1949, the British High Commission in South Africa started to make plans for getting Seretse and Ruth out of Bechuanaland.

Clark wrote to Sir Godfrey Huggins in Salisbury to warn him that the Khamas might need to drive through Southern Rhodesia on their way to catch the flying-boat in Livingstone. This made Huggins uneasy. 'I am rather perturbed about Seretse and Ruth travelling by car,' he replied, 'in case of an unpleasant incident should one of our lunatics hear of the journey.' But the train, he realized, would be even worse. If they *had* to go by car, then the 'only thing would be for them to have a European male in the car to camouflage things. As you will gather, I do not like the idea.' As far as he was concerned, flying would be the safest option, although even that was risky – 'What I fear is one of our Afrikaners hearing of the journey – they must refuel somewhere.'[16] Clark came up with a solution. 'If our tiresome couple are summoned to London,' he said, 'we will arrange for them to fly from Francistown to Livingstone direct. They will then have to traverse only a tiny bit of Southern Rhodesia to get to the flying boat landing stage on the south bank of the river.'[17]

Attlee had still not seen the Harragin Report: the affair had been put on hold when Noel-Baker went to Ceylon for a conference of Commonwealth Foreign Ministers. But Gordon Walker, his Parliamentary Secretary, decided it was time for action. He had been having lengthy discussions with Sir Evelyn Baring, who was still in London, but who would be leaving for Africa in a week's time. On 21 January 1950, Gordon Walker sent a top-secret memorandum to the prime minister, with a copy of the Harragin Report. He explained that he had taken this initiative, even though the Commonwealth Secretary was abroad, because the Seretse problem had become pressing. Dr Malan, he said, was about to present another demand for the transfer of the High Commission Territories to South Africa, and Ruth's pregnancy was an additional worry:

Seretse's wife is due to give birth to a child in May or thereabouts. Seretse is unlikely to leave Serowe willingly without her; I am most reluctant to leave them both in Serowe for much longer. There may be some risk in inducing his wife to travel to London but I think we must face it, and the risk will be least if she can be brought to make the journey at once. An offer of the best medical attention in London in her confinement may prove a strong inducement.

The whole question must be put before Cabinet at an early date, argued Gordon Walker. This urgency was increased by the imminent general election, which meant that parliament would be dissolved on 3 February 1950.

Attlee agreed. 'This matter must come to Cabinet,' he scrawled at the bottom of Gordon Walker's memorandum. Then he added a note about the Harragin Report:

The document is most disturbing. In effect we are invited to go contrary to the desires of the great majority of the Bamangwato tribe, solely because of the attitude of the governments of the Union of South Africa and Southern Rhodesia.

'It is as if,' he observed unhappily, 'we had been obliged to agree to Edward VIII's abdication so as not to annoy the Irish Free State and the United States of America.'[18]

The matter came to Cabinet very shortly afterwards. Members were circulated beforehand with a copy of the Harragin Report, as well as a draft White Paper. The White Paper was based on the information that had been collected by Baring in Africa and had been given by Noel-Baker to Attlee. It was designed to show that Seretse's character was not, after all – despite the contrary finding in the Harragin Report – suitable for a man in the role of Chief. An earlier draft had been shown to senior officials at the Colonial Office, who read it with derision. They objected to the argument that 'the weight of opinion among responsible Africans is against recognition', because the only evidence offered for this was a single telegram about West Africans.[19] It was also ludicrous to accuse Seretse of being a drinker:

I do not think that the fact that Seretse has been drinking liquor is a legitimate argument against his recognition . . . there are many Chiefs both in Bechuana-land and elsewhere who do this contrary to traditional custom. There is no suggestion that Seretse drinks to excess.[20]

When the Cabinet met on the last day of January, they were unsure how to deal with the problem of the Harragin Report; they were also critical of the White Paper, which was put on hold. But they agreed with the proposal of the CRO – which had been decided at the meeting on 16 December – that Noel-Baker should see Seretse while he was still in office, before the general election in late February. The Khamas should be brought as soon as possible to the UK. On arrival, Seretse should be invited to renounce the Chieftainship.[21]

10

Tricked by the British Government

As soon as the Cabinet had given a green light to the plan of bringing Seretse and Ruth to London, the High Commission in South Africa booked two seats on the flying-boat leaving Johannesburg on 9 February 1950. In fact, the Khamas were obliged to join the flying-boat at the Victoria Falls, because they were prohibited immigrants in the Union. But it was hoped that booking the extra leg would put journalists off the scent: 'we are to warn BOAC *as late as practicable* that the passengers will embark at the Victoria Falls and that [the] seats must be kept empty'.[1] Nicholas Monsarrat, the United Kingdom Information Officer in South Africa, was told to settle details and, most importantly, to keep them from the press. Monsarrat, a handsome man with piercing blue eyes, was well equipped for the job as he was acquainted with a wide circle of journalists and understood their world. He was a writer himself and was shortly to make his name with the publication of *The Cruel Sea* in 1951.

Sillery drove to Serowe to see Seretse and Ruth, to tell them of the plan to send them to London. They were astonished – and immediately suspicious. 'Why should I be asked to London to discuss tribal affairs,' wondered Ruth, 'when women in Bechuanaland take no part in politics?'[2] In any case, it seemed very peculiar to invite them to the UK just before a general election. On the morning of 5 February, Sillery and Nettelton met the Khamas at the office of the District Commissioner in Lobatse, to tell them of the arrangements that had been made – they would leave for Francistown on 8 February and catch the flying-boat at the Victoria Falls on the afternoon of the following day. Then they took them to lunch at the hospital. But although the Sisters had prepared an excellent meal, reported Sillery to Baring,

Seretse had a poor appetite and 'kept bringing the conversation round to his return journey. We skated fairly easily over this thin ice.' Seretse wanted a guarantee that he and Ruth would be returning to Serowe. This stumbling block had been anticipated by the High Commissioner's Office as early as 28 November, when the idea of calling Seretse to London had first come up. 'The question which Seretse will almost inevitably ask, when presented with the summons to London,' Clark had warned Sillery, was

'Will I be allowed to return and will my return fare be paid?' The only answer which we could presumably give is that this is entirely dependent on the outcome of his discussions with the Secretary of State and that, if the talks resulted that way, his return fare would certainly be paid. The implication of this reply would of course be very obvious to Seretse, but we can see no other way out of the difficulty.[3]

The Khamas went to see the Bradshaws in Palapye. As Doris wrote to her sister:

Ruth and Seretse called us out of bed at midnight last night to tell us that the Resident Commissioner has told them it is necessary for them to fly to England to consult with Noel Baker over their future. At the moment, all this is very hush hush in the B. P. and S. Africa. They will fly to the Victoria Falls on Thursday and leave by flying boat on Friday 10th, arriving in England on 13th ... They are coming to say goodbye to us, before they leave, and I'm looking after her two kittens while they're away. They expect to be in London a week.[4]

A Kgotla was called, so that Seretse could hear the opinion of the Bangwato elders.[5] Many of them were suspicious that the invitation to London was a trick to remove Ruth from the Reserve, although they assumed that Seretse would be able to return. At first they said they did not want her to go, but after further discussion they decided to trust the Government. Next day, a delegation – twelve elders and Seretse – went to see Sillery to report on their decision. Sensing their hostility, Sillery felt reassured to know that 100 Bechuanaland Protectorate police had recently arrived in Serowe and that reinforcements from Basutoland were on their way.[6]

On 8 February – the day that Seretse and Ruth were expected to go to Francistown – Sillery sent a junior official to the Khamas' house to make the final arrangements. But he soon came back, accompanied by Seretse, to report that the plan had collapsed. At a further Kgotla, to which Percy Fraenkel had been invited as adviser, it had been decided that Ruth should not leave unless Sillery provided a written guarantee that she would return. Sillery had not been able to give this guarantee, which confirmed the general fear that there was some trick in the invitation.[7] The full discussion of the Kgotla was described in a press report:

An old grey-bearded Bamangwato tribesman stood up in a sun-baked clearing at Serowe, Bechuanaland . . . and told his chief-designate, Seretse Khama, that the tribe would not allow his London-born wife Ruth to leave the country.

'One after the other,' added the report, 'elders of the tribe heatedly urged Seretse to turn down the invitation . . . If he did decide to go he should leave Ruth behind.' One of the senior men said he believed there was a plot between the South African and British Governments. It had therefore been decided not to let Ruth go: Seretse should go on his own. Seretse accepted their decision, saying he would be back within three weeks.[8]

Sillery told Seretse that he could not accept Ruth's refusal unless she gave it herself, so Seretse went to fetch her. After about an hour Ruth appeared, 'extremely nervous and apparently downcast'. She was now faced with the prospect of yet another – immediate – separation from her husband. But she was firm in her decision not to go.[9]

'Top Secret,' Sillery cabled Baring. 'Ruth has jibbed at last minute. We all have impression that Ruth is prisoner of Seretse's supporters.' As soon as he had sent this message, he realized that it might be taken literally and swiftly sent another: 'Reference Ruth's refusal to move I did not make it clear that Ruth's decision was conveyed personally by her to Nettelton and me. Word prisoner was of course metaphorical.'[10] By this time, Sillery was thoroughly fed up with Mrs Khama. 'Ruth wears the trousers,' he complained, 'and we think she has a carping disposition.'[11]

There was still a chance, hoped Sillery, that Ruth might play ball. Next morning, he and Nettelton went to Francistown, where an aircraft had been chartered to pick up Seretse and Ruth and take them to Livingstone. There they found the Khamas, with a number of friends, including Kgosi Mokgosi of the Balete. But Ruth was clearly not dressed for travel – she was wearing a summer dress and no hat.[12] Even the wild elephants, observed Margaret Bourke-White, who had driven up to Francistown, seemed to oppose Seretse's departure for London: the night before, 'a herd of playful elephants tore up a grove of trees along the airport road just for the king-sized sport of it.' Seretse had to stop repeatedly on the way to the airport, to chop the tree-trunks and scattered branches which blocked the road.[13]

Seretse hugged Ruth tightly, kissing her, then climbed into the tiny aircraft. As the plane taxied and then took off, Ruth watched quietly in her car.[14] Then she started up the engine and drove off at top speed.[15] 'It was a sad day for both of us,' said Seretse later, 'when I kissed her goodbye at the airport and waved to my tribesmen as the plane lifted into the air.' Down below he could see the sparse, dry, cattle-land of his beloved country. As the little plane climbed higher and higher, 'I somehow had a feeling of foreboding that I was flying to certain disaster.'[16]

Shortly afterwards, Noel-Baker received a letter from the Bangwato Office in Serowe. 'We regret,' it stated, 'that our Queen has been unable to come to you as you wished.' But when they had asked for a promise of her safe return, this had been refused; consequently, 'we have not found the way clear to permit her to undertake the journey to you'. Their apprehension had arisen from the 'inimical talk' of South Africa and Southern Rhodesia –

Throughout our history both these countries seem to have sought to dispossess us of our land and our rights and it was on account of this very apprehension that we originally sought the protection of Great Britain . . .

Assuring you of our genuine loyalty to His Majesty and his Government, we are, Sir, the Bamangwato.[17]

Ruth returned to Serowe from Francistown with a heavy heart. Three weeks without Seretse seemed unbearable, especially now that she was pregnant. But she had not been home for very long before her spirits were unexpectedly lifted. Margaret Bourke-White, who was about to leave Bechuanaland, had dropped in for a last cup of coffee.

Suddenly, through the open window, they heard the sound of ululating women – it began as a faraway sound, a blend of wailing and yodelling, which died away and rose again. As Ruth and Margaret looked far down the hill, they could see a procession of women winding single-file through the low bushes. They went out to the front porch as the file of women approached the house, and saw that each one carried on her head a pail of water or a basket of grain. Crooning and raising folded hands, they filed in a stately parade past the porch:

'Isn't it staggering!' Ruth exclaimed. 'Isn't it simply staggering!'

Then a handful broke from the ranks. Led by a handsome young woman, they darted in swift circles, their tongues working visibly like little clappers as they shrilled [their] greeting . . .

Ruth sat down on a canvas chair under a spreading thorn tree, and the women seated themselves on the ground with their offerings of grain and water, which they had brought all the way from the well as gifts for Ruth. 'We are glad our queen did not go with our chief to England,' their leader said. 'We were afraid they would keep her there. We have come to tell you we are happy our Mother has stayed with us.' Then they sang a song which they had composed:

> When the chief comes back
> > We will be waiting for him,
> Seretse has dogs, and his dogs are the
> > Bamangwato people.
> Our Queen will come with rain, and all will be
> > Well in the land.

Margaret was clicking away with her camera, absorbed in taking pictures. But then it grew suddenly darker:

'Why is the light fading so?' I wondered. I looked up toward the sky and dark clouds scudding in. 'It can't be!' I thought to myself. Then a large drop fell on my wrist, followed by three drops on the lens. The tribal women, still singing, rushed for shelter on the porch. It seemed miraculous, but it was true. Their Queen had come with rain.[18]

Margaret had grown more and more fond of the Khamas. She saw that they were in a maze of troubles – 'but the deeper their trouble, the closer they grew together'. She had enormous respect for Ruth, 'for the fact that she was genuinely in love with her husband'.[19] Aware that Ruth was unable to go to any of the cities in South Africa to do any shopping, she gave her all her spare clothes. At least, she thought, Ruth would have the company of the cats, Pride and Prejudice, while Seretse was away.[20]

Seretse's flying-boat reached Southampton Marine Airport on 15 February 1950. 'Authority turns out to meet him with everything short of an Iron Curtain,' observed a Pathe newsreel sympathetically, as it showed Special Branch officers milling around him, as well as numerous press photographers and newsreel cameramen. As Seretse put on his hat against the cold wind of the British winter, he looked tired; he gave a 'half smile' to the press but made 'no comment', reported the Pathe newsreel.[21] John Keith was waiting for Seretse on the dock. He immediately whisked him up to London, to the offices of the CRO in Whitehall. Here, at ten minutes past six in the evening, Sir Percivale Liesching was waiting for him in his office.

Liesching had a challenging task ahead – persuading Seretse to summon his wife. Before any discussions began, Baring had insisted, they *must* get Ruth to London. But what would happen, wondered Herbert Baxter, a CRO official,

if Seretse refuses to send for Ruth, at least until hearing what we wish to say? He might well say that, if meanwhile we have nothing concrete to put to him, he will forthwith go back to Serowe. Could we then stop him going? And, if he went back, could we possibly repeat the process and summon him (and Ruth) again? We should have got into a position at once dangerous and ridiculous.

The furthest they could go, he thought, would be to put pressure on Seretse to send for Ruth. If he refused, then the secretary of state would just have to get on without her. The priority was to put to Seretse the proposals that had been agreed by Cabinet.[22]

Liesching had been carefully briefed for the meeting by Baxter, who had consulted Keith on ways of approaching Seretse. He was advised that it wd be better to refer to the lady as your wife or Mrs Khama, rather than as Ruth or Ruth Khama. The form of address to the young man is more of a problem: on the whole he thinks you cd suitably address him as Seretse, as from an older man to a younger. When at Oxford, the boy called himself Mr S. Khama; but Seretse is more analogous to an English surname than to a Christian name, and Khama is an added patronymic.

Baxter proposed that Keith, who would be bringing Seretse to the meeting, should remain during their talk, 'in case of distortions'.[23]

As soon as Seretse had arrived at the CRO and been introduced by Keith, Liesching launched into the object of the meeting. He told Seretse that the Commonwealth Secretary wanted Mrs Khama to join in discussions, because a matter affecting him so closely affected them both. Then, reported Liesching to Noel-Baker,

I paused for some reply but none came. It was not that we had not succeeded already in putting Seretse at his ease with us or that he looked either dour or obstinate. In fact he looked quite relaxed and cheerful.

Concluding that his silence was deliberate, he decided not to press him and the meeting came to an end.[24]

Seretse may have appeared 'relaxed and cheerful' to Liesching, but he was seething inside. After the meeting, he told Keith that he had been very annoyed by Liesching's references to the absence of his wife. He added that if the Government were not going to let him be Kgosi, then he was determined to go home: he certainly did not wish to be in England. He hoped to see the Secretary of State next day and to return to Bechuanaland by the end of the week. He said, too, that in the view of the Tribe it was the British Government – and not Tshekedi – who was the villain of the piece.[25]

After the meeting, Seretse was taken to the little flat that had been provided for him at Airways House, off Haymarket. Just a few days before, he had been living with his wife in a peaceful, slow-moving village in southern Africa; now he was being driven through the fast streets and bright lights of London's West End. Next morning, he was summoned to a meeting with Noel-Baker at 11.30 a.m. It was also attended by Viscount Addison, who was the Lord Privy Seal, Liesching, Sir Sidney Abrahams, as legal adviser to the CRO, and

Lord Rathcreedan, who had been engaged as a legal adviser to Seretse. Noel-Baker began the discussion by asking Seretse to bring Ruth to London. Seretse explained that the Tribe had seen no reason why Ruth should come and were afraid that this was a trick on the part of the United Kingdom Government. He felt bound to share these suspicions, he added, since the Resident Commissioner had refused to give a guarantee of her return. He then asked whether a guarantee could now be given, but Noel-Baker ignored the question.

'The dangers of disintegration and faction within the Tribe,' said Noel-Baker, disingenuously, 'had caused Ministers great anxiety.' He then came to the point: that Seretse should voluntarily relinquish his claim to the Chieftainship. If he accepted, he would receive an allowance to enable himself and his wife to live in the UK. Tshekedi, he added, would not be allowed to return to the Reserve or to become Chief, and the Tribe would be administered through the direct rule of the British Government. It would be 'in the interests of all', he added, 'that the nature of the solution should not be publicly disclosed until the Election campaign was over'.

Seretse was taken aback. He was so surprised by the proposal that he treated it as a joke. Would a condition of his acceptance, he asked drily, be that he refrained from political activity – for example, from 'Communist activities'? Noel-Baker treated this as 'semi-jocular', saying that he 'did not think himself that a Labour Government would stop the allowance if Seretse chose to engage in Communist activities'. Then Seretse became grimly serious. He pointed out that in the autumn of 1948, Tshekedi had asked the Protectorate Government to intervene in the Tribe's affairs, but it had refused. Then, after the June Kgotla the year before, the High Commissioner had assured him that he would be confirmed as Chief in a few weeks. But thereafter, 'apparently doubts had arisen and a Judicial Commission had sat; then there was silence and the Tribe had been told nothing until the recent invitation to come to London was received'. Noel-Baker felt uncomfortable. He made a vague reference to the British Government's 'wide experience in other parts of Africa where similar difficulties had arisen from time to time'.

Then Seretse raised the issue of South Africa and Southern Rhodesia. The Tribe believed, he said, that confirmation was being refused for fear of annoying Dr Malan and Sir Godfrey Huggins. Both of their Governments believed in the persecution of native people – but it appeared that the UK Government thought it better to annoy the Tribe than to annoy Dr Malan. Noel-Baker flatly denied this. 'It was no part of the policy of the UK Government to placate the South African Government at the expense of Seretse or of the Tribe,' he lied. He wished this categorical statement, he said, to be clearly understood. Seretse repeated the accusation, but again Noel-Baker lied. 'The Cabinet had not and would not,' he declared, 'deal with the matter on this footing at all, or look at it in this way.'

Seretse said that he alone could not respond to the Secretary of State's suggestion. The Tribe had to be consulted, he insisted, 'and it was now in the dark'. He warned that an interim period of direct rule would lead to trouble – 'an imposed solution would not be welcome'. It would also destroy confidence throughout the Protectorate, because other tribes would ask, 'Who next?' He then proposed an alternative to Noel-Baker's suggestion: that he be confirmed as Chief, but for a trial period. This was dismissed out of hand by Noel-Baker. Finally Seretse asked for a copy of the Report of the Judicial Inquiry, which was refused.[26]

Next day, Seretse complained to Keith that the Government were 'not being wholly frank with him'. He was planning to write a memorandum before the next meeting with Ministers, setting out the terms he was ready to accept. He had cabled Fraenkel in Mafikeng, asking him to come to London, because Rathcreedan seemed to him to have no real understanding of the issues. Keith submitted a report of his meeting with Seretse to the CRO, adding that 'Seretse was a gentleman, and had a lot of moral courage, and was behaving very well here, especially in his attitude to the Press.'[27] But Seretse was miserable, and smoking heavily. He missed Ruth badly and wrote to her every day.[28] He was adamant, though, that she should not be brought to London.[29]

But suddenly the Government dropped the Seretse Khama affair. Having brought Seretse to London and installed him in a flat 6,000 miles away from his pregnant wife and his people, they turned their attention to the imminent election.

This took place on 23 February. The contest was close: although Labour were returned to power, they had a majority of only six seats and there was a strong swing to the right. Attlee made Gordon Walker, who had been Noel-Baker's Under-Secretary, his new Commonwealth secretary; he believed Gordon Walker had shown 'exceptional ability' and deserved promotion.[30] His rise to power had been stellar: after just five years in Parliament and only 43 years old, he had now become a Cabinet Minister. The son of an Indian civil servant, he had grown up in the Punjab and gone on to shine as an academic – but then abandoned the life of an Oxford don for the world of power and politics. He was a tall, balding man, who smoked a pipe.

Noel-Baker, who had never impressed the Prime Minister, was sent to the Ministry of Fuel and Power. Liesching was delighted with the appointment of Gordon Walker, with whom he got on well. He was also relieved to see the departure of Noel-Baker – who always suspected that Liesching had been instrumental in his removal.[31] Possibly it was Noel-Baker's sloppy performance on the Seretse issue that had convinced Attlee: if Gordon Walker had not intervened in such a forceful way, the Prime Minister might still have been waiting to see the Harragin Report.

Godfrey Huggins, the Prime Minister of Southern Rhodesia, was as delighted as Liesching with the replacement of Noel-Baker by Gordon Walker.[32] He liked Gordon Walker and the warmth was mutual: when Huggins arrived at London Airport in 1950, the Commonwealth Secretary not only came to welcome him, but took his arm.[33]

Seretse Khama was waiting impatiently for his stay in London to end. Usually a mild and good-humoured man, he was now thoroughly exasperated. Then, five days after the general election, towards the end of February 1950, Liesching resurrected the affair. He wrote a secret memorandum to his new Secretary of State, Gordon Walker, and to Addison, the Lord Privy Seal, to report on a recent communication by Sir Evelyn Baring, who had argued that little progress would be made until the Government said clearly that they were not able to recognize Seretse. Liesching said he shared this view. He and Baring also agreed, he added, that it would be 'very dangerous' to allow Seretse to return to Serowe, even temporarily; he might be allowed to visit Lobatse, but he should be kept out of the Bangwato Reserve. Ruth's pregnancy should not be allowed to prevent her from coming to the UK: she was not due to give birth until May or June and she could be accompanied by a suitable person or nurse. 'But the fundamental need,' concluded Liesching, 'is for a firm decision by His Majesty's Government on the question of recognition'[34] – that is, a firm decision of *non*-recognition.

Once again the Cabinet took up the issue of the chieftainship of the Bangwato at Gordon Walker's instigation. At the second meeting of its new term, on Friday 3 March, it was the first of just two items on the agenda. Gordon Walker put to Cabinet members a new strategy: that Seretse should be banished from Bechuanaland. Any decision about the chieftainship should be postponed for five years, during which time Seretse and his wife should not be allowed to live in any part of the Protectorate. Tshekedi should also be exiled, but only from the Bangwato Reserve; and the Bangwato should be governed through direct rule. He asked the Cabinet for authorization to carry this through. It was a brutal plan.

The Cabinet initially recoiled from the proposal, but Gordon Walker argued persuasively. It was the best way forward, he insisted, for the Bangwato themselves – to protect them from South Africa. His fellow Cabinet members agreed in principle and the matter was put on hold until the next meeting of the Cabinet.[35] This took place on 6 March, when it was the second of two items on the agenda. Approval of the plan was confirmed, so long as the Attorney General agreed that the banishment would be legal.[36] Within only a week of taking office, Gordon Walker had forced through a decision on the Seretse issue – to disregard the decision of the Bangwato and to exile their acclaimed kgosi.[37]

Seretse and Fraenkel were summoned to the CRO straight after the Cabinet meeting on 6 March. As soon as they were ushered into the meeting room, at 6 p.m., Seretse sensed that a decision had been taken against him. But he was stunned when Gordon Walker read out to him the details of the Cabinet's decision. 'All talk of British justice sounded empty and hollow in my ears,' he said later. 'Exiled for five years! I simply could not believe it.' The Secretary of State's 'calm and unemotional manner,' he said,

was as unfeeling as if he was asking me to give up smoking, or surrender old school [examination] papers that I had accumulated while at Oxford. I doubt that any man has ever been asked to give up his birthright in such cold, calculating tones.[38]

Seretse protested that he could not under any circumstances accept this judgement and suggested a two-year trial as Chief. But Gordon Walker dismissed the idea without a second's thought. He asserted, falsely, that one of the reasons for the decision was to introduce direct tribal administration, as a way of giving the Bamangwato 'a more democratic' say in their own affairs.[39]

Seretse had been in London for three long weeks. Throughout this period, he had refused to speak to journalists. But now, from his tiny flat, he chose to issue a statement to the press. A newsreel entitled 'Seretse Khama Talks to Movietone' filmed him as he spoke, looking troubled and grave:

I wish to say that I am thoroughly disappointed with the undemocratic decision of the British Government in exiling me from my country . . .

The worst I expected after the Judicial Inquiry was that I would be officially recognized as chief but with a greater adoption of council assistance.

The step that had been taken, he warned sadly,

will lead to the disintegration of the Tribe and will have serious repercussions in the African continent and throughout the colonial world. I am sure the British public and all right-thinking people will not tolerate such injustice to me and, more seriously, to my suffering people who have also been loyal to the British crown and believed in British justice.[40]

The news of Seretse's banishment was broadcast to the world over the BBC Overseas Service. Ruth, who was sitting in her house listening to the radio, could hardly believe it.[41] Not long afterwards, she received a cable from Seretse:

Tribe and myself tricked by British Government. Am banned from the whole Protectorate. Love, Seretse.[42]

'Everyone here extremely distressed,' she wired back. 'Please advise if coming back at all.'[43] Another cable was sent by a tribal elder: 'Not our wish to be ruled directly by British Government. Please challenge.'[44] Concerned for Ruth's safety, the headmen posted guards around Ruth's house, day and night.[45]

III

Lies and Denials from Whitehall

11

The humiliation of
Sir Evelyn Baring

Gordon Walker was furious with Seretse for speaking to the media. 'He thus got 40 hours' start on me,' he fumed in his diary, 'and it took me several weeks to catch up.'[1] He would now have to make an immediate statement to the House of Commons – a task that should not have been necessary for another week. He was fairly confident of support from the Conservative Party, because of its traditional ties of 'kith and kin' with white settler groups in Kenya and the Rhodesias. But he was worried about critics from within his *own* party. Its razor-thin majority had up to now persuaded dissenters to toe the party line, but this was less certain on a matter that aroused suspicions of a colour bar.

No decision had yet been made on what to do about the Harragin Report – which contained 'so much explosive material', Gordon Walker warned Attlee that it would be better not to publish it. He had spoken to men on the Conservative front bench, he said, who had agreed not to press for publication. He left the final decision with the Prime Minister:

I'm sorry that (owing to Seretse's irresponsibility) this has come up so suddenly that it will be difficult, if not impossible for you to consult the Cabinet. May I, therefore, have your decision about which course I should adopt?

'I agree it would be better not to publish,' answered Attlee.[2]

The day after Seretse's press conference, he and his legal advisers, Fraenkel and Lord Rathcreedan, were summoned to the CRO for a meeting with Gordon Walker, Liesching, and other senior officials. The Commonwealth Secretary immediately took the moral high ground, accusing Seretse of a breach of understanding; Seretse did not bother to reply. Gordon Walker and Lord Addison then left the CRO for Westminster, to deliver a statement on Seretse's exile: Gordon Walker to the House of Commons; Addison to the Lords. Just after 2.30, Gordon Walker stood up to speak to his fellow Members of Parliament. Banishing Seretse had been necessary, he said, in order to achieve 'the disappearance of the present tendencies to disruption which threaten the unity and well-being of the tribe'. It would be for a minimum of five years, at which point the situation would be reviewed. Tshekedi would be exiled from the Bangwato Reserve, though not from Bechuanaland, for so long as the chieftaincy was in suspense. In the meantime, the British Government was going to replace the current system of administration in the Reserve with direct rule. But, he added, a council of Africans would be set up as quickly as possible, in order to give the Bamangwato people a fuller say in the conduct of their affairs.

On the issue of the Harragin Inquiry, the Secretary of State explained that the Government had decided not to make its findings public, because they were simply 'advisory':

It is only one of the many factors we have had to take into consideration in coming to our decision. It would give a disjointed appearance if this one factor of those we have had to take into account were made public. I hope, therefore, that I shall not be pressed to make the Report public.[3]

Seretse would be given the opportunity to return to Bechuanaland to attend the hearing of a legal case about his property, which had developed out of his conflict with Tshekedi. The dates of the visit would be arranged in such a way, he added, that he could be there before and during his wife's confinement. But he would only be permitted to go to Lobatse: he would not be able to go to Serowe or to any other part of the Bangwato Reserve. The Government hoped, added Gordon Walker, that Ruth would join Seretse in Lobatse and give birth there; it had good medical facilities, he said, and the distance from Serowe was 'a small journey' (in fact, it was close to 250 miles of rough, dirt road).

Many MPs heard the Commonwealth Secretary's statement with deep misgivings. Gordon Walker was subjected to a 'fairly rough passage' for half an hour and had to answer questions from all sides of the House, reported Egeland in London to Malan in South Africa.[4] Fenner Brockway, a Labour MP, attacked the front bench. 'I have rarely been more angry,' he wrote later, 'than when I heard the Minister announce that he had deposed Seretse . . . It was beyond my belief that such a thing could happen under a Labour Government.'[5] Brockway, who had been born in Calcutta, was the son of a missionary in the London Missionary Society. He was a highly principled man and had been elected a month earlier as the MP for Eton and Slough. Now 62 years of age, he had been an energetic champion of colonial freedom for a long time, with the result that some of his fellow MPs referred to him as 'the Member for Africa'. As far as Brockway was concerned, the exile of Seretse highlighted the issue of the colour bar and he made 'quite a scene' in the House. Quintin Hogg (later Lord Hailsham), MP for Oxford, joined in the protest from the Conservative side.[6]

Was this the first time, asked Sir Herbert Williams caustically, that 'any British Government had imposed a colour bar in any part of the British Empire?' When Reginald Sorensen, a Labour backbencher, asked if South Africa had had any influence on the Government's decision, Gordon Walker denied it categorically: 'we have had no communication from the Government of the Union nor have we made any communication to them. There have been no representations and no consultation in this matter.'

Winston Churchill, the leader of the Opposition, 'led a persistent and prolonged interrogation' of Gordon Walker, according to *The Times*.[7] He did not question the decision to withhold the chieftainship from Seretse, but he did want to know 'whether this chief is being treated quite fairly as between man and man'. That was a point, he said, 'which causes some anxiety'. In particular, he wanted to know whether Seretse had been warned that if he came to the UK he might be forbidden to return home. Or had he been 'enticed' to Britain under false pretences? 'Where is Mrs Khama at present,' he asked –

and where was she at the time when Seretse Khama took leave of her? Will the right hon. Gentleman not consider that Seretse has a right to go back to that very place and meet her at that very place before the Government take any further action in the matter?[8]

Gordon Walker argued strenuously that Seretse had not been tricked in any way, and 'got away with it,' wrote Brockway afterwards – 'but only just'.[9]

Churchill was not convinced, however. 'It is a very disreputable transaction,' he growled.[10] When Ruth heard of Churchill's protest, it gave her 'great heart', reported Noel Monks. Like her parents, she was a longstanding supporter of the Conservative Party and she believed that if it had been in power, her husband would never have been exiled. 'When the Tories get in,' she said, 'they will change it.'[11] Seretse, too, though his political views were further to the Left than Ruth's, was encouraged by Churchill's intervention.[12]

In Cape Town, Sir Evelyn Baring was becoming increasingly worried about the prospect of Seretse being allowed to visit the Protectorate. The best solution, he wrote to Liesching, would be to get Ruth out of Bechuanaland.[13] But Gordon Walker was far less worried about difficulties in Africa than about those at home in Britain, where opposition to the exile of Seretse was growing. On 10 March he complained to Baring:

You do not apparently propose to deal with what may prove perhaps at your end and certainly at ours to be one of the most criticised points in our decisions. It is that, whereas Tshekedi is excluded from the Reserve only, Seretse is excluded from the Protectorate.

Even those who sympathized with the Government's difficulties, he added, were regarding Seretse's banishment from the whole of the Protectorate for five years as unnecessarily harsh. 'I should like you to consider,' he added with evident irritation,

whether there is a possibility that we have gone too far in excluding Seretse and Ruth from the Protectorate . . . If you still maintain your view that they cannot be permitted to reside there (or to reside within the Protectorate within such area as could be prescribed) for the full five-year period, I should need to be provided with the most cogent and convincing arguments for this.[14]

Baring parried. 'Am most grateful for firm line taken by the United Kingdom Government,' he cabled Gordon Walker. 'A major disaster has been avoided and [the] effect on relations with Union Government has been admirable.' He promised to do everything he could to ease difficulties in London. He was willing for Seretse to come to Lobatse at any time after the Kgotla in Serowe on 13 March, when he would announce the terms of Seretse's banishment to the Bangwato. But, he insisted, the removal of both Seretse and Ruth *had* to be enforced once their child had been born. In the meantime, he hoped Ruth would join Seretse in Lobatse. 'I will try to suggest this to her,' he said, 'but am told that she is so perverse that a direct suggestion might have [the] effect of confirming her in her idea of staying at Serowe.'[15]

The colonial administration was preparing for the Kgotla. 'British do *not* expect trouble,' said Robert Stimson, a BBC journalist, to the US attaché in Pretoria, because '[they] consider the Bamangwatos "gutless" – and have enough troops to handle anything'.[16] The Protectorate police were on high alert and the Southern Rhodesian government had sent reinforcements from their own police force.[17]

But the press were far more difficult to manage than security. Almost as soon as Seretse had given his statement to the media on 7 March, the world's press had swooped down on Serowe. 'You never saw such comings and goings,' wrote Ruth's friend Doris Bradshaw in a letter to friends in Britain – 'aeroplanes galore with hundreds of reporters and photographers from all over the world.' The correspondent for the British *Daily Telegraph*, she said, was on a mission in Cairo – 'but he abandoned that and flew to Serowe'. The *Daily Express* reporter was on a mission in Accra – but he too 'abandoned that and flew to Serowe'. It was a delightful change in the daily routine of the Bradshaws. 'We had a lovely time meeting all these famous people,' she said, 'and could just about have swum in the drinks they offered, as they wanted news from us.'[18] Monsarrat and Clark hoped to encourage reports that were favourable to the government: they were planning to go early to Serowe 'to feed material to the press, to try to drop ideas'.[19]

At midday on Saturday 11 March, Baring flew in his private aircraft to Mafikeng, where he met with Tshekedi and then Sillery. Meanwhile, British officials in Serowe were getting ready for the High Commissioner's visit. At the kgotla ground, chairs were put out for the dignitaries and junior officials practised taking the salute.[20] This would be Baring's first visit to Serowe. 'It will always seem incredible to me,' observed Noel Monks,

that, up to this moment, Sir Evelyn Baring, in Pretoria, had not come to Bechuanaland to see for himself what lay behind the Seretse Affair, whether the marriage was a good thing or bad for the Bangwato. Indeed, he had never met Ruth or Seretse in his life.[21]

But just before Baring left Mafikeng on the night train for Bechuana-land, alarm bells started to sound. News arrived that a petition had been received from Fraenkel's office, requesting a postponement of the Kgotla on the grounds that without a Kgosi, it was not possible to hold an assembly. Baring's reaction was firm: the Kgotla would go ahead. Then he and his staff embarked on the long rail journey north to Palapye.

But the alarm bells grew louder as they went further north. When the train eventually steamed into the station of Palapye, the District Commissioner was waiting with worrying news – that the day before, the headmen of the Bangwato had come to tell him that the Kgotla would be boycotted.[22] The High Commissioner quickly consulted his staff, recalled Sillery later:

Baring asked Sullivan what the chances were, and I heard Sullivan say, 'Fifty-fifty, sir.' But Nettelton said that the Ngwato were too keen on politics to forgo a meeting, and the High Commissioner, who had Clark with him, decided to proceed.[23]

The government party went on to the Residency, on a hill high above Serowe.

That night, Peto Segkoma delivered a message to the press. In his soft voice, he explained that at a meeting on Saturday afternoon of thirty-five leading headmen, it had been decided to boycott the Kgotla. The meeting had been attended by Fraenkel's legal partner, A. A. Gerricke, who had flown to Serowe earlier that day; Fraenkel himself had not been able to come as he was still in London with Seretse.[24] They had tried to warn the Government, explained Peto, because they didn't want to embarrass the High Commissioner – but officials just wouldn't believe them.

Throughout the night, Peto, Goareng Mosinyi, Serogola Seretse and

Lenyeletse Seretse went around the villages talking to people, making sure that everyone knew about the boycott.[25] Concerned that their action might provoke the enforced removal of Ruth, they posted a secret guard in the hills surrounding Serowe, to keep a close watch on her safety, night and day, in addition to the bodyguard they had appointed to be with her constantly.[26]

When Baring drove up to Serowe early in the morning of 13 March, there was no sign of the thousands of men who had been expected to arrive.[27] 'The BP Gov officials were running round Serowe in circles,' wrote Doris to friends in the UK, 'begging natives to go to the meeting.'[28] But still nobody came. The dusty kgotla ground remained silent and deserted, except for the press and about twenty-five European spectators sitting under a tree. 'There were no Africans,' observed John Redfern, the *Daily Express* reporter, with amusement. 'Sir Evelyn had travelled 1,000 miles to speak to the Bamangwato and the Bamangwato were missing.' The whites had been at the kgotla ground long before it was supposed to start:

The men wore well-pressed tropical suits and ties, and looked quite different from their normal shorts-socks-and-shirts. They were bursting with loyalty and anxiety and stood about, a baffled group.

Where were the Africans? Fifteen minutes after the High Commissioner was due to receive the opening salutes, there was *one* African, by name 'Basket', Mrs Page Wood's employee. He was on duty, looking after his mistress's requirements.[29]

A quarter of an hour before midday, just five minutes before the High Commissioner was due to drive in state from the Residency, Monsarrat hurried from the Kgotla to one of the few telephones in Serowe and announced in his low voice: 'There is no one here. Better tell H. E. not to come.' So Baring put down his cocked hat, unbuckled his sword and changed out of his uniform.[30] 'In these circumstances,' Baring reported to the Secretary of State, 'vigorous police action was clearly undesirable and would in any case have been ineffective. I therefore cancelled the Kgotla.'[31]

It was a humiliation for Baring. He had looked majestic in his white uniform and sword, crowned with the tall cocked hat and white feathers, and with his Star of St Michael and St George on his chest.[32]

But this finery now looked absurd. 'The boycott of the Kgotla,' wrote Monsarrat, 'was, in its context, an atrocious personal insult.' He felt personally humiliated himself – 'the white uniform, white helmet, medals and sword which I had donned for the great occasion seemed ridiculous'. They were also, he complained, very hot.[33] 'Never before, in British Africa,' wrote Monks, 'had the Crown's representative been so insulted.'[34] The boycott was a very public defeat of the British Administration by the Tribe they claimed to govern and was covered in painful detail by a Movietone newsreel. As it showed a close-up of a reporter in the deserted Kgotla, with a typewriter on his knee, it observed mockingly, 'As you see, the press turned up in *full* force.'[35]

Yet again, the Khama family had embarrassed the British. Clark told officers at the US embassy that one of the reasons for the British decision to exile Seretse had been to get rid of the 'trouble-making' Khama ruling house. 'This small group of wretched Bamangwatos who have caused His Majesty's Government so much trouble in the past,' said Clark, 'are not worth it.' From the 'puritanical Khama the Great down to Seretse,' he added, they had been a source of trouble. But at least now, 'a unique opportunity' of getting rid of them had presented itself.[36]

Baring had still to deliver the terms of the Parliamentary statement on Seretse's banishment. He arranged for a written instruction by the District Commissioner, acting as Native Authority, to be delivered to twenty-four senior men, asking them to appear before him. But only twelve of these orders were successfully delivered, and not one of the recipients obeyed. 'Only if we are handcuffed and carried will we go to the Kgotla,' said one headman.[37]

As a last resort – so as to deliver his statement to *somebody* – Sir Evelyn gave a press conference at the Residency. In any case, he needed to offer some kind of explanation to the journalists. The press event took place in the Sullivans' beautiful garden, with chairs set out on the well-watered lawn in a semi-circle for the twenty-two press men and photographers. They were plied with drinks and made as comfortable as possible, but it was 'not a happy experience', said one of the local officials. 'The press were in a destructive mood, for they all sided with Seretse and questioned Baring with cheerful contempt verging on open hostility.'[38] Baring told them that the boycott was a case of simple intimidation and he emphasized the threat of conflict between Seretse and Tshekedi. The history of the Bamangwato people, he said, was one of quarrels and feuds. The government's objective 'has been to stop the development of what we feel might become one of the biggest and the worst dynastic feuds that has ever been':

There is a danger to peace and good order if you have either of them [Seretse or Tshekedi] ... We thought that you would get the position of the feud between Tshekedi and Seretse, whatever the position at this moment is, that there would develop one in which the feud between Tshekedi and Seretse would become worse, and then you have disasters ... We think that with either in the saddle we are going to have almost endless trouble in the near future.

Then he developed the idea that Gordon Walker had put forward to the House of Commons – that Seretse's banishment was a progressive measure aiming at greater democracy.[39]

The first questions of the press were about the role of South Africa, to which Baring unhesitatingly lied, just as Gordon Walker had done in the House of Commons:

PRESS: Has the present position arisen through the Union Government?
HE [HIS EXCELLENCY, BARING]: The Union Government has taken no action whatever.
PRESS: I mean by action an approach to the United Kingdom Government saying if you do this then we will do something else.
HE [HIS EXCELLENCY, BARING]: The Union Government has taken no action, except banning Seretse Khama from Union territory. The Union Government has made no approach to the British Government.[40]

Redfern was impressed by the way in which Baring carried the press conference off. 'This was the British colonial chief at his best,' he thought. 'So calm, so cool, an oasis in a desert of exacerbation.'[41] But however calm Baring appeared, deep down he was apprehensive. He had even been boycotted by Ruth, who had gone to Palapye to spend the weekend with the Bradshaws, in order to avoid him.[42] He had the uncomfortable knowledge that news of his failure would very soon reach Britain and every corner of the Empire, through newspaper reports and newsreels. Liesching sent him a message of sympathy.

'This Seretse business is very troublesome,' he said, 'but we always knew it would be.' He put the blame squarely on Seretse: 'I am sorry that the Serowe situation turned so sour on you for the Kgotla. Our original plan would of course have timed the announcement of the decision here with your appearance in Serowe.'[43]

Baring was afraid, he confided to his wife Mary, that he might get the sack over the Seretse Khama affair.[44] He suspected that the Government were considering plans to rescind or modify the exclusion order on Seretse – and he was right. On the very day of the failed Kgotla, even before the news reached London, Gordon Walker told Liesching that he was increasingly doubtful about their policy. 'We have had a very bad reception: not too good even in some Union papers,' he observed in dismay. 'We cannot ignore this,' he added, 'indeed it may in the end prejudice our whole policy. We must, there-fore, see what we can do, whilst keeping our principal policy intact.' The policy of non-recognition must be sustained, he thought, but he hoped for a compromise on Seretse's return to the Protectorate:

The question of where Seretse resides is I think a matter only of law and order. I don't think the mere residence of Seretse plus Ruth in the Protectorate or Reserve would unite and inflame S. African opinion.

And he added:

It strikes me that if Seretse's appearance in Lobatse at this moment does not endanger order, his permanent residence could not do so either. Indeed, we will be on weak ground if, basing ourselves on the law and order argument, we let him go back now and remove him later. There is also the point that Seretse in the Protectorate may be much less of an embarrassment and a source of disorder than in London, where he has organisations and the whole Press at his disposal.[45]

Then the situation in Bechuanaland deteriorated even further. The boycott of the Kgotla was now being followed by a boycott of the Administration. Six senior headmen signed a letter stating that the tribe would not obey any orders 'by or emanating from a newly constituted Native Authority and would not pay further taxes with-out the authority of Seretse'.[46] Nor would they elect a new Kgosi – because he was born, not elected.[47] In other words, the Bangwato were on strike. The Tribal Treasury stayed open, but collected no revenue; the Kgotla was deserted except for a few old men; and in the course of their work, government officers were met by polite preoccupation.[48] Nobody attended a Kgotla called by the District Commissioner, in his position as Native Authority, and the native courts ceased to function.[49] The campaign was further strengthened when the diKgosi of other nations in the Protectorate joined in.[50] Feelings ran high.[51]

The boycott drew on the precedent of the civil disobedience campaign that had been led in India by Mahatma Gandhi against British rule. Gandhi had first used this method of protest – *Satyagraha* – in South Africa, in the Transvaal, between 1906 and 1912, to resist the racist laws of the Government.[52] It was a form of opposition that suited the people of Bechuanaland, who preferred to negotiate a solution to a problem, rather than to fight. 'We are sure the natives won't raise a hand and use violence,' wrote Doris Bradshaw to her family in the UK. 'They are just taking it quietly and resisting passively.'[53] She believed that the Administration would have *preferred* violence. 'There's been such a lot of dirty work by the Gov,' she wrote to her sister in the UK. 'You've no idea. They seem to be trying hard to *create* disturbances but the natives are too shrewd to be stampeded into anything the Gov could use against them or Seretse.'[54]

Baring assumed that his problems with the Bangwato had been caused by a few ringleaders and he was especially bothered by the 'participation of certain local Europeans'. The worst offender, he told Gordon Walker, was the representative of the Native Recruiting Corporation, Alan Bradshaw. He resolved to remove him from Bechuanaland without delay. 'When passing through Johannesburg,' he reported to London, 'I asked formally for his transfer and was told that this would be arranged at once.'[55] Within just three days, Bradshaw got a telegram telling him that he was on 'immediate transfer' to Vryburg in South Africa, about 150 kilometres south-west of Mafikeng.[56] When the telegram arrived, Doris was helping Ruth make baby clothes. She showed it to Ruth, who commented sadly, 'Doris Bradshaw is the only white woman in this whole territory whose home is open to me. She is the only white woman I can confide in at this rather trying time for me.'[57]

'We don't like Vryburg very much,' wrote Doris shortly after her arrival,

though we have a nice house in the centre of the town, with electric light and indoor sanitation – a treat after Palapye. But it's so cold here, the people are all Afrikaans and speak only Afrikaans and don't like us because we are English.

They were especially unpopular because of their known support for Seretse and Ruth. 'Poor Seretse,' sighed Doris, 'they're treating him like a leper aren't they? Ruth has all the guts and courage in the world . . . We feel ashamed of being English when we see what's going on.'[58] The tribe 'do not and never have trusted the Administration, who only order them around and never hardly listen to their point of view,' wrote Alan to Doris's sister.[59]

Baring decided to inject some fresh blood into the Administration in Serowe. He brought in Forbes MacKenzie, the Government Secretary of Swaziland, who was a Rhodesian and famous throughout the Protectorate for his height – 6 feet 7 inches. MacKenzie was told on 1 April 1950 'to take control of the situation'[60] and was appointed the new District Commissioner. This meant that he was also designated 'Native Authority', under the new regime of direct rule by the British Government. MacKenzie started to develop the machinery for the direct rule of the Bangwato Reserve and appointed Keaboka Kgamane as 'Senior Tribal Representative' and Senior Judicial Officer. Keaboka was one of Seretse's principal supporters and was fourth in the line of succession to the kingship of the Bangwato.

Throughout Bechuanaland, there was dismay and concern at the idea of direct rule in the Bangwato Reserve. In Maun, in the north of the country, the Regent of the Batawana, Mrs Moremi, who was well known as a progressive and just administrator, said that it raised 'an important point of principle'.[61] Not only in Bechuanaland, but also in Basutoland and Swaziland, the other two High Commission Territories, there were protests. From their point of view, it created an unhappy precedent – 'This might happen to us.'[62]

I2

Cover-up

In London, Seretse was taking legal advice on what course to follow to return to his wife and his country. He was much heartened by messages of support. 'Britain's 20,000 Negroes rallied around me,' he wrote, gratefully.[1] The day after Gordon Walker's speech to the House of Commons, concerned individuals and organizations in the UK – including the West African Students Union (WASU), the African League, the League of Coloured Peoples and the Council for Overseas Indians – met together in London and immediately formed the 'Seretse Khama Fighting Committee'.[2]

Learie Constantine, a veteran campaigner on issues of injustice relating to colour and race, played a leading role in setting up the Committee and was appointed Chairman.[3] Nii Odoi Annan, a law student from the Gold Coast and Financial Secretary of WASU,[4] was Joint Secretary of the Fighting Committee along with Billy Strachan, a Jamaican who was the Secretary of the Caribbean Labour Congress and had served with distinction as a pilot in RAF Bomber Command during the war. Joe Appiah, President of WASU, was also involved. The Committee was based at the WASU hostel on the Chelsea Embankment and was publicly supported by numerous other organizations, ranging from the University of Oxford Socialist Club to the Birmingham Trades Council.[5] The Afro-American Association in the USA, which had a membership of 15 million people, had sent representatives to Britain and was in touch with Seretse.[6] Edinburgh set up its own Fighting Committee, to support the campaign from Scotland.

The Committee organized a Mass Protest Meeting at Denison House in London on the evening of Sunday 12 March, which was chaired by Constantine and attended by about 800 people. Seretse attended the meeting although he was not feeling very well; he was fit and athletic, but the blow he had been given in the past week had sapped his strength. On behalf of the Bangwato he thanked the audience for coming: 'I am sure that the people back home, disappointed as they are at what I consider a rather undemocratic decision, will take heart when they know they are not the only ones in this battle.' 'I am happy to say', he added warmly, 'that, even though this action has been taken by the British Government, the British people have not associated themselves with it.'[7]

At the meeting a resolution of protest was passed and it was agreed to distribute a copy of this to the King, the Prime Minister, Churchill, the United Nations, the world press, embassies in different parts of the world, and the National Council for Civil Liberties – to make them aware of 'the stand of all the Colonial People'. The Fighting Committee also resolved to send frequent cables to Ruth in Bechuanaland.[8]

A week later, on 19 March, a large rally was held in Trafalgar Square, at which Seretse and Fenner Brockway both spoke. The Labour Party had been asked to send a speaker, but had said they were unable to supply one. The Reverend Reginald Sorensen, however, although a Labour MP, joined the protest in a private capacity. He said he was attending on behalf of many friends inside and outside the House of Commons.[9] Sorensen, a Unitarian minister, took a keen and active interest in movements for colonial liberation.

The exile of Seretse was seen to highlight the evil of the colour bar in Britain and her colonies. It was high time, asserted the African League, that 'the world knows the root of the troubles in Africa. In their relations with Africans, most Europeans consider themselves "gods" and "goddesses". They take this fantastic attitude in order to prevent the Africans from attaining equality with them.'[10] This was the reason, claimed the Fighting Committee, that British newspapers had made such a great play of the story that Ruth was a typist – the idea being that a white woman would only marry a black man if she were a 'social reject'.[11]

The Colonial Office was gloomily predicting increased trouble with nationalist elements in all of the African colonies because of the Seretse affair.[12] The Foreign Office, too, said one of the CO officials, was 'seriously concerned (like us) as to the disastrous effect of this on world opinion'.[13] Certainly the effect on opinion in the Commonwealth was disastrous. Krishna Menon, India's High Commissioner in London, went to see Gordon Walker to register a protest from the Indian Government.[14] In the Ceylon Parliament, it was announced that the banishment would 'rouse the opposition of all coloured people against the Commonwealth'.[15] In Kingston, Jamaica, all the political parties joined together to warn the British Government that it risked losing the support of 'countless millions of colonial people'.[16] Citizens of Trinidad pledged to support any move to release 'the monarch of Bechuanaland'.[17] From all over the Commonwealth, letters and telegrams of objection and complaint poured in – to the CRO, to the Colonial Office, and to the Prime Minister.

'Embassy believes British have blundered,' reported the US embassy in South Africa to the office of the American President. 'Believes British action jeopardizes their reputation for fair dealing with Natives.'[18] Most of the American press, though, were taking a 'moderate line'.[19] This was hardly surprising, given that thirty out of the forty-eight states had legislation prohibiting mixed marriage and enforcing segregation; in the Southern states, a system of laws known as 'Jim Crow' segregated black people from whites in all areas of society, ranging from schools and buses to theatres and parks. American liberals, however, were generally shocked by the British Government's treatment of Seretse, and the African-American community was outraged.[20] W. E. B. Du Bois and the Council on African Affairs telegraphed Sir Oliver Franks of the British diplomatic corps, as well as Trygve Lie, Secretary-General of the UN, to protest against Seretse's exile. There were 65 signatories to the telegram, including many pastors.[21] 'The Negro press – which is a highly influential medium – is full of the Seretse debacle,' reported a leading trade union journalist. It was the first time, he added, that 'the Negro press has ever, to my knowledge, been critical of the British Labor Government. It's lost a good many friends for the Government among our Negroes.' It would be difficult, he added,

to exaggerate the repercussions of the Seretse affair among some quarters here. Some of us like to think that the Labor govt policy is pretty free of the common stultification of American racial attitudes. Our Negro performers and troops come back from England raving about the British enlightenment etc etc. Then this.[22]

Among blacks in Africa, there was bitter condemnation. Walter Sisulu, the general secretary of the ANC, sent a telegram to the Resident Commissioner in Mafikeng, deploring the decision. He feared that it had 'destroyed perhaps forever what confidence Africans had in the integrity and honour of the British Government'.[23] The Kroonstad African Community sent a similar telegram to Attlee, as did the South African Indian Congress.[24]

But white South Africa, with few exceptions, approved.[25] The Anglican Bishop of Bloemfontein asserted:

We who know South Africa well and its native life know the aversion which most natives have to mixed marriages ... It is no question of morality – presumably an Englishman can morally marry an Eskimo or a Hottentot – but it is very decidedly a question of wisdom. All I have seen of 'coloured' people in South Africa makes me perfectly aware that it is a terrible mistake. The coloured hate their strain of black blood, and the natives despise them. That is just sheer fact, and has to be faced.[26]

'The natives have got more insolent since Seretse and his wife came here,' complained a white in Cape Town to Attlee:

Riots in Durban and Jo-burg, sly pushes as they pass the whites, cheeky in the shops, and innumerable pin pricks which will certainly grow if they aren't checked. I suppose by now they think they are as entitled to a white woman as Seretse.[27]

The opinion of South African newspapers followed predictable lines. Of the 'white' papers supporting the United Party, there was approval of the banishment from the *Argus* in Cape Town and the Afrikaans *Suiderstem* and *Volkgtem*. On the other hand, the more liberal *Rand Daily Mail*, the Johannesburg *Star*, and Durban's *Natal Mercury* were critical. The *Cape Times* took a position between the two: that the decision might have been justified, but no single argument had been put forward. Among the Nationalist papers, *Die Burger* in Cape Town and *Volksblad* in Bloemfontein praised the courage of the UK Government; the same line was taken by *Vaderland*, the Afrikaner Party paper. The *Transvaler*, an extremist paper, rebuked the British Government for slowness in reaching its decision.

All the leading vernacular papers in southern Africa were published by 'Associated Bantu Newspapers', an umbrella group that was heavily controlled by the editorial director, B. G. Paver, and based in Johannesburg. This press group published, among many other newspapers, *Naledi ya Batswana*, which was aimed at Bechuanaland, and *Bantu World*, the main newspaper read by black South Africans.[28] The leader columns of most of his newspapers, Paver assured Baring, supported the British Government's policy, although *Umthunywa* did not toe the line. 'Our associated paper *Umthunywa* published a leader attacking the British Government,' explained Paver in a report to Baring, 'but I consider that this is of no special significance, for *Umthunywa* is run by a private printer who is inclined to leave his leaders to a rather wild and woolly African editor.' He added, reassuringly, 'When we have the capital, we shall take over this paper.'[29]

In Britain, public opinion was growing increasingly hostile. 'If the Bamangwato do not object to a white consort and the prospect of a half-breed succession,' argued *The Times*, 'it would not seem to be for the imperial Government, pledged before the nations to respect the equal rights of all races, to overrule them in their own domestic concerns.'[30] Many letters to newspapers were describing the affair as another Munich, except that this time it was South Africa that had been appeased.[31] A letter of protest, signed by over 100 students, was sent to *The Times* from Balliol, Seretse's college at Oxford.[32]

'From all this,' wrote Gordon Walker wearily in his diary, 'I have learned to stand up to much abuse and publicity.' But he was also enjoying his high profile. 'Though it has not been a pleasant experience,' he observed, 'I have not altogether disliked it. There is something to be said for having oneself talked about, whatever the cause.'[33] He was helped by the South African High Commissioner in London, Leif Egeland, who had long discussions with influential people in the media, warning them against any agitation that would play into the hands of 'Communist exploitation' of the colour issue. But he had done this discreetly. 'Nothing will play more surely into the hands of our enemies and enemies of the present United Kingdom Government,' he told Malan, 'than any overt sign of intervention on our part.'[34]

Egeland reported to Dr Malan that Gordon Walker did not think the Conservatives would want to bring down the government on the Seretse issue – 'a *damnosa hereditas* to which they would not wish to succeed'. But Egeland was worried about Winston Churchill. 'Churchill has got out of step with his Party,' he told Malan, 'most of whom would like to see [the] issue played down.'[35] Churchill was deeply troubled by the Seretse affair. According to his friend Violet Bonham Carter, he had told her: 'I believe firmly in 2 principles: (1) Christian marriage, & (2) the bond of strong animal passion between husband & wife. Both exist in this case.'[36] On 15 March, two days after the failure of Baring's Kgotla, Churchill sent an urgent telegram to Smuts in South Africa: 'Should be grateful for full information about your views Seretse by swiftest airmail. Feeling here very strong against Government muddle. Winston.'[37]

Smuts replied immediately with a telegram, promising to send an air-letter by the next day's mail, 'which advises caution from Commonwealth viewpoint'.[38] The letter set out this caution in detail. There was much to be said, acknowledged Smuts, for Churchill's view that Seretse had been tricked into the London visit. But he did not see how the Government could change their decision without 'very grave damage' from the South African point of view. 'A form of passive resistence [*sic*], or boycott,' he pointed out, 'has already been started by the tribe against the Government, and any change now by the Government will be looked upon as a capitulation . . . and it would be an inducement to Natives in the Union to do likewise,' with far-reaching consequences. 'Natives traditionally believe in authority,' he argued, 'and our whole Native system will collapse if weakness is shown in this regard.'

If the British Government were to ignore South African hostility to Seretse's marriage, warned Smuts, public opinion would harden behind Malan's claim for the annexation of the High Commission Territories. And if this claim were refused, the 'extreme course' of declaring South Africa a republic would at once become an issue. This would undermine the Commonwealth. But such a calamity would be prevented if the situation were managed properly.

I believe the feud between Tshekedi and the Seretse factions is [a] plausible excuse which the British Government may have for banishing both from the Territory. Whether they will make use of this I cannot at present say.

'But from all this,' he concluded, 'you will see that the Seretse case in its full implications is full of dynamite.'[39] Churchill was persuaded. From now on, he ceased to confront the Labour front bench on the issue of Seretse.

But as Gordon Walker had feared, Labour backbenchers started to press their opposition. At a long meeting of the Parliamentary Labour Party, many of them accused Attlee and Gordon Walker of instigating a colour bar.[40] Then there was a new challenge: the Liberal Party – which viewed 'with deep misgivings' the treatment of Seretse – tabled a motion for debate in the Commons.[41]

Gordon Walker needed to find some way of taking the initiative. He seized on the idea of a White Paper, as an alternative to the Harragin Report, that would satisfy the repeated requests to the government for a clear statement of its case. One of the people making this request was Isobel Cripps, the wife of the Chancellor of the Exchequer, Sir Stafford Cripps. 'I am finding, even amongst people who try to take an unbiased view,' wrote Lady Cripps to Gordon Walker, 'that there are certain suspicions which are aroused, and if I were not as close to the picture as I am, I myself would probably be tainted by these suspicions.' She understood, she said, that the chief point was 'the very real danger which I gather exists of civil war being caused intertribally if Seretse went back'.[42] This was not, of course, the chief point at all – rather, it was the 'plausible excuse' advocated by Smuts. Lady Cripps was deluding herself in the belief that she was 'close to the picture'. But since it was the very point that Gordon Walker had been trying to make, he replied gratefully. 'This has been a hideously difficult matter,' he confided to her. 'I am sure it has been right to take the immediate unpopular line, but it hasn't been exactly fun.'[43]

Lady Cripps appears to have genuinely believed the official story. It had a trace of truth: the difference of opinion between uncle and nephew. But this difference had been puffed up and magnified to such an extent that it really did seem to threaten the good order of the

Bangwato. Lady Cripps herself was free of racist prejudice: not only did she publicly denounce it, but also she did not object when her daughter Peggy announced in 1952 her wish to marry Joe Appiah, Seretse's friend from the Gold Coast.

A Cabinet meeting was arranged for 16 March. One of the items on the agenda was the question of the conditions under which Seretse would be able to return temporarily to Bechuanaland. Gordon Walker had asked Baring for his views. 'I am more than grateful for your decision to consult me again,' replied the High Commissioner. He suggested that Gordon Walker grant permission for Seretse's visit – but only for so long as Seretse's behaviour did not make it impossible to maintain order. This proviso, he argued, would create a 'loophole', which he thought was necessary to maintain stability in the reserve.[44]

At the Cabinet meeting, Gordon Walker explained to his colleagues that he had offered to pay Seretse an allowance of £1,100 a year for so long as he was in exile. Subject to good behaviour, he added – thereby building in Baring's 'loophole' – Seretse would be allowed to visit Bechuanaland briefly in connection with his lawsuit. But Cabinet members objected. They could not see why it was necessary to prohibit Seretse from taking up residence in the Protectorate, so long as he was outside the Bangwato Reserve. If Tshekedi was allowed to live in the Protectorate, then why not Seretse? They also thought that the Commonwealth Secretary should say at once that he would be prepared to review the whole matter, if Seretse's presence in the reserve did not prejudice good government.[45]

The day after the Cabinet meeting, Gordon Walker went to the Colonial Office for a meeting with representatives of the Seretse Khama Fighting Committee, who included Learie Constantine and Nii Odoi Annan. The meeting was also attended by James Griffiths, who had replaced Creech Jones as Colonial Secretary after the February election. The Fighting Committee put forward strong views. The feeling of 'the coloured people in this country and throughout the Colonial Empire,' they protested, 'was one of extreme anger' at the British Government over this affair, which should have been left as a domestic affair for the Bamangwato. They described a general feeling that – as Joe Appiah was to put it in his memoirs – 'Labour in office, as in the Seretse case, [had] adopted a policy of drift unworthy of any responsible government.'[46] Some extremists on the Fighting Commit-tee, they said, wanted the whole colonial empire to boycott British goods and even to shoot British officials; but they had been firmly told to conduct the fight on constitutional lines. Constantine added that so far as he was concerned, the Seretse Khama affair was just one more example of racial discrimination. He gave examples of insulting treatment received in London by himself and his family and, in addition, he produced a copy of a concise *Pocket Encyclopaedia* published by Asprey, an exclusive shop in London's Mayfair district, 'which included as part of the description of a Negro the words "breeds fast and is showing menace".'[47]

Meanwhile, in South Africa, Baring felt under increasing pressure. On opening the *Cape Times*, an English morning newspaper, on 20 March, he was horrified to find a leading article with the title, 'Seretse will win'. Two Labour MPs in London, reported the news-paper, were saying that the Government was retreating from its origi-nal position and that Seretse would be Chief of the Bamangwato before the end of the year. Baring hurriedly arranged a meeting with General Smuts. 'He spoke very seriously to me about the serious risks of such an eventuality,' he reported to Gordon Walker. The possibility of Seretse staying indefinitely in Bechuanaland, he added, filled him with dismay and great anxiety.[48]

The White Paper – 'Bechuanaland Protectorate. Succession to the Chieftainship of the Bamangwato Tribe' – was finally released on 22 March. It made a great deal of the danger to tribal unity posed by the rivalry between Seretse and Tshekedi and of the future attitude of the tribe towards the children of Seretse's marriage. No colour bar, it said, had been imposed on the tribe:

His Majesty's Government are fully aware of the very strong feelings that are aroused on the subject of the merits or demerits of mixed marriages, but that is not the issue which is here raised. This particular marriage assumed impor-tance because of Seretse's position as a prospective Chief of the Bamangwato tribe.

Regarding South Africa, the document repeated the lie that Gordon Walker had given two weeks earlier:

His Majesty's Government were of course aware that a strong body of European opinion in Southern Africa would be opposed to recognition; but, as stated in the House of Commons on the 8th March, no representations on this matter have been received from the Government of the Union of South Africa or Southern Rhodesia.[49]

The full text of the White Paper was cabled to every British colony throughout the Empire.[50]

The White Paper had a mixed reaction in the UK. As far as the Seretse Khama Fighting Committee was concerned, it had not disclosed anything that was not known before.[51] From Lambeth Palace, the Archbishop of Canterbury sent a letter to the Prime Minister, expressing deep concern that the Government seemed to be taking a new – and unacceptable – policy on race relations. He enclosed with his letter a set of resolutions on the Seretse Khama affair, which had been passed by the British Council of Churches.[52] The serious weeklies remained unanimous in their disapproval of the Government and letters to the editors were running about three to one in Seretse's favour.[53] But *The Times* and the *Manchester Guardian* thought the White Paper put a somewhat better face on the banishment. The *Daily Telegraph* welcomed the Government's decision to release a written account of the situation. Some of the Labour Party members who had complained about the banishment now felt reassured.

In Britain's colonies, there was widespread disgust. From Lagos an angry telegram was sent to the Colonial Secretary: 'Nigerians advise hands off Khama and let him rule his people as Britons do theirs.'[54] The United Gold Coast Convention complained that, 'We in the Gold Coast deplore any act likely to worsen the deterioration of colonial Africa's shaken confidence in the British justice.'[55] 'I am afraid the White Paper has been very badly received,' wrote the head of the Bureau of Public Information in Georgetown, the capital of British Guiana, to the Colonial Office, 'to judge from the conversations wherever I go.' He added, 'I should myself have wished that the White Paper had been worded with an ear for possible West Indian reactions. I do not think I have seen people of African descent, in all strata, so indignant since the Italo-Ethiopian war, and that is saying a lot!'[56] In

Jamaica, a resolution of 'profound regret' was passed in the House of Representatives.[57]

In the USA, reported the British embassy in Washington, the case had had 'a very bad effect on Negroes generally, who felt much moved and almost personally affected by it.'[58] The Council on African Affairs, of which Paul Robeson was Chairman and W. E. B. Du Bois Vice-Chairman, was appalled by the White Paper. It sent a letter of objection to the Secretary-General of the United Nations, pointing out that the British Government had violated the provisions of the Universal Declaration of Human Rights, Article 7 – 'No one shall be subjected to arbitrary arrest, detention, or exile.'[59]

The Government had intended to publish the White Paper while Seretse was en route to Lobatse, well out of the way. But Seretse was determined to see it before he left and he postponed his flight for a day. The contents saddened him. From his flat in Airways Mansions, he wrote a long and thoughtful letter to *The Times*. 'As hard as I tried,' he said, 'I have failed to discover one single charge against me where I have done wrong.' He had committed no crime: all he had done was to marry an Englishwoman.[60]

Two days after the release of the White Paper, the Commonwealth Secretary was faced with a new crisis. He was told that in the House of Assembly in Cape Town, Sam Kahn, the Communist member, had confronted Dr Malan on South Africa's role in the Seretse Khama affair, asking whether 'any representation' had been made to the British Government. Malan had been evasive in his answer and referred Kahn to the White Paper.[61] But Gordon Walker was horrified. He knew that if the truth emerged, his lies to the House on 8 March and in the White Paper would be exposed. He quickly telephoned South Africa House and summoned Egeland to Whitehall.

For three hours, they sifted through the details of the meeting on 30 June 1949, when Egeland had presented Malan's point of view on Seretse to Philip Noel-Baker, Gordon Walker's predecessor. Liesching joined in the discussions. They were anxious to find a way of showing that the South African High Commissioner's communication was '*not* a "representation" made on instructions from Dr Malan'.[62] They looked at Noel-Baker's record of the meeting, which stated that

Egeland 'was making only semi-official or private representations' – even though, as Egeland now pointed out, Noel-Baker had fully understood that Egeland had been instructed by Malan to come and talk to him.[63]

This was the first time, cabled Egeland to his Prime Minister, that he had seen this record; he himself had kept no written account of the conversation. He did not remember every detail, but he was 'extremely surprised' to find that this had been Noel-Baker's impression. And even though the issue was one of 'interpretation and perhaps of rather fine distinctions', he knew that he had left Noel-Baker 'in no doubt about your attitude which, of course, would have been well-known to him in other ways'.[64] In other words, Malan *had* made a representation to the British Government. This telegram from Egeland to Malan was copied to the Commonwealth Relations Office, from where it was forwarded to Attlee, to other senior officials in the British government, and to Baring in South Africa.[65]

Egeland also wrote a private letter to Malan, which was intended for his eyes only. Noel-Baker's note, he said,

set out quite fairly and fully the implications which I had stressed and at the very start made it clear that my call was on your instructions. Noel-Baker's reference lower down to 'non-official' representations may, I think, be fairly ascribed to the 'woolly-mindedness' which cost him his place in the Cabinet.[66]

It is unlikely, however, that Noel-Baker – as Secretary of State – would have written this record himself. Almost certainly it was written by a Private Secretary and its contents may have been influenced by Liesching, the Permanent Under-Secretary, as an insurance against any accusation of collusion with the South African Government.

But in any case, what Egeland described as Noel-Baker's 'woolly-mindedness' was his successor's lifeline. In a statement to Attlee, Gordon Walker insisted that his statement to the Commons on 8 March had been borne out by Noel-Baker's record. And although Dr Malan had claimed in a speech to the Nationalist Party Congress in 1949 that he had sent a telegram to the UK Government, this was demonstrably untrue: 'No such telegram was ever received by us from the Union Government.'[67] No evidence existed, therefore, to suggest that South Africa had made an official representation to the British Government.

Egeland received a swift reply from Douglas Forsyth, the South African External Affairs Secretary. 'Prime Minister appreciates, of course, delicacy of situation,' he assured Egeland, 'and wishes Secretary of State to understand that should question again be raised here he will deal with it with all possible discretion so as to avoid embarrassment to Gordon Walker.' The Commonwealth Secretary was hugely relieved. 'The most helpful and understanding reply which you returned to my telegram of the 24th', wrote Egeland to his Prime Minister, 'has been received with warm appreciation by the CRO.'[68]

But no sooner had Gordon Walker dealt with the issue of representations from South Africa, than once again he was on the defensive in the House of Commons. A debate on the Seretse Khama issue started two minutes before midnight on 29 March, lasting well over an hour. It was listened to by Seretse himself, sitting at the back of the Chamber. It began with Fenner Brockway describing the case as a symbol – 'an issue of the division of the world between the white and what are known as the coloured races'. The colour bar, he said, 'is the real issue behind the decision . . . against which this House should protest with its last breath'. Quintin Hogg was equally critical. 'What we have to discuss here tonight,' he said acidly,

is whether the Government have acted wisely, not in endorsing or refusing to endorse the marriage between a Bechuanaland prince and a London typist, but in over-riding the decision of the Bechuanaland tribe to accept this man and his wife as their prince and princess.

'It seems to me,' he added, 'that this is the matter upon which the Government have virtually offered no case at all.'[69]

Gordon Walker found the debate heavy going. 'I went over to the attack, having been so far conciliatory,' he recorded in his diary. 'I asserted our rights and said the critics had done harm by spreading misconceptions.' But he found that:

The repercussions were altogether bigger than I had expected – though not nearly so big as the papers made out. Unfortunately the thing is news as a personal story. There is clearly a powerful world negro opinion – not as rich or well organised as the Zionists – but similar.[70]

Fresh calls were made for the Harragin Report to be published. In desperation, Gordon Walker resorted to the threat of Communism. If the arguments in the Report were published, he said, 'they would be made use of by Communists all over the world – and not only by Communists but by all sorts of people – as official Government policy'.

Fenner Brockway and Liberal MPs interrogated the Secretary of State about South African involvement, to which Gordon Walker repeated the lies he had given earlier. Then Brockway tackled the main reason given by the White Paper for Seretse's banishment – namely, the rift between Tshekedi and Seretse. The logical conclusion of this, he pointed out, was that if there were a reconciliation between the two men, there would no longer be any need to keep Seretse in exile. 'Of course,' replied Gordon Walker evasively, 'a reconciliation between the two is very much to be desired. It would certainly, I think, reduce the tension and difficulties among these people.' But he would not commit himself to any review of the situation: 'I cannot give an absolute, categorical answer to a hypothetical question.' He could not give an absolute, categorical answer, because he knew that, whatever happened, he could not allow Seretse to return home as the chief of the Bangwato.

When it was time for members to vote, the atmosphere was charged with emotion. It had been hoped that a free vote would be allowed, but the Government issued a three-line whip. Even so, seven Labour rebels voted against the Government – Richard Acland, Richard Crossman, Tom Driberg, Michael Foot, Jennie Lee, Woodrow Wyatt, and Ian Mikardo, who acted as the teller for the Noes.[71] Others registered a protest by absenting themselves from the vote. The Conservative MP Reader Harris described the scene:

Members of the Labour Party went into the Lobby with tears running down their cheeks when they had to vote for their own Government's motion in relation to Mr Seretse Khama. Mr Seretse Khama was sitting at the back of the Chamber, and I saw Labour Members go to apologise to him because, on the whips' orders, they had to vote against him.[72]

But the Government had managed to pull through. 'We are lucky in having Gordon Walker as Secretary of State,' observed Egeland with satisfaction to Dr Malan. 'He is showing great courage and common-sense.' Egeland still regarded the Seretse issue in the UK as 'explosive and delicate', but believed that it had become less urgent.[73] Now, he cabled Malan two days later, the 'centre of interest has shifted to Bechuanaland'.[74]

13

In Africa, but kept apart

Seretse arrived at the Victoria Falls on 30 March 1950, after nearly two months in the UK. He stayed overnight in Livingstone and then flew south by charter plane to the airfield near the small town of Gaberones, which was the closest landing strip to Lobatse. The whole airfield had been cordoned off with wire fencing by police, and the only people allowed inside were members of the press and British officials, as well as Fraenkel. The waiting Bangwato were kept firmly at a distance. For days, they had been arriving in Gaberones by train and by lorry, staying in an improvised camp under thorn trees near the station.[1] They had come to welcome Seretse home, but none of the officials bothered to give them any information. Only Fraenkel supplied them with any news and the time of Seretse's arrival. A Movietone newsreel showed Fraenkel and Peto Segkoma walking together towards the camp: Fraenkel was handing Peto a telegram from Ruth, saying that Seretse's arrival would be delayed for twenty-four hours.[2]

When the sound of an aircraft was heard overhead, everyone looked up at the sky – to see a bizarre sight. For Seretse's plane did not arrive alone. It was preceded by five other tiny planes, all carrying journalists, which landed in a fairly haphazard manner.[3] Seretse climbed out of his two-seater aircraft and, reported one of the newspapermen, 'a roar of welcome went up from tribesmen waiting to greet him'.[4] Seretse was dressed in a dark suit, with a trilby and sunglasses to protect him from the glare of the sun.[5] He had a cigarette in his mouth and looked weary and drawn – he was no longer the carefree, almost boyish figure who had married Ruth less than two years before.

Four senior Bangwato men had been allowed to stand on the edge of the airstrip, with the diKgosi of the Balete and the Batlokwa. Seretse went straight over to them, to shake their hands. They led him under a nearby tree, where he spoke to the thousands of men seated on the ground, waiting to welcome him home.[6] He was clearly unhappy that he had not been allowed to return to Serowe and as he wiped his brow with his handkerchief in the baking heat, he gesticulated in angry frustration. 'As for Seretse,' commented Movietone – 'well, his gesture was certainly expressive.'[7]

The British officials thought they had prepared for every eventuality. But a crisis developed that took them by surprise. The night before Seretse's arrival, an urgent message came through to Nicholas Monsarrat, the UK Information Officer, who had come to Gaberones to look after the press. The message stated that Seretse's plane was not in fact flying directly to Gaberones, but was going to land at Mahalapye airfield – about eighty miles from Serowe. A large crowd and Ruth, too, Monsarrat was told, were waiting there for Seretse. This was a distinct departure from the plans that had been so carefully drawn up by the Administration. It had been contrived by Noel Monks, as a way of arranging for Ruth and Seretse to meet together briefly. Like the other newspaper correspondents covering Seretse's return, Monks was treating it as a big story and hoping for a scoop. And, like them, he had gone to Livingstone to wait for Seretse's flying-boat. But before leaving Serowe, he had told Ruth that his paper wanted a picture of her being reunited with Seretse – and asked if she would cooperate with a plan to get them together. She agreed readily. So did Seretse, when Monks spoke to him in Livingstone. Then Monks worked out the details with the pilot. They decided that the plane should land at Mahalapye, on the pretext of needing to refuel; this would seem perfectly reasonable, as he was flying in a small, light plane. Monks sent Ruth a telegram: 'Be Mahalapye airfield at noon tomorrow.'

But the plot was foiled. 'Somewhere along the line,' wrote Monks years later, 'an Administration official, who saw my telegraph through service channels, had a brainwave. There was a plot afoot to kidnap Seretse! Else why should Ruth want to go all the way to Mahalapye?' This interpretation of the telegram was fed to the South African press, with the result that – just before take-off – Seretse's pilot was ordered not to land at Mahalapye. The kindly pilot, who felt sorry for Seretse and Ruth, made repeated requests. But Monsarrat strictly forbade it.[8]

Monks planned afresh. It was now too late to stop Ruth making the hard drive to the Mahalapye airstrip, but the pilot of Seretse's plane saw no reason why he shouldn't fly low enough – while not actually landing – for husband and wife at least to see each other. Seretse and Monks thanked him for the idea. Monks's plane was faster than Seretse's, so he flew ahead to Mahalapye, landing some twenty minutes before Seretse's plane was due. He found an 'amazing scene':

Ruth was there all right. So was my photographer. So, too, were hundreds of tribesmen and many police. Nobody knew that Seretse's plane wasn't landing there. The chief police officer told me the place was excited but orderly. He laughed his head off when I showed him a South African paper with kidnap-plot splashed all over the front page. 'Bloody rubbish!' he said.

There was just time to get Ruth to the centre of the field as Seretse's plane came over. True to his promise, the pilot flew low across the field, and then back again. Seretse spotted Ruth. They waved to each other, blowing kisses.[9] Ruth was seven months pregnant now and her figure was cumbersome, but in her joy and desperation at seeing Seretse, she managed to jump about on the dry grass of the airstrip, waving her parasol in the air.

If Seretse *had* been able to land at Mahalapye, to touch and to hold his wife, his return to Bechuanaland would have been blessed with at least some happiness. But as it was, his return to the Protectorate was painful and distressing. Almost as soon as he had landed in Gaberones, he was told that an order was going to be served on him, confining his movements to Lobatse.[10] This came as something of a shock: that he was going to be detained by the force of the law. He and Fraenkel were taken from the airstrip to the District Commissioner's office, where Sullivan served the order. Seretse insisted that he wanted to see his wife, but he was told this was under review.

Seretse then drove to Lobatse with his uncle Peto, in his lorry. There, on the outskirts of the little town, surrounded by high granite hills, he saw the temporary home that had been arranged for him by the administration. They were appalled: it was a two-roomed house, furnished with a metal bed, two chairs and a table, two tin mugs, two tin plates, and two tin knives, forks and spoons. Such rudimentary accommodation was clearly regarded by local officials as appropriate for a 'native', but it was wholly inappropriate for the son of Segkoma, the grandson of Khama III. Peto immediately went out to buy proper furniture, crockery and cutlery.[11]

Seretse was miserable in Lobatse. Police officials kept a watch on the house and paid him periodic visits. Initially, there had been a plan to post a guard on his house, until Baring realized this might lead to criticism in the press. He instructed his officials to persuade the newspapermen to use different language in their reports. 'The press consistently talk of "headmen", "tribesmen" and the "tribe" when referring to Seretse's advisers and supporters,' he complained crossly. 'We should try discreetly to get them to use "followers" and "supporters" if we can.'[12] Forbes MacKenzie, the Serowe District Commissioner, believed he had found the best means of influencing the press – alcohol. 'Relations with the Press representatives are good,' he reported. 'Several of them have consumed a decent quantity of my gin so there will be opportunities to try and get at them informally.'[13]

Monsarrat was annoyed at the journalists' constant interest in Ruth. 'The press have reverted to their bad habit of packing close round Ruth,' he told Clark in ill temper, 'and ignoring official channels (in any case we have nothing much to give, and she has plenty).'[14] But Ruth had no time for journalists who supported the Government and she was furious at the man who had ruined her chance to be reunited with Seretse, however briefly, at the Mahalapye airstrip. On one occasion, the journalists hanging around her house joked that he was outside. Monsarrat was told by one of the correspondents that:

One evening we told Ruth, for a joke, that Godfrey (*Rand Daily Mail* man who broke the 'kidnapping' story) was outside and wanted to see her. She shouted: 'I won't let that bastard into the house! Keep him out, keep him out!'[15]

Tensions in the Bangwato Reserve were rising. On 11 April, a group of people in Serowe tried to stop some of Tshekedi's supporters from taking cattle and wagons to the Bakwena Reserve. The police intervened, using tear-gas and injuring one man with a baton blow to the leg. MacKenzie addressed an assembly of about 400 people, telling them to stop interfering with the movement of cattle and goods. It was a stormy meeting and the police made a number of arrests.[16] 'The Govt and Tshekedi are only asking for trouble,' observed A. J. Haile, the LMS missionary.[17] The Administration had been on edge ever since they knew of Seretse's imminent return, because of the success of the boycott. Numerous rumours about the insubordination of the Bangwato were spreading among the white residents and officials. One of these had warned of a strike of African servants at Serowe just before Seretse's return, but it did not materialize.[18] 'If possible,' Sillery had cabled Baring, 'keep me advised when Seretse leaves England. I am keeping police at full strength and retaining those of other countries until [the] situation clears.'[19]

Tshekedi was travelling around the Bangwato Reserve, collecting evidence for the lawsuit over Khama's will; he was separating his own cattle from those belonging to the herds of Sekgoma, which were the property of Seretse. He was accompanied by Michael Fairlie, a colonial officer, because he had argued that the pro-Seretse communities were so violently against him that he was in danger of assault. In fact, said Fairlie,

this threat was all in Tshekedi's mind and it was no great hardship to move around the district with him. He was himself amusing and easily moved to laughter when his sights were not set on some consuming issue which drove everything else from his mind.[20]

Meanwhile, Seretse was stuck in Lobatse. He was making little headway in his negotiations to visit Serowe and had now been told that any application to leave Lobatse must be in writing, setting out the destination, purpose of the visit and its duration. He arranged to get a letter supporting his case from Ruth's physician, Dr Moikangoa, who did not mince words:

Dear Seretse,

This is to advise you that I have become rather worried about your wife's health since you left here for England. Since your arrival the condition has deteriorated further . . . She has stood quite [a] lot and I have fears that she will further deteriorate both physically and especially mentally. You will appreciate too that she has almost reached term and the possibilities of

deterioration into psychopathic states which have to be seriously reckoned with.

'The British Government', he went on, 'is taking rather long about getting you to Serowe. Please consult with your legal adviser about this situation.' Seretse alone, he said, could give her 'the necessary comfort to relieve her of the mental tensions and strains that have been her lot for so long. I consider that your coming back is quite imperative, and that too as soon as possible.' He added in a postscript, 'It is impossible for Mrs Khama to do any travelling whatsoever in her position and not for any distance either.'[21]

Dr Moikangoa also communicated his concerns to the High Commissioner's Office and told Clark that Ruth had threatened suicide unless Seretse came quickly. This worried Clark. 'Even discounting hysterical outburst,' he told the High Commissioner, 'there is reason for thinking that at one time at least in her pregnancy her physical health has not been good.'[22] In London, too, British officials were starting to feel anxious. 'You will see from the press,' sneered a senior official at the Commonwealth Relations Office to a colleague, 'that it is now argued that Seretse should be allowed to go to see his wife at once because the lady is pining away through his absence.' Then he added nervously, 'How easily we may be squeezed into a general retreat from the decisions in the White Paper!'[23]

The High Commissioner's Office decided to send the Director of Medical Services, Dr Mendi Freedman – a white doctor working for the Government – from Mafikeng to Serowe, to see Ruth. But she refused to see him. She had no wish to see a doctor she didn't know, she said, and had received a telegram from Seretse that morning, telling her not to submit to any medical examination. She also refused to see Dr Gemmell, the Senior Government Medical Officer at Serowe.[24] Dr Freedman was annoyed. 'If Mrs Khama were really ill,' he argued,

she would have no hesitation in seeing me. If, however, she were medically fit, she would take steps to ensure she were not 'found out' and would not submit to a medical examination as she might erroneously believe that this might prejudice the chances of Seretse being permitted to visit Serowe.

He asked Dr Moikangoa to persuade her to see him. But Dr Moikan-goa soon returned, saying that Mrs Khama still refused a visit from the director. 'I left Serowe the same evening without having seen Mrs Khama,' reported Dr Freedman to Mafikeng.[25] He added that in the opinion of Dr Moikangoa, Ruth was not in a fit state to undertake even a train journey to Lobatse. But, added Dr Freedman, he had had a chat with the Serowe district commissioner, who had 'expressed the opinion that there were valid reasons for doubting the "bona fides" of Dr Moikangoa in this matter, and that his medical report was very probably biased by his political opinions'. A copy of Freedman's report was sent to Clark by Nettelton, with the comment, 'This seems a fairly good sample of double-crossing on the other side.'[26]

At the very least, reasoned Baring, Dr Moikangoa's reports had been exaggerated. After all, Ruth had recently driven from Serowe to Mahalapye.[27] Nevertheless, he started to worry. 'It is clear that [an] early visit by Seretse would help allay her anxieties,' he wired the CRO. 'This may be bluff but Resident Commissioner thinks there may well be something in it.'[28] His attitude to Ruth was calculating and ruthless: he assumed that whatever she did was political. His own wife had given birth to three children, so he must have had some idea of the risks and discomforts involved. Moreover, he himself suffered badly from problems with his liver, so he knew what it felt like to be vulnerable physically. But he had no sympathy for Ruth: he had lost sight of her as a human being.

Sir Evelyn was also afraid that Ruth was planning to bring her sister Muriel to Africa. For one thing, the prospect of having to deal with yet another young woman from the Williams family appalled him. For another, he had heard a rumour that 'Seretse's closest supporters hoped that Ruth would be successful in her efforts [to bring Muriel] as this would give them an opportunity to emulate Seretse's successful wooing.'[29] There was no foundation whatsoever for this rumour, but Baring was predisposed to believe it and it frightened him.

It was true that Muriel had hoped to join her sister and support her in her pregnancy. But she was unable to raise enough money for the long and expensive journey to Serowe.[30]

Ruth was missing Seretse badly. Their only means of contact was by letter: 'Easter came and went. Still there was no news of Seretse

being allowed to visit me.'[31] She 'paced the veranda of her home overlooking the Bechuanaland bush,' reported the *Sunday Express*, 'and said with anger in her voice: "When is this waiting for my husband going to end? It is torture." '[32] She *could* have gone to Lobatse, to join Seretse – and the Administration were keen for her to do this.[33] But as Dr Moikangoa insisted, it would have been risky for her to make the journey. In any case, it would have been very unpleasant for Ruth to give birth in Lobatse Hospital, as she would be surrounded by hostility. She had been told that the hundred or so Europeans living in Lobatse had objected to the idea of Seretse living near them. They had made so many threats against him that Nettelton had even found a private farm several miles outside the town – so that if things got too bad, Seretse could be moved there.[34]

As she waited to hear whether Seretse would be allowed to visit her, Ruth prepared their home for the new baby. The women of the village watched anxiously as she drew closer to term, doing everything they could to help. 'Ruth is our Queen,' said one older woman to a reporter. 'We and our children will stay with her and die with her. Her child will be our child.'[35]

Finally – and grudgingly – Baring decided to let Seretse visit Serowe. 'I felt that given the anxiety of pressmen to be present at Seretse's first meeting with his wife,' he reported to London, 'we would lose more than we would gain by withholding permission.'[36] The visit was granted for five days: from Sunday 16 April to Thursday 20 April. The climax to Seretse's long wait took place on 15 April in the High Court at Lobatse: Nettelton tip-toed into the tense atmosphere of a murder trial and handed Fraenkel, who was the defending counsel, a copy of the permit allowing Seretse to visit his wife. As soon as Seretse was given the news, he packed hurriedly and ran out to Peto's lorry, planning to reach Serowe by midnight – so that he wouldn't waste a single moment of the precious time he was allowed with Ruth.[37]

Seretse was followed by the inevitable pressmen and also by Monsarrat, who never forgot the journey:

The heat, the dust, the bumpy ride, and the sheer hard work of that drive have stayed in my memory until this day. The [car] left behind it a towering yellow cloud of dust, but the stuff was everywhere – eyes, ears, nostrils, hair, and neck-band . . . Towards dusk on the first day, I ran over an enormous boa-constrictor which was slithering across the road.

Then the car hit a bump and was thrown into the ditch: 'There was no traffic; just the dust, the heat, a few vultures weaving overhead . . . I was stranded on the edge of the Kalahari. All I could think of was that boa-constrictor.' He was eventually rescued by an old man driving an ox-cart, who 'raised his bee-hive hat with great courtesy' and then, without a word, pulled him out of the ditch and towed him the last nine miles to Serowe. 'If anyone is making out an itinerary,' added Monsarrat, 'a span of eight oxen towing a 2½-litre Riley with no brakes and a broken transmission does 1½ miles an hour.'[38]

A few minutes after midnight, Seretse arrived in Serowe. 'My wife was waiting up for me,' he recalled later:

She must have spotted me first, for when I brought the truck I was driving to within 500 yards of where she stood, she began running toward me, stumbling, half-crying, half-laughing like an overjoyed child.

It was all he could do 'to hold back the tears of knowing what she must have had to live through'.[39] As the truck stopped, reported *The Times*, 'she opened the door and flung herself into her husband's arms'. She clutched at his sleeve in the darkness, sobbing, as he drove the last short distance to their home. As they arrived, there were joyful shouts of '*Pula!*' from the men and women who had been waiting outside their house since early evening. Family and friends surged towards the door of the house to greet Seretse and he, with one arm closely embracing Ruth, joyfully shook their hands.[40]

He had accepted the conditions put on his visit: that he would not obstruct the Administration and that he would not hold or attend any public gatherings. Even so, he and Ruth had to endure constant observation by plain-clothes policemen from the moment of his arrival.[41] Seretse had been instructed to report to the District Commissioner as soon as he arrived. But Ruth was his priority and he stayed with her. Next morning, he and Ruth arrived at MacKenzie's office at 11.20 a.m. The DC was frosty. He had been very annoyed, he told Seretse, to hear that he had been seen talking to a group of men at Mahalapye.[42] But as Seretse reasonably pointed out, he could hardly help people gathering round and greeting him.[43] Then MacKenzie announced that the Kgotla in Serowe was strictly off-limits. Seretse was now thoroughly exasperated. It was customary for men to go and sit there, he pointed out, as part of the daily routine of the village. But he was flatly forbidden to go anywhere near the kgotla.

Wherever he went, Seretse was greeted by crowds of people, many of them weeping.[44] As soon as his green Chevrolet was seen, people gathered around, some of them climbing to the tops of huts to get a better view. There were happy calls of greetings and many women danced around the car. Others touched Seretse's arm and kissed his wife's skirt.[45] 'The reception he got from his people,' said Ruth,

was tremendous. Each day hundreds and hundreds of Africans trekked to our house. I saw them coming for miles in the distance. The women, especially, were wildly excited, dancing around weeping and making their traditional greeting of ululation.

After these demonstrations, she pointed out, 'no one could possibly doubt Seretse's popularity'.[46] But Seretse was aware of the risks involved. On Monday, when a crowd of about 400 people collected at his house, he warned gently that if this were to happen again, his visit to Serowe would be immediately cut short.

On Wednesday afternoon, the head teachers of the five schools in Serowe brought their pupils to the Khamas' house, 'to greet the chief and to sing'. Irritably, Monsarrat watched the start of the event from a police truck; he then went to the top of a hill, to get a better view. Contingents from the various schools started to collect and to move along the route together; groups of adults also arrived, by car or lorry, by foot, or on horseback. By 3 p.m. everyone was assembled and Monsarrat estimated that, altogether, there were 1,200 children and 300 adults. At 3.05, he reported,

Ruth and then Seretse appeared from the side door of the house, and sat down in the centre of a row of chairs. The audience closed in round them, calling to them. At 3.15, after a number of short speeches, an entertainment began, the various groups of children taking it in turns to sing. Subsequent police reports, after I had left, indicate that at the close of the proceedings

Seretse made a short speech, thanking the children for their efforts and for coming along.[47]

'This seems to me,' complained Monsarrat sourly to Clark, 'like a press-promotion: it will have good photographs, a heart-rending story, and tears in Ruth's eyes as she pats a tiny head. But it seemed to us that it could hardly be forbidden, except at the risk of making us look ridiculous.'[48]

Seretse went back to Lobatse on 21 April. The visit had been for only a few days, said Ruth, 'but how precious those days seemed to us! We had been apart for two and a half months.'[49] And now, once again, they were apart. This time, it was even more painful: they would have to wait separately for the birth of their baby at the beginning of June, just over one month away. The Administration heaved a sigh of relief when Seretse left Serowe and congratulated themselves on their success at controlling the situation.[50] As far as Monsarrat was concerned, the visit had been 'a series of pin-pricks, small in themselves, adding up to an annoying total'; for the full five days, he added, Seretse had been 'an uncooperative nuisance'.[51] In fact, Seretse had been remarkably cooperative – and it was this that had kept Serowe peaceful. If he had called for any kind of demonstration against the British, it would have happened at once.

In the early weeks of May, Seretse started to collect evidence for his lawsuit against Tshekedi. He went on a tour of his cattle-posts with Michael Fairlie, who had also accompanied Tshekedi. 'I had not met him before,' recorded Fairlie, 'and, to my surprise, in view of the provocation he had suffered, I found him friendly and genial.' They drove in a convoy, in two lorries: Seretse was in the lead, with a dozen or so helpers. A compassionate man, Fairlie felt 'slightly embarrassed at having to supervise another person in the conduct of his private business'. It was ideal weather for touring: the start of the winter season, when the days were bone-dry and warm under a clear blue sky. In the evenings, Seretse chose a campsite for himself and his followers and Fairlie parked his lorry about fifty yards off. Some years later Fairlie wrote:

Although we were naturally polite to each other, there was no fraternization, for the racial barriers in Southern Africa were still high and we spent the

1. Seretse Khama aged four, in Scottish Highland dress, at the installation of his uncle Tshekedi as Regent of the Bangwato, 1925. He is with Semane, Tshekedi's mother.

2. Law students in London, late 1940s: Seretse (*right*) with Charles Njonjo from Kenya, his old friend from their days at Fort Hare University, South Africa.

3. Tshekedi Khama leaving the Office of the British High Commissioner in South Africa after a meeting with Sir Evelyn Baring. Pretoria, 1949.

4. Seretse Khama in contemplative mood, Serowe 1950.

5. Ruth Khama in Serowe with her kittens, Pride and Prejudice, 1950.

6. Seretse and Ruth sharing a meal with Seretse's friend Kgosi Mokgosi of the Balete. Above the fireplace are Seretse's law books; the kittens play on the antelope skin rug.

7. Seretse and his lawyer Percy Fraenkel at a kgotla to discuss his summons to London, February 1950. 'Elders urged Seretse to turn down the invitation . . . If he did decide to go he should leave Ruth behind.'

8. 'We have come to tell you we are happy our Mother has stayed with us' – Bangwato women bring gifts of food and water to Ruth, who is six months pregnant, after Seretse's departure.

9. Gathered round the radio while Seretse is in London. News of his exile was immediately broadcast to Africa over the BBC.

10. A rally in Trafalgar Square, March 1950, organized by the Seretse Khama Fighting Committee to protest at Seretse's banishment, which was seen to highlight the evil of the colour bar in Britain and her colonies.

11. Daniel Malan, Prime Minister of South Africa and architect of apartheid, at tea with his family in Pretoria, 1950. He called on the British Government to exile Seretse and his white wife.

(Below) 13. Ruth, Seretse's sister Naledi (to Ruth's left), and Seretse, with Ruth's family. Ruth's sister Muriel holds baby Jacqueline, her father is second from left, and her mother stands by Seretse (1950–51).

(Above) 12. From Victoria Falls to Southampton Marine Airport: the Khama family disembark the flying-boat to start their exile, August 1950.

14. Seretse and Ruth with Jacqueline, nearly three, and baby Seretse Khama Ian, shortly after his birth in February 1953.

15. The Bangwato delegation to London. The six men, including Seretse's uncle Peto Sekgoma (*second from left*), arrive on 9 April 1952 to plead for Seretse's return.

16. The Council for the Defence of Seretse Khama, created 1952. *Seated from left*: Canon John Collins, Jennie Lee MP, Seretse Khama, Fenner Brockway, Ruth Khama, Jo Grimond MP. *Standing*: Reg Sorenson MP is far left, Tony Benn MP fourth from left, and George Williams (Ruth's father) seventh; Learie Constantine is eighth from right, Dorothy Williams (Ruth's mother) is sixth, and Muriel Williams is third.

17. Seretse talks of his hopes at a press conference in London, 1956 – 'to assist my people to develop a democratic system, to raise our standard of life, and to establish a happy and healthy nationhood'. Three-year-old Ian is in the foreground.

18. A jubilant Seretse at London airport on his way back to Africa, sharing a joke with Ruth, Muriel (*centre*) and Clement Freud (*left*).

19. Seretse returns to Serowe to a rapturous welcome in October 1956, as joyful crowds surge round him crying *Pula!* – 'Rain!'

21. Campaigning in Bechuanaland, 1965. Seretse Khama's political party won an overwhelming victory, making him President of newly independent Botswana the following year.

20. 'The New Africa'. Dr Hastings Banda of Nyasaland (Malawi) is released from prison by Harold Macmillan in 1960, as British colonies throughout Africa demand their independence.

22. Seretse and Ruth Khama, Botswana, 1960s. 'I thank God,' said Ruth, 'that I picked Seretse to be my man for life.'

evenings apart. One day I ventured to ask him for an evening meal in the bush and he accepted, but I did not dare tell Forbes MacKenzie of this grave social transgression.

The tour was pleasant and uneventful until they reached Mahalapye. They stopped at the police station, just outside the village, when Seretse said he wanted to visit the Kgotla in the village and to see his uncle, Manyaphiri. Fairlie told him he could not agree to this, because the Administration had expressly forbidden any kind of meeting. Then Seretse's temper snapped. He shouted that he would go anyway – and jumped into his truck. Time stopped still for Fairlie as he waited to see in which direction Seretse would go:

Just ahead of the police station there was a fork in the road. One led to the village, the other to the Tuli Block. A lot happened in the next few seconds. Seretse considered the pros and cons of entering Mahalapye, while I prayed that he would resist the temptation.

Seretse *did* resist the temptation: he took the other road, to the Tuli Block, and Fairlie heaved a sigh of relief. He was immensely grateful to Seretse. A few days later, he received a note of congratulations from Sir Evelyn, on the way he had handled Seretse. But if any congratulations were due, thought Fairlie, 'they belonged to Seretse for his mature bearing and good nature'.[52]

Seretse had just got back from his tour of the cattle-posts when – several weeks before their baby was due – Ruth went into labour. On the morning of Monday, 15 May, she lay in bed feeling restless. For four hours, from three to seven, she dozed, occasionally waking with a pain in her back. By seven she decided to see Dr Moikangoa. At first he thought it was a false alarm. But at nine o'clock she was admitted into the general wing of the Serowe hospital. 'I could have gone in the European wing,' she explained later, 'but I chose the tribal wing because I wanted to encourage Bamangwato women to accept the new world of hygiene that medical progress had brought to their country.'[53] Ruth wanted to set an example, as Seretse's wife, because the maternal and infant death rates were very high in the Protectorate and many women were suspicious of modern medicine.

The news of Ruth's confinement reached Seretse at lunchtime. He rushed off to find Peto and his lorry, which they quickly filled with fuel for the nine-hour drive to Serowe, 250 miles away. By 2.30 p.m. they were ready and went to collect the pass which local officials had arranged, giving Seretse permission to go home. At first, Seretse took the wheel. But after just five miles he drew to a halt and asked his uncle to take over. He was so anxious to get to the hospital and in such a state of excitement that he had been driving too fast and recklessly along the dirt roads. He knew that if he carried on, they would never get to the hospital at all.[54]

But Ruth had given birth before they even left Lobatse. At 1.25 p.m., after a quick and easy labour, she welcomed their daughter into the world – a healthy 7lb 4oz.[55] Ruth was euphoric. But she desperately needed to see her husband and refused to go to sleep until he had arrived. Concerned that she should rest, Dr Moikangoa injected her with a powerful sedative. But she willed herself not to sleep. Fourteen hours later, when Seretse arrived, she was still awake. He was given the good news that mother and daughter were well and told that Ruth was sedated. But when he and the doctor looked in on her, she shouted out, 'Seretse!' He rushed over and clasped her in his arms. As he held her, she fell asleep.[56]

Seretse was overjoyed with his new daughter – 'a little crinkle-faced baby,' he said with pleasure.[57] 'Everyone said how like her father she was,' said Ruth. 'She had jet black hair and even her father's snub nose.' They named her Jacqueline Tebogo. Tebogo, meaning 'thankfulness' in Setswana, was the name of Seretse's mother, and quickly became a popular name for girls born that year in the Bangwato Reserve, as people celebrated the birth of their Kgosi's daughter.[58]

There was immense relief at the CRO and in the High Commissioner's Office that the Khama baby was not a boy, who would then be next in the line of succession after Seretse. As early as January 1949, before Ruth had even fallen pregnant, Clark had referred to the damage that would be done if Seretse were to 'produce a half-caste heir – a matter in which we are now powerless'.[59]

Seretse had been given permission to stay for a month in Serowe. For the first week, Ruth was in hospital and he went to see her and their baby three times a day. Then he brought them home. *Life* magazine described Seretse's pride as he went to collect his family:

'He took Ruth's arm and supported her as she walked unsteadily to a car to be driven to the six-room bungalow which she and Seretse had expected to make their home.'[60]

'We, the press, who had hounded this couple for nearly two years,' recorded Monks, 'were waiting at the bungalow to welcome them home. I have never seen Ruth look prettier, or happier, than on the day she brought Jacqueline home. The marriage that had rocked Africa seemed to be making out fine.' Every day, the women of the Bangwato came to the house to see the baby and to pay their respects, bringing gifts.[61]

14

Together in Lobatse

When the time came for Seretse's return to Lobatse, he and Ruth decided to go together – now that Jacqueline had been born, the prospect of separation was too painful to bear. 'So we settled in Lobatse,' said Ruth. 'At times it seemed that we had hardly left Serowe, for so many of the tribe followed us down to camp near our new house.'[1] This house was the 'hovel' – as Monks described it – that had been arranged by the Administration for Seretse. It was hardly suitable for a one-month-old baby. 'In any decent community,' said Monks, 'the place would have been condemned. But the only hotel in Lobatse wouldn't put them up, so they had to live somewhere . . .'[2]

Lobatse was very different from Serowe – it was a 'European' town like Francistown, where black people had to live in the 'African location'. Whereas in Serowe the white traders had to be careful not to offend Seretse, there was no such constraint on the whites in Lobatse, who looked on the Khamas with loathing. A few weeks after their arrival in the town, a journalist called Weighton, who had come to Lobatse to do a story for the London *Daily Express*, telephoned Baring in Pretoria in a state of hot indignation. He angrily complained that the Lobatse Hotel had refused to serve him lunch because of his guest – Mrs Seretse Khama. The hotel proprietor, said Weighton, had said this refusal was 'in accordance with British Government's policy'.[3]

Baring, who was continually worried about publicity, ordered an immediate investigation and Richard Sullivan, the District Commissioner, went to see the proprietor. He discovered that Weighton, with his wife and another couple, had been staying at the hotel and, after leaving it briefly, had returned with Mrs Khama as their guest and had ordered a round of drinks in the lounge. A little later the proprietor anxiously noticed the group talking to the head waiter and went to investigate. When he discovered that they had reserved a table in the dining room for lunch, including Mrs Khama, he approached Weighton. It would have been more courteous, he told him, if he had come to see him about his wish for Mrs Khama to eat in the hotel – and then suitable arrangements could have been made. He could, for example, have arranged for them to eat in a separate room. This blatant endorsement of the colour bar made Weighton furious. He asked for his bill and the party left the hotel.[4]

The fact that Weighton had stormed out of the hotel, Sullivan observed, had actually saved the proprietor. For it forestalled any need to refuse serving lunch to Mrs Khama – if he had done so, there would have been some justification for a charge of discrimination. For although segregation was practised freely by the whites, it was not allowed by law, as was the case in South Africa. Defending the proprietor, Sullivan said that he lived at Lobatse and had to consider the effect of his actions on his livelihood: 'European feeling is still as strong as ever against Mrs Khama. Were she to be served once, she would expect to be served again and her presence in the hotel might expose her to unpleasantness if not to insults.'[5]

One morning in Lobatse, when Seretse and Ruth were in a shop, she noticed that people were staring and that everybody had gone quiet:

Seretse went up to an African standing by the counter, said 'Hello, uncle,' and turning to Ruth, called, 'Come and meet my uncle.' Ruth had met many uncles and thought, as she shook hands, that this was yet another, until, instead of greeting her with 'Dumela Mma,' he said 'How do you do'. This, then, was Tshekedi Khama.[6]

Later that day, Tshekedi visited their home to see baby Jacqueline. Ruth said afterwards that she had found him 'perfectly charming'.[7] Until now, they had never met and he had appeared to be implacably opposed to her, but this was the start of a reconciliation between uncle and nephew, after nearly two years of acrimony. They reached an agreement about their cattle: that Tshekedi would hand over to Seretse the Sekgoma estate and that Seretse waived all claim to the Khama estate. This meant that the lawsuit and the hearing at Lobatse was off.[8] The two men then spent many weeks riding round the vast, widespread cattle-posts together. 'Seretse has been to me during our recent trip together my Seretse of old,' wrote Tshekedi with heartfelt pleasure to his lawyer Buchanan.[9]

But Tshekedi noticed that local officials were perturbed to see the two men coming together. They ought to have been delighted, if the animosity between the two men had been the genuine reason for Seretse's exile, as the Government had claimed. But as it had been merely a pretext, they regarded their reconciliation as a threat to the viability of the Government's cover story. Tshekedi and Seretse understood this weakness in the Government's case and started to talk together about the possibilities of a joint strategy to deal with the Government.[10]

Meanwhile, in the Bangwato Reserve, the boycott was growing from strength to strength: no one would serve on the Finance Committee, School Committee or Livestock Improvement Centre Committee. There were no 'native' taxes coming in, except from Bangwato miners in South Africa, whose tax was taken at source.[11] Forbes MacKenzie called a meeting in the Kgotla in Serowe, but only one person turned up. This made his job impossible, he seethed, especially as there had been an outbreak of foot-and-mouth disease and he needed to regulate the movement of cattle. As a last resort, he drove through the village in his Land Rover, broadcasting instructions through a loud-hailer; but his instructions were politely ignored. When he sent word to Mahalapye that he was going to hold a meeting there, Manyaphiri sent a message that he was too ill even to read the District Commissioner's telegram.[12]

MacKenzie decided it was time to force the Bangwato into cooperation. He sent an official to withdraw sales permit books from all the villages refusing to present their cattle for inspection. If he found the culprits, he said, he would deal with them – and if there wasn't enough evidence for a prosecution, they would be made to report daily to his office.[13] But when he started to make arrests, Seretse cabled a report on them to the Fighting Committee in London, who immediately passed this information on to the press. This led to questions in the House of Commons and MacKenzie was instructed to back down.[14]

While MacKenzie was failing so publicly to hold meetings with the Bangwato, Seretse's lawyer Fraenkel was being invited by villages throughout the Reserve to come and talk to the headmen. This infuriated MacKenzie. He insisted that Fraenkel be accompanied by a Government representative and that full transcripts were made of everything that was said. Fraenkel went to five different assemblies. At each one, he reported on the opposition in the House of Commons to the exile of Seretse, quoting Winston Churchill's judgement that it was 'a very dishonourable transaction'. He explained that many of the press in the UK were on the side of the Bangwato and also told them about the Seretse Khama Fighting Committee.[15]

Wherever Fraenkel went, the headmen asked him to act as their legal adviser. 'May God help you in our sorrow,' said a man in Mahalapye – 'We send you as our ears and spokesman.' 'Please plead with the Government as we have no power,' asked Manyaphiri, in distress.[16] At a meeting in Shoshong, Goareng Mosinyi recalled the sacrifices made by the soldiers from Bechuanaland who had joined up to help the Allies in the Second World War. 'Next war,' said Mr Mosinyi, 'we shall not listen when the government asks us to fight, and then forgets us in times of peace. Our hearts are sore.' 'You can rest assured,' promised Fraenkel, 'that I and the barristers are trying hard to comply with your wishes.'[17]

Once Seretse had returned to Bechuanaland, the issue of his banishment had been put on hold in London. 'We decided, in effect,' wrote Gordon Walker in his diary, to let Seretse stay 'on good behaviour'. There was a general feeling, he recorded, that Seretse had been treated badly: 'The PM and [Herbert] Morrison stood firm: also McNeil. Lord Addison weakened on the question of return: but not on recognition. Bevan was hostile throughout and probably egged on the dissidents in the Party.'[18] But the High Commissioner was determined to get Seretse out of Bechuanaland. So long as he was there, observed Clark to Baring, the Administration was 'on a very sticky wicket'.[19]

In the second week of June, Gordon Walker brought the High Commissioner from Africa to London, for further discussions. Baring welcomed the visit, as an opportunity to build up pressure on the Government.[20] As soon as he arrived, he attended a special meeting in the Commonwealth Secretary's room at the House of Commons, which was also attended by Liesching and other senior officials. Baring drew the meeting's attention to the problem of non-cooperation in the Bangwato Reserve and proposed the banishment of Serogola and Peto Sekgoma – an idea which was not taken up. Then Baring argued that people would start to turn to Tshekedi once Seretse had gone – and Seretse *had* to go. There was some talk of producing another White Paper; in that case, said Baring, examples should be included of the 'threats' to good government that had been made by Ruth.[21]

As far as the Bechuanaland Administration was concerned, Ruth had become an intolerable irritant. 'If Seretse leaves and Ruth returns to the Bamangwato Reserve,' Sillery believed, 'she will be set up by Seretse's supporters as titular head on [the] same basis as Mrs Moremi, widow of the Kgosi of the Batawana, and will be [the] focus of continued trouble.' The Administration's dislike of Ruth was bordering on hatred and Sillery argued that she was 'by far the greater danger at present than is Seretse'.[22] The High Commissioner's Office warned that

Ruth has not learned Sechuana. S[eretse] has an obvious taste for Eur. habits. They are bound to seek the company of Eurs. or of Coloured persons. There will therefore undoubtedly be unfortunate incidents and these will receive a great deal of publicity. Moreover, every complaint made by every discontented African in the Bam. Res. will continue to find its way into the newspapers as long as pressmen wander about the Prot. waiting for [a] new development.[23]

There were two further risks, believed Baring, if Ruth were to stay in Bechuanaland. The first was that 'if she became ill – and we know already that she is quite capable of feigning illness – it would be very difficult for humanitarian reasons to oppose visits by Seretse to her'. The other risk, which continued to bother him, was that 'she would invite her sister to join her, whose intention it is to become engaged to another African'.[24]

At the end of June, Gordon Walker circulated the Cabinet with a memorandum, arguing that the time had come to remove Seretse from Bechuanaland and bring him and Ruth to the UK. The reason for this, he said, was the need to placate South Africa. He did not specify any particular reasons, but the memorandum would have been read by Cabinet members against the background of the surprise attack on South Korea by the North, starting just a few days before, on 25 June, and horrifying the West. The drive to obtain uranium from South Africa had now become more urgent, as had the neeed to protect defence agreements with the Dominions. 'Commonwealth forces were prepared, if occasion offered,' recorded Attlee in his memoir, 'to resort to war. It became necessary, therefore, to strengthen the armed forces of the democracies.'[25] It was not a good time to alienate South Africa.

Nevertheless, the memorandum was read with uneasiness. Norman Brook, the Cabinet Secretary, wrote to the Prime Minister about his concerns. For one thing, he objected, Ministers had already made it clear – on 8 March and then again on 16 March – that they were unhappy about the idea of Seretse's exclusion. Secondly, the tenor of the memorandum suggested that there was no real prospect of Seretse *ever* being recognized as Chief – even though it had been clearly under-stood that the Government would keep an open mind and that the pos-ition would be reviewed at the end of five years. Furthermore, argued Brook, the Cabinet should consider 'whether they are going to allow the possible reactions of South African opinion to influence their decision at all'.[26] Hartley Shawcross, the Attorney General, was asked for his views. 'I do not,' he answered with distaste, 'like the idea that an Order deporting a British subject from his home territory could be made on the ground that the Governor or High Commissioner does not like his moral character.'[27]

But when the British Cabinet met on 29 June 1950, it agreed to remove both Seretse and Ruth from the Protectorate in August.[28]

15

Into exile

Seretse and Ruth had been in Lobatse for just six weeks, when they were told by Gerald Nettelton that it was time for them to leave Bechuanaland. They were extremely upset: they had become hopeful about the possibility of being able to stay in Africa and had even bought a new car – a 1950 model fawn-coloured Ford Custom. If the High Commissioner wanted him to leave, argued Seretse, then he would have to order him to go. But Nettelton ignored their distress and got on with his job. He asked them to think about preparations for leaving and the young mother was appalled to learn that her tiny baby, just eleven weeks old, would have to be inoculated against yellow fever. This was a requirement for travelling through Egypt, which was on the route of the flying-boat to the UK. 'Wife asked', reported Nettelton, 'whether Government could not issue what she termed a "phoney" certificate, namely a false certificate since she asserted this had been done before.' This was 'obviously a try on', he commented callously, 'to see what Government would do'.[1]

The issue of certificates for Jacqueline had in fact been causing the Administration considerable worry earlier that week. When Seretse signed the notice of birth for his daughter, he described his occupation as 'None (Exiled Chief)' and listed Ruth's occupation as 'Exiled Chief's Wife'.[2] This had been annoying, which was bad enough. But then Protectorate officials noticed that Seretse had registered baby Jacqueline on a form under Proclamation Number 59 of 1939, which provided for the registration of births and deaths of persons *other* than natives. 'Natives', explained the form, were defined as 'any aboriginal native belonging to any tribe of Africa and also any persons of mixed race living as members of any native community, tribe, kraal or location in the Territory'. But was the tiny baby a 'native' – or not? In Mafikeng, Ellenberger consulted an expert. He was told:

I think we must look to Section 1 of Proclamation 59/1939 for the definition of 'Native' in this matter.

The question is whether the child, admittedly of mixed race, is living with her mother as members of a native community, tribe or location. If the answer is 'Yes' then the child is a 'native' and cannot be registered under the Proclamation 59/1939. If 'No' then she can.

The problem was further complicated by the fact that Seretse had described himself on the form as a 'Mongwato' – a member of the Bangwato. 'It seems quite clear,' observed Ellenberger in dismay, 'that registration cannot legally be effected.'[3]

Baring was horrified to hear of this dilemma, which was just the kind of detail that the press would blow up into a major news story. He instructed his office to sort out Jacqueline's registration straight-away. The High Commission staff and their lawyers put their heads together and finally came up with a formula to solve the problem: 'Child is of mixed race and is living with its European mother presum-ably after style of a European. It is not repeat not living as a member of a native community, etc.'[4] Baring heaved a sigh of relief.

When Nettelton had brought his bad news to the Khamas, his last words to Seretse were that they should work on the basis of departure by flying-boat on 18 August.[5] As it turned out, these were quite literally his last words to Seretse. For he was a very sick man, with high blood pressure and kidney trouble, and he died just days later.[6] Baring now had to find another Resident Commissioner and in the meantime, Clark took over the implementation of the Government's policy on Seretse. On 3 August, he flew to Lobatse and drove to the Khamas' home, to deliver their exclusion orders. They had been expecting his visit and had been waiting with Fraenkel, but nonetheless they were shocked when the orders were produced. They withdrew to discuss matters and when they came back, said Clark, Ruth looked 'a little upset' and the atmosphere was polite but strained. He explained that they would be flown from Gaberones to Livingstone on 16 August, to catch the flying-boat two days later. Seretse said they would like to take with them his sister Naledi, who was nursing in Durban.[7]

'Circumstances of interviews were trying,' reported Clark. But, he added with a respect that he had not expected to feel, 'their attitude most of the time was reasonable and correct'.[8] This was the first time Clark had met Ruth and he was compelled, he wrote to Liesching, 'to some admiration of Ruth ... She has obviously been through a lot including loneliness, but she was neat in appearance and composed in manner. She displays a quick but limited intelligence and a ready wit. She undoubtedly has courage.' Of Seretse, he wrote that he 'undoubtedly feels very sore; his often lethargic manner cloaks deep feelings'.[9]

Discussions continued about Jacqueline's inoculation, to which Ruth finally consented when Dr Moikangoa assured her of its safety. But she was anxious about the practical details of taking her little baby on the long journey by flying-boat. 'Ruth made a pathetic last-minute request to my wife, who had been one of her two white women intimates,' recalled Noel Monks later. 'Baby Jacqueline was very young to fly – two months – and Ruth wasn't allowed to go into Mafikeng, the nearest town, to shop. Did we have such a thing as a carry-cot?' Mrs Monks was glad to help and handed over the carry-cot they had used for their own baby.[10]

Ruth's 'attitude' was a source of searing irritation to MacKenzie, who had replaced Nettelton as the Acting Resident Commissioner of Bechuanaland. He ordered an intensification of the watch on Seretse's house in Lobatse, as well as twenty-four-hour wireless communication between Lobatse, Serowe and Mafikeng. This would ensure an immediate warning of any attempt by Ruth to get back to Serowe – 'where there could be a fine old scene with hordes of native women grappling with police if she refused to go. Such a scene would be better staged in Lobatse or Gaberones where it would perforce be on a smaller scale!'[11] Three white women from the British South Africa Police were secretly brought from Southern Rhodesia into Gaberones, in case Ruth had to be forced against her will to leave the Protectorate. Baring felt he could cope with Seretse. But, he wrote to Sir Godfrey Huggins, 'I would be most chary of having to carry out an arrest of Ruth with male police. You can imagine the row which this would create in the press!' He arranged with Huggins to send some of your very excellent police-women to stand by in case of need for a few days about mid August. If so, I would suggest that they might travel in plain clothes and take a few days holiday at the Protectorate's expense in the hotel at Gaberones. Our Commissioner of Police could then mobilise them immediately in case of need. This arrangement will be kept strictly secret.[12]

Baring had heard about the reconciliation between Seretse and Tshekedi and was anxious to know more. In the second week of August, he arranged for MacKenzie to bring Tshekedi down to Pretoria, where he managed to obtain from him a general sense of his discussions with his nephew: that they had talked about renouncing any claim to the chieftainship and hoped to return to the Reserve as citizens. Baring was horrified. He warned Tshekedi that if Seretse were to return, South Africa would lose no time in pushing her claim for the High Commission Territories. He persuaded Tshekedi to put any plans on hold – to wait until Seretse and Ruth had left the Protectorate. They could resume talks, he pointed out, at a later date in London.[13]

Then Tshekedi left Pretoria and went to Lobatse, to the Khamas' bungalow. As soon as he had greeted Ruth and the baby, he and Seretse left the house for discussions outdoors, in the hills outside the town. They wrote down some guidelines and principles upon which they might work together – that they would carry out the orders of the Government, but under protest. They would also consider the possibility of giving up any claim for themselves and their children to the kingship of the Bangwato – though, of course, this would have to be discussed fully at the Kgotla, since it was not in their power to make such a decision. As well, they would press the British Government to allow them to live in the Bangwato Reserve and serve their people in some capacity, and they advocated the formation of a Tribal Council. They agreed not to publish any of these views without further consultation with each other, and to meet in England as soon as possible, for a fuller discussion.[14] They both signed this document, but it was not in any way binding – it was simply, as they wrote at the top, an 'Aide-Memoire'. For now, they would keep it secret.[15]

Then Tshekedi and Seretse asked the Administration for more time. They had every hope, they said, of reaching an agreement on a joint statement urging cooperation between the Bangwato and the

Government. They also asked for transport facilities to bring representatives of the Bangwato to Gaberones, so that the joint statement could be delivered.[16] Clark was greatly heartened to hear of this idea – for by now the campaign of non-cooperation had more or less paralysed the Reserve.[17] He telephoned Baring, who agreed to grant twenty-four more hours to Seretse and Ruth; it would make scheduling tight, but there would still be enough time for the Khamas to make the flying-boat as planned.[18] He also agreed to provide transport, and a fleet of trucks, cars and jeeps drove off to collect about 200 Sub-Chiefs and headmen from places as far away as Francistown.[19]

But Seretse was keenly disappointed. 'I expected postponement for life, not twenty-four hours,' he remarked bitterly.[20] Until the late hours of the evening, he and Ruth had been hoping for a last-minute reprieve. Now that Seretse and Tshekedi had settled most of their differences, the reasons for exile that had been given in the White Paper were redundant. 'I have never really believed that we would have to go back to England,' Ruth told a reporter that evening. 'Notwithstanding what has been published in the British press, I do not want to leave Bechuanaland . . . my home is out here now, and I really belong to this territory.'[21] But they had to go. Sullivan called on Ruth at nine in the evening, to give her a final set of travel details.[22]

Seretse and Tshekedi were working on their joint statement a few miles away from Lobatse, with Kgosi Bathoen. When it was ready and Clark had approved it, the three men said they wished to hold a meeting with some of the elders of the Bangwato in secret, to avoid the intrusions of the press. Clark readily agreed, especially as they offered to keep Government officers informed of their whereabouts and said they were welcome to attend. Clark was appreciative. 'There was really no obligation on them to do this,' he reported afterwards. 'Had they wished, they could have gone ahead by themselves jointly or independently with results which might have been embarrassing or disastrous to us.' They borrowed lamps, typewriter, paper and carbons, and disappeared. They were hard at work until nearly midnight, when Seretse and Tshekedi delivered signed copies of their joint statement to the Administration, for Monsarrat to issue to the press next morning.[23]

They also sent a telegram to Baring. Their exclusion from the

Reserve, they argued, had created a transitional period in the life of the Bangwato – from rule through traditional Chiefs to rule through another body. This was a drastic change. The institution of direct rule, they pointed out, was unwelcome and contrary to the declared principles of the British Government. Accordingly, they requested the Government

to appoint a Council of experts (both African and European) in British Colonial Administration, to consult with our people in their own country regarding the formation of a workable system of Tribal Administration, before any scheme of a permanent nature is tried. We feel that this request is both urgent and necessary.[24]

Clearly, the two men were thinking hard about models of government that would be most appropriate for their people, and how such models should be created. These were questions that had become pressing for many African leaders at this time, who were looking ahead to majority rule and self-government for their nations.

Despite their late night, Seretse and Tshekedi were up before dawn the next day and left Lobatse for the rocky slopes of a hill five miles from Gaberones, where hundreds of men were waiting for them. As the sun started to rise into the sky, the meeting began. Seretse read the joint statement, which emphasized the two men's reconciliation, in a voice quivering with emotion:

While Tshekedi's views on the effect of Seretse's marriage on the Tribe remain unaltered, both Tshekedi and Seretse have reached the conclusion that a basis of cooperation between them and their people and the Government is not an impossible solution to find.

They had agreed, they said, to meet in London at some future date and they insisted that

A perpetuation of the present friction between those who support Seretse's views and those who support Tshekedi's views on the question of the marriage will only make the solution impossible of attainment. Differences of opinion should not interfere with common interest.

Then they called upon the Bangwato to start cooperating with the Government. 'This cooperation is most essential,' they urged, 'to the eventual establishment of a fully representative and efficient system of Native Administration run by Africans.'[25] Seretse and Tshekedi shook hands and Tshekedi said, 'We shall meet in London soon and get this business fixed up.' Clouds of red dust rose into the air as the audience stamped their approval.[26] Tshekedi, sitting huddled and tired on a rock on the outskirts of the circle, wearing a greatcoat to keep warm against the chill of the early morning, waved his hand.[27]

Seretse then went on to make a speech of his own, to say farewell.[28] He had not mentioned this in advance to Clark, who surmised afterwards that he had written it before producing the joint statement with his uncle.[29] He was leaving the Protectorate against his will, he explained: he was not abandoning his claim to the kingship. It was important for Seretse to emphasize the fact that he had been forced into exile and that he had not accepted the British Government's decision to deprive the people of their Kgosi. This statement did not represent a departure from the 'Aide-Memoire' he had signed with Tshekedi, since that document had only set out guidelines for discussion; it had been clearly understood between uncle and nephew that any renunciation was a matter for the people to decide, after full discussions at the Kgotla.

Since his return from England at the end of March, continued Seretse, representatives of every subordinate group of the Bangwato had visited him – 'and have convinced me that the whole Bangwato Nation is now more united than at any time in living memory'. This fact, he said, 'has brought me solace at this moment when I have to leave you with deepest sorrow'. He had planned, he added, to introduce reforms for the advancement and happiness of his people – and it was a 'sad and bitter disappointment' to be deprived of this opportunity.

He encouraged the Bangwato to pay tax and to obey all the lawful orders of the government. 'Above all,' he said, 'pay due homage and remain loyal to His Majesty King George VI.' He looked forward to his return to his people: 'Hard words have been spoken, misinterpretations and misconceptions have taken place and injustices have resulted. Let us call a temporary truce and with the help of Almighty God I look forward to the day not far off when the Bangwato Nation will be united with me in person for the welfare and progress of our country.' He concluded:

To each one of you my wife and I with sorrowful hearts express our deep appreciation of your loyalty and unlimited kindness. Your welfare and happiness will be our constant concern wherever we may be.

May God bless each one of you and protect you.

SALANG SENTLE [Stay well].[30]

Fraenkel handed out copies of Seretse's speech to the press, which had been printed as a broadsheet. It was entitled '*Go batho ba me*' – 'To my people'.[31]

The press picked up on the reconciliation between Seretse and Tshekedi. 'Tshekedi Reconciled to Nephew's Marriage to White Woman,' reported the *Rhodesia Herald*.[32] But the Administration played it down, pointing out that it was not far-reaching. Clark suspected, in any case, that Tshekedi had been surprised by Seretse's speech of farewell and was not at all happy about it.[33]

Meanwhile, outside the general store in Gaberones, men and women waited to catch a glimpse of Ruth, who was driving the new family car from Lobatse. When she arrived in the town, they crowded round to see baby Jacqueline, in the arms of Naledi, who had now arrived from Durban.[34] The two women and baby then drove to the airstrip, accompanied by the District Commissioner and his wife. They were fifteen minutes late, complained Clark, as Ruth 'insisted on driving in their own car, which had not yet been run in'.[35]

The Khamas were scheduled to leave at 12.15 and would be flying for the first leg of the journey in Sir Evelyn's official aircraft. This had been arranged because, unlike most aircraft in the region, it would not need to stop in Francistown to refuel – an extra stop that would require more policing.[36] There was much anxiety about what could still go wrong. Once again, there were rumours of a kidnap plot and Monsarrat stayed up half the night coding up a message to ask for extra security – with the result that next morning the airstrip at Gaberones was surrounded by policemen and the aircraft was ringed by guards.

In the event, the Khamas' departure took place without incident, although the aircraft took off about thirty minutes behind schedule – 'owing to Mrs Khama's slow driving,' grumbled Clark.[37] Seretse and Ruth showed the strain of the last few days: he looked tired from the intense negotiations with both Tshekedi and the Government; and she had clearly been weeping. They were both wearing sunglasses. Ruth was dressed in a plain, unfussy suit, with a scarf neatly tied around her neck, and low heels; Seretse was dressed in a suit and tie, with a trilby. Naledi wore a turban round her head, with a scarf around her neck. Solemnly, they passed down a line of headmen, shaking hands with them.[38] These men, some of them old and grizzled, 'bowed their heads in sorrow,' reported the Johannesburg *Star*, 'and the many Europeans present to see the send-off were visibly moved'. Even among the officials, added the *Star*, 'there was some biting of lips'. Monks, who was there, said that a police officer, of long service in the Protectorate, blew his nose and said, 'Poor devils.'[39] Ruth and Seretse held each other's hands tightly. 'Anyone who lived as close to this story, as I did,' said Monks, 'couldn't help being impressed with their devotion to each other and with the sincerity of their relationship, whatever our feelings about the marriage.'[40]

At one o'clock in the afternoon, the Khama family walked together across the tarmac, slowly and with great dignity. The air was still and dry and the veld around the airfield looked parched: there had been no rain for many months. Ruth and Naledi carried between them the carry-cot – provided by Mrs Monks – in which Jacqueline slept.[41] As they neared the aircraft, Oratile – her face creased in grief and sobbing – rushed forward for one last look at the child and then turned to Ruth, whom she kissed and embraced; Ruth clung to her.[42] All along the perimeter fence of the airfield, Bangwato men and women shouted farewell. Tears ran down their faces. On the step the banished couple turned round for one last look and a wave of the hand. Mrs Khama was overcome. Then, as they took their seats in the aircraft, Seretse buried his face in his hands.[43] As the plane went off, a spontaneous moan ran through the crowd.[44]

The aircraft swooped low over the heads of the crowd and set course for the north.[45] Monsarrat was designated the 'conducting officer'. After the plane had taken off, he recalled later, 'both Seretse and Ruth Khama were glum, as I would have been myself. I walked forward to the tiny cockpit, and had a look at the chart. It showed that, with a very small alteration of course, we could fly directly over Serowe, the capital, and Seretse's own birthplace.' This he proposed to Seretse:

I went back and asked him if he would like that. The answer was Yes, and we spent ten minutes circling the vast spread of mud huts, maize patches, herds of cattle, and dusty tracks before getting back on course again, and steering for the swirling cloud of spray, a thousand feet high, which marked the point where the Zambezi River thundered over the Victoria Falls.[46]

This recalled the stunt arranged by Monks when Seretse had returned to Bechuanaland in March. At the time, Monsarrat had been furious. But when faced with the Khamas' grief, he felt a need to do something to ease their pain. Although an abrasive man, he was deeply romantic and did not fit naturally into the world of the British colonial Administrator.

The aircraft arrived at Livingstone at 5 p.m. and the Khamas were taken under the wing of the District Commissioner. Monsarrat had to get them off safely the next morning, which proved a challenge. They were to catch the flying-boat very early – and it was important to get them on that boat, because it only flew once a week. But Seretse did not share Monsarrat's sense of urgency:

I think he liked his breakfast; he was certainly enjoying this one, and it was not to be hurried. I could not really blame him; he had me by the tail anyway, and my impatience as he worked his way through the mealie porridge, the eggs and bacon, the soft rolls with chunky marmalade, the cup after cup of coffee, must have been laughable – especially as it was the last laugh he was going to enjoy in this part of the world, for a very long time.

By courtesy of our faithful ally, BOAC, I managed to hold the flying-boat until the last crumb was disposed of, and there was no egg left on anyone's face. Then Seretse caught his plane.

I telegraphed Arthur Clark, in our agreed code: 'EXIT'.[47]

The flying-boat lifted slowly into the air. The Khamas would soon leave southern Africa behind them: they would arrive at Kampala in the afternoon, to spend the night at the BOAC hotel, before the next leg of the long journey.

Baring was immensely relieved. 'We succeeded in getting the Khamas out and the press was bitterly disappointed there was not a scene . . . I received a row of congratulations, not very well deserved, including one from Clem [Attlee],' he wrote with satisfaction to his wife. 'I will be relieved to be rid of the Seretse problem next July,' he told her, referring to the forthcoming end of his term of office. 'Malan and I are now practically blood brothers!' But he was afraid that the British Government had been undermined by the reconciliation between Seretse and Tshekedi: 'All the same we are not out of the woods since Seretse and Tshekedi now think they will both resign the chieftainship and both come back as private individuals.'[48]

Five senior Bangwato men went to see MacKenzie. They said that on Seretse's instructions, they would now pay tax. They asked him to call off the police who were chasing defaulters and also for permission to hold a large meeting, where everyone would be told to pay tax and cooperate; Oratile's name, they suggested, should be put on the tax receipt. MacKenzie's manner was cold and abrupt. He said that the tax receipt should be left blank and refused the request for a meeting, arguing that they had insulted the High Commissioner in March and had also refused to come to the meetings that he had called. Referring to Peto Sekgoma and Manyaphiri as 'scoundrels', he said that if they were to offer a public apology, he might be more favourable. They seemed to think, he complained, 'that everything in the past should be wiped off the slate and that we should start afresh'. But, he warned nastily, they were not going to get away with it so easily.[49]

The headmen of villages throughout the reserve were infuriated by this request for an apology. 'We cannot understand,' they said in a message conveyed by Fraenkel, 'why this Government is being so persistent with many requests for the Bangwato to *apologise*'. They had had no intention of being discourteous to Sir Evelyn when they boycotted his Kgotla, and had done their best to warn his officials beforehand. The blame for the fiasco, therefore, rested squarely on the Government and not on the Bangwato.[50]

IV

Exile

16

Living in London

Six days after leaving southern Africa, on 24 August 1950, the Khama family arrived at Southampton Marine Airport. Photographers and cameramen gathered round to film them as they walked up the gangway from the flying-boat onto land. Ruth's mother and Muriel rushed up to welcome them, waving with broad smiles, accompanied by an official from the CRO. 'The first interest', announced a Pathe newsreel,

is baby Jacqueline. Next comes Ruth herself. Almost overlooked in the excitement is Seretse Khama himself, the man who lost his chieftainship of the Bamangwato, through his marriage to a white girl. With his wife and daughter, now three months old and weighing ten and a half pounds, he begins his five years exile. While they find a home they are guests of the government.

'With them is Seretse's sister, to share the exile,' it added, showing Naledi and Seretse carrying Jacqueline between them in Mrs Monks's carry cot.[1] It was a chilly summer's day, but the newsreels showed a close-up of Seretse wiping his brow with a handkerchief. Now that they had arrived on British soil, he was faced with the reality of exile and his enforced removal from his people and his land.

A government car drove them to London, where a large crowd was waiting to see them as they reached the Grosvenor Court Hotel in the West End.[2] This was to be their home for the first six weeks – as 'guests of the government'. The first few weeks were hard. For, as Ruth remarked, 'hotel life with a baby is no joke'.[3] She was also continually pestered by journalists, who wanted to know how she had coped with life in Bechuanaland, especially the food. She replied that it was no different from Britain, except for Mopani caterpillars –

which provoked horror. 'But the English eat crabs!' remonstrated Seretse.[4]

The British public were fascinated by the Khamas. A play called *The Baker's Daughter* was written about their marriage and exile, with a performance planned for September in Bridlington.[5] But it was 'Not Recommended for Licence' by the Lord Chamberlain's Office. 'This, without any disguise,' judged the Reader's Report, 'is the story of Seretse Khama's marriage':

The baker's daughter is a London girl into whose family Gbor-Gbor (pronounced Bo-Bo) Chief designate of the Beruba tribe, is introduced by her married brother Brian, a student at what is obviously London University. Rose, the girl, falls in love and insists on marrying Bo-Bo, in spite of the opposition from all her family except Gladys, Brian's wife.

They get married and go to 'Jammatoland, the protectorate where Bo-Bo is Prince. There Rose, now pregnant, is snubbed by the white residents and has a violent scene with Bo-Bo's uncle, the Regent.' The government then exile Rose and Bo-Bo from Jammatoland:

Rose rushes hysterically out into the monsoon (if they have monsoons in Africa, which I doubt) and is nearly killed by a native who mistakes her for a tiger (in spite of the fact that this is Africa). She is picked up by Bo-Bo who nearly runs her over in his car.

Then Bo-Bo abdicates, the child is born healthy, and they go to England. The Reader's Report listed some 'offensive vulgarities', including the line: 'I bet there isn't one of those old trollops wouldn't like a night with him.'[6]

One day, Muriel, who worked for Deloitte, a firm of accountants, was told by one of the junior partners, 'Miss Williams, I do hope you don't tell these newspaper reporters that you are related to Seretse Khama and that you work for Deloitte.'[7] But CRO officials had 'nothing but praise', reported the US attaché in London to Washington, for the manner in which Seretse and his wife had been conducting themselves since their return to London:

There has been little of the sensational publicity which the CRO feared and Seretse has refused to allow himself to be used by Communist-inspired political groups in their trouble-making. Although the CRO are somewhat less enthusiastic about Mrs Khama and find her on occasion 'aggressive in manner', they pay tribute to the restrained manner in which she has dealt with the press since her return to London.[8]

'One of the biggest comforts during the trying first weeks of our return to England,' said Ruth, 'was a complete reconciliation with my own family. My father met Seretse, and from the first meeting the two of them got on famously.'[9] He and Ruth's mother came to see them often, as did their old friends, especially Charles Njonjo.[10] A special pleasure for Seretse was the opportunity to share in the success of the West Indian cricket team, who had beaten England at Lords for the first time in June that year. It had been front-page news and was regarded by many black and Asian colonials as a real and welcome challenge to established beliefs about racial superiority.[11] Seretse and Ruth were invited by the West Indian Students Union to a dance at Hammersmith Town Hall in West London, to celebrate the Test victory and to say farewell to the West Indies XI. 'The joint's jumping!' reported Pathe News, introducing viewers to the special guests – Seretse and Ruth, with the Colonial Secretary James Griffiths, and the Jamaican athlete MacDonald Bailey and his wife.[12]

After six weeks at the Grosvenor Court Hotel, Seretse and Ruth took a six-month lease on a flat in Chelsea, on the third floor of a small pre-1914 block. The flat had three bedrooms, a small dining room, and a lounge. Seretse had arranged to study with a firm of law tutors, Gibson and Weldon, starting in January; he planned to take his final Bar examination the following May, which would qualify him as a barrister.[13] He and Ruth also made plans for Jacqueline to be baptized by an Anglican minister, who came round to see them. The minister was convinced, he wrote to a friend, that Seretse was acting in good faith. He liked Ruth, whom he thought was practical, stable and sensible, and surprisingly devoid of bitterness 'Quite frankly,' he said, 'I doubt very much the Brit Govt want a rapprochement between Seretse and Tshek – too embarrassing in respect of SA and SR. Why has the Govt not tried to bring Tshek and Seretse together? Why ignore both?' He saw the persecution of Seretse as part of a larger picture of racialism. What was the use, he asked, 'of fighting racialism in the Union when we soft-pedal it in Bech?'[14]

A CRO official, Peter Lewis, visited the Khamas on the evening of 13 November 1950. He had helped them in Southampton, when they first arrived, and his seniors, believing he had won their confidence, encouraged him to build on this – 'establishing an informal channel of contact for us'.[15] The day after his visit to the Chelsea flat, he wrote a report. The flat, he said, was 'fairly well, but not over well, furnished'; he had admired the leopard-skin and springbok-skin rugs on the floor and Seretse had told him that the best one, a lion's skin, was still on its way. He thought the Khamas looked much better and more cheerful than when they had first arrived, especially Seretse. 'They both, in fact, seemed to be very happy,' he said, 'and in excellent spirits. When I arrived the baby, Jacqueline, was being prepared for bed in front of the sitting-room fire. She was looking well.' The household had been increased by a young woman, a German refugee, who helped Ruth with the cooking and washing. Naledi was set to go to Hammersmith Hospital in January, at the start of the new nursing students' term, but she had been feeling a little homesick.

Lewis was invited to stay for a meal. The menu was tomato soup, then curry, followed by stewed fruit and custard. 'The curry was quite alarmingly hot,' said Lewis, 'and Ruth confessed to having overdone the chillies.'[16] This may not have been a mistake. Ruth was an experienced cook and often made curry, which had been Seretse's favourite ever since his student days at Nutford House.[17] She and Seretse may have suspected that the visit would end up in a report and were enjoying some harmless fun at Lewis's expense. He was astonished by the civility they showed towards the British Government and their apparent sympathy for Baring: 'They both, strangely enough, seemed to have a soft spot for Sir Evelyn Baring. Seretse spoke with concern of Sir Evelyn's state of health and thought the job a very onerous one for someone who was not of robust health.'[18] Lewis accepted these comments at face value – but it was possible that he was being gently mocked. For Seretse, who was teaching Jackie to grimace whenever Gordon Walker was mentioned, had a mischievous sense of humour.[19]

After dinner, there was a break in the conversation while Seretse listened to the closing stages of a fight between champion heavyweight boxers, Bruce Woodcock and Jack Gardner. Their own wireless was out of action, so Seretse rang up a friend and got him to put the telephone mouthpiece near the loudspeaker of his set. Then there was some further conversation: 'In politics Ruth proclaims herself a "true blue Conservative". Seretse is a "Socialist". I was also given an outline of the political views of various members of Ruth's family.'[20] The Secretary of State enjoyed Lewis's snapshot account. 'Very good report,' he wrote. 'I would like to see Mr Lewis.'[21]

Seretse became involved again in the activities of the Seretse Khama Fighting Committee, which was still busy campaigning. One of the new people he met on the Committee was John Stonehouse, who was then a student at the LSE with an interest in colonial and African affairs. Stonehouse later became a Labour Government Minister and then shocked the world when he faked his own death; when he was found, living with his secretary, he was imprisoned for fraud. But in 1950, he was unknown and an idealist. He had great respect for Seretse, describing him as 'impressive in stature', with 'a brilliant faculty for interpretation and expression', and he enjoyed his warm personality and generosity of feeling. One night, they went together to address a meeting in Basingstoke, at which Seretse was in fine form:

His analysis of democracy and politics was as good as any political philosopher could muster. The audience was fascinated and entranced. When it came to my turn to make the appeal for the Seretse Khama [Fighting Committee] the pound notes and cheques came up in healthy profusion, including a very generous donation from the local Tories.[22]

The Khamas started to make new friends. Clement Freud invited Seretse to speak at a celebrity Club Supper at the Arts Theatre Club off Leicester Square, which he was managing. 'A hundred members and their guests', explained Freud in his autobiography, 'bought tickets, got a decent meal and listened to a speech by a man or woman of the moment' – and in the autumn of 1950, Seretse Khama was the 'man of the moment'. Other celebrity speakers had included Bernard Shaw, Peter Ustinov, Christopher Fry and Laurie Lee.[23] Freud understood the difficulties faced by the Khamas and wanted to help. He also found Seretse agreeable company and thought Ruth was an admirable and very courageous woman. He and his wife Jill invited them home and he cooked – which always made for a successful evening, as Seretse appreciated good food.[24]

The Labour MPs Jennie Lee and her husband, Aneurin Bevan, gave parties in their home for Seretse and Ruth. Although they followed the doctrine of collective responsibility in relation to the Labour Party, in private they followed their own principles – and they believed that the Labour Party had treated the Khamas very badly.[25] Bevan organized a party at Cliveden Place, where Seretse and Ruth met Cheddi Jagan and Forbes Burnham, leading politicians from British Guiana.[26] Bevan publicized this party as much as possible, to draw attention to the problems suffered by the British colonies.

Seretse and Ruth became good friends with MacDonald Bailey, the famous sprinter known as Black Flash, from Port of Spain in Trinidad; Bailey had also married a white Englishwoman and was living in Britain. Over six feet tall, Bailey ran for Britain in the Olympics of 1948 and was to become a medallist in the 1952 Olympics. Movietone filmed a newsreel showing the Khama family and the Baileys enjoying Christmas together in the Khamas' flat, the adults serving sandwiches and cake to the children, and pulling crackers. The four adults laughed happily together in the living room, next to a huge framed photograph – about two feet square – of Seretse's father, Sekgoma, in military uniform, standing beside Khama III.[27]

The Khamas visited Ruth's aunt and uncle in Norfolk, where Seretse enjoyed evenings in the pub with the local farmers, discussing crops and cattle.[28] But Seretse longed for his own land and people. 'He visited our beauty spots – Devon and Cornwall, North Wales, the Lake District, the Scottish Highlands,' wrote Fenner Brockway, 'but when I asked which part of Britain he liked most, he said, "East Anglia, its flat distances to the horizon took me home".'[29]

Towards the end of January, Lewis, the CRO official, went again to see Seretse and Ruth.[30] He found them in good spirits: 'Ruth, I fancy, is a trifle plumper, and amid the domesticities of home and preparing baby Jacqueline for bed, is very much the young matron. The baby continues to flourish and to manifest a certain winsome charm.' Since his last visit, Seretse had a supply of bigger and better karosses, reported Lewis, 'so that the flat was now almost entirely carpeted by animal skins of various kinds.'

The lease was due to end in March but they had arranged to rent it on a month-by-month tenancy until they found somewhere more permanent. Seretse had begun his law course. 'He has, I think,' said Lewis, 'an agile and intelligent mind, and I think he is taking his studies seriously.' Lewis had made arrangements to take them out to dinner at a Hungarian restaurant in Soho. When the baby had been put to bed and instructions given to the babysitter, they departed by bus. The dinner passed off well, reported Lewis, 'although Seretse somewhat disconcerted the waiter at the beginning of the meal by fiercely demanding "steak"'. But meat was still rationed and was not on the menu:

the waiter retaliated by explaining that there was no steak, but that Seretse could have a selection of meats cooked on a skewer. Ruth followed me in choosing chicken goulash . . . Rather cavalierly I omitted to ask them what they wished to drink with their food and ordered a bottle of red wine. Seretse confessed later that he would sooner have had beer.

At one point Lewis remarked that W. A. W. Clark had moved from South Africa to the UK and was now the Head of the High Commission Territories Department of the CRO. Then he asked his guests if they had seen Clark in London, to which Seretse replied that he had – 'whereupon his face fell, and he seemed anxious to change the subject. I made no attempt to pursue it, and the conversation resumed its lighter-hearted tone.'

At about 10 o'clock they finished their meal and Seretse invited Lewis to go on with them to a club. Partly out of curiosity, he agreed, and went with them to a club called Sugar Hill, in a small backyard off Duke Street, St James:

The club consisted of a very small room with a very heavy carpet on the floor, shaded lamps, a stream-lined bar tended by a white bar-maid and a black barman, and a small mixed company of black and white – with the black element the more numerous. Seretse and Ruth seemed to be quite well known.

Seretse saw Lewis was finding it dull and they left after about half an hour. Lewis reported:

I had gone quite prepared to find the place slightly vicious, but instead found it only boring. It appears to be merely a drinking club for rather wealthy coloured gentlemen, and the only interesting moment for me was when Seretse introduced me to Macdonald [*sic*] Bailey, the Jamaican athlete, a rather poor specimen, I thought, with a fish-like handshake.

'My relations with Seretse and Ruth remain very friendly,' said Lewis, 'and I must confess I find them an interesting pair. There is no sign that the marriage is other than a great success, and they seem much attached to each other.' Lewis then added that he wished to record one further opinion, based on his growing acquaintance with Seretse. 'He seems to me', he noted, 'to possess good qualities of character and intelligence which, if all goes well, bode well for his future.' He had doubtless many weaknesses, including a full share of the fecklessness of youth, he thought, but beside these,

there are qualities which I think are probably remarkable in an African – determination, a strong ingrained respect for authority and above all an honesty and directness in dealing with people, and a right judgement of them, which I find impressive.

In Lewis's view, it would be

a tragedy if these qualities were to be frustrated by bitterness, or inactivity, or neglect. If they are fostered, they seem to me just the qualities which could be a help to the administration of our African Colonies, especially in the present stage of development.[31]

This was also Clark's view. 'I agree with him about Seretse's potentialities,' he commented on Lewis's report. 'Once he completes or abandons his legal studies we must interest ourselves seriously in his future.' He added in brackets, 'I am sure Tshekedi would not approve of the Sugar Hill!'[32]

After six months in Chelsea, in March 1951, the Khamas moved to a flat on Albany Street, not far from the gardens and fields of Regent's Park in the centre of London. But it was not an easy time. There was massive inflation and the cost of living was high, so it was difficult for Ruth to manage the housekeeping budget on their allowance from the Government. At least the rationing of food was starting to ease up:

'A second lamb cutlet' and 'a bar of chocolate', according to Clement Freud, were gradually reappearing in the everyday vocabulary of ordinary folk, at least in London.[33]

They settled into a routine: Ruth was looking after baby Jacqueline and running the home; Seretse was applying himself to his law studies, but was also taking a keen interest in politics and frequently went to the Visitors' Gallery in the House of Commons to watch debates.[34] On one of these visits to the Commons in 1951 he met Kwame Nkrumah, who had stopped in London for a few days on his way back to the Gold Coast from the USA. Nkrumah went to the House of Commons, where he discussed his country's problems with a group of MPs in one of the committee rooms. Seretse was in an adjoining committee room, holding a meeting with MPs – and as soon as he heard that Nkrumah was next door, he immediately left the meeting to go and shake his hand.[35]

But it was a difficult time in many ways. Naledi had started nursing at Hammersmith Hospital, but it had refused to recognize her qualifications from South Africa and insisted that she re-train.[36] They also felt unwelcome as a mixed-race family in their local community. 'The general atmosphere was shall I say "cool" towards us,' commented Ruth several years later. 'Perhaps the kindest thing would be to say they didn't seem to understand that Seretse and I loved each other, were decently married, and intended to stay that way for the rest of our lives.'[37] At times, Seretse felt discouraged. When John Stonehouse told him that he and his wife were planning to go to Uganda to work for the African Co-operative Movement, Seretse had his doubts. 'I met him in the cafeteria of the House of Commons one night,' wrote Stonehouse, 'when he was in a particularly dejected mood':

> He was quite disparaging when I told him about my prospective mission.
> 'They will either buy you out or ban you, if you haven't already given up in frustration.'
> 'They', of course, meant the Colonial Government or the settlers.[38]

But however much they felt downcast at times, the Khama family were clinging to their hope of returning home to Africa. 'I have not given up the fight on my banishment,' Seretse told the American magazine, *Ebony*. Ruth, he added, felt as he did:

I have heard her say so often to visitors how deeply she feels the injustice that has been dealt us. 'The Tribe has accepted me,' she will say. 'It is not the tribe which is against me. It is the white people of South Africa. They need something to knock them off the pedestals they have set themselves on.'[39]

17

Six thousand miles away
from home

As W. A. W. Clark had suspected, Tshekedi had been very annoyed by Seretse's separate speech of farewell to the Bangwato, after their joint statement. Shortly after his nephew's departure, he told Baring that he had now shifted away from Seretse and was opposed to the idea of him ever being Kgosi.[1] Six thousand miles away from home, Seretse had heard reports of his uncle's changed attitude and, in October 1950, he wrote to him from London, emphasizing the need for them to work together:

even though we have given away our fatherland through our dispute we are nevertheless ready to forget the things which have caused misunderstandings between us so that we can redeem our land from the control of the Europeans so that it may return to the Bamangwato.

Government officials were eager to see conflict between them, he argued, 'so that they could say that when we were together we would continually be at loggerheads'. He urged Tshekedi not to play into their hands. 'I refuse,' he said, 'to quarrel with you further.'[2]

But Tshekedi ignored the warning in his nephew's letter. He felt isolated in Rametsana and was keenly aware of the hostility towards him from so many of the Bangwato, which had led to skirmishes in several villages. The final straw was the burning down of his house at the Kgotla in Serowe, in the middle of the night of 17 October 1950. Arson was suspected, though not proved, and Tshekedi was bitterly hurt that no one had even tried to put out the fire.[3] His entire library was destroyed, as were irreplaceable family memorabilia, including the Bible which Queen Victoria had presented to Khama III.[4]

On 12 November, Tshekedi publicly ruptured his reconciliation with Seretse. He published the 'Aide-Memoire' that he and Seretse had signed, claiming that this document proved that Seretse had agreed to renounce his own, and his children's, claim to the chieftainship. But now, he complained, Seretse was trying to return to Bechuanaland as Chief. Tshekedi added that he had taken this step after several conferences with the British High Commissioner, Sir Evelyn Baring. He told the press that he could see no end to the dynastic feud.[5] This choice of words – 'dynastic feud' – was resonant of the White Paper and gave a sense of inevitable and ceaseless quarrelling between the two men. It was exactly what Baring and Liesching wanted. Just two weeks before, Liesching had told Baring of his worry that Tshekedi might be 'tempted into a combination with Seretse that would be fatal to our plans'.[6]

Seretse was appalled. He explained to reporters that he had never signed an agreement renouncing his claim to the chieftaincy – that the 'Aide-Memoire' was merely intended to set out 'certain lines along which we might work'. This included the *possibility* of them both renouncing their claims, but only after discussing the matter in London and as a basis for discussion at the Kgotla. There could be no question of taking such a momentous decision without the involvement of the Bangwato people as a whole. 'This was fully understood by my uncle at the time,' he said firmly in a statement to the press. He denied that he was trying to return as Kgosi. He simply wanted to find a way in which he might serve his people in any responsible position they might wish him to occupy:

I feel I have the right to live in the territory, no matter in which capacity. The statement [by Tshekedi] has confused the whole issue. We shall probably have to start negotiating all over again. As far as I can see the British Government will never let me return as Chief.[7]

Seretse's genuine wish to be reconciled with Tshekedi was confirmed by a source close to David Astor, the editor of the London *Observer*. This source had examined the situation fully and reported that he could find no evidence whatsoever that Seretse had broken his agreement.[8] He said, too, that a colleague who had visited Seretse had found him 'very understanding and anxious for reconciliation'.[9] Astor was taking an interest in the matter because he was a sympathetic supporter of the struggle against imperialism in Africa. He and Michael Scott, an Anglican minister in South Africa, were loyal friends of Tshekedi and were doing their best to support him.

On 13 December 1950, Seretse was summoned to the CRO. The purpose of the meeting was to consult him on a forthcoming visit to southern Africa by Gordon Walker – and whether or not it would be a good idea to include a few days in Bechuanaland. Seretse said that he welcomed the idea of such a visit, which would enable the Commonwealth Secretary to 'see things on the spot'.[10] Gordon Walker was convinced that he should go, though officials there had warned against the plan. 'It's never any use being cowardly – I can't really go furtively around,' he wrote in a note to Liesching.[11] One of the officials who had discouraged the visit was the new District Commissioner of Serowe, Jean Germond. With his goatee beard, Germond not only looked different from other whites in the reserve – he *was* different. He tried to diminish the unofficial apartheid in the Reserve and had the partitions between Africans and Europeans removed in Post Offices and, so far as was possible, on the railways.[12] He got on well with Keaboka Kgamane, Senior Tribal Representative, and unlike his predecessor, MacKenzie, was generally liked by the Bangwato.[13] Germond insisted that if the Secretary of State were to visit Serowe, then he would have to hold a Kgotla, or it would do more harm than good – 'I can see no other convincing pretext for his visit here.' He added that members of the Tribe would expect to give speeches themselves, on the matters uppermost in their minds: their wish for Seretse's return and their determination never to let Tshekedi back.[14]

It was the worst time of year for the Bangwato to attend an assembly in Serowe – the season when everybody hoped for rain and went out to their lands to plough. But plans went ahead anyway for the first visit of a Cabinet Minister to Bechuanaland. Some rail coaches were brought up to Palapye from South Africa, to be used as his sleeping-quarters, and ox-teams neatened the road between the railway and Serowe. Red, white and blue ribbons were wound around the poles supporting the front of the Tribal Office.[15] The police kept a careful watch on movements into the Reserve and turned back any of Tshekedi's supporters who ventured near.[16]

Colonel Beetham, the new Resident Commissioner – a large and overbearing man known as Ted – wanted to lay on a 'European/African tea party'. 'If you can work in an odd unofficial into the tea party,' he wrote to one of his officers, meaning a white who did not work for the government, 'I think it would be a good thing.' But, he added, 'I don't know whether you have any prominent unofficials and if you have whether they would object to having tea with Africans.'[17] Germond told Beetham that he was asking all the local government officers and their wives to a luncheon on the lawn under the poplar trees at the Residency – but 'I am not asking any of the local Europeans except Mrs Page-Wood. The rest have little to recommend them and did not show up very well during the Seretse troubles.'[18]

But the big event was Gordon Walker's Kgotla on 1 February 1951. About 10,000 people turned up, some of them arriving as early as 5.30 in the morning.[19] From Francistown, in the north of the territory, more than 1,000 people – women as well as men – were brought in special trains. Several thousand also came in lorries and buses, all laid on by the Administration. Some arrived by ox-wagons.[20] One reason for the large numbers was that Germond, who was widely trusted, had been travelling around the country, encouraging people to attend. But it was also because people were eager to hear from Gordon Walker when their Kgosi would be returned to them; some people hoped that he would be bringing Seretse with him and would produce him at the meeting.

At 10.30 a.m. Gordon Walker arrived at the kgotla ground under a blistering sun, accompanied by the High Commissioner and the Resident Commissioner.[21] Sporting a blue flower in his buttonhole, he sat in front of a table covered with a Union Jack, under a flag-draped roof. The breeze blew up the dust across the ground. First there were prayers and then a choir of school children sang '*Morena boloka sechaba sa rona*' – 'Lord, save our nation'. Gordon Walker was welcomed by a speech from Keaboka, whose pinched, thin cheeks and wrinkled forehead reflected the gravity of his feelings. Keaboka described the sorrow of the Bangwato at the banishment of Seretse and asked the Government to order Tshekedi's followers out of the country.[22]

After his speech, Keaboka called on the representatives of the nine districts of the Reserve to speak; each one came from one of the allied clans ruled by the Bangwato, whom Tshekedi had claimed were on his side. Gordon Walker gave a nod or a wave to each of these men as they stood, then listened for several hours to their speeches, which were translated from Setswana into English by a man with a booming voice. 'Loudspeakers were in use for the first time,' reported John Redfern, the *Daily Express* correspondent, 'and they really rattled under the assault of the men's harsh and sorrowful voices, pleading for Seretse's return.'[23] Then Monametsi Chiepe, a prominent intellectual and a former Tribal Secretary, spoke for everybody there in a long, eloquent speech:

The eyes of a sorrowing people behold you today and hope is kindled in their hearts . . . We pray that it may please His Gracious Majesty's Government to reconsider in due course this decision and return to us Seretse Khama who is by our law and custom the only legitimate heir to the Bamangwato Chieftainship. We do not want Tshekedi back in our country.

Chiepe reminded the Commonwealth Secretary of Britain's obligation to protect Bechuanaland from South Africa:

Requests for the transfer of our country to the Union have been made from time to time. These requests come to us like a chilly and biting wind. We pray that whenever these requests to transfer us are made our Mother stretch her protecting wings all the closer about us and keep us warm, happy, confident and hopeful of growing into what we are destined by nature and healthy impulses to be.[24]

One woman near the front row held up her parasol to hide her tears during the speeches. Some of the speakers had told Mr Gordon Walker they thought he would be bringing Seretse with him to Bechuanaland. 'Anyway,' said one with a bitter chuckle, 'we still feel that our Chief is in his pocket.'[25]

Then the Commonwealth Secretary began his address. He understood, he said, that it had been inconvenient for people to attend a kgotla at Serowe 'at this difficult time of harvest when most of you would wish to be at work in your fields'. But, he added, 'It is also very nice to see your women and your children in such great numbers singing.' Then he moved on to the core of his speech: that nothing could be done about Seretse for five years, and possibly not even then. Referring to the White Paper, he said that His Majesty's Government were keen for a system of District Councils to be set up, which would be given increasing responsibility until they had all the functions of a Native Authority. Then Gordon Walker made a promise. 'I want you to know further, in reply to the speeches you have made to me,' he told the many thousands of people facing him, 'that the Government will never impose Tshekedi or anyone as Chief of the Bamangwato against the wishes of the majority of the people.'[26]

Straight after the Kgotla, Gordon Walker sent Liesching a telegram. 'Ten thousand were present, extremely orderly,' he reported with satisfaction. 'Received nice lion skin.' Then he went to Mafikeng to meet Tshekedi, who he thought was an 'extremely able, ruthless, and unforgiving man'.[27] There was evidence, he told Liesching, of extremely strong feeling against Tshekedi, so they would have to abandon the idea of involving him in the affairs of the Bangwato. Otherwise, he believed, the pro-Seretse feeling would be fuelled. 'Only policy now,' he cabled, 'is to make it clear Tshekedi is out and to allow anti-Ruth feeling to develop.'[28]

Gordon Walker may have wanted 'to make it clear Tshekedi is out' – but Tshekedi had other plans. The former Regent had been living at Rametsana in the Bakwena Reserve for well over a year, with the 1,200 people who had followed him there. But the move had only been intended as a temporary solution to hostilities and now Tshekedi wanted to go home to the Bangwato Reserve. In April 1951 he sailed to the UK with Buchanan, and embarked on an intense and energetic campaign to argue his case. It was 'tremendously exciting if dreadfully exhausting', commented Mary Benson, who became his assistant and later his friend and biographer. 'Brilliant, fiercely energetic, obstinate, humorous, sagacious,' she wrote, 'he marshalled his arguments as a general would his troops ... he ceaselessly lobbied MPs of both Houses as well as newspaper editors.'[29]

It was not long before his campaign produced results. There were many letters to the press protesting against his banishment, as well as a long letter to *The Times* from Tshekedi himself.[30] He had the support of the *Observer*, the *Manchester Guardian*, *The Economist*, the *News*

Chronicle and *Tribune*, the left-wing Labour weekly, and the backing of groups ranging from the Anti-Slavery Society to Christian Action.[31]

To some extent, Tshekedi's high profile was the result of his charismatic and forceful personality. It was also because of his reputation as an enlightened leader. Frequent references were made in the press to Tshekedi's concern to educate his people and, especially, to the building of Moeng College: hardly anyone in Britain was aware of the sufferings this project had caused for the Bangwato. 'His schemes of education,' enthused Fyfe Robertson in *Picture Post*, 'showed him at his far-seeing best.' Robertson described him as the 'Black Smuts':

Lords and Commons have discussed his fate, and to millions of Africans, his treatment, and the use that is made – or not made – of an outstanding man who understands the difficulties on both sides of the black–white problem, will show the way the wind is blowing for black people in Southern Africa.

Tshekedi, he added, 'is the African chief best known in Britain today. He had made himself a legend in his thirties, and now at 46 he is one of the most influential Africans in all southern Africa.'[32]

So successful was Tshekedi's campaign that on 26 June 1951 the Labour Government was threatened with defeat in the Commons, on an Opposition motion calling for an end to his banishment from the Bangwato Reserve. Gordon Walker's back was now against the wall. But he was an agile politician and, as if out of a hat, he produced a last-minute strategy to buy time. Recalling the Kgotla he had attended in February that year, he proposed sending a delegation to the Protectorate, to obtain the views of a general Kgotla on whether or not Tshekedi should return as a private citizen.[33] This quick thinking saved the vote.

During Tshekedi's visit to London, efforts were made by David Astor to bring Tshekedi and Seretse together. With the help of Mary Benson and Michael Scott, he tried to arrange an overnight stay for the Khamas at his home in Berkshire, where Seretse would have consultations first with Scott and then with Tshekedi; he described the planned meeting as the 'Two Power talks'.[34] But Seretse was evidently unwilling to discuss such important matters on territory that was dominated by Tshekedi's friends, entirely on their terms. He scrawled a curt note to Scott: 'Unable to come willing to meet Tshekedi my place any time except Saturday and Sunday. Seretse.'[35]

On 24 July 1951 the government finally sent to Bechuanaland their team of observers – Professor W. M. Macmillan, Director of Colonial Studies at St Andrews University, Daniel Lipson, a one-time Independent MP for Cheltenham, and H. L. Bullock, a former President of the Trades Union Congress.[36] When the three men arrived in Palapye, they were met by Sir Evelyn Baring for a briefing. Railway carriages in a siding had been arranged for their accommodation. As they toured the region, the Observers were given the same message again and again – that the Bangwato people wanted Seretse back as their Kgosi. One speaker pointed out that however hard they tried to tell the Government their views, they were never heard: 'we don't know what happens to words we tell people when they return overseas. As we speak it seems that we are singing a song – the words simply go into the air.' First they had told Sir Walter Harragin, then they had told Gordon Walker, but still Seretse wasn't allowed to come home. 'Now we suspect,' he said, 'that nothing will happen to the words we speak to you.'[37]

The Observers' itinerary included a visit to Tshekedi, who had now returned to Rametsana from London. Tshekedi, wrote Bullock to Gordon Walker afterwards, may have been a tyrant but he was 'a great man' and also charming, with 'an answer for everything'. But everywhere they went, he added, the cry was for Seretse, though some people said that Tshekedi could return if Seretse was there. There was a danger, he warned, 'of the Tribe going to pieces. This would be a great pity as they are a polite, courteous, friendly folk, whose strongest weapon seems to be their tongue. They can talk an Englishman out of existence.'[38]

In the afternoon of 16 August, at the school-house in Serowe, an unprecedented event took place – the Observers met a group of at least 1,000 women, at their own request; they were dressed in 'brilliant coloured frocks and headdresses', according to the *Rand Daily Mail*, and had their babies and children with them.[39] When the meeting was opened to the floor, there was a short silence. Then, hesitating, a woman put up her hand. She asked, 'Where is Seretse? Where is Ruth, and where is the baby?' She was followed by speeches from twenty women in turn, who spoke with great feeling. Without exception, each one said that she did not want Tshekedi back, in any capacity. He was a 'hard hearted man,' complained one woman, starting to weep, 'whose judgements were severe even to widows. They were beaten and banished and all the widows remember him with bitterness.' At this point many of the other women burst into tears as well, and it was some minutes before the meeting could continue. The women handed over a memorandum. According to their custom, it stated, 'a wife of a chief (no matter what the colour of her skin is) contributes very little or nothing at all to communal manual work, and in the circumstances Seretse's wife will be exactly in the same position'. It was therefore not true that Ruth would not be able to do the work of a chief's wife and the women begged the Observers to let her come back.[40]

On 30 August, the Observers had their last meeting in Bechuanaland and left for the UK. Although they had argued with each other on some matters, with the result that Macmillan and Bullock produced a joint report and Lipson wrote his own, shorter, report, their conclusion was the same: that Tshekedi's return to the Reserve would be bitterly resented. In the course of his period in power, he had exiled many royal relatives who opposed him, used regimental labour freely for public projects that people did not want, and had a reputation as a man 'who never forgets or forgives'. The crisis over Seretse's marriage, they said, came at a time when Tshekedi was engaged in his greatest enterprise – the building of the Bangwato National College at Moeng, for which a prohibitive levy of oxen was imposed on the community and for which regimental labour was used on a monumental scale. 'The chief fear', emphasized Macmillan and Bullock's report, 'is that if Tshekedi returns in the absence of a superior he will and must step as of right into the position of Chief and bring about a counter-revolution – and this in spite of what amounted to his constitutional displacement by the Kgotla in 1949.'[41]

After the observers had gone, the Bamangwato Women's Association in Serowe asked the Government for the return of Ruth and her daughter, if only for a short visit. 'We, on behalf of the women of the Bamangwato Tribe,' they wrote to Germond, respectfully request that you make representations to His Majesty's Government to allow our mother Ruth Khama and her baby to visit us at Serowe for two or three months.

We had grown to love and cherish them when they were snatched away from us. We have grieved and suffered through their absence and the absence of our Chief Seretse. We still grieve that our mother is being kept away from us and we are puzzled at the reason for their banishment.

We humbly request therefore that they soon be allowed to return to their home and take their rightful place among us and so bring peace and happiness to the unhappy and heartbroken people.[42]

The Observers' reports were ready in September but they were not published, because a general election had been set for 25 October 1951: the Cabinet was worried that publication might weaken Labour's standing with the electorate. But, as it turned out, Labour lost in any case – the Conservative Party was voted into power, with an overall majority of seventeen seats. Winston Churchill was now Prime Minister. For Seretse and Ruth, who had now been living in exile for over a year, there seemed real grounds to hope for a reversal of Government policy. For one thing, Churchill had told the House of Commons in March 1950 that Seretse's banishment was a 'very disreputable transaction'. For another, Gordon Walker had been replaced as the Commonwealth Secretary, so was no longer in a position to exert power over the Bangwato. Nor was Sir Evelyn Baring, whose appointment as British High Commissioner in South Africa had ended in September 1951.

G. M. Kgosi immediately wrote from Kimberley, South Africa, to congratulate the new Prime Minister:

Sir, re: Recent British General Elections: Churchill's victory: Bamangwato welcomed British *New Government: Pula Pula Pula!!!*

Please convey to the British Parliament and People, the warmest *congratulations* of the Bamangwato, a *Chiefless tribe*.

He had no doubts, he said, that the new Government would send Seretse home.[43]

18

Banished forever

The new Government *was* planning to change the policy: not to reverse it, however, but to make it even more brutal. Although there had been outward changes in the Government, two key players in the Seretse crisis at the CRO were still firmly in post: Sir Percivale Liesching and W. A. W. Clark, who carefully briefed their new Minister, Lord Ismay. They produced a brief document on Bangwato affairs, which drew heavily on discussions with Sir Evelyn Baring and advocated a new scheme: to keep Seretse and Ruth out of Bechuanaland on a permanent basis, creating a vacuum in the chieftaincy that should be filled by Rasebolai Kgamane, who was Tshekedi's leading supporter and third in the line of succession. Tshekedi himself should be allowed back into the Bangwato Reserve, if at all possible.[1]

During the last months of his appointment as British High Commissioner in South Africa, Baring had worked tirelessly to convince influential people – including Sir John Le Rougetel, his successor – of the need to make Seretse's exile permanent.[2]

In June 1951, Baring had reported to the CRO on discussions with J. G. N. Strauss, who had succeeded Smuts as the leader of the South Africa United Party. Strauss had argued, he said, that if the British Government did not take a very firm position on Seretse, anti-British feelings in South Africa would be even fiercer than in 1949. This was largely because of recent developments in the Gold Coast, which in February 1951 had become the first British colony in Africa to achieve self-government. Nkrumah's party had swept to victory in the elections, forcing the British Government to release him from prison. 'In a sweltering town on the Gold Coast [Accra]', wrote Learie Constantine, the doors of Fort James prison swung open, and the figure of a released African prisoner stood there, wearing a white shirt and green trousers and blinking in the sunlight. A roar of voices greeted him: 'Nkruma! Saviour! Nkruma!' The crowd swept the police aside and tossed the prisoner shoulder-high, riding him in triumph through the cheering streets.

'Across the Gold Coast, nearly 4,000 miles from Cape Town,' added Constantine, 'falls the malevolent shadow of Dr Malan, Premier of South Africa. He does not approve of self-government for Africans under a Negro Prime Minister.'[3]

Baring's case for banishing Seretse permanently also drew on the fact that legislation in South Africa now provided for maximum separation between the races. This meant that the recognition of Seretse as Chief, while married to Ruth, would be even more starkly at variance with South African racial policy than it had been in 1949.[4] Furthermore, insisted Baring, hostile reaction in Southern Rhodesia to the possibility of recognizing Seretse, 'is to my mind certain and would endanger acceptance of new federation proposals'.[5] These proposals were the British Government's plan to create a Federation of Southern Rhodesia, Northern Rhodesia and Nyasaland, which was bitterly opposed by Africans, who suspected – rightly, as it turned out – that it would increase their domination and persecution by whites. A powerful struggle was being played out in Africa at this time. 'If African nationalism was on the march in Africa in the 1950s,' one historian has acutely observed, 'so too was white power. Kenya's white settlers cast envious glances towards Rhodesia and South Africa.'[6]

Lord Ismay, the new Commonwealth Secretary, was easily persuaded that Rasebolai should be groomed as prospective Chief and that Seretse should be permanently excluded from the chieftainship. He was also keen to help Tshekedi, who had flown over to London to see him after the election. With Clark smoothing his way at the CRO, Tshekedi had been granted a meeting with the new Secretary of State and the two men got on well:

Ismay shook hands and sent everyone except Clark out of the room. He ushered Tshekedi to a sofa and sat down beside him. Within ten minutes agreement had been reached. Tshekedi would be given increasing freedom to look after his cattle in Bamangwato country and, if all went well, would be able to return as a private person.[7]

The Colonial Office also supported the plan. Baring had prepared the way for this by having a quiet but effective word in August with Alan Lennox-Boyd, who became the new Minister of State for the Colonies after the election.[8]

This new strategy on the Khamas was endorsed at a meeting of the Cabinet on 22 November 1951 and again on 27 November. But it was decided not to make an announcement for the time being, in case it had an adverse effect on plans for the Federation of Rhodesia and Nyasaland. Opposition to the Federation from Africans in the region was already getting publicity and this would increase if there were also complaints from the Bangwato – that their wishes, too, were being ignored.[9]

The first stage of the new policy was implemented on 6 December in the House of Commons, when the Parliamentary Under-Secretary for Commonwealth Relations, John Foster, made a commitment to Tshekedi's return to the Bangwato Reserve as a private citizen, as soon as possible.[10] This was heard with astonishment – for the Observers' reports, which had just been published, had stated clearly that the Bangwato did not want Tshekedi back.[11] Foster also made a statement on Seretse: that nothing had changed.[12] That day, Seretse issued a statement to the press. He expressed his disappointment that the Government were keeping to the 'disastrous policy' of the previous administration, which was directly contrary to the wishes of his people. The unrest in the Reserve, he warned, was bound to deteriorate further.[13]

Less than two weeks after Foster's statement on Tshekedi, on 19 December, the Cabinet decided that the time had now come to act on Seretse – 'So long as this was left in uncertainty, relations with the Government of South Africa would be made more difficult.'[14] But they were worried about the effect on British public opinion, so the mandarins at the CRO embarked on a strategy to make the policy seem more palatable, by offering Seretse an appointment under a colonial government outside Africa. They finally agreed on Jamaica –

a choice, explained Clark, that had been reached with the Colonial Office:

Although anxious to be helpful, the Colonial Office were compelled to point out that in East and Central Africa there might be social embarrassments, in West Africa imported Africans are resented by local Africans even more than Europeans (the cry is 'Nigerian jobs for Nigerians' etc.) and in some of the West Indian Colonies there are colour bars. Remote islands would sound too penal.[15]

Sir Thomas Lloyd at the Colonial Office was given the job of approaching the Governor of Jamaica, Sir Hugh Foot. 'We fully recognize that at first sight it may seem to you a surprising and perhaps distasteful suggestion,' he wrote apologetically, admitting that 'there are formidable arguments against it.'[16] The Governor was altogether taken aback. 'The suggestion in your letter certainly seems odd to me,' he replied to Lloyd. He was confident, though, that Seretse would be welcome in Jamaica.[17]

On 13 March 1952, Ismay produced a paper for Cabinet on Seretse. 'His recognition as Chief is, in my opinion,' he declared, 'out of the question. It would outrage white opinion in South Africa and Southern Rhodesia.'[18] Churchill consulted Lord Salisbury for his view. Salisbury's opinion was important, because in less than two weeks he would be taking over the role of Secretary of State for Commonwealth Relations, when Ismay went to a new appointment at NATO. 'I am personally in complete agreement with the action which [Ismay] now proposes,' replied Salisbury to his Prime Minister. 'Indeed, as you may remember,' he added,

it is broadly speaking the course for which I pressed in the interview which he and I had with you before Christmas . . . I do not believe that the Bamangwato Tribe will ever settle down until they have been told definitely that Seretse can never come back. Then they will look at other alternatives. That is Sir Evelyn Baring's own view . . . We are bound to have this row sooner or later and if we leave it for another 3½ years (when the original five years' grace given him by the late Government runs out), we are likely to have to take the same decision on the very eve of a General Election here.

At such a critical time it would be an even greater problem. 'By all means let us try and get the Jamaicans – or anyone else – to take him,' he added. 'But if they won't, I am in favour of grasping the nettle now.'[19]

The Cabinet met on 18 March 1952 and approved Ismay's plan. Then things moved swiftly and Seretse and Ruth were summoned to the Commonwealth Relations Office for a meeting on Monday 24 March with Lord Ismay. Lord Salisbury, who would be taking over Ismay's appointment in a couple of days, was there too. They all sat round a conference table, recorded Ismay afterwards, so that the Khamas were able to take notes if they wished – and they did so, 'copiously'. He started off the discussion with a few friendly observations, saying he had spent more time on the affairs of the Bamangwato than on any other, since taking up office. Then he told the Khamas that the Government had serious misgivings about the idea of Seretse returning to Bechuanaland. He had married the girl of his heart, he said, without taking into account the wishes of the Tribe:

I for one would not think of blaming him for this, and would very likely have done the same thing myself. But Rulers whether they were Kings of great Empires, or Chiefs of Tribes had not the same liberty of choice in their consorts as is enjoyed by their subjects ... Quarrels and factions would continue.

He went on to give them some news that took them completely by surprise: that the Government of Jamaica had now offered Seretse 'a most attractive appointment as an officer in the Jamaican administration'.

Then he announced that Seretse's exclusion from political life was to be made permanent. The Khamas were staggered – and at this point Ruth showed signs of distress. Seretse was given two alternatives: to abdicate, or to compel the Government to make an Order-in-Council excluding him. He was asked for an answer in two days; an announcement would be made in Parliament the following day. 'I begged him to be very discreet about the advisers he consulted,' recorded Ismay. 'They must be people on whose discretion he relied, and they must also be people who had Seretse's own interests at heart and were not merely out to make mischief.' In that case, replied

Seretse with a bitter laugh, he had better not consult any Members of Parliament.

The whole meeting had taken just over half an hour. 'It had been quite friendly and unstrained,' noted Ismay. 'Neither of them by look or word gave any clue as to what their decision was likely to be. Seretse would make a good poker player.' Once these notes had been typed up, he added by hand, 'So would his wife.'[20]

Seretse and Ruth went home, stunned. By now they had moved out of central London into a rented house in the suburban village of Chipstead, in Surrey. The village was surrounded by open country, which helped to ease Seretse's and Naledi's homesickness for the vast spaces of Bechuanaland. There, for two days, the family discussed Ismay's extraordinary proposal.

On Wednesday 26 March, at 3 p.m., Seretse and Ruth were back at the CRO to give their answer. Ismay had now been succeeded by Salisbury.[21] At the first meeting, Ismay had done the talking and Salisbury was quiet; at this one, it was the other way round. Rathcreedan, Seretse's lawyer, and Clark were also present. Seretse began by saying he could never desert his people. Then he said that he knew perfectly well that the reason for his exile was intervention by South Africa. He dealt with the points that Ismay had made in the previous meeting, one by one. He did not, he said, claim any particular ability. But because of his birth and his people's affection for the hereditary succession, he would be able to put an end to all the difficulties in the Reserve if he were allowed to return. He asked for a trial period. The Jamaican post was no solution – if the Government was really sincere, why did it not offer him a similar post in Bechuanaland, preferably in the Bangwato Reserve? He warned that if the Government in the UK appeased the Union on a matter like this, white South Africans would be encouraged in their repressive policies and race relations would deteriorate even more quickly.

He then said that, as he had indicated on a number of occasions, he was prepared to renounce his claim to the chieftainship, so long as he was able to take part in the political life of the tribe. This was out of the question, replied Salisbury quickly. But here Lord Ismay intervened – he had not, he said, realized that Mr Khama had ever considered renouncing his claim to the chieftainship. If this were the case, then surely the situation was rather different and ought to be considered. But this was an avenue that Salisbury did not want to go down. He interrupted to say that they had had a very long discussion and that it would be a good idea to adjourn for fifteen minutes or so, to review its course.

When the meeting resumed, Ismay kept silent. Salisbury informed Seretse that his suggestion of renunciation, while retaining his political liberty in the Reserve, was unacceptable. They were therefore making the refusal to recognize him as Chief permanent and final.[22]

Seretse and Ruth walked out of the office, in a state of shock. 'He came home,' said Ruth, 'and buried his face in his hands and said, "To think that I can never go home again. Never, ever".'[23] He gave a press conference the next day. The offer of a job in Jamaica, he said, meant that the Government was trying to placate South Africa, even if it meant alienating thousands of Africans. He had always believed, he added, that in Britain and elsewhere in the Commonwealth it was 'no crime to marry anyone you love'.[24] Seretse took the news, said Ruth, 'like the man he is. You know, Seretse's ability to take things, good or bad, with complete equanimity is one of the things I love about him. He just refuses to be cast down.'[25]

The Secretary of State's announcement about Seretse was given in the Serowe Kgotla at 5.30 in the evening by Colonel Beetham. About 1,000 people listened silently. 'The decision of which I have just told you', warned Beetham, 'is absolutely final.' The Tribe would have to choose a new Kgosi, he said, but until then the District Commissioner would continue as Native Authority. At this point there was angry murmuring and people stood up, as if to go; some of them walked out of the Kgotla.[26] One man pointed his switch at Beetham and shouted, 'You go. I will see you.' He was supported by two young men, who were both 'storeboys' for European stores, who shouted, 'What beer does he drink? *Marete* [balls].' The 'distinct rumbling heard then, and the absence of the Pula Salute usually accorded to the Resident Commissioner,' noted one man who was there, 'were sure signs of discontent.' It was only because Keaboka appealed to the people to sit down, he believed, that they did not leave the Resident Commissioner alone in the Kgotla.[27]

On the same evening, meetings were held at Mahalapye and

Palapye.[28] The meeting at the Mahalapye kgotla was addressed by Dennis Atkins, a local official, and it ended in disorder. When Atkins gave Manyaphiri Ikitseng some copies of the Commonwealth Secretary's address to Parliament in London, one man stood up and said that he should not accept them; he repeated this three times. Another man stood up, saying the same; and then the entire meeting stood up and said the papers should be handed back. Atkins left. As he went, the papers were thrown in through the window of his car. Then, as Atkins started to drive off, another man stood up and shouted, 'Hold the DC's car! Do not let him get away, ask him where he obtained the papers. They are not from England.' Some men picked up their stools and shouted that if Tshekedi were to come back, there would be trouble – and accused the Europeans of wanting to take their country. At this moment, Manyaphiri's wife – who was in her fifties and was regarded as 'tough', the equal of any man[29] – approached the Kgotla with about 100 women, all shouting. She said that Atkins was lucky to have left before she arrived, as she would have taken him from the car and thrashed him. Scenes of fury and despair were repeated in every village that Atkins visited over the next few days. Many of the Rametsana, too, regarded it as a terrible injustice.[30] It was a disastrous time for the Bangwato, made even harder to bear by a severe shortage of water: the dam in the reserve was dry and the cattle were gasping from thirst.[31]

The decision was given to the Commons in London at the same time as the announcement in Serowe. It was heard with dismay and Anthony Wedgwood Benn made an application for an emergency debate, which was successful. Seretse Khama was in the Visitors' Gallery. 'A ray of sunshine', reported *Time* magazine, 'reached down through Britain's gloomy House of Commons . . . and glanced brightly off a pale gold wedding ring on the hand of a young Negro.' It was a fortuitous spotlighting, went on the article, of the matter then before the House: 'under sharp debate on the floor was the political consequence of the gleaming wedding ring'.[32]

'Tonight in Serowe,' said Wedgwood Benn, opening the debate, 'feelings would not be dissimilar from the feeling here in 1936 at the time of the abdication of King Edward VIII.' The Government had argued that Seretse had demonstrated his 'total incapacity' for any office – but now they were told the Government hoped he would have a successful career in Jamaica. They knew, he argued, that if Seretse were to set foot in Africa again he would be seen as a national hero, so they wanted to send him to another, distant, part of the world. He said Africa was facing a choice: either to go the way of apartheid, or towards cooperation. He asked:

What effect is this decision going to have on Prime Minister Nkrumah on the Gold Coast and on Nigeria, Tanganyika and even as far north as the Sudan?

What effect would it have on the African delegation which was coming to London next month to discuss Central African Federation?[33]

Wedgwood Benn was speaking from a deeply felt conviction. He had come across the colour bar and racial inequality in southern Africa in 1944, as an RAF officer in Southern Rhodesia, and had been shocked and disgusted by it.[34]

The Government's action on Seretse was a 'disgraceful way to introduce the principle of the colour bar,' said Fenner Brockway. It was helping the South African Government at the very moment when the liberal element in the Union was waging war on the issue. 'Why Jamaica?' wondered Hynd, a Labour MP, drily. 'Is there no suitable opening at St Helena?' Gordon Walker, too, condemned the government's decision. 'It is calculated,' he said, 'to create the worst possible impression in the tribe, and to appear to them to be a deliberate provocation of their expressed views.'[35] When Lord Salisbury heard about Gordon Walker's intervention, he seethed with anger and later wrote:

At the time of the Troubles over Seretse Khama he came to see me at the CRO and told me that he felt personally that the Govt were doing the right thing, but he felt sure that I would understand if, for party reasons, he did not say so; and then he went down to the House of Commons and made a most violent speech on the other side. Politics are politics; but I remember being very shocked at the time.[36]

Sir Ian Fraser, Conservative, defended the Government. 'I think it would be wise as well as gracious of members of this House,' he said, not to bring South Africa into the discussion:

I understand Dr Malan did not intervene at all, that he made no recommendation or representations directly or indirectly, and that the British Government did not ask for any advice or help from South Africa.

After the debate, there was a vote. MPs approved by 308 votes to 286 the Government's decision to exclude Seretse Khama permanently.[37] The Government had held firm. Seretse quietly left the Visitors' Gallery and went home.

Ismay gave the announcement to the Lords. 'Both in its substance and in its timing,' said Earl Jowitt, the leader of the Opposition, 'there is obviously grave matter for criticism here.'[38] He then asked for a debate. This took place on the following Monday, when Ismay argued that the previous government had been mistaken to banish Tshekedi, 'for he was guilty of no fault as Seretse, in his character of ruler, had been'. Tshekedi had committed no offence, whereas Seretse had committed 'I do not say a crime or an offence but a most serious breach of all the tribal customs and traditions'. Ismay was accused of trying to bribe Seretse with the offer of a job in Jamaica. His reply was an implicit compliment to Seretse: 'I can assure the House that it was not intended in that way. Indeed anyone who has talked to Seretse for five minutes would realise that on that basis it would not be likely to be successful.'[39]

In the view of *The Times*, at least the Government's decision had the benefit of being definite, and the *Daily Telegraph* said that the decision was courageous. The *Manchester Guardian*, however, believed that it would shock many people in Britain and 'will give mortal offence to millions of Africans throughout the continent'. The *Daily Express* said it was a 'bad deed which should arouse shame and anger throughout the country'. Many people were disgusted. 'This case really makes me ashamed I am English,' wrote 'Miss X' in London, 'and proves what sort of hypocrites we are . . . I am afraid our "bossing" days are over and we must wake up.'[40] Oliver Messel, the celebrated theatrical designer, wrote personally to the Foreign Secretary, Anthony Eden. 'I am wildly distressed at the issue about Seretse Khama,' he said:

I am a staunch Conservative supporter but this injustice and change of policy gives me a shock, which I feel so strongly about that I have to write to you

. . . Surely you cannot approve of the attitude in South Africa. It will have to change as it has already in America, or end in bloodshed like the French Revolution.[41]

The British Council of Churches sent a deputation to the Secretary of State, led by the Archbishop of Canterbury. Even if the policy were right for the Reserve, said the Archbishop, it could not be isolated from its effect on African opinion elsewhere at a time when Africans were putting great faith in Her Majesty's Government.[42]

A cable from the African National Congress was sent on 1 April to Lord Salisbury. The ANC, representing 10 million Africans, it said, was shocked at the 'arbitrary and harsh exclusion of Seretse' and it warned of serious repercussions throughout Africa.[43] Reaction in the white South African press was muted. 'There has been no public comment,' reported the High Commissioner to London, 'and it would appear almost as if there had been a general tacit understanding that the subject should be avoided.'[44] The only papers to comment directly on the decision were *Die Transvaler* and *Die Volksblad*, which heartily approved.

In less than six months after the start of their term in office, the Conservative Government had ended the exile of Tshekedi and had made Seretse's exclusion final and permanent. In Chipstead, 2-year-old Jacqueline Khama said she liked gooseberries and other berries – but not 'Salisberries'.[45] Her parents were now faced with the prospect of spending the whole of the rest of their lives in exile, away from Africa and away from the Bechuanaland Protectorate. Without Ruth, thought John Redfern, Seretse might have been 'knocked hard' by these years of frustration. But with her, 'he has taken all his misfortunes with a shrug of the shoulders. Occasionally cutting, he is never sour.'[46] Seretse and Ruth were admired by their friends for their restraint. 'Throughout this ugly period,' wrote Joe Appiah in his memoir,

Seretse displayed regal dignity and calm worthy of his royal ancestry. And as for his dear wife, Ruth, her courage and defiance, her devotion and steadfastness will forever be remembered wherever the story of this inhuman treatment is told . . . Like her biblical namesake, Ruth went with Seretse, making his God her God and his people her people.[47]

19

Envoys for justice

There was a cloud of sadness and despair over the Bangwato. The usual self-help projects had ceased and the whole of the Malekantwa regiment – Seretse's age group – now wore beards: they had vowed to shave only when Seretse returned.[1] Every time a plane passed over Serowe, the children looked up to the sky and called, 'Seretse come down!'[2]

The Bangwato had pleaded with the Government for Seretse's and Ruth's return on three separate occasions – at the Harragin Inquiry in November 1949, at Gordon Walker's Kgotla in Serowe in February 1951, and during the tour of the Observers in August 1951. But it had made no difference. Tshekedi, on the other hand, had managed to persuade the Government to end his exile from the Bangwato Reserve. It occurred to Keaboka that they needed to adopt a new strategy: to follow Tshekedi's example. The former Regent had gone to Britain to press his case – and had been successful. In 1895, the diKgosi Khama III, Bathoen and Sebele had gone to Britain to appeal for protection against the Boers – and they, too, had been successful. It was now time for Seretse's people to go to Britain, to plead with the Secretary of State: 'Black as we are we can think. Government is doing something unjust to us.' He proposed the idea to a meeting at the Kgotla and it was immediately taken up, with renewed hope for Seretse's return.[3]

A request was made for the use of Tribal Treasury funds for the journey, but it was refused. This meant that all the money had to be collected from individuals in the Reserve, which called for great sacrifice. Most people were very poor, and even if they did have some kind of means, it was likely to be in the form of cattle or goats – they had little access to cash. Much of the money had to be raised in loans, against future payments of cattle.[4] Almost daily, the women of Mahalapye met together to organize the fund-raising campaign. Many of their meetings were addressed by Manyaphiri's wife, in her hut.[5]

Colonel Beetham told the tribe firmly that a delegation to Britain was 'not only an utter waste of time, but moreover a complete waste of large sums of money contributed by you Bamangwato'.[6] But the Bangwato didn't agree. Plans were well advanced when suddenly the situation became even more pressing – for they were given the shocking news that the exclusion order against Seretse had been made permanent. On the morning of 28 March 1952, an urgent meeting was held at the Serowe Kgotla, attended by Keaboka, Fraenkel and over 500 people. Fraenkel said that he had made arrangements for six men to go to London, flying from Johannesburg on 6 April. There were Government spies at the meeting: one of the headmen went up to two men, identifying them as plain-clothes policemen, and ordered them to leave.[7]

The six men who were eventually selected as ambassadors for the Bangwato were: Keaboka Kgamane; Peto Sekgoma; Kobe Baitswe, the headman of Selika village in the Tswapong district and a retired trooper in the Bechuanaland Protectorate Police; Mtultwatsi Mpotokwane from Tonota, who had been a Supervisor of Schools; Mongwaketse Mathangwane, a headman from the Bokalaka district; and Gaothobogwe Leposo, a headman from Madinare. Fraenkel would also go, as their legal adviser. The Bangwato asked for a Government official to accompany the delegation, but this was refused.[8] There was a new spirit of hope abroad in the reserve and a request was made to the LMS missionary, Alan Seager, for prayers to be said in the church for the success of the delegation. These were held every Monday and Thursday at seven in the morning and were well attended.[9]

The delegates left Johannesburg by air on 6 April and arrived in Britain in the late afternoon of Wednesday 9 April 1952, after an exhausting journey involving many stopovers. As they descended the steps of the Portuguese airliner which had brought them from Lisbon, their last stop, they were met by a battery of press representatives and newsreel cameramen.[10] Movietone observed that Salisbury had promised to listen to them – 'but offered no hope for their plea'.[11] The

Pathe newsreel was equally pessimistic – 'These visitors *will* be heard, though no change is expected.'[12] John Redfern, the *Daily Express* correspondent who had been sympathetically following the story ever since Ruth's arrival in Serowe in 1949, was one of the waiting journalists. He observed that the visitors from Bechuanaland were dressed in light-coloured, snap-brim hats, and had a worried air.[13]

Lord Rathcreedan was waiting at the airport to welcome them. When he had first agreed to act as Seretse's lawyer, he had taken it on as just another brief; but now, having got to know and like Seretse and Ruth, he was angry about the injustice that had been done to them and the Bangwato. Fenner Brockway, too, had come to the airport, but had to return to the House of Commons before they arrived. The British Government had not sent anyone to greet the delegation. When this was pointed out by the press, one of the delegation remarked that before leaving their homeland they had made a special journey to pay their respects to the Resident Commissioner. 'The implication,' observed Redfern, 'was that courtesy had begun, and ended, at home.'[14] The delegates went straight to Chipstead to be received by Seretse and Ruth and to bring news of home to them and to Naledi. A photograph was taken of them in front of the house, dressed up warmly against the chill of the British spring, with Seretse standing in the middle of the group.[15]

Almost up to the time of their arrival, the Government had flatly refused to see them. All the arguments were already known, insisted John Foster to the House of Commons. This was greeted with cries of 'Shame' from some members, and one MP warned that 'The decision to refuse to see the representatives of the African people who desire to come here to see the Minister is a policy calculated to lead to grave damage to our reputation in Africa.' In the Lords, the Commonwealth Secretary said he would not see the delegation, because there was nothing to be achieved.[16] But he, too, was so heavily criticized that he gave in – an announcement that was met with cheers.[17]

The visitors from Africa were made to wait for nearly two weeks before they were granted a meeting with Salisbury. As they waited, they were frequent visitors to Chipstead, where they spent long hours discussing their strategy with Seretse. The Khamas also went to see them in their hotel in Bloomsbury. 'As Seretse strode into a corner of the lounge,' reported Redfern, 'the six men jumped to their feet. He was their Chief all right.' Some well-wishers took them on tours of the capital:

The visitors thought that the Underground was 'a miracle', as one of them put it. They were particularly delighted by the escalators ... The traffic worried them. Apart from Keaboka, acting as their Chairman, they had hardly any acquaintance with big cities. Mafikeng was a big city to them.[18]

They also attended the meetings that had been arranged by the Seretse Khama Fighting Committee and other organizations. On 15 April, they joined Seretse and Joe Appiah on the platform of Caxton Hall in Westminster, at a meeting organized by Racial Unity, which numbered Mary Attlee, Clement Attlee's sister, among its founders. The delegates did not speak, as they had still to meet with Salisbury and they were afraid it might prejudice their hopes. But they sat behind Seretse on the platform. Ruth and Naledi sat together in the front row; Ruth wore a black spring coat over a lavender dress, with a black hat.

Seretse gave his first public speech since the Government's decision to exile him on a permanent basis. He had been offered a post in Jamaica, he said, where people were much more advanced than the people of Bechuanaland. 'Would I not be more useful in my own country?' he asked. He had been told that his marriage was contrary to native custom, but he could prove this was not the case:

I am not bitter, but I am frustrated ... I am compelled to live here and do absolutely nothing. I find it difficult, for all my Oxford training, to understand the people I have been dealing with – even though some of them have been to Oxford. Perhaps they went to a different college.

'We are a peace-loving people,' he told his audience, then urged:

Don't let your Government teach us racial prejudice. We don't have it. We don't want it. We in Bechuanaland still regard ourselves as British and we still have a great deal of confidence in British justice, fair play and decency. Don't destroy it by allowing your government to carry out this unjust decision without a protest from you.[19]

Seretse made a very good impression and demolished the government's reasons, especially the one concerning his 'lack of responsibility', recorded the Secretary of Racial Unity. It seemed to him that the Government were putting out 'scapegoat reasons' for their policy, which were unfairly – and without any justification – raising doubts about Seretse's personal reputation.[20]

Joe Appiah then spoke. An African Chief, he said, could marry anyone – Seretse's crime was that he had dared to fall in love with a member of the super-race. He added:

We of the Colonial world – we of the coloured world know it as abundantly clear that this matter of Seretse is something that Malan wanted. Both the Labour and Tory Governments flatly deny this, but we know that expediency is always in the background. What has happened on the Gold Coast has given Malan a headache.

'But,' he added, 'there is always the last laugh. What has happened on the Gold Coast will happen in Gambia, Nigeria and elsewhere.'[21]

Officials from the CRO went to the meeting and made careful notes. They estimated that it was attended by 184 people, 80 per cent of whom were female. The women, they observed, were divided into roughly '50% tense bobby-soxers, and 50% elderly suburban matrons, half of whom wore coloured scarfs [sic] as head coverings, and the others a bewildering and staggering array of Lady Baldwin specials [large hats]'. It was a new crowd, they thought – a new generation of activists. There were no India Leaguers, no women like Agatha Harrison, who had supported Gandhi, and no Quakers.[22]

The CRO did not take the members of the delegation from Bechuanaland at all seriously, describing them variously as 'country hayseeds'[23] and 'a band of Chipstead minstrels'.[24] 'I should like to stress', W. A. W. Clark told Herbert Baxter, a senior official, 'that this delegation is unlikely to cut much ice, once the press have got over the glamour of its arrival. I do not think we should be too greatly exercised about its activities. Its members will soon expose their own shortcomings.'[25] What these shortcomings were, he did not explain. Meanwhile, the envoys of the Bangwato were preparing carefully for their meeting with the Secretary of State. Rathcreedan phoned the CRO to explain that

The Delegation was anxious to be able to speak in Kgotla fashion, which meant that each speaker would have his say and Keaboka, the leader, would conclude. He said that he would do his best to ensure that the speeches were as short as possible but he was afraid that they were all naturally rather long-winded. Moreover, as he told me, only one of the Delegation speaks really fluent English and he will be interpreting for the other five. The interpreter, incidentally, will not be Keaboka.[26]

'It is a wearisome prospect for the S of S,' commented Baxter dismissively.[27]

The Secretary of State was given some confidential notes before the meeting. Peto, he was told, was 'a bad type and bitterly hostile to Tshekedi'. Apart from Peto and Keaboka, the men came from allied tribes and were 'of no great standing'. There was no information about how the men had been selected, but the Secretary 'should refrain from treating them as in any way plenipotentiaries of the Tribe as a whole'.[28] It was decided that only Clark and Peter Lewis should attend the Secretary of State at the meeting, so as to diminish the importance of the occasion.[29] The delegation would be attended by Rathcreedan, Fraenkel and Matthew Crosse, Seretse's press agent. 'Lord Rathcreedan is a solicitor,' Baxter told Clark, 'and is agreeable and helpful so far as his duty to his clients allows. Mr Fraenkel, the lawyer, is tough and unfriendly. Mr Crosse is a respectable "public relations" adviser.'[30]

The meeting finally took place on Monday 21 April 1952, shortly after 3.00 in the afternoon. Lord Salisbury spoke first, saying that he regretted the decision about Seretse as much as the tribesmen did, but it had only been taken for the sake of their welfare. Each member of the delegation then spoke in turn, insisting they wanted Seretse to return to them as Kgosi. 'The tribe believed', said Mpotokwane, 'that they had been deprived of their Chief because of a colour bar, and because they were a small nation.' By exiling Seretse, the Government were losing a competent and cooperative helper, who knew Western ways and would be able to bridge the gap between native law and custom and Western ideas.

Kobe Baitswe implored the Secretary of State 'not to give them a snake when they asked for a fish, or a stone when they asked for bread'. Gaothobogwe Leposo said he represented nine villages outside Serowe. He pointed out that after the decision had been announced in March 1950 the Government had called a meeting of the tribe but they had not attended, because they were so grieved. They had stopped paying tax. It was only at Seretse's request, on his departure from the reserve, that they had resumed cooperation with the Government. He added:

In 1895 Chief Khama came to England to ask for protection from those who would intrude into his country. He was very glad when this protection was given, and to show his gratitude he had given Her Majesty's Government a part of his country. To deny the Bamangwato their rightful Chief was a poor return for such loyalty.

'But if Seretse was allowed to return,' Peto assured Salisbury, 'there would be no troubles of any kind. Let the Government try Seretse out for even a fortnight, and this would be proved true.' This was one of the proposals that had been put forward by Seretse himself on several occasions, but without success.

Keaboka introduced himself as the head, for the time being, of the Bangwato. But, he insisted, it had never been his wish to have this position – it had been forced on him, because there was no one else to act as intermediary between the Government and the tribe. It was a very difficult position. The Tribe were aware of the large number of additional police posted to the Reserve, watching the Bangwato leaders as if they were about to do something violent. But, he said,

they were not inclined to violence, and did not wish to fight the Government. The Tribe at present were like a baboon whose little one had been taken away. When this happened the baboon did not think of biting but just came and begged for its child to be returned.

When he went back home, added Keaboka, he would no longer be willing to act in any official capacity:

In 1941 he had been a soldier and had gone to Italy. There the troops had been issued with currency inscribed with the language of Mr Churchill's Atlantic Charter declaration about the four freedoms. These freedoms were now being denied to the Bangwato although they had fought loyally in the war. The Bangwato needed protection from Rhodesia and the Union, but the banishment of Seretse meant that the government favoured the Union.[31]

As he came to the end of his speech, he threw forward his hands and said, 'We ask for bread and you give us stones! Release our Chief!' He handed Salisbury a written memorandum, which had been signed by all six men. The Commonwealth Secretary then shook hands with the delegates, saying he would give them a reply in a few days.[32] The meeting came to an end at 4.50 p.m.

After the meeting, the delegation issued a copy of the memorandum to the press, who wrote sympathetic reports.[33] On the following day, the envoys were invited to meet with Liberal MPs, including the leader, Clem Davies, at the House of Commons.[34] These activities gave the envoys a high profile and on 24 April, three days after the meeting with Salisbury, indignant questions about the treatment of the Bangwato were raised in the House of Commons. One MP commented that very few honourable Members had a good conscience about 'this sad story'.[35]

One week after seeing the delegates, Lord Salisbury met them again, to deliver his reply. He repeated his earlier statement: that a ruler could not enjoy the same freedom as an individual – 'particularly in respect of his marriage'. He handed out copies of the White Paper for them to take back to the Protectorate.

'I pointed out that their claim to represent the tribe was not unchallenged,' Salisbury told the House of Lords the next day. 'Quite recently, for example,' he added, 'persons of high standing in the tribe had seen fit to petition my predecessor [Ismay], contesting their right to speak for the tribe.' This was an attempt to undermine the significance of the delegation. It was immediately picked up by Lord Stansgate, who shared the distaste of his son, Wedgwood Benn, for the Government's treatment of Seretse Khama. Stansgate asked the Commonwealth Secretary for the source of his information and was told that these details could not be given 'for obvious reasons'. This led to a bitter exchange, reported *The Times*:

> *Viscount Stansgate* said that it could not create a good impression if people were told that undisclosed information was available to the Secretary of State which had influenced his mind.

The Marquess of Salisbury said that this was always so in public life. There were always things which could not be disclosed . . . it was a case of what was in the public interest.

Viscount Stansgate It is a question of good faith.

The Marquess of Salisbury I hope the noble lord is not charging the Government with breach of faith. Certainly there is no reason for that. Out of the two hours I listened to the Bamangwato delegates, about three quarters of the time was occupied with complaints of what happened under the previous Government (Ministerial laughter).[36]

John Foster gave an account of the delegates' visit to the House of Commons. He acknowledged that they

represented a majority of the tribe – (Opposition cheers) – but that the views of the majority of the tribe were not the paramount reason for the decision (Opposition cries of 'Oh!').[37]

The members of the delegation gave a press conference. Mpoto-kwane, acting as spokesman, explained that the Bangwato accepted Seretse's marriage. 'We are convinced that we are being very unjustly and unfairly treated,' he said. 'We consider ourselves as human beings and entitled to the same rights and liberties as any other individuals.' The Government's decision, he believed, 'amounts to nothing but cowardice. We are sure that the British public will not tolerate the racial discrimination that the British Government are adopting.'[38]

The envoys were now painfully aware that their mission to Britain was hopeless. But they were determined to bring Seretse home some-how, even if they had to sacrifice the great wish of the Bangwato people – to have Seretse as Kgosi. Accordingly, they proposed the same compromise that had been suggested by Seretse to the Government on various occasions. 'As we informed you,' they wrote to Salisbury in a letter on 5 May, 'we do not think that the Tribe will nominate anyone other than Seretse as Chief. Even if some members of the Tribe were prepared to do so, we cannot see that there is anyone who would command the support of the majority of the Tribe.' This meant that a prolonged period of direct rule was the only way forward, which was unpopular. The only solution, therefore, was for Seretse to return in some capacity other than Chief:

We are convinced that the presence of Seretse in the tribal area is essential if peace and good government are to prevail, and if he cannot be there as Chief, then he should be allowed to return to the area in some other capacity. The Tribe needs his counsel and advice and it is unfortunate that the Government considers that his marriage prevents them from confirming him as Chief.[39]

They asked for another interview, to explain their plan. But this was refused.

On 10 May, a few days before the envoys from Bechuanaland were to return to Africa, they went with Seretse to a meeting organized by Fenner Brockway at Denison House, the home of the Anti-Slavery Society in London. Now that they had seen Salisbury, they were free to speak and they were glad of a chance to give their views. 'We sent our Chief here for education so that we should reap the benefit,' argued Mongwaketse – not so that he should be sent to some other country, like Jamaica. 'When we get home,' he added unhappily, 'there will be no cooperation between us and the Government.' Another member of the delegation, reported the *Manchester Guardian*, expressed surprise that they had been asked to 'appoint' a new Chief when Seretse was still alive and had not abdicated. 'It would be difficult for you,' he pointed out, 'if you were asked to go and appoint to the Throne someone not in the royal line.' He was surprised that Salisbury did not understand the issue of succession, 'for Lord Salisbury, after all, has inherited his title from his father'.

Fenner Brockway was unsparing in his condemnation of the Government's decision – that it was an outrage against democracy, committed by those who claimed they were teaching democracy to Africans. He repeated his argument that one way of solving the racial problem in South Africa, without violence, was by setting an example of racial equality and social justice in Bechuanaland and the other two High Commission Territories.

Seretse, reported the *Manchester Guardian*, was 'dryly ironic' in his comments on the attitude of both the Labour and the Conservative parties. From his experience, said Seretse, it seemed that the Colonial peoples were being used 'only as playthings, or rather as sticks with which to beat political opponents. The Socialists could use him to knock the Conservatives and vice versa.' He argued that the 'black and ignorant' men sitting on the platform – the Bangwato delegates – knew the wishes of their own people better than Lord Salisbury. Probably, he added, he himself was the first black man that Salisbury had ever met. According to the *Guardian*, his speech was 'nicely detached'. Seretse had often protested he was not bitter, it added, but there was something like bitterness in his speech.

John Collins, who was the Canon of St Paul's Cathedral, also spoke, with great force. He was a keen reformer, who had founded Christian Action and wanted the Church of England to take on a much greater level of social responsibility. He urged the audience to do more than simply show sympathy – he told them to work up 'a white heat of fury against the evil of racial discrimination . . . Everyone knew that South Africa was the spectre behind the scenes. Malan and his followers were re-creating the master race theory and threatening the peace of the world.'[40] In 1948, the year he had been appointed Canon of St Paul's Cathedral, Collins had read and been powerfully moved by *Cry, the Beloved Country*. He invited its author, Alan Paton, to preach at St Paul's and to undertake a lecture tour of England – and in this way, Christian Action became committed to opposing apartheid and fighting for racial equality. Collins was very sympathetic towards Seretse and Ruth and had been horrified by the role played by the Anglican Church and the Bishop of London in forbidding their marriage. Many years later, Ruth wrote to Collins's wife to express her gratitude for 'the immense moral support that John gave us in those bad days . . . he was very influential in restoring my faith in the Church and its priests'.[41]

The day after this meeting in London, three of the delegates went with Seretse and Ruth to Birmingham, to attend a large public rally in the Town Hall, which had been organized by the United Nations Association's Midland Regional Council. More than 2,000 people attended and the *Birmingham Post* commented that Seretse 'faced the biggest audience of his life'. This assumption was mistaken, as it was nothing like as large as the Kgotla at Serowe in June 1949, when Seretse was acclaimed as Kgosi – which was attended by about 9,000 men. The meeting in Birmingham was presided over by Daniel Lipson, one of the three Observers sent to Bechuanaland by Gordon Walker. Seretse told the audience that he and his Tribe had lost faith in the

British Government. They had the impression, he said, that they did not belong to the category of first-class British citizens. 'Even if we are coloured and our country is very small and cannot make a military contribution to the Western world,' he said, 'we are entitled to enjoy the rights that belong to every free man throughout the world.' Of his marriage to a white woman, he said, 'This is not a matter that can be put into a little compartment and called an injustice to one or two people. It is a principle that is involved.' He had been in the UK for two or three years, he went on, and during that time

I have been a very good boy. But where has it got me? If it is true, as it has been said, that I am not fit to rule, that I am irresponsible, how can I hope to serve ably and properly the Jamaican people? If I am fit to be the assistant governor of Jamaica, I think I am more fit to be the ruler of my own people.[42]

He asked if Britain was prepared to sacrifice the loyalty of 60 million Africans for the doubtful friendship of Dr Malan.

Then the members of the delegation spoke. Prefacing their speeches with references to 'My Chief and the Mother of my Tribe', they spoke sadly of their disappointments. They still regarded Seretse as their Kgosi: nobody could take his place. He who was born Kgosi, they said, was Kgosi for as long as he lived. They appealed to the British public for their help.[43]

The envoys from the Bangwato Reserve left London for Africa on Thursday 15 May 1952. 'The delegation left the UK empty handed,' noted the CRO with satisfaction.[44] It was certainly true that they had not succeeded in their primary aim: to end the exile of Seretse and Ruth and to bring them home. Nevertheless, their visit had not been without some positive outcomes. As a result of their visibility in the newsreels, the reports of the press, and their appearance at meetings, they had touched the sympathy of the public and put the government on the defensive. They had also made British people more aware of issues about racial inequality, as had the media spotlight on Seretse. 'As I look back on all the publicity,' he had remarked in 1951, 'perhaps the sacrifice of my privacy did some good for at least it exposed the hypocrisy in high places and won the sympathy of most men of good will for the cause of racial equality and understanding.'[45]

But as the envoys journeyed home, they were faced with a painful task: to report on the failure of their mission to Britain. They knew that, ever since their departure, people had been pinning their hopes on the success of the delegation.[46] They would be bitterly disappointed. The Administration were well aware of this and were now on edge: they were regularly spying on the Bangwato and were also tapping telephones and opening letters. If anyone wanted to guarantee that a letter would not be opened by officials, they had to go to South Africa or to Southern Rhodesia to post it.[47] The gentle Germond had been replaced as District Commissioner by Gordon Batho, who had been brought in as a strong man. Batho was a strapping South African in his late thirties, with dark, wavy hair parted in the middle. His attitude was confrontational and, wherever he went, there seemed to be trouble.

20

Sorrow in Serowe

The delegates arrived back from London in Serowe in the early hours of 21 May 1952, weary and troubled. They went straight to the Kgotla, where about 1,000 people were waiting for them. In silence, Salisbury's written reply to their mission was read out and translated. As the news slowly sank in, a sense of bitter disappointment spread through the Reserve.[1] Later that day, Keaboka resigned his office as Senior Tribal Representative.[2]

A Kgotla was arranged for Monday 26 May, so as to allow five days for people to travel to Serowe from the outlying areas. A large gathering turned up, of between 2,000 and 3,000 men, to hear the delegation give the full details of Salisbury's reply. But they were angry. They did not stand up when the British officials arrived, as they usually did, but continued to sit in the shade of the makala trees. Seretse's supporters had their backs to the seats occupied by Batho and his four white officials, while followers of Tshekedi faced the platform. There were angry murmurings and when Batho called on Peto to quieten things down he did not respond.[3] The District Commissioner had difficulty at the best of times when he gave orders to the Bangwato, many of whom disliked him and thought it was strange that in Setswana, his name – *Batho* – meant 'people'.[4]

There was a call for 'the usual prayer', but this simply added to the tension. Two men prayed at the same time: a supporter of Seretse with his back to the platform, and a supporter of Tshekedi facing it.[5] Then Batho started to read Lord Salisbury's reply. He was interrupted by people saying they wanted Seretse back, which was met with loud applause. Batho argued that they did not seem to understand Salisbury's reply; he said he would read it aloud and 'if necessary explain what it means'. This made the assembly furious – because they understood perfectly well what it meant. Men stood up, shaking their fists and hurling insults. Batho tried to call the meeting to order, but by now there was so much noise it was impossible for him to be heard.[6]

Suddenly, a group of women burst into the Kgotla. 'For the first time in the history of the tribal Kgotlas,' reported the *Rand Daily Mail*, 'women came into the picture':

> They stood in front of the dais, shouting and gesticulating and screaming: 'We want Seretse' and 'May you die where you're sitting.'
> Said Mr Batho: 'I'll give you a hearing when you've given me one.'

One woman shouted: 'Seretse should lead us . . . You have tried to rule us with a rod of iron. You treat us like ants. We won't have you.' Then a group of women surrounded the offices near the Kgotla, at which point Batho fled to his car. They chased after him as he drove off.[7]

Next day, Keaboka and the Serowe elders wrote a letter to the British High Commissioner, stating their refusal to accept any Kgosi other than Seretse and announcing a fresh campaign of non-cooperation.[8] Sir John Le Rougetel worried that the Administration was losing control. He decided it was time to take action against 'the Keaboka group' and authorized the Resident Commissioner to close the Kgotla.[9]

On the morning of Saturday 31 May, officials toured Serowe in a lorry. They shouted out through a loud-hailer that the Kgotla was closed, which was met with shouts of angry protest. Four policemen were then stationed in the Kgotla and a white line was drawn across the mouth of the entrance, beyond which no one was allowed to go. In the afternoon it was announced, again by loud-hailer, that the law against brewing and the consumption of liquor would be strictly enforced. At 5.30 p.m., Batho was told that over 100 people had pushed past the police pickets and assembled in the Kgotla. He went straight there and gave them five minutes to disperse, but about forty men – including Peto and Keaboka – refused to go and were taken to gaol. About 300 people, including women, followed them and sang hymns outside the gaol. The prisoners were released the following morning, but were warned that a summons would be issued against them.

The Administration had called for reinforcements from Basutoland of African police, who arrived before daybreak on Sunday morning. Then some people started to assemble outside the Kgotla – about 50 men and 200–300 women. They wanted to hold a religious service in the kgotla and had asked Reverend J. Cidraas, a minister of the LMS, to conduct it for them. Cidraas consulted Batho, who said that so long as it remained a religious service he would not interfere – but people must disperse immediately, once it was over.[10] Hymn-books were issued and people started their service, singing hymns for several hours; speeches were also made, demanding the return of Seretse. Batho went to the Kgotla and tried to speak, but each time he did so, his voice was drowned out by a crescendo of hymns. Eventually he shouted through a megaphone that they must finish their singing before 2.30 p.m.[11] At lunchtime, people left.

By three in the afternoon, about 600 people had assembled outside the Kgotla and were shouting loudly. Dennis Atkins and a 'European' Sub-Inspector tried to take charge, standing in front of the police and trying to calm the people down. But the police were rushed at by the crowd and Atkins was attacked by stones and knocked down; he was rescued by the police, all of whom were wounded.

Shortly afterwards, the Basuto reinforcements occupied the Kgotla. Then the police took up a position across its mouth, in a double line. They were faced by a huge crowd – over 800 people. Then Batho arrived, at 3.30 p.m. He ordered a police lorry to be driven right into the Kgotla and warned the crowd that if they did not disperse within five minutes, tear gas would be released. No one left. A police officer fired a gas shell and immediately there was panic and confusion. Some of the ex-servicemen were familiar with tear gas, because of their wartime experience. But many people had no idea what it was, so the gas had the opposite effect to that which was intended: people surged forward and rained showers of stones on the police, many of whom were themselves overcome by the gas.[12] The scene was chaotic and an officer sounded a retreat, instructing the policemen to drive off in the waiting lorries.

Some of the policemen had became separated from the main party and were left behind. One Basuto sergeant escaped to a village about a mile away but was found and hammered to death. Two other Basuto policemen were killed as well. One of them appeared to have been killed as he fell off the lorry that was driven into the Kgotla, crushed under the wheels of the lorry behind.[13] In addition, about twenty policemen were admitted to hospital. Many of the Bangwato were badly injured, too, but few sought medical care at the hospital in case they were picked up by the police. Until late that evening, every Government vehicle moving within Serowe was stoned on sight.[14]

The Police Superintendent from Francistown arrived to take charge and moved the police from the security camp to the low hill occupied by the European residents, who were terrified. The white women and children were corralled together. By this time, the telephone and telegraph line between Serowe and Palapye had been cut at several points and the only means of communication left was by wireless, for which conditions were poor. During the night, the police officer in charge of the Northern Protectorate arrived, as well as the Commissioner of Police from Mafikeng. Fraenkel phoned from Mafikeng and offered to go to Serowe and intervene, to avoid further bloodshed, but Beetham did not accept his offer.

'Not a single police vehicle has now any glass left in it,' reported Sir John to London next day.[15] The first plane-load of British South Africa police from Southern Rhodesia arrived at 9.30 in the morning, with 'ten Europeans and 70 African ranks'.[16] By four in the afternoon there were about 5,000 people at the Kgotla, but no action was taken against them – there were just too many people to be dispersed. Seager and Cidraas went to the Kgotla, where people were singing hymns. Seager took a service, 'choosing hymns as carefully as I could'. After the service the men explained why they were so distressed – 'The Kgotla is ours.'[17]

Police set up road-blocks, stopping every lorry, and the atmosphere throughout the Reserve was heavy and tense. The Administration was panicked by the fact that 'everywhere in Serowe there is an inexhaustible supply of stones which tribesmen use as ammunition' and several women collecting stones in buckets were arrested.[18] But early patrols on Tuesday found the village quiet. There was now only a handful of people in the Kgotla: during the night there had been an exodus from Serowe by lorry and on foot. Thousands of people had packed up their things and trekked off to their cattle stations.

In the late afternoon, lorries full of police, armed with tear-gas bombs, rifles and bayonets, truncheons, pick-handles and wickerwork shields, carried out sweeps of the area and made many arrests, including Keaboka and Peto.[19] At Palapye the police encountered serious resistance: a crowd of about fifty men and women were waiting for them, armed with sticks, stones, pieces of iron and an axe.[20] The crowd was eventually dispersed by tear gas and batons, but suffered many casualties in the struggle.[21]

Nearly 170 people were arrested altogether, including 40 women.[22] Fraenkel, who had come up to the Reserve at the urgent request of the Bangwato, protested against the violence of the police. On one occasion, he complained, the prisoners were beaten up by African police in the presence of European police, who looked on and laughed. They were also kept in miserable conditions. Seventy-eight men, with only one blanket each, were gaoled in a motor shed that was open on one side to the chill night of Bechuanaland's winter. When Peto, Keaboka and nineteen other men were moved from Serowe in the middle of the night to Gaberones gaol in the south of the Protectorate, 200 miles away, they were taken in an open motor truck, with nothing to wear except the clothes in which they had been arrested. Keaboka was sentenced to fourteen days intensive hard labour for spitting at a white Sub-Inspector. Women prisoners had the additional humiliation of being conducted by male police into the veld when they needed to relieve themselves.[23]

The High Commissioner had no illusions about the reason for the riot. 'We must accept as a fact,' he stated in a telegram to London on 9 June, 'the general desire of the tribe to have Seretse as their Kgosi.'[24] He added that he was hoping to rally the support of the many tribesmen who – however much they wanted Seretse back – were opposed to violence. For this reason, he asked the CRO to be extremely careful to avoid giving the false impression that the rioters were a mob, and the worse for drink. 'Any suggestion that responsible tribesmen are already on our side or that the rioters were merely a drunken rabble', he warned, 'will have precisely the opposite effect.'[25]

But Sir John's request went unheeded. John Foster reported to the House of Commons that the attacks in the Serowe Kgotla on 1 June had been made by a big crowd – 'many of them the worse for drink and among whom were many women'. The rioters, he added, were 'a minority rabble'.[26] Churchill summed up his account: 'Indeed a terrible position. An angry mob, armed with staves and stones, inflamed by alcohol, and inspired by Liberal principles.'[27]

But Jennie Lee was convinced this was not true and tackled Foster on his statement, especially his allegation that the women were drunk. 'There was one passage in the hon. and learned Gentleman's statement,' she said, 'which I should like to have clarified' –

when he used the phrase 'the worse for drink', he at the same time said that the women took a very active part in those demonstrations. I know we all want to be careful about statements which go out from this House, and I think the impression could legitimately have been given that the women were drunk, and that therefore their action was irresponsible and unrepresentative.

I think it is very important that we should have this point clear, because Mrs Seretse Khama got on very well with her husband's tribeswomen. There is a good deal of strong feeling there.

Then she reminded MPs of the excellent impression that had been made by the recent envoys from Bechuanaland:

Many of us were impressed by the members of the delegation to this country. They seemed responsible and, in fact, distinguished men, and therefore it is very hard for us to accept the impression given in the statement that this was just an unrepresentative rabble and that the women taking part were drunk.[28]

Because of Jennie Lee's intervention, the CRO was obliged to ask the High Commissioner's Office for a report on whether or not women had been drunk. The reply from Africa was unmistakeable: 'On 1 June women were in state of extreme excitement but there is no evidence that this was due to drink. Of the men only some appeared to be drunk.'[29] But no statement was made to the House of Commons to correct Foster's earlier announcement.

Of the 167 people arrested, twelve men were charged with murder, all of whom were imprisoned in a barbed-wire cage in the thorn scrub at Lobatse, including one man who was blind.[30] Bail was set so high – as high as £1,000 for each of thirteen people – that no one could possibly afford to pay.[31] In London, the Seretse Khama Campaign

Committee opened new committee rooms near Paddington to raise money for the defence of those on trial. The *Guardian* reported that among the first to come forward were Africans attending British universities.[32] The Campaign Committee had changed its name from 'Fighting Committee' under its current Chairman, Monica Whately, a Catholic feminist and pacifist, who was a strong advocate of colonial freedom and had worked with Ellen Wilkinson and Krishna Menon in the 1930s in the India League, which had campaigned for self-rule.

The defendants' counsel, Mr Vieyra, argued that one of the policemen killed in the riot had not been murdered, but struck by a lorry. Under cross-examination, a police lieutenant admitted that the crowd had been orderly when the police arrived.[33] Mr Vieyra described the closing of the Kgotla as the trigger for the violence:

the riot took place for closing the Kgotla – an unprecedented incident. The Kgotla is their traditional meeting place and this closing annoyed them. Although the action of the District Commissioner, as Native Authority, may be justified in law ... it is against native law and custom and such action would not be understood by the accused.[34]

The trials reached their conclusion in November 1952. Seven of the men charged with murder were sentenced to three years' hard labour, including Keaboka and Peto. 'Hard labour' meant long hours of useless and exhausting work in the hot sun – such as breaking rocks or digging a hole and then filling it up.[35] The remaining men who had been charged with murder were either discharged or acquitted. Twelve months' hard labour was the sentence given to two young mothers, one of whom had a baby only a few weeks old.[36]

The riot of 1 June 1952 had left the Bangwato Reserve in a state of shock and grief. 'We are very surprised at the recent happenings and to see women in riots,' commented one man unhappily – but the whole community was suffering without Seretse. 'If you pass small children not more than three years old in this village,' he said, 'you will hear them talking about the nomination of Seretse. Even the children are sad about it.'[37] The memory of the riot would remain vivid for a generation and the babies born at that time were called Mokubukubu, 'the children of the riots'.[38] The atmosphere remained tense. The police reinforcements from neighbouring countries were kept in the region and ammunition permits were refused to Africans, who were told to use poison to keep down lions and leopards, instead of guns.[39]

Now that Keaboka and Peto were in prison, there was a vacuum in the leadership of Seretse's supporters. To maintain the campaign for the return of their Kgosi, a new organization called the Bamangwato National Congress was founded by Leetile Raditladi, with the support of Lenyeletse Seretse, Monametsi Chiepe and some others. One of their aims, explained Raditladi in *Naledi ya Batswana* on 2 August 1952, was to find a way of uniting the different factions of the Bangwato. As part of their manifesto, they nominated Oratile as acting Kgosi – 'Princess Oratile Sekgoma Khama, the highest scion of blue blood in the land, to be the Head of the Bamangwato People and Administration', assisted by a representative and elected body of men.[40] Oratile, whom Ruth described as 'a lovable and generous person',[41] commanded wide respect and affection. After the riot, she was often in Lobatse, supporting and helping the men and women on trial at the High Court.

This was the second time that Oratile had been put forward as a leader to replace the banished Seretse. Two years earlier, she had been nominated as President of a Council and the proposal had been rejected outright by the Resident Commissioner and the Government. But this time, the Resident Commissioner thought that Oratile might offer a solution to their problems: a Chief who would be approved by the Tribe as an alternative to Seretse.[42] He sent this view to the High Commissioner's Office. But next day a strongly worded message came back from Sir John – that Oratile would *not* do.[43] London took the same line. The appointment of Oratile, wrote Salisbury to Sir John was 'out of the question' – she was not suitable and Tshekedi would never rest so long as she was in office. The Tribe had to be reminded, he said, that there was 'no precedent in Bamangwato history for [the] appointment of a woman as chief'.[44]

Salisbury was right that there was no precedent in the history of the Bangwato for a woman Chief. But women in other parts of the Protectorate had taken leadership roles. Among the Bangwaketse, Gagoangwe and her daughter Ntebogang had served as Regents for Kgosi Bathoen II from 1923 to 1928.[45] And when Oratile's name was put forward in 1950 and 1952, Mrs Moremi was the Regent of the Batawana.[46] The reason for Salisbury's objection to Oratile was not that she was a woman, but that she was closely linked to Seretse. As Le Rougetel warned, many Bangwato would regard her appointment 'as keeping the Chief's chair warm for Seretse'.[47]

The Commonwealth Secretary set out to the British High Commissioner the details of a three-point programme: getting Seretse out of the Chieftainship and the Protectorate for a long time; getting Tshekedi back into the Reserve as a private individual; and promoting the appointment of Rasebolai Kgamane as Chief.[48] Rasebolai was next in royal seniority after Tshekedi. However, he was not of the House of Khama, like Seretse, Tshekedi and Oratile, but of the House of Kgamane, Khama's brother, which had a reputation as warriors rather than statesmen. The CRO argued that Kgamane's war record, as the only regimental Sergeant-Major from Bechuanaland in the Second World War, made him eminently suitable for office. In the view of his Commanding Officer, 'RSM Rasebolai had not only all the real dignity of an African of good breeding, but he had a modesty of demeanour and above all, that rarest of all things in the African, a capacity for understanding the white man.'[49] But the chief reason for Rasebolai's appeal to the CRO – especially to those mandarins who continued to back Tshekedi, notably W. A. W. Clark – was his close relationship with the former Regent: he had gone with Tshekedi to Rametsana in 1950 and was his leading supporter. If he were to become Kgosi, he would become a channel through which Tshekedi could exert control over the Bangwato.

In August, the exclusion order on Tshekedi was finally lifted. He was now allowed to return to the Bangwato Reserve, though he was not allowed to take part in political affairs. But he and his followers did not return to Serowe, knowing they would not be welcome. Instead, they established a new village called Pilikwe, south of the Tswapong Hills, about fifty miles from Serowe.[50] Under Tshekedi's iron rule, Pilikwe swiftly became a model village. A new junior official from Britain, George Winstanley, was impressed. 'The thatching was immaculate,' he found, 'and untended sheep and goats were not tolerated in the village. There was not a scrap of litter to be seen.'[51] In his office, Tshekedi had a plentiful library – classics, Shakespeare,

Dickens, modern novels, works on law and colonial legislatures, history and economics, horse and cattle breeding, irrigation and education, as well as manuals of instruction on mechanics, fruit-growing and football.[52]

Winstanley was surprised, though, by the extreme deference accorded to the former regent. One day, when he was taking tea with Tshekedi on his veranda, one of Tshekedi's women servants brought him a message. When she approached her master, she was 'so low that she was almost on her knees and after he had received the message she retreated in similar fashion'. Winstanley wondered if the woman was disabled, but Tshekedi explained that his servants usually approached him in this way. 'Nobody ever walked past him without acknowledging his presence,' said Winstanley. 'The villagers stopped and bowed and greeted him with a gentle soundless clapping of their hands.'[53]

Le Rougetel was putting pressure on the Administration to deliver the results demanded by Salisbury. At the start of September, Beetham distributed letters throughout the Bangwato Reserve, in English on one side and Setswana on the other, announcing the return of Tshekedi and the need to choose a new Chief.[54] Batho held a meeting with royal headmen of the Bangwato as well as diKgosi from other parts of the Protectorate, who agreed that an Assembly should be held on 11 November. For this, the Serowe Kgotla would at last be opened.[55]

But many people were unhappy about the proposed Assembly, especially because Keaboka and Peto were still in prison. At a meeting in the village of Sefhare, strong feelings were expressed. 'The government is a snake, or chameleon,' complained one man, 'it changes colour every day.' Then he referred indignantly to the presence at the meeting of an informer:

I see a policeman at the meeting. I know that he represents the DC and I know that he will report the things that we say in this meeting. We are going to fight again. If a Rametsana man were to touch me now, I will fight him. I do not care if I am arrested. I have been in gaol before.

The policeman who was exposed made careful notes. The overall tone of the meeting, he reported, was highly charged: 'Most men appeared to be very angry. They seemed to shiver as they spoke.'[56]

Early in the morning of Monday 10 November 1952, the Kgotla

was officially opened by Batho, for the first time in over five months. Security police stood by, with two armoured cars. Up to 2,500 men had come from every direction and the diKgosi of six other nations had also arrived. So had Fraenkel, at the request of the Bangwato. Tshekedi, who had been visiting Serowe, greeted the diKgosi and then left, as he was debarred from taking part in politics.[57]

Batho told the Assembly about the need to appoint a new Chief and he renewed the Government's promise that no Chief would be imposed. Then he opened up the discussion. Raditladi made the first speech, in which he argued that Rasebolai had not been accepted back in Serowe by the Bangwato people; this was heard with enthusiastic applause.[58] By the next day, well over 3,000 men had assembled. 'Government promised not to force a Chief on us,' objected Oabona Nthobatsang, 'and it is shameful that Government should now try to force one on us. You can kill us but we stick to our decision – we want Seretse only. He has committed no wrong.' This was followed by long and hearty applause and *pulas*.[59] On the third day of the Kgotla, low rain-clouds hung over Serowe and the men looked anxiously at the sky, reported the *Star*, 'thinking of their lands, which should have already been ploughed'. No decision had been reached, but Batho dispersed the assembly:

I can see that the Tribe as a whole has not made up its mind to designate a Chief. I have, therefore, decided to disperse this meeting until after the ploughing season is over. You may now go to your lands and plough.[60]

'My closing speech,' he reported, 'was received in complete silence.'[61]

Batho had not got the consensus he wanted in favour of Rasebolai. But at least the Bangwato of Serowe had got their Kgotla back. Every day, groups of men met there informally to talk together.[62] Life had returned to normal in many ways and the ploughing season passed uneventfully. But life in Serowe had lost its centre. A correspondent for *The Times* reported that it seemed to have gone downhill. 'The huts have a dilapidated air,' he noticed, 'and where they have fallen into disrepair have not been attended to.' This was no doubt caused by the problem of drought followed by rains but it also, he thought, 'reflects the listlessness of the people and is one of the disadvantages of not having a Chief'.[63]

V

Colonial Freedom
'The Big Issue of This Century'

21

A watershed in opinion

At the end of the 1940s there had been little expression of concern in Britain about the welfare of the people of Africa. But by the start of the 1950s, argued Trevor Huddleston, an Anglican churchman and human rights campaigner working in South Africa, this was starting to change: questions were being asked about the practice of imperial rule and the future of the African colonies. One important reason for this was the growing awareness of the evil of apartheid. Before the election of the Nationalist Party, few people had understood what was at stake in South Africa. After all, wrote Huddleston, Jan Smuts had been one of the great wartime leaders and had also played a major role in drafting the constitution of the United Nations – and he was a South African. Furthermore, even if he had been defeated by Malan in 1948, the fact of Malan's election was proof of the democratic structure of his country, even if the electorate was an all-white one.

But since then, there had been a string of laws increasing the divide between whites and blacks and diminishing even further the quality of life of black people. The passing of the Natives (Abolition of Passes and Coordination of Documents) Act now meant that all African men were compelled to carry a pass or reference book. Canon John Collins drew attention to these evils in 1952, when he preached a sermon at St Paul's Cathedral in which he described Malan as 'this poor wretched man hag-ridden with fear'. After this, the press began to pay serious attention to the issue of racism in a Commonwealth country – that, as Huddleston put it, 'anti-Semitism and the atrocities perpetrated by the Nazis were not the *only* forms of racism alive and kicking in our world'. It would be hard, said Huddleston, to exaggerate the importance of this change at that time, because it was 'a kind of watershed dividing the South Africa of the Empire and Common-wealth . . . from the South Africa in which the majority, being black, had begun their struggle for freedom and deserved support because they were oppressed'. This made people think hard not only about South Africa, but also about the inequalities of British rule in Africa. One could say, believed Huddleston, 'that it was an awakening in every way comparable to that at the beginning of Wilberforce's campaign against the slave trade'.[1]

An additional influence on this watershed in opinion was the move-ment of the Gold Coast towards the installation of an all-African Cabinet Government, which was the first of its kind to be established in British Africa. In 1952, Kwame Nkrumah became the country's first prime minister. All over Africa, following the end of the war, demands within British colonies for self-rule had grown louder and stronger, and were at last bearing fruit. What had seemed impossible before the war – African independence – was clearly going to become a reality in the near future. This had led to a sense of futility among some colonial administrators: the Colonial Office observed the preva-lence of a feeling that 'the show isn't going to last much longer anyway and it doesn't matter'.[2]

There was growing concern about racial inequalities and exclusion. A series of minutes between officials at the CO discussed a need to 'arouse interest in and friendliness towards Africans as human beings (and not only as domestic servants)', and the CO wrote to the Arch-bishop of Canterbury to ask for help with ideas to reduce friction from racial antipathies.[3]

The injustices suffered by 'natives' in British colonies were exem-plified in Kenya. In every sphere of life, there was segregation of Africans, Asians and whites – in terms of where they lived, where their children went to school, and in clinics and hospitals. Nor were they just segregated: essential services for black people were scant and inadequate. Nearly all the good land had been seized by white settlers, who prosecuted the colour bar vigorously. In the early 1950s, these injustices led to an outbreak of unrest which became known as the Mau Mau uprising and which was mercilessly put down by the Col-onial Government, under the leadership of Sir Evelyn Baring, the Governor – the very same Evelyn Baring who had pushed through the exile of Seretse Khama. As soon as Baring arrived in Nairobi on 30 September 1952 to take up his new appointment as Governor – fresh from his position as the British High Commissioner of South Africa – he was immediately put under immense pressure by the European settlers to crush the rebellion. Just over a week after his arrival, on 9 October, he cabled London to advocate a state of emergency; he also asked for more troops to be rushed to the colony.

Six months later, Baring had Jomo Kenyatta, who had returned to Kenya from the UK the year before, convicted for being the leader of the 'terrorist' movement of the Mau Mau. Kenyatta's trial, which took place at Kapenguria, was based on fabricated evidence. Baring had set him up, just as he had tried to set Seretse Khama up at the Harragin Inquiry in Bechuanaland in 1949, which effectively served as a rehearsal for Kapenguria.[4] Up to this point, the Mau Mau rebellion had been relatively minor. But now, in response to Baring's ruthless measures, it erupted into a mass movement, leading to a colossal loss of life and suffering by the Kikuyu people.[5]

Before Baring's arrival as governor, the Kenya African Union had articulated a clear and firm opposition to the appointment, because of his role in the exile of Seretse. It passed a resolution describing him as 'an official closely identified with the policy of appeasement of South Africa who has apparently approved South Africa's racialist policies'. Such a Governor, who had handled Bechuanaland's affairs so disastrously, stated the resolution, could never be acceptable to Africans – and urged Her Majesty's Government to appoint someone else.[6] But their plea went unheeded.

As far as Fenner Brockway was concerned, the Mau Mau crisis was of a piece with a larger picture of colonial inequality, like the treatment of Seretse and Ruth Khama. In the summer of 1952, he decided to intensify the campaign to end their exile.[7] The Seretse Khama Campaign Committee had served a valuable role, but it was largely a fringe organization and had little impact on mainstream public opinion. What was needed, reasoned Brockway, was an all-party committee, in order to make use of the sympathy and support of well-known people across the political spectrum and from the fields of education, the arts, religion and athletics.

The outcome of Brockway's thinking was the creation of the

Council for the Defence of Seretse Khama and the Protectorates. He was Chairman, the Vice-Chairman being Jo Grimond, a Liberal MP; the Treasurer was Anthony Wedgwood Benn. Members included the Conservatives Earl Baldwin and Lord Boyd-Orr, and Labour supporters such as the Reverend Sorensen, Lord Stansgate, and the campaigner Sir Richard Acland. Other members included Canon Collins, the cinematographer Frank Byers, Learie Constantine, MacDonald Bailey, the actors Alec Guinness and Dame Sybil Thorndike, the writer Sir Compton Mackenzie, Kingsley Martin, who was the editor of the *New Statesman*, the playwright and Labour politician Benn Levy, and Charles Njonjo. The Council was not intended to replace the Campaign Committee, which continued its work, but to bring Seretse's case more directly into the public eye.

The aim of the Council was primarily to secure 'the recognition of the right of Seretse Khama to return to Bechuanaland as Chief of the Bamangwato Tribe', but it also called for the right of Tshekedi to take part in the political life of Bechuanaland. These demands were made within the context of a larger objective: the need to develop all three of the High Commission Territories 'educationally, socially, and economically, so that they may become models of racial equality and African development'.[8] In this way, believed Fenner Brockway, they would be able to influence South Africa, 'where the colour bar operates so viciously'.[9]

Officials at the Commonwealth Relations Office watched the formation of this new Council in dismay. 'The organisation chiefly concerned hitherto,' observed one, 'has been the Seretse Khama Campaign Committee, which has been a small affair under Communist influence'. But the new Council under Fenner Brockway's chairmanship, they realized, was 'clearly intended to be a much more influential body with a wider basis'. But there was nothing to be done, 'except to prepare for the projected assault on the Government'.[10] The campaign began in earnest on 16 February 1953, with a deputation to the Commonwealth Secretary. Signatures were collected for a huge petition to Parliament, supported by well-known people including the playwright Christopher Fry, the artist Augustus John, Bertrand Russell, the novelist Ethel Mannin, the actor Michael Redgrave, and A. J. Cummings of the *News Chronicle*. When 10,800 signatures had been collected, the petition was presented to Parliament on 23 March 1954.[11]

For quite a while, CRO officials had been carefully watching meetings at which Seretse spoke; they did not think of him as an instigator, but simply as 'a pawn in the hands of the "woolly-woollies"'.[12] But now, as he started working closely with the Council in the autumn of 1952, his speeches became more powerful and more effective.[13] 'Whenever Seretse speaks,' reported the Council in a letter to the people of the Bangwato Reserve, 'he wins the sympathy and support of the British people.'[14] He went all over Britain – to Glasgow, Edinburgh, Leeds, Sheffield, Port Talbot and other parts of Wales – to tell the British people about Bechuanaland, its people, their customs and their problems.[15] Many local newspapers had articles like one in the *Yorkshire Post* entitled 'Seretse Khama pays a visit', with a photograph of Seretse with smiling schoolgirls.[16] There was a large meeting at Hammersmith Hospital in London, where Naledi was working as a nurse. His listeners were particularly struck when he told them that in Bechuanaland elderly people were looked after by their families, not put in homes for the aged.[17]

The Council was a leading organization in the growing movement for black Africa in the UK. Another organization was the Africa Bureau, set up in March 1952; it was financed by David Astor and directed by Reverend Michael Scott, with considerable help from Mary Benson. Journalists for the *Observer*, such as Colin Legum and Anthony Sampson, were also involved. Out of the activity that led up to the setting up of the Bureau emerged a book called *Attitude to Africa*, published by Penguin in 1951. 'A whole continent is stirring into political life,' observed an editorial in the *Observer*, 'and we in Britain are as directly responsible for the political fate of whole African communities as the people of America are for what happens in their Southern States.' The Bureau felt particularly strongly about the planned creation of the Federation of Rhodesia and Nyasaland, on the grounds that it was opposed by the Africans in the territories. Although it did identify the exile of Seretse as an injustice that needed to be addressed, it was far more concerned about Tshekedi and worked energetically to support him.[18]

*

On 27 February 1953, the Khamas had a second child – a boy, Seretse Khama Ian Khama. His second name was requested by a group of Serowe elders, in memory of the Great Khama III. Seretse Khama Ian's birth changed Tshekedi's position in the Bangwato nation, because he superseded Tshekedi in the line of succession after Seretse. On 10 March 1953, when baby Ian was just twelve days old, the Council for the Defence of Seretse Khama called a press conference in a room at the House of Commons, which was attended by Seretse. Cables were read from leading members of the Bangwato, pledging loyalty to Seretse and his son. It was known 'all round the Ngwato tribe', said one telegram, 'that the 4th Khama is born. Again WE humbly request the Government to return our Chief Seretse and family back . . . We can never change our opinion.'[19] Another cable congratulated

both Chief Seretse Khama and Ruth Khama for having a baby boy whose only name is Khama – *Pula! Pula! Pula!* We ask that he and the family come and live amongst us. We want to nurse him ourselves . . . We, the Bangwato, Seretse's people, want that child here.[20]

'We are like sheep in a jungle and there being attacked by a leopard,' was one sad message.[21]

Brockway briskly announced the start of a new nationwide campaign to annul the banishment against Seretse.[22] Seretse himself spoke briefly, recalling that the chieftainship was hereditary: 'So long as it is the desire of the tribe that I should be Chief – and information from Bechuanaland indicates that this is so – I am ready to serve them to the best of my capacity.'[23]

Towards the end of this busy year, Seretse and Ruth decided it was time to leave Chipstead. With their growing family, they needed more space, and they also wanted to find a friendlier neighbourhood, where people were less conscious of racial difference. They found a house in Addiscombe, a suburb near Croydon, twelve miles from London, where things started to change. 'People have seemed more friendly to us,' said Ruth, relieved. 'Whenever I go shopping in the market with Seretse, people chat with us, and seem pleased to see us. Little Jacqueline has made friends at school, and she brings them home for little spreads and things.'[24] The house had a small strip of garden around it, where the children could play. A special pleasure for Seretse, who badly missed the vast spaces of Bechuanaland, were the open fields nearby, where he and Ruth went horse-riding.[25] Brockway often came to visit and was pleased to see that in Addiscombe they were treated by their neighbours 'without a trace of colour feeling'. Three of the neighbours had cars and they would take it in turns to give the children a lift to school.[26]

England was becoming an easier place to live, without the austerity and controls of the early postwar period. Meat stayed on the ration books until July 1954, but other foods that had been rationed for a long time, such as eggs and sugar, were now widely available. Televisions and refrigerators were found in more homes, as well as other modern amenities. By the time of the next election, in 1955, observed Brockway, the Tories were able to say with some truth, 'You've Never Had it so Good.'[27]

Every Sunday, Ruth cooked a curry or a joint for lunch and the house was full of friends. The Khamas' Croydon home, recalled Charles Njonjo years later, was 'a haven to many people from everywhere' – Ruth, he said, was very welcoming and proud of her home. Seretse had his 'own' pub, where he was popular; he and Charles used to go there on Sunday morning, while lunch was cooking.[28] The Khamas were finally able to enjoy a settled family life. People seemed to think, said Ruth, that the pressure of exile must have led to a 'good old family tiff', but this was not the case – 'We have them, of course. But they are mostly over the children. Seretse wants to spoil them. I have to do all the disciplining.' But they were perfectly united in their marriage. 'Seretse and I', she stated firmly, 'are one race. Colour doesn't enter into it. It never has.'[29]

A reporter from the *Evening Standard* came to Addiscombe to interview Seretse in their 1936 Tudor-style house, with black beams and leaded windows. In the firelit lounge, she said, leopard-skin karosses hung on the old walls, adding 'a magnificence that the Tudors never knew'. She heard Seretse telling his children about life in Africa – 'You don't like animals,' accused his daughter Jackie, as he described a lion hunt. 'Yes I do,' he explained gently, 'but lions must be killed because they eat the cattle.' Then Jackie, wearing jodhpurs because she had just come back from her weekly riding lesson, took 'a spectacular leap' into her father's lap and his reflective face burst into a smile. One thing was certain, said the reporter – this was a marriage that would last. She quoted a crisp comment made by Ruth: '*All marriage is an experiment. It is not the race, or races, of the couple concerned, but the couple themselves.*'[30]

'Our house became quite a cosmopolitan centre,' said Ruth. 'We were visited by West Indians, Africans, Indians, Arabs and Americans.'[31] Visitors from Africa included a number of South Africans who were leaders in the struggle against apartheid. Walter Sisulu, the Secretary-General of the ANC, came to Addiscombe during a visit to London for political reasons. He found Seretse especially impressive in his understanding of the South African situation and he raised with him the possibility of reviving political activity in the High Commission Territories.[32] Sisulu was accompanied to the Khamas' home by Lionel Ngakane, a South African film maker who had gone into exile in the UK after his work on the 1951 film of *Cry, the Beloved Country*; this film of Alan Paton's novel, starring Sidney Poitier, was a powerful and harrowing portrayal of the suffering caused by racism, and contributed to the growing criticism of apartheid among the British public. Like Seretse, Ngakane was a graduate of Fort Hare and had also been to Wits.

Joe Appiah and Peggy Cripps were frequent visitors. Joe, who was appointed Prime Minister Nkrumah's Personal Representative to the UK in 1953, had married Peggy in London on 18 July of that year. Their marriage did not lead to exile, as had Seretse's and Ruth's, because Joe's nation, the Gold Coast, did not border on South Africa. And whereas Ruth came from an ordinary middle-class family, with no influence, Peggy was the youngest daughter of Sir Stafford Cripps, who had been Chancellor of the Exchequer in the Labour Government. Perhaps, too, it helped that the Gold Coast, was under the aegis of the more enlightened Colonial Office, rather than the Commonwealth Relations Office – and also that attitudes among the general public in Britain had started to change since the Khamas' marriage in 1948. Even so, Joe and Peggy did not escape racist abuse, such as the foolish questions from the press at their engagement party. 'The most audacious of them all,' recalled Joe in his memoir, was to Peggy by a female reporter: 'Why are you marrying a coloured man?' This question nearly, very nearly, made me feel like giving her an uppercut had not Peggy delivered a quick and beautiful retort: 'Because I love him. And love is a greater thing than colour or creed or race – or anything.' I still remember the 'hear, hear' from most of the press people that greeted this spontaneous reply. I was satisfied with her reply and proud of her indeed.[33]

Their marriage was a brilliantly colourful ceremony. While Peggy wore a very English cream satin gown, heavily embroidered in many-coloured silks, and a small cream satin cap, from which hung a tulle veil, Joe's countrymen and other African friends

were in dresses of their several native lands – *kentes*, *agbadas*, smocks and what have you. Indians were there in their saris and our British and continental friends in tails and top hats, with waistcoats of lavender or lounge suits of various colours.

'It was a veritable "United Nations" assembly in session right in the heart of Mayfair,' observed Joe with pleasure – 'It did something to my heart and soul.' Kwame Nkrumah was going to be best man but an urgent affair of state prevented him from travelling to London, so George Padmore took his place; Padmore, Hugh Gaitskell and Krishna Menon gave speeches after the wedding. 'We shall need your prayers and help in a world ridden with hatred and bigotry and racism,' said Joe in his speech as bridegroom. 'We hope that because of us others will take courage!'[34]

Their marriage gave much delight to the gossip columnists – and much disgust to the South African Government. Charles Swart, the Minister of Justice in South Africa, held their wedding photograph before the South African Parliament, saying, 'It is a disgusting photograph of a wedding between the daughter of a former British Cabinet minister and a Nigerian blanket [*sic*] native. If such a thing were ever to happen in South Africa, it would be the end.' The *News Chronicle* in London picked up the story and reprinted the same wedding photograph, but with a different caption: 'A Picture we are proud to print.' Then, quoting Swart's words, the newspaper went on:

This is what we say. If Britain were ever to take the cruel and reactionary way Mr Swart is now travelling, it would in truth be the end – the end of

Christian tolerance; the end, almost certainly, of the British Commonwealth. And the use of such an illustration to arouse racial bitterness comes close to establishing a twentieth century record in the realm of the disgusting.

It published the picture again a few days later, along with letters of support from readers.[35] 'What a problem for Mr Swart,' observed one letter, 'if, on arriving in Heaven, he should find his God to be a Man of Colour.'[36]

In December 1953, the Khamas' circle of friends was increased by a man with whom Seretse suddenly had a great deal in common – another African leader who was exiled from a British protectorate in Africa. This was Edward Mutesa II, often nicknamed King Freddie, who was the Kabaka – or King – of Buganda, the wealthiest province of the British Protectorate of Uganda. In 1942, he had been crowned the 35th Kabaka, in a line of kings dating back to the sixteenth century. Then, after a spell at Makerere College in Kampala, he went to the UK in 1945 to study History and Colonial Administration at Magdalene College, Cambridge. After his studies, the Kabaka served for a short time with the Grenadier Guards. Urbane and debonair – and always immaculately dressed – he developed the style and bearing of a perfect English gentleman, which he retained until the end of his life.[37]

He returned to Buganda in 1948. In 1952, the British began discussions about making Uganda into an independent country, incorporating Buganda. To this the Kabaka vehemently objected, demanding independence for Buganda as a country sovereign from Uganda; he also objected to a suggestion by the British of a federation of the three East African territories, similar to the model developed for the Federation of Rhodesia and Nyasaland. This was a source of worry to millions of people in East Africa, who were afraid that if they were forced into a federation, they would be dominated by the white settlers of Kenya. The Kabaka refused to cooperate with the British Governor on any of these terms. The response of the British was swift and uncompromising – they simply banished him from his country and he became the second African leader to be exiled within three years.

As with the exile of Seretse, the banishment of the Kabaka from Buganda caused immense anger and grief among his people. It was also heavily criticized by much of the world's press and Church leaders, including the Archbishop of Canterbury and the former Bishop of Uganda. As Learie Constantine observed:

The story of the Kabaka has been reported and misreported, accompanied by streams of propaganda which seem to have misled nobody, not even the British reading public. Most Britishers feel uneasy and unhappy about it, as about so much else that concerns Africa.

The annual Christmas broadcast of the British sovereign continued to give a picture of a happy and harmonious Empire, but doubts were growing.[38]

The Kabaka's years at Cambridge were largely concurrent with those of Seretse at Oxford, but their approach to their studies was very different: Seretse was serious and purposeful, while the Kabaka chose to play hard rather than to study hard. When John Stonehouse met the Kabaka in London, after his exile, he was struck by the difference between the two men:

I tried to discuss politics and economics in Africa with him [the Kabaka]. This had been possible with Seretse, who was intensely interested, but it soon became evident that the Kabaka was not. He had none of the fervour and enthusiasm of Seretse.[39]

Nor did the Kabaka share Seretse's commitment to democracy. When the two men met in the UK and discussed the political situation in Africa, Seretse argued that it was changing rapidly, due to the rise of nationalism and pan-Africanism, and that soon there would be no monarchs left in Africa.[40] This was not the Kabaka's view. Nonetheless their shared situation of exile and their longing for their own country forged a bond of friendship.

Lord Swinton had replaced Salisbury as Commonwealth Secretary in mid-December 1952. Now, in the English spring of 1953, he decided that it was time to resolve, once and for all, the whole question of the Bangwato. Nothing, he told Le Rougetel, the High Commissioner in South Africa, should be left undone to secure completion of the outcome they wanted. This had now become particularly important, because campaigners for Seretse in the UK had resumed activity. Liesching assumed that the pro-Seretse faction in Serowe was not likely to riot again, after the 'salutary drubbing' it had suffered the previous June – although it was 'never safe', he added, 'to predict the reactions of Africans.'[41]

Sir John instructed his administrators in Bechuanaland to arrange another Kgotla in Serowe on 4 May, to push through the nomination of a new Chief – Rasebolai. By now, Forbes MacKenzie had taken over as Resident Commissioner from Colonel Beetham. MacKenzie was well known to the Bangwato: not only because of his extraordinary height, but more especially because he had been such a tough and unforgiving District Commissioner of Serowe during the passive resistance campaign of 1950. MacKenzie quickly got to work, as did Batho, who had been 'in very close contact with Rasebolai, and [had] been bolstering him up'.[42] He had also distributed a letter to the Bangwato, which stated that, 'The great Khama of his own will yielded his sovereignty to the Queen.' And now, it went on, 'the Queen has ordered that neither Seretse nor any child of his shall be eligible to be chief of the Bamangwato.'[43]

Heavy pressure was put on senior members of the tribe to attend the Kgotla and they were fined or imprisoned if they failed to turn up at preparatory meetings organized by British officials.[44] When the Kgotla finally began, on the morning of Monday 4 May, Batho told the assembly that the nomination of Rasebolai Kgamane was still valid. But the great majority persisted in nominating Seretse – this was useless, warned Batho. Some people were angry at the letter distributed by Batho, which they complained was blaming the Queen for the injustice against them. They objected that 'Her Gracious Majesty had nothing to do with the exile of Chief Seretse Khama and that her name was being used to mislead us.' Batho replied with the words, 'Talking nonsense' – a remark which was described as very offensive.[45] *The Times* reported that 'one Mosinyi, an educated Native . . . expressed his views freely on the frustration of the tribe and laid his grievances all at the door of the white man'. Mosinyi was 'another example', argued *The Times*, 'of hostility bred unwittingly by education'.[46]

Batho brought the Kgotla to an end after three days. He really had no choice, reported Fraenkel, who was there, to Rathcreedan. 'If the Kgotla had continued for another half day,' he pointed out, 'there would have been no speakers left supporting Rasebolai and Seretse speakers would have spoken for another week.'[47]

But the Administration had another plan up its sleeve. The Kgotla meeting was recalled less than a week later, on 12 May, to hear a statement by the Resident Commissioner. MacKenzie began his speech by carefully distinguishing between the office of Kgosi and that of Native Authority. Then he made a shocking announcement – that an order was being issued that day to make Rasebolai Native Authority. Rasebolai would hold this appointment, he said, until the tribe agreed to designate a Chief. After giving this terrible news to the stunned men in front of him, MacKenzie shook hands with Rasebolai and congratulated him. Rasebolai gave a short speech, saying that he wanted peace in the Reserve and he knew that there were others who felt the same.[48]

Most people wanted peace – but they did not want Rasebolai. They were furious. They had been promised again and again that no Kgosi would be imposed upon them: but now, Rasebolai had been given a position that was tantamount to that of Kgosi. In the past, the Kgosi and the Native Authority had, without exception, been one and the same man. The former title symbolized the power vested in this man by the people; the latter symbolized the authority devolved upon him by the Administration.

The Commonwealth Relations Office, working closely with the High Commissioner's Office, had worked out the details of this plan even before the Kgotla of 4 May, the week before. Realizing that the tribe were unlikely to nominate Rasebolai as Kgosi, they adopted a Machiavellian strategy to produce the same outcome. In notes for Lord Swinton at the end of April, a week before the Kgotla started, Clark insisted that 'no indication should be given that we have another move up our sleeves if the resumed Kgotla proves abortive. The High Commissioner is convinced that, if news of this leaked, the whole plan would be jeopardised.'[49]

The Government was given a hard time in Westminster on the transfer of authority to Rasebolai. Was it correct, asked the Labour MP James Griffiths in the House of Commons, mockingly, that the 'person now appointed to this rather unprecedented post of Native Authority was rejected by the Bamangwato?' Was it *really* possible, asked Lord Hailsham in disgust in the House of Lords, that this new Native Authority was the very same man 'whom the Tribe made it perfectly clear they were not prepared to accept in the office of Chieftain?'[50]

Seretse was staggered by the news, of which he had been given no warning whatsoever. He immediately issued a statement to the press. 'I hope the Bamangwato tribe, in spite of this provocation,' he said, 'will continue to refrain from conduct which might lead to disorder. But I wonder how long the wishes of the African people, peacefully presented, will be disregarded by the Government?'[51]

22

The campaign intensifies

In April 1953, the Nationalists in South Africa were re-elected with an increased majority by the white electorate, showing their support for the systematic and relentless implementation of apartheid. In the same year, the Bantu Education Act decreed that blacks should be provided with separate and inferior educational facilities, using the vernacular languages; the Act was justified by Hendrik F. Verwoerd, the Minister of Native Affairs, with the statement that, 'There is no place for the Bantu in the European community above the level of certain forms of labour.'[1] The passing of the Reservation of Separate Amenities Act, also in 1953, restricted non-white use of libraries, galleries, public transport, beaches, and entrances to public buildings; it legislated that all races should have separate facilities and that these need not be of an equivalent quality. All over South Africa, signs with the words 'Europeans Only' or 'Non-Europeans Only' were posted. On the Durban beach, for example, there were signs proclaiming that, 'Under Section 37 of the Durban By-Laws, this bathing area is reserved for the sole use of members of the white race group.'

Further north, in central Africa, the political and economic interests of white settlers were consolidated by the creation of the Federation of Rhodesia and Nyasaland in October 1953, despite bitter opposition from the black population of the region. It had been finally pushed through by Sir Godfrey Huggins, the Prime Minister of Southern Rhodesia, and Roy Welensky, the trade unionist white leader of Northern Rhodesia, in association with the Colonial Office. It was described by the CO as a racial partnership, but Huggins – far more accurately – described it as a relationship between 'a horse and its rider'. It was to prove a cruel and dismal failure.

Kenya was now dominated by the Mau Mau uprising, as Baring implemented his savage policy of confining the Kikuyu in protected villages and hunting down the Mau Mau soldiers in the forest. Under the 1952 State of Emergency, more than 20,000 Mau Mau rebels were killed in combat in the 1950s, while at least 150,000 Kikuyu spent some time behind the wire of a British detention camp and 1,090 Kikuyu went to the gallows for Mau Mau crimes; 32 white settlers died.[2] British colonial officials running the camps were responsible for appalling conditions, which involved deprivation of food, water and clothes and widespread torture that included castration.[3]

Dedan Kimathi, a Mau Mau guerrilla fighter (who was executed by the colonial Government in 1957), regarded the exile of Seretse and of the Kabaka as consistent with the oppression of Kenyans by the British. 'We, in Kenya,' he wrote to a supporter of the Kabaka in Entebbe, 'are horrified and terrified that the British have seen fit to depose and exile our two great Kings, namely Seretse Khama and Kabaka Mutesa II.' What disturbed Kenyans the most, he added, was

the realisation that although these two great Kingdoms – Baganda and Tswana – existed before the coming of the European imperialists to our Continent, it is now clear that the primary aim of the British is to use all weapons to destroy them. This evil design is clear proof that the British don't want any other kingdom to exist except their own.

Kimathi pointed out that if the people of Uganda had detained Queen Elizabeth when she was visiting their country, the British would have used 'blood and fire' to release her.[4]

Fenner Brockway and some other activists, including Jennie Lee, decided that the time had come for a major anti-colonial campaign, which was based on a single principle: the right of colonized nations to self-determination. In April 1954, at a conference attended by about 350 delegates from organizations all over Britain, the Council for the Defence of Seretse Khama amalgamated with over 300 other organizations – ranging from the British branch of the Congress Against Imperialism, the Central Africa Committee, and the Kenya Committee – to form the Movement for Colonial Freedom. It was hoped that this amalgamation would bring an end to the many little councils and committees, each dealing with a single colonial issue.

Anti-colonial energy had been dispersed among rival groups, believed Brockway, and too much work was duplicated – the MCF offered a real opportunity for consolidation. Parliamentary committees were set up and much of the Movement's work concentrated on pressurizing MPs to raise colonial issues in both the House of Commons and the House of Lords. The British colonies of particular concern were Kenya, Nigeria, the Gold Coast, Malaya, British Guiana, Uganda, the High Commission Territories, Somaliland, Tanganyika, the Federation of Rhodesia and Nyasaland, Zanzibar, Cyprus, and the islands of the West Indies.

The movement's manifesto stated its commitment to human equality, regardless of colour or race.[5] 'Wonderful! That is the only word to describe the advance of our Movement,' wrote Brockway in a fundraising letter. 'I know you will give,' he wrote to supporters, 'because you believe with us that "all persons are born equal in rights and human dignity". It is the big issue of this century.'[6]

Brockway's views differed from those of Arthur Creech Jones and Rita Hinden, colleagues in the Labour Party who were also involved in issues of colonial policy. Creech Jones and Hinden were leaders of the Fabian Colonial Bureau, which believed that colonies needed to 'mature' under British guidance, before they were ready for self-government. The Movement for Colonial Freedom, however, put forward a wide-ranging critique of colonialism and maintained that Fabian 'nation-building' could only start once the colonial relationship had been broken, through the grant of full and equal political rights. It aimed to challenge Ministers rather than lobby them privately, and to extend its influence beyond the small metropolitan audience reached by the Fabians. The Movement also wanted to develop relationships with the nationalists themselves – unlike the Fabians, who limited their links to liberals among the colonial administrators.[7]

The General Secretary of the MCF was Douglas Rogers and the Assistant Secretary was Joseph Murumbi, the General Secretary of the Kenya African Union, currently in exile in the UK (later to become the Foreign Minister of newly independent Kenya, and then Vice-President). The Treasurer was Anthony Wedgwood Benn, Brockway's Parliamentary ally on the Labour Left. 'Now,' wrote Wedgwood Benn with satisfaction to a fellow member of the Movement, 'we have a chance to be really effective!'[8]

Sufficient funds were raised – through membership, cultural events and appeals, as well as affiliations with organizations ranging from the Fire Brigades' Union to constituency Labour parties – to pay for modest offices on Regent's Park Road in London, a small staff, the publication of a bi-monthly journal, campaign material, and private and public meetings. The Movement was sponsored by up to 100 MPs and it had an individual membership of about 1,000; its regional, national and international affiliations brought the total number of people involved up to about 3 million.[9] For the first time, the issue of imperialism and the future of British colonies, especially in Africa, was being pushed high up the national and colonial agenda.[10]

The MCF had many different committees, including the Southern Africa Protectorates Committee, which carried on the campaign to end the exile of Seretse Khama; Monica Whately, who had been the Chairman of the Campaign Committee, was appointed Chairman of this Committee too. Seretse and Ruth were grateful for the efforts made on their behalf. But they also continued to search for other ways to negotiate a return to Bechuanaland. One Labour MP complained that he had seen Seretse in the House of Commons having interviews with representatives of each of the political parties, which he regarded as unscrupulous.[11] But Seretse's bitter experience at the hands of both the Labour Party *and* the Conservative Party had taught him not to put his faith in any particular political colour.

On 17 May 1954, Seretse once again proposed to the Government that he renounce the Chieftainship of the Bangwato and be allowed to take his family home. He and Rathcreedan met with John Foster and senior officials at the CRO. If he resigned his claim to the Chieftainship, he suggested, and undertook to go round the Reserve to persuade the Bangwato to accept his resignation, would the Government allow him to return? But the answer was no. The first objective, said Foster, must be the establishment of a new Chief: 'The programme . . . might be first the renunciation of the Chieftainship by Seretse, the establishment of a new Chief, short visits and then finally his return.' But it would not be possible, he added, to give any guarantee of a return or to say how long the process might take. Foster asked Seretse to make a statement of renunciation on these terms. But Seretse refused. He objected that the guarantee would be all on his side, and none on the Government's.[12]

In Bechuanaland, Rasebolai had been installed as native authority and he was living in the house of the Kgosi, by the Kgotla in Serowe – the house which had been burnt down in anger against Tshekedi in 1950, and had now been rebuilt.[13] He was vested with all the powers of a Chief that depended on Government proclamation; and of those powers that were traditional, he assumed what he could. He and Batho had selected a number of subordinates to carry out his rule.[14]

The Bangwato were miserable and adopted a policy of non-cooperation, just as they had done in 1950, although they continued to pay tax.[15] Despite their loyalty to the British monarchy, there was barely any celebration of the Coronation of Elizabeth II on 20 June 1953. 'Only 30 tribesmen turned up at Serowe,' reported Fraenkel to Rathcreedan. 'In spite of there being many pots of cooked meats and invitations extended to people walking in the street to participate,' he added, 'they refused to do so saying they were not vultures.' No disrespect was intended to the Queen, explained Fraenkel – it was simply a protest at the imposition of Rasebolai upon them.[16] At the end of a sports event in Serowe to celebrate the Coronation, the District Commissioner called on the schoolchildren to give a vote of thanks to the Native Authority and his committee. But the children responded with shouts of disapproval.[17] 'As a result of the unfair treatment of the tribe by Government,' reported a letter to London, 'the Coronation day was characterised by a gloomy atmosphere around Serowe and the whole Reserve in general.'[18]

The Administration was edgy and nervous about its ability to control the Reserve, relying heavily on intelligence reports. The 'Relationship between European and African' was a regular item in these reports and was described in June 1954 as 'good except for Mahalapye where once again Lenyeletse and Theo Tamoucha have indicated their anti-European feelings': 'They attempted to sit in chairs reserved for Europeans at a circus on the 10th. They were heard to say that there was no colour bar and that their money was [as] good as that of Europeans.'[19] Leading members of the Bangwato who remained adamantly loyal to Seretse were regarded with deep suspicion by the Administration. George Winstanley, a junior British official, who had recently arrived in the Protectorate, noticed that their names 'figured largely in the various intelligence reports that landed on our desks'. On each of these pages were the words, in deep red, 'UK Eyes Only'. 'I thought this was very curious,' wrote Winstanley later, 'seeing that many of the senior officials who compiled and read them had been born in South Africa.'[20]

Rasebolai was firmly backed by the District Commissioner, Bruce Rutherford, who had taken over from Batho in September 1954. Rutherford was also a harsh, unfeeling man and the people of the Reserve complained that they were unfairly treated. Although the customary fine for killing an eland or giraffe was one ox, a man was fined eighteen head of cattle, two horses and his rifle for shooting an eland. People were being flogged for minor misdemeanours, and fined or imprisoned for not turning up to meetings. Members of the Zionist Church – which had been forbidden by Khama III from operating in the Reserve – were arrested and imprisoned for two weeks. During their imprisonment they were forced to work without payment and were ordered to carry water with their hands tied to poles; they were also made to sleep sitting up. In addition, people objected that they were denied their right to free speech in the Kgotla and to hold meetings; they were not even allowed to meet their legal advisers.[21] Rasebolai was demanding unpaid labour in the Kgotla, which was considered unjust.[22]

On 8 September 1955, the last of the men imprisoned for the riot of 1 June were finally released, triggering another clampdown by the Native Authority. In November 1955, Peto Sekgoma complained to the Commander of the Police that a man who had visited him had been tied by a trek chain to lion traps for some days and that he had also been flogged – simply because he had gone with Peto over the border to South Africa, to buy goods for his shop. He complained, too, that women and children were being flogged in the Kgotla in public.[23] A copy of this letter found its way to the desk of Fenner Brockway, who immediately called for an investigation.[24] The CRO duly made inquiries and were given some background to the complaints – though no denials. Where there were no tribal lock-ups, it was explained, it was necessary to tether people to poles and lion traps; the women who had been flogged were prostitutes.[25] The CRO dismissed the allegations about the flogging of women in public, on the grounds that they were 'general and therefore unworthy of attention'. But on 7 August 1956, Martin Wray, who had by now replaced Forbes MacKenzie as the Resident Commissioner of Bechuanaland, telephoned the CRO in London to report that he had 'found to his horror that the stories about the flogging of women in the Kgotla are indeed true'.[26]

Bechuanaland was visited in 1955 by John Hatch, the Labour Party's Commonwealth officer. He was sent to find out the opinions of the Tribe, so that the party could carry out its commitment to a review of the case after five years. The Bangwato found it hard to take seriously yet another investigation into their opinion, which they thought was bound to be overlooked. As a letter handed to Mr Hatch in Francistown pointed out, the attitude of the Tribe had already been given on several occasions to the British Government:

1. The Commission of Enquiry,
2. Mr Gordon Walker,
3. The Three Observers,
4. The Bamangwato Delegation,
and you are the fifth.[27]

But, polite and courteous as always, they answered the questions that were put to them. Many of the older men had tears in their eyes as they explained that everyone was waiting for Seretse to return. Rasebolai and his advisers, too, said that they still regarded Seretse as the rightful Kgosi and wanted him to return. In fact, said Hatch, Rasebolai had told him that his own position with the people was weakened whenever the Government suggested that he was replacing Seretse.[28]

Hatch came back to the UK with no doubts – the Bangwato would never appoint anyone as an alternative Kgosi to Seretse. He also returned with a strong distaste for the racial attitudes and the discrimination he had seen in the Protectorate. Officially, there was no colour bar and the separate entrances for Africans had been removed from the post offices, but an unofficial apartheid still operated. In shops, the whites walked behind the counters to be served, while

Africans remained on the outside. The schools and healthcare facilities were segregated according to colour – and the services provided for whites were immeasurably superior to those for blacks.[29] Hatch had discovered that an African with the same responsibility and doing the same job, was paid on a lower scale than a European.[30] He discovered, too, that in the hospitals there were no African Sisters: 'what concerned me most was not the absence of African sisters, but the apparent absence of intention or desire by European Matrons to encourage their African nurses to the point of becoming efficient Sisters'.[31]

Hatch's return, which was heavily publicized in the UK, raised the profile of Seretse's case. So too did the publication in July 1955 of a book by John Redfern – *Ruth and Seretse. 'A Very Disreputable Transaction'*. It was the outcome of the many years he had spent reporting on the story. The *Manchester Guardian* was full of praise. 'He brings out perhaps more clearly than has been done before,' it said, 'the human side of the story, the dignity and decency of Ruth and Seretse Khama, the clash of personalities, the dissolving doubts and later the passionate loyalties of the tribesmen.' All these things, it went on, 'add weight to the case for reconsideration'.[32] The Nationalist newspaper in the Transvaal, *Die Transvaler*, was annoyed about the fuss made of the book and responded with an article entitled, 'The Bamangwato are only a handful. The British public is not aware of this.'[33]

Yet another event which reminded the public of the injustice against Seretse was the return home in October 1955 of the exiled Kabaka of Buganda, to the great joy of his people. All along his route from Entebbe airport to the royal palace, triumphal arches were erected. When he arrived, there was a long procession of cars to greet him, decorated with leaves from banana trees. As he drove slowly along the 25 miles to Kampala, the road was lined on both sides by cheering crowds, waving banana leaves; when he passed, people knelt down and clapped to show their respect and their happiness to see him back.[34] But the CRO in London was not happy at all, as they feared that the end of the Kabaka's exile would fuel the campaign on behalf of Seretse. In 1954 Lord Swinton had warned:

Public opinion regards the two cases as parallel; and when a comparison is made it will be said with truth that the Kabaka's behaviour was more reprehensible than Seretse's. Indeed, the removal of Seretse can only be justified as an act of State in the interest of the Tribe.[35]

By the end of 1955, there had been a significant change at the top of the CRO: in April, Lord Swinton had been replaced as Secretary of State by the patrician Alec Douglas-Home, the 14th Earl of Home (who became Prime Minister in 1963). He was a considerate and courteous man and someone, observed Macmillan, 'who represents the old governing class at its best'.[36] Although he was widely criticized for his backing of the Federation of the two Rhodesias and Nyasaland, on most other issues regarding the empire he took a progressive – though paternalistic – approach and he strongly denounced apartheid in South Africa.[37]

There had also been substantial changes in the senior officials at the CRO who were dealing with Seretse's case. Sir Percivale Liesching, who as the official head of the CRO had been instrumental in Seretse's exile, had gone to South Africa to take up the appointment of High Commissioner to South Africa in March 1955. The new Permanent Secretary was Sir Gilbert Laithwaite, a very different sort of man. They were almost the same age and had both served with distinction on the front line in the First World War. But whereas Liesching was old-fashioned in his spirit, and a model of the Establishment – and even, with his lean figure and sharp features, looked the part – Laithwaite was rather different. Solidly built, he was a Roman Catholic and a homosexual, who never married, with a keen interest in fine arts. He had a reputation for fairness and got on well with the Deputy Under-Secretary, Joe Garner, who had been in post since 1953. Garner was the son of a draper and was married to an American. He was a personable man of integrity, who condemned racism.

Another fresh and progressive recruit to the senior levels was Eleanor Emery, who had moved up the ranks of the civil service and joined the CRO in 1955; she had been born in Glasgow and then grew up in Canada. She was the first woman official to be involved in the Seretse Khama case – indeed, one of the first women ever to be appointed as a principal at the CRO – and she quickly introduced a more human and sympathetic approach. Michael Fairlie, another principal, had worked as an official in the Bechuanaland administration and had regarded the racial segregation and treatment of Africans as inhuman. This new stable of mandarins at the CRO held modern attitudes and was very different from the one that had backed the exile of Seretse and Ruth. As a consequence, Lord Home was given far more enlightened advice than that which had been given to previous Commonwealth Secretaries – Noel-Baker, Gordon Walker, Ismay, Salisbury and Swinton.

On 9 August 1955, Home met with a delegation from the Labour Party, led by James Griffiths and including John Hatch, who recommended a conference of tribal representatives in London to find a settlement. But Home replied that 'it was necessary to face the fact that Seretse could not go back as Chief with a white wife'.[38]

At the Labour Party Conference in Margate in October 1955, Seretse and Ruth sat in the front row of the Press Gallery. 'On the question of Seretse Khama,' observed one Labour MP, 'we cannot pat ourselves on the back overmuch.' Fenner Brockway was more blunt. Seretse's only crime, he argued, was that he had affronted Dr Malan and South Africa.[39] Griffiths, speaking for the National Executive Committee, observed that the period of five years, for which Seretse had been excluded from the Bangwato Reserve, was shortly to expire. He said that Labour had made a commitment in 1950 to review Seretse's case in five years – and they were determined to do this. On the strength of the evidence gathered by Hatch, he added, they hoped to arrange a meeting of tribal elders in London.[40] When he had finished speaking, the Conference Chairman extended a welcome to the Khamas, sitting together in the Press Gallery. There was an outburst of applause, which swelled into an ovation when Seretse and Ruth responded to shouts of 'Stand up!'. As they left the Conference Hall, they were loudly cheered again.[41]

The Commonwealth Secretary, Lord Home, a principled man, was troubled by the Seretse Khama issue. On 29 November, he sent a paper on the situation in the Bangwato Reserve to the Prime Minister, who was now Anthony Eden. 'I thought I would show you this,' he said, 'because these situations are apt to blow up quickly, and I do not want to be unprepared.'[42] The paper by Home described increased unrest in the Reserve, which he attributed to Hatch's visit. In the previous few months, he added, Rasebolai had been opposed in the Kgotla by the pro-Seretse faction on important issues, and it had been necessary to send a security force to the north of the Reserve, to deal with an outbreak of violence. He was wondering, he said, whether the Government ought to review their policy on Seretse, though on balance he supposed they should leave it as it was.[43] He asked Eden for advice about whether or not to circulate this paper to Cabinet. Eden replied promptly, telling him to go ahead. 'Socialist party', he added, referring to Hatch's visit and to Labour's demands for a review of the permanent banishment, 'appears to be behaving very badly.'[44]

Meanwhile, in Addiscombe, the Khamas waited and hoped. One great pleasure during this period was a visit to their home by Mrs Lilian Ngoyi, a leader in the struggle against apartheid. The daughter of a washerwoman, Mrs Ngoyi had become the National President of the Federation of South African Women in 1954. In 1955, she went to the World Congress of Mothers in Lausanne with Dora Tamana, a leader of the ANC.[45] Then they travelled through various countries, including England:

In Uganda, she sat in the same cinema as white people . . . At the hotel in Rome, an Italian man opened a door for her.

For a dreadful moment Lilian thought she was being shown to the kitchen, but the man simply smiled and asked her what she would like to drink . . .

More eye-openers awaited the two of them in London. They saw white men digging in the streets, swinging huge pickaxes as they worked . . . On an overcrowded train, two white men stood up and offered Lilian and Dora their seats. Lilian was amazed. 'Am I dreaming?' she asked herself.[46]

During her visit to London, Lilian struck up a firm friendship with Ruth.[47]

A correspondent from *The World* went to visit the Khamas and asked Seretse if he would like to return to Bechuanaland. 'I should like to go very much,' he replied. 'Otherwise I would not be continually approaching the Commonwealth Relations Office.' He talked about his wish to improve people's lives:

The Government, I know, have big plans for Bechuanaland. Big plans which they cannot at present push ahead because there is no life, no enthusiasm, among the people there.

They feel they have been deprived of something. Those plans concern not only administrative matters but matters of development in the way of agriculture, cattle, minerals and so on.

I believe I could help in bringing those plans to a good end and it would be my aim and joy to try and do so.

He was asked if he would miss the stores, the big football matches, and he replied – as he looked through his sitting-room windows at the bleak and grey February sky – that he could just as easily watch football in Bechuanaland. 'I think I might put it this way,' he explained:

I think I should like it here if I came from my own country on an occasional holiday.

But as I am living now I feel very much an exile – as though I had been banished here.

All the time I feel restless – an urge to get back to where I rightly belong.

'I have no doubt,' he said, that 'if it rested with the ordinary British people, I should be allowed back any time. But it is the British Cabinet that must give the decision.' The Bangwato were asking for Ruth back, he added, as well as wanting him: 'It is only the Government that seems to mind about her being white.'[48]

23

The ending of exile

Tshekedi was smarting under his restrictions in the Bangwato Reserve and longed to resume political life. The only way of changing this, he knew, would be through a common front with Seretse – but he was adamant that Seretse would have to renounce the kingship. This for him was a sticking point, as he explained in a letter to Creech Jones towards the end of 1955:

I wish to say that if I am invited by any Party in power to come to London for discussion with Seretse, I will gladly do so, but my attitude would be to inform Seretse that I would not take any part in his case if his line of action is to continue to fight for his return as chief.

But should Seretse abandon his claim and fight for his return as an individual – 'then I would support such an action'.[1]

The Bangwato now needed Seretse's return more than ever before. For there had been a new and significant development in Bechuanaland: mining companies were showing interest in the minerals of the Protectorate. Geological surveys had been carried out and copper, gold and silver had been discovered in exploitable quantities.[2] The Anglo-American Corporation was particularly interested in the Bangwato Reserve and they were now keen to start negotiations. In March 1956, senior headmen met twice in Serowe to discuss the issue of mineral development with the District Commissioner. He was encouraging them to give their consent to concessions, but the Bangwato – although they accepted the idea of mineral development in principle – opposed any kind of agreement in the absence of Seretse and Tshekedi.[3] They were afraid that, without the guidance of the Khamas, they would be taken advantage of by the Government and the mining companies. As well, many of the men had worked in the harsh conditions of the mines of South Africa, and they were determined to make sure that this brutal system was not replicated in their own country.

Some of the diKgosi in the Protectorate had anticipated the discovery of minerals and prepared for it. In 1953, Kgosi Mokgosi of the Balete had engaged lawyers in Johannesburg to find out what rights the British Government had in relation to their land and to the minerals that might be found on it.[4] He was assured that as the law stood the consent of the diKgosi and their people was necessary for any concessions.[5] Fenner Brockway made sure that this point was put on record during discussions in the House of Commons in London: Commander Alan Noble, the new Commonwealth Under-Secretary of state, was required to give an assurance 'that no leases will be given to any firms, South African or otherwise, without the consent and the knowledge of the African Native Authorities concerned'.[6]

The Bangwato now had leverage over the British Government. Finally, for the first time since Seretse's marriage, they had something to offer that the Government wanted. This put Tshekedi and Seretse in a very strong position. On 29 March 1956, three days after the second Kgotla at which the Bangwato refused to grant mining concessions, Tshekedi wrote to David Astor to tell him that he would be coming to the UK with his wife Ella, to take their sons to school in Ireland. He was 'a shackled man', he complained, heavily restricted by the Government. The question of the moment for Bechuanaland, he went on, was the exploitation of minerals, to which the people were not opposed – 'but took the line that they needed advice from the two sons of Khama viz. Seretse and Tshekedi'. It was clear, he said, that

there was a pronounced spirit of unity where there has been disunity and it would be most advantageous for the Government to try and bring the parties who differed on the effects of the Seretse marriage together. But the Government does not seem to be anxious to do this. Do not be led away to believing that there is any strong objection to mining developments, because there is none.[7]

Tshekedi and his family went to Britain in June and met with Seretse and Ruth. Seretse welcomed his proposal that they work together and told him that he was willing to give up the kingship. But he insisted on being able to take part in politics, out of a sense of duty to his people.

With this agreement from Seretse, Tshekedi now embarked on a relentless series of meetings with his many admirers in England and people of influence. One of the first men he went to see was his legal adviser in the UK, Graham Page, who reported on this meeting to Commander Noble. There were ways, argued Page, in which the Protectorate could be developed – notably, through the mining concessions sought by the Anglo-American Corporation. These concessions particularly affected the Bangwato Reserve, he explained, but the people were hesitant about supporting the project because they did not have their chief. Since Tshekedi had returned to the reserve without trouble, why shouldn't Seretse return in a similar capacity?[8] The same argument was being energetically pressed by the Movement for Colonial Freedom. In June it published a glossy pamphlet, *Bechuanaland. What Seretse's Exile Means*, with a foreword by Seretse and an introduction by Fenner Brockway. 'As we colonials have no direct representation in the British Parliament,' wrote Seretse, 'our appeal for justice must be directed at the British public, regardless of party beliefs.'[9]

On 1 August 1956, just before the summer recess, the banishment of Seretse was raised once again in the House of Commons. James Griffiths repeated his demand that the Government should convene in London a conference of tribal leaders, including Tshekedi and Seretse. But, he argued, a new factor had entered into the situation – the interest of certain mining companies in the minerals in Bechuanaland. And since Bechuanaland was a protectorate, not a colony, the mineral rights were vested in the population living there – 'the written consent of the Tribes is essential for a concession; indeed, that it is obligatory upon us, by our act of protection, to obtain that consent'. The Tribe would not come to a decision, he added, in the absence of Seretse, and without his position being finally settled. But if an agreement *was* reached, then the lives of the people in the Protectorate would be transformed.

Jennie Lee insisted that Seretse be allowed to return as Chief. 'We must all be impressed by the dignity with which Seretse Khama and his wife have gone through those difficult years,' she said. 'It is not easy for a young couple to have to face, early in their married life, all the difficulties which they have had to face.' But even if Seretse had been 'far less able and distinguished a man than he is, and his wife Ruth a less lovely and gifted lady than she is', the moral argument remained. It was time, she argued with conviction, to right the wrong which had been done to the Bangwato. Brockway took up her theme, asking how it was possible for the government to dare to say they held democratic principles:

A Tribe in Africa, year after year, despite all the circumstances against it, says, 'We want this man to return as our chief,' while the Government, claiming to accept democratic principles, have the impudence and arrogance to sit on the Front Bench of a Parliament thousands of miles away, here in Westminster, and say to that Tribe, 'You have no right to choose your own Chief. We shall not allow him to return and we impose a Native Authority on you.'[10]

Bechuanaland, he observed sadly, 'has become a symbol of the colour bar because of our treatment of Seretse and Ruth Khama'.

Wedgwood Benn then sought to push the Labour Party into an irrevocable position of support for Seretse. The Conference that was planned, he said, should not be to discuss *if* Seretse Khama should be allowed to go home, but *how* – the conditions under which he would return. 'The view of my right hon. Friend and the party as understood by myself and others,' he declared, 'is that the return of Seretse Khama is something which is now the policy of the Labour Party.'

Clem Davies, the leader of the Liberal Party, referred to Seretse's banishment as a 'great evil'. Another Liberal MP linked this injustice to the one against his uncle: he said he had met Tshekedi that very afternoon and wanted to see something done to put Tshekedi 'not in charge of his own Tribe but at a higher level, because he is an outstanding African'. Clearly Tshekedi had been working his usual charm on the gentlemen of the British Establishment. Commander Noble, too, expressed his admiration:

. . . may I add my word of praise to Tshekedi Khama? All of us know that he was Regent for many years, and we know what a forceful and enlightened person he is. I am very glad to have met him on two occasions during the past few days.[11]

Seretse and Tshekedi were now working in partnership. On 14 August, they went together to the Commonwealth Relations Office and asked to see Lord Home. They were told that he was 'very much pre-occupied with Suez' – the nationalization by Egypt of the Suez Canal in July 1956, which was perceived as inimical to British overseas economic interests. Nonetheless, a meeting was arranged for the next day.[12] The Commonwealth Secretary could hardly refuse their request, as the opposition would make political capital out of any refusal by Ministers to see the leaders of the two Bangwato factions, who were now cooperating with each other. The quarrel between Seretse and Tshekedi was so well known to the British public that one day, when Tshekedi was shopping in London and signed a cheque, the salesman exclaimed, 'So *you're* the wicked uncle!'[13]

Uncle and nephew returned to the CRO the following day and handed to the Secretary of State a document in which they both unconditionally renounced for themselves and their children any claim to the kingship of the Bangwato. They added that all the previous differences of opinion between them, relating to questions of law and custom, had been resolved. But they both expected complete freedom to serve their people as members of a Tribal Council. The document ended, 'We appeal to the Protecting Power to allow both of us to return to our country with our families as full citizens.'[14] Lord Home took this document extremely seriously and gave it his full attention, despite the demands of the Suez crisis. He arranged for a telegram to be sent that night to Sir Percivale Liesching, the British High Commissioner in South Africa, in which he commented that, 'Seretse's renunciation of Chieftainship is obviously an important development'. He did not seem to realize that it was not a *new* development: that Seretse had made this very suggestion on several occasions already, to previous Secretaries of State.

There were aspects of the suggestion that worried Home, especially the question of whether Seretse should be allowed to go home before a Chief had been designated by the Tribe. But he made short shrift of the problem of South Africa, which had assumed so much importance when the issue of Seretse and his white wife had first come up in 1949. The Union's attitude might well be an issue, he acknowledged in a cable to Liesching – 'but I think we may have to face whatever objections they might raise'.[15]

There were many good reasons for disregarding the views of the Union. In the past few years the South African Government had become a villain in the eyes of many people in the world, especially after Dr Malan was replaced in December 1954 by Johannes Strijdom, who was even more right-wing and had backed Hitler. Policy differences between South Africa and Britain had now become very marked. A few months earlier, in April 1956, the Tomlinson Commission, which had been set up in South Africa to advise on plans for the country's social structure, had issued a summary report advocating total apartheid, through the creation of so-called Bantu Areas, or Bantustans, as separate ethnic homelands for all African citizens. This policy was intended to excise Africans irrevocably from the body politic and to consolidate the supremacy of whites. It would protect and preserve the status quo, in which three million whites owned 87 per cent of the land. Eight million Africans would be relegated for ever to the remaining 13 per cent, with the least fertile land and a lack of basic amenities.[16]

Although racial discrimination was still practised in many countries, observed Father Huddleston, only South Africa 'openly asserts it as a legitimate and even desirable basis for Government . . . There can be no doubt, in a Commonwealth of Nations numerically non-European, South Africa is a hideous embarrassment.'[17] It was also – as were the white settlers of Kenya and the Federation of Rhodesia and Nyasaland – running against the trend of other Western countries. In the USA, 'Jim Crow' was starting to be seen as unacceptable by the general population, and when Rosa Parks, a 42-year-old seamstress, was arrested in December 1955 for refusing to give up her bus seat to a white man in Montgomery, Alabama, her act of courage sparked a black boycott of the buses. It also triggered a campaign of non-violent protest, led by Dr Martin Luther King, which brought about the outlawing of segregation on buses and the start of a mass movement for civil rights.

International concern about apartheid focused in June 1955 on the

Congress of the People at Kliptown, near Johannesburg, where the Freedom Charter was adopted, which became the programme of the ANC. Nelson Mandela and Walter Sisulu, although they were banned, drifted around the edges of the meeting in disguise as the Charter was recited in three languages, each clause approved by shouts of 'Africa!' from the crowd. The Freedom Charter began:

We, the people of South Africa, declare for all our country and the world to know that South Africa belongs to all who live in it, black and white, and that no government can justly claim authority unless it is based on the will of the people.

On the second day of the meeting, police with sten guns burst into the crowd and announced that the names of everyone there would be recorded on suspicion of high treason. Later Mandela wrote that the raid that day 'signalled a harsh new turn in the fight for emancipation'.[18]

When John Hatch had examined the Seretse question in 1954, he had consulted various people on the likely reaction of the Union Government if Seretse were allowed to go home with Ruth. The Director of the South African Institute of Race Relations, Quentin Whyte, thought that South Africa might simply ignore it, particularly if Seretse did not come back as Chief, although there was a chance that it might be used to whip up reaction against British African policy.[19] Julius Lewin, a Lecturer in Native Law at the University of Witwatersrand, believed that the National Government were unlikely to take any kind of position, because of the risks of publicity at the United Nations. Nor, he added, has the 'atmosphere or temperature here been such as to require the Nats to do anything by force. They are now more securely and safely in the saddle of office than in 1949.' Seretse's return as Chief, he acknowledged, might be used as a cry in the republican issue. But, like the transfer of the Protectorates, 'this question will be raised *anyhow* in the coming years, not just because of Seretse'.[20]

Even the issue of transfer, however, had slipped off the agenda, as far as Britain was concerned: it would have been folly in the mid-1950s for any British Government even to consider the possibility of transferring the High Commission Territories to South Africa. As Prime Minister in 1954, Churchill had made a statement to the House of

Commons in which he warned the South African Government against 'needlessly' bringing up the incorporation issue.[21] The Tomlinson Report had referred to Bechuanaland, Basutoland and Swaziland as 'heartlands' for the Bantu Areas, but the CRO swiftly and firmly responded, making it clear that the transfer of the HCTs was simply not an option. There was now a consensus outside South Africa and Southern Rhodesia that, as the Freedom Charter of the ANC stated in one of its clauses, 'The people of the Protectorates – Basutoland, Bechuanaland and Swaziland – shall be free to decide for themselves their own future.'[22]

In June 1956, Strijdom was in London and addressed the South Africa Club on what he described as a 'great problem': the survival of the white man and his heritage in southern Africa. To 'all clear-minded people,' he said, it should be plain that if the whites in southern Africa, far outnumbered as they were by the non-whites, should allow the control of their countries to pass out of their hands, 'they would be doomed either to leave or to be absorbed by the huge majority of blacks'. He argued that whereas it had

taken the European 2000 years or more to emerge from barbarism to his present degree of development, the Negroes and Bantu have during all that period, with few exceptions, clung to their primitive and native way of life. Many decades and probably generations will pass before they will, generally speaking, reach the white man's stage of development – and that notwithstanding all the assistance that they are receiving.[23]

Next day, Strijdom, with Eric Louw, his Minister of External Affairs, met with Lord Home and Commander Noble. He expanded on his themes of the night before, emphasizing the danger to white South Africa if any of Britain's colonies in Africa were granted self-determination. 'Any form of political association in one State which gave the blacks political rights and a vote, however qualified,' he insisted, 'would be the end of the whites. It might take time but the end would be inevitable. Ninety-nine per cent of the whites in the Rhodesias would share his view.' Home parried. Time alone, he said, 'would show whether his system or ours was right but that as political realists we must recognise that his apartheid policy had roused passions which would take time to cool'. Another issue discussed was that of the Protectorates:

when [Strijdom] raised the problem of the Protectorates he only asked that South Africa should be allowed to explain their objectives in the Territories: either South African officials could go to the Territories or leading personalities in the Territories could go to the Union.

What had we to fear? If the leaders were happy and wanted to join the Union as he was convinced that they would, our troubles with the Protectorates would be at an end.

Home made it clear that the transfer would simply not be allowed. 'Time was up,' he recorded, with evident distaste. 'So I repeated my piece on "no political change" and said we would resume.'[24]

Seretse's and Tshekedi's meeting with Home on 15 August 1956 led to a series of further meetings at the CRO over the next few weeks.[25] Initially, the Commonwealth Secretary maintained his view that Seretse could not be allowed to return before an alternative Chief had been approved, preferably Rasebolai. But, keeping an open mind and feeling his way forward, he was gradually won over by the arguments of Seretse and Tshekedi. From South Africa, Liesching warned repeatedly of trouble with South Africa,[26] but Home believed that he had sufficient political support to ignore this threat. Finally he made up his mind: to accept the Khamas' offer of renunciation, on their terms. Now he had to persuade others to support his decision. His first move was to write to the Prime Minister to explain his reasons. He was concerned, he said, that there might be a leak of information and

Seretse's renunciation will become public property. That will stir up the Labour Party here to enquire what we are going to do about it, and on this they will not be helpful, while it will start rumours and speculation and perhaps trouble in the tribe.

His instinct was to move 'pretty fast' and he hoped to bring off a comprehensive settlement – 'If you agree I will do so. I am preparing a short paper for Cabinet as I think they must be kept up to date.'[27] Eden replied immediately. 'This seems a courageous course,' he wrote, 'if we really have to stir up this hornet's nest . . . I agree that a talk with Cabinet is desirable.'[28]

A final meeting on the issue was held at the CRO, for which Bechuanaland's Resident Commissioner, Martin Wray, was specially flown to London. Joe Garner, the Commonwealth Deputy Under-Secretary of State, wrote a letter to Sir Gilbert Laithwaite, the Permanent Secretary, who was abroad, to bring him up to date. 'Suez takes up practically all our time', he said, but the other development is that 'we have brought our affairs with your African friends to what I hope will prove to be a very satisfactory conclusion'. Then, with much satisfaction, he added that

there was a complete volte-face on the part of Percivale [Liesching] and his advisers. As you know, they have throughout been recommending the utmost caution and going slow and had thought that it would be necessary to go through all sorts of hoops before matters could be finalised.

'My own hunch', he told Laithwaite, 'is that we have turned a very important corner and that a new and untroubled future may well lie ahead.'[29]

'I know we are taking risks,' Home told Liesching firmly, 'but I hope all this will now go well. I have seen Jim Griffiths and Clement Davies and both are well pleased.'[30] When the Cabinet met, Home achieved a consensus without any difficulty. Finally, and for the first time in the story of the Khamas' marriage, morality had triumphed over expediency in the policy of the British Government. But Liesching was bitter. In the course of discussions, he had referred to the 'skilful exploitation' by Tshekedi and Seretse of the political embarrassments they could cause.[31] It was not intended as a compliment.

In the Khama household, everyone had been on tenterhooks for weeks. 'Life became one long whirl of meetings, discussions and consultations,' wrote Ruth. But then came the day of the last meeting:

When Seretse arrived home from Westminster, I did not need to ask him the result. His beaming face told me everything.

All I asked was: 'When?'

'It has got to be kept secret for two weeks,' he said. 'A fortnight after that we can return.'

We celebrated the great news by forgetting to eat any dinner and talking wildly all the evening.[32]

On 26 September 1956, an official statement was issued by the CRO, announcing Home's acceptance of the renunciation by Seretse Khama of all claim to the chieftainship. Seretse and Tshekedi would return to Bechuanaland and would take part in tribal affairs.[33] The statement was greeted with enthusiasm by the broadsheets in the UK. *The Times* pointed out that the two main political parties in Britain had both behaved badly. 'The fundamental mistake', it argued, 'was committed when this decision having being taken for deeply based imperial reasons, the attempt was made to disguise it as a concession to the wishes of the tribe.' All the subsequent embarrassments, it added, 'have flowed from the intellectual dishonesty of this unhappy procedure'.[34] Home was praised in the UK and throughout the empire. It had taken only a month for him to reach his decision, once Seretse and Tshekedi had presented him with their document, and he came out of it well politically.[35]

'This is a great day for me,' Seretse told reporters outside his home.[36] He had always imagined that there might be some kind of slip, he explained, but now that it was definite he was immensely relieved. He had been due to take his final law examinations in December but he was unlikely ever to finish them – he wanted to get home as soon as possible.[37] Asked about his relationship with Tshekedi, he commented that,

We have always been good friends, but we had our political differences. My uncle came over to England in July and we talked over the position.

We decided to sink these differences for the sake of getting a settlement and in the interests of the progress and development of the Reserve. I am hopeful for the future.[38]

After six years and two months of exile, Seretse and Ruth were at last getting ready to take their family home. Naledi had already gone back to Bechuanaland in February 1954, having caught tuberculosis while nursing at Hammersmith Hospital. 'Reason for her return', reported the CRO to the High Commissioner, 'said to be that tuberculosis condition is *not* improving and she thinks Bechuanaland climate will be better for her.'[39] Once home, she recovered quickly.[40]

'We seemed to get hardly enough sleep during the next few weeks,' wrote Ruth, happily. She would leave Britain without the slightest regret. 'I thank God', she added, 'that I picked Seretse to be my man for life. No woman could have a better husband than I, nor is there a father more crazy about his children':

I'm not starry-eyed about this. I'll admit right here that these past seven years have been difficult ones.

We have lived in a sort of half-world, uncertain of our future, unhappy at our predicament. Life hasn't been easy, and some marriages might have come unstuck under the strain. But not ours. Seretse's cause was mine. My worries were his.[41]

Throughout the whole wretched affair of their exile, she said, Seretse 'has never lost his head, never let fly, never "gone on the town" to relieve his feelings – as well he might have done. He is a man with the sweetest temper imaginable.' He had never forgotten a single anniversary –

one of those little things a wife cherishes. He thinks I'm a good cook, and will eat anything I set before him. He is regular in his habits and not once through our married life have I been left at home heel-tapping waiting for my 'hubby' to come home. We have two lovely children. What more could a wife ask for?[42]

A press conference was called and the whole family came to the film studio, laughing together and clearly in excellent spirits. Six-year-old Jackie stood quietly next to her father, smiling and listening carefully to his words. Three-year-old Ian looked excitedly about him, fascinated by the cameras and bouncing up and down on Ruth's knee. On leaving Britain to return home for the first time in over six years, stated Seretse, he wanted to express his thanks 'to all those people here who have shown friendliness to my wife, my children, and myself. I should particularly like to thank those who have worked so hard to secure my return to my people.' Asked why he had given up his claim to the chieftainship, he replied:

I have renounced the chieftainship as I have always been prepared to do. Now I hope to assist my people to develop a democratic system, to raise our standard of life, and to establish a happy and healthy nationhood.[43]

Rasebolai was told of the settlement by Wray. He was pleased and cooperative, saying that his own position as native authority would be strengthened, as the people would no longer be waiting for Seretse to return as Kgosi. He remembered what most of the mandarins and politicians had forgotten: 'that just before Seretse had finally left the Protectorate in 1950 he discussed the possibility of his renunciation with Tshekedi'.[44] Wedgwood Benn made the same point in a letter to the press, a little later. The first memorandum of renunciation had been drawn up by Seretse six years before, he pointed out, and the British Government had known about it ever since.[45]

The momentous news of Seretse's and Tshekedi's renunciation – and their imminent return – was made to sixteen assemblies in different parts of the Bangwato Reserve. Very careful preparations had been made by the Administration. A British official in Mahalapye, George Winstanley, was surprised to receive a 'Top Secret for UK eyes only' letter, which was delivered by special courier. It instructed Winstanley to make the announcement in the main villages in his sub-district. This was quite a task, because of the great distances between villages. Next day, he set off early and visited each of the principal villages, explaining to headmen that he would be returning the following day and asking them to summon their people. One of these villages was Sefhare, which had been very active in its support of Seretse. Here there was great jubilation: 'Gasebalwe Seretse stood up and facing the Kgotla with his arms raised above his head shouted *Pula!* three times with great emphasis. The Tribe responded and shouted *Pula* over and over again.'[46]

Martin Wray came from Mafikeng to deliver the news to the Serowe Kgotla. Wearing brimmed hats against the blaze of the sun, 200 men sat on stools or squatted quietly, as Wray slowly and clearly explained that Seretse Khama had formally renounced for himself and his children all claim to the chieftainship of the Bangwato Tribe; and that Tshekedi Khama, who had previously renounced all claim to the chieftainship, had reaffirmed his renunciation. And he added:

In furtherance of the policy of Her Majesty's Government, a Tribal Council of an advisory nature is to be established for the Bamangwato. Rasebolai Kgamane, as the African Authority, will be Chairman of this Council when it is established. Both Seretse Khama and Tshekedi Khama have declared that they are in full agreement with the establishment of a Council and will lend their full support to Rasebolai Kgamane in his capacity as Chairman.[47]

'As Resident Commissioner,' he concluded, 'I am confident that this settlement will make a great difference to your future and will result in a happier period for the tribe. I wish you all a safe return to your homes. *Pula*.'[48] As soon as the translation of Wray's announcement had been completed by the interpreter, reported Reuters, the men jumped up with shouts of '*Pula!*' and for a few minutes no single voice could be heard above the uproar.[49] When copies of the announcement, written in Setswana, were handed out, they 'scrambled eagerly for the typewritten sheets' and gathered in groups to discuss them.[50]

The Nationalist Party newspaper, *Die Transvaler*, was heavily critical of the British Government's decision. A leading article stated that, 'Condonation of mixed marriages in a territory intended to be incorporated in the Union will upset the public in the Union.' It was fatal, the article went on, that the British should follow a policy in neighbouring territory which clashed with South African policy: it could do nothing but obstruct the solution of racial problems in the Union and would disturb good relations and order in the sub-continent. That the British should approve the Seretse marriage and allow the pair with their 'chocolate babies' to come and contaminate tradition in southern Africa, it went on, was on a level with her most short-sighted policy elsewhere in Africa.[51] This 'short-sighted policy' was a reference to the UK Government's undertaking, which had been announced to the Dominion Governments in 1955, to grant independence to the Gold Coast by the end of 1956 (though it did not take place until 1957) and subsequently to Nigeria in 1958 (1960).[52] The *Rhodesian Herald* was as bitter as *Die Transvaler* and also used the image of 'chocolate babies'.[53]

But there was no comment from the South African Government. Nor was there any comment from the Government of Southern Rhodesia.

Between 26 September 1956, the day of the official announcement, and 10 October, when Seretse was expected in Bechuanaland, there was a stream of conflicting rumours and reports in the Reserve about what would happen when Seretse actually arrived. These varied from statements that, whatever happened, he would be Kgosi, to reports that he would be forcibly installed as Kgosi by his supporters in Serowe. 'An important factor', reported Wray to London with some apprehension, 'was the large numbers of women who are devoted followers of Seretse.' He feared they might attend the Kgotla and cause disturbances – 'not so much according to any fixed plans but brought about by their enthusiasm for their hero'.[54] Excitement and tension mounted through the week. But Rasebolai, the Native Authority, was unworried. 'The troubles of the Bamangwato are over,' he told a correspondent from the *Rand Daily Mail*. 'I think everything will go smoothly. The tribesmen will wait for Seretse to return before they speak.'[55]

24

'Before their eyes it rained'

At last, Tuesday 9 October 1956 arrived – the day that had been scheduled for Seretse's departure. Well-wishers came with Ruth and the children to the airport to see him off, including Clement Freud, John Hatch and Muriel.[1] 'Then with a last hug for the children and myself,' recorded Ruth, 'he followed the air hostess out to the plane.'[2] Seretse was smiling broadly. But he looked tired and older than his 33 years: the years of banishment and worry had taken their toll.[3]

Seretse was leaving first, to be followed by Ruth and the children three weeks later. Ruth explained to the *Daily Mail* why they had made this decision:

Well, it is simply this: Seretse's return to Serowe will be HIS day. I want him to have it all to himself.

Much as I would have liked to be at his side for that great moment I feel that it belongs to him and him alone.

Seretse is bursting to be off now, and, husband-like, has little interest in the minor details of packing up, selling off, and so forth. But I don't blame him.

'If you had been exiled for six years from your homeland, through no fault of your own,' she asked the reporter, 'wouldn't you like to get back at the earliest possible moment?' Then she added,

I have been so proud of Seretse throughout his exile. Not once has he had the 'grumps' or taken it out on me for his misfortune. I wonder how many men would have behaved with equal consideration of his wife's feelings?[4]

The flying-boat service had been replaced by land planes in late 1950, just a couple of months after the Khamas had journeyed into exile. Now, Seretse flew to Salisbury in a propeller aeroplane, stopping to refuel at Rome, Cairo, Khartoum and Nairobi. At about 2.00 p.m. next day – after seventeen hours of travel – he reached Salisbury. Here he transferred to a tiny charter aircraft which took him to Francistown shortly before dusk.

Seretse's face lit up with joy as he stepped onto the tarmac, where he was greeted by Rasebolai and Tshekedi, as well as Fraenkel and the British officials of the region. When he saw his sisters Oratile and Naledi, he rushed forward to kiss and hug them. He was then welcomed home by headmen and local leaders, one by one; for each of them, he had a handshake and a few words.[5] Outside the aerodrome, more than 3,000 men, women and children were cheering and waiting to greet him; many of them were from the Bangwato Reserve and had travelled the long journey to Francistown in lorries and by train. Seretse wanted to speak to them, but they were so excited – and there was so much noise – that he had to abandon the plan. At one point the Police Commander was afraid the crowd was going out of control and ordered rifles to be handed out to his men.

But the crowd broke up when Seretse was driven away from the airport.[6] As the car passed out of the aerodrome, reported the *Bulawayo Chronicle*, people jammed the entrance, so that it was impossible for the car to get through for ten minutes:

Men threw their hats into the air, and while some women flung themselves to the ground, others kissed the car's bonnet.

Those who could not get near stood on lorries to get glimpses of Seretse, or screamed and jumped on car bonnets and roofs.

Eventually, Seretse's car had to be forced through the crowd.

Men and women scrambled into lorries and followed.[7]

When they arrived at the Divisional Office in the town, at least 2,000 people were waiting under a fluttering Union Jack and broke into a rousing hymn. Seretse spoke briefly to them, but was inaudible in the noise; he raised his arms and appealed for quiet, and an official banged on the side of a police truck. But nothing helped: the throng was too excited. After twenty minutes, Seretse gave up the attempt to speak. Then he went on to Oratile's house in the location and the people melted away into the darkness of the evening. He was planning to drive the 150 miles to Serowe the following day.[8]

Next day, the fleet of lorries that had brought the Bangwato to Francistown took them back in the early hours, to wait for Seretse outside Serowe and to escort him into the village.[9] It had seemed a good idea for Seretse to arrive in Serowe just before dark, as a way of diminishing the excitement. 'The great welcome given to Seretse,' reported the Johannesburg *Star*, 'was more than was expected, even though the former Chief has virtually leaned over backwards to discourage demonstrations.'[10] But all day, people had waited in little groups, eager to catch a glimpse of him. The elders waited patiently under the kgotla tree, the children were shrieking, and the women, with every false alarm, began trilling their welcome. For the last five miles of the journey, the road was lined with cheering, happy crowds. When, in the gathering sunset, Seretse finally arrived, with Tshekedi, Rasebolai and James Allison, the District Commissioner, they leapt to their feet with a delighted '*Pula! Pula!*'

Seretse went on to Rasebolai's house in the centre of the village, where the welcome, reported the *Sunday Times*, 'was fantastic. The crowd surged and swayed, then swarmed around Seretse, stretching out their hands to touch him, pat him, caress him. It was sheer joy, almost untouched by political feeling.'[11] Seretse went to the Kgotla, where 2,000 people had collected – but neither he nor the District Commissioner could be heard above the applause. The welcome he was given at Serowe exceeded even the reception in Francistown on the previous evening. Eventually Rasebolai took Seretse back to his house and Allison addressed the crowd from the veranda. Then everyone dispersed, in the best of spirits.[12]

Ever since *Life*'s photographer, Margaret Bourke-White, had come to Serowe in 1950, the magazine had taken a keen interest in the story of Seretse and Ruth's exile. They sent a correspondent to cover the happy ending – Seretse's return. The fact that Seretse was returning as a private citizen, not as Kgosi, he reported, was a fine distinction that seemed to be lost on the Bangwato. He was greeted with the traditional cries of welcome – '*Pula, Pula*' – and then, added *Life*, 'before their eyes it rained'. It was not even just a drizzle, but a heavy storm. When Seretse reached the tribal offices, recorded a local official, 'thunder and lightning rent the air and the rain came down in torrents'.[13] The *Bulawayo Chronicle* reported that

The first crash of thunder split the air. Flashes of lightning followed each other and clouds erupted over the Bamangwato Reserve.

'Seretse's home and it's raining,' screamed the mob. 'Seretse has brought the pula.'[14]

Seretse still had to make a public statement about his renunciation of the kingship. On 12 October, he, Rasebolai and Tshekedi conferred with Allison and they agreed that although plans had been made for a Kgotla in three days' time, it should be delayed until Thursday 18 October, to allow time for the excitement to subside – 'with special reference', wrote the Resident Commissioner anxiously to London, 'to the large numbers of women who were already a problem in Serowe'. The delay would also give Seretse an opportunity for informal conversation with the people of Serowe, to prepare them for the Kgotla. Moreover, said Wray,

Seretse's general behaviour and attitude towards Government officers has been exemplary ... I am now much more hopeful that the outcome of the Kgotla and subsequent tour will be completely successful than I was before it was possible to gauge his reactions to a tumultuous welcome by his own people. So far he has been extremely level-headed and helpful.

Wray reported on the security measures that had been put in place to cope with any sudden and unexpected outbreak of violence at Serowe, such as 'anti-European riots'. It had been arranged with the Witwatersrand Native Labour Association, the agency which sent Bangwato men to the mines in South Africa, that an aeroplane would be standing by at Francistown. If there was a sudden emergency, extra security forces could be flown immediately to the Serowe airstrip.[15]

Thanksgiving services were held at the London Missionary Society Church in the centre of Serowe. Seretse attended one of these services and made a speech to the congregation, expressing his joy at returning home again. The light streamed through the arcs of the church windows into the dark, cool interior, lighting up the figure of the man whom everyone had been waiting for.[16]

The day came for the Kgotla in Serowe, at which Seretse would publicly renounce the kingship and explain his reasons. There was a vast assembly: 5,000–6,000 people, including women. Despite the

October heat, many of the men were wrapped in their old army greatcoats. In front of them sat Seretse, Tshekedi and Rasebolai, with Seretse in the middle; all three men wore dark suits, reflecting the solemnity of the occasion.[17] Prayers were said and then, just after nine o'clock, Rasebolai opened the Kgotla. He ordered a large number of women to go to the back, and they obeyed. Keaboka was the first to speak. He described his immense pleasure at seeing Seretse, Tshekedi and Rasebolai together and said that he and others looked to 'the big three' to guide them.[18] It was Keaboka's full, public support right from the start, believed Allison, that assured the success of the Kgotla.[19]

A deep silence fell when Seretse rose to speak. He said that he was giving up the kingship for the sake of tribal unity. 'If I can cooperate with my elders,' he told the assembly, 'so can you, who are their juniors.'[20] He reminded them that the idea of his living in the Reserve as a private citizen was not new – it had been raised in 1950 and when the delegation had gone to the UK in 1952, they had proposed this to the Government on behalf of the people. He would assist Rasebolai with his tribal duties. Kingship was over: it would be replaced by Councils, under Rasebolai as Chairman. Either he or Tshekedi, or both of them, would probably be elected. This would be a new form of Government, he explained, which would allow the Bangwato, for the first time in their history, to take part. Rule by one man would now be over. In the past, people had complained of unfairness and oppression, but a Council would end this. It would allow everyone in the Reserve to take part – to know what was happening, to correct wrongs and to contribute to the common good. 'You should not be worried,' he assured his listeners, 'for such a system means you will be able to take part.' He would not have renounced the kingship, he assured them, 'if it was not the greatest step towards advancement of the tribe'.[21]

He had heard that when he stopped speaking he was to be invested with a lion skin and declared Kgosi – but, he said, he did not have two tongues like a snake.[22] Seretse spoke 'firmly, resolutely and convincingly', reported Allison, returning at frequent intervals to his main theme – peace, progress, welfare and unity, and the absolute necessity of setting aside the old divisions and hatreds.[23] He empha-sized that political development in the Bangwato Reserve was to be on modern lines. He finished his speech to the sound of three long, deep *pulas*.

Then Tshekedi spoke, underlining his support for the Council. He traced the history of the Bechuanaland Protectorate under the protection of the British Crown, which had been accepted by the diKgosi. There was no need to worry about not having a Kgosi, he said, because many countries did not. In any case, he said,

Seretse is still the son of our Chief. We still give him the respect due to a Chief and we will always in our hearts regard him as Chief, but now Rasebolai is the head of the Tribe and Seretse will help him. In this way he is not lost and his advice and help will always be available to us.[24]

He reassured the Bangwato that Seretse would rule them with Rasebolai, through the Council. He spoke with great force, almost as if the Council had already been set up. He added that after his four years' absence from the Kgotla, he would now be dealing with tribal affairs.[25]

The last 'nail in the coffin of any possible non-acceptance', reported Allison, was driven home by Oabona Nthobatsang, who was a powerful orator and had been a leading supporter of Seretse. He said that he had little to say except to offer his thanks. He was grateful to God that the sons of Khama were now together and he prayed they might be as united as their diKgosi. And now, he said, it would be possible to pursue the mineral development of Bechuanaland: 'We refused to give any concessions in the absence of Seretse. Now he is back and this can be considered again.'

Rasebolai stood up. Everyone who had contributed to the discussion so far, he commented, had spoken for the same thing. He asked if anyone wished to speak differently. No one answered and there was a 'sudden almost fierce murmur from the front of the crowd – "No, these men have said all our words." '[26] There was a unanimous acceptance of Seretse's renunciation.

Then Rasebolai said that, as was customary, he would ask the visiting dikgosi to speak. Kgosi Molefi spoke first, 'forcefully, picturesquely and amusingly, greeting the [Bangwato] on behalf of the Bakgatla, expressing his joy at seeing the sons of Khama together'. He said that the Bangwato had been a proud people and then became a laughing stock – but, he added jokingly, 'Now the Bakgatla had seen Seretse, they were finished.' Bathoen spoke next and likened the Bangwato to an iron pot with three legs:

The three children of Khama were the three legs of the pot. In the pot food was boiled, and they were the food in the pot. If there was unity in the home, there would be unity in the Tribe. The troubles of the past should be left. Government made every effort to help the Tribe. The latter should replace evil with good, and Government should regard them with trust and confidence and forgive them.

Then it was the turn of Kgosi Mokgosi of the Balete, Seretse's good friend. He said he agreed with everything that had been said and he emphasized Bathoen's call for deeds as well as words: 'But deeds will show. Let us be careful of what we say. Seretse and Tshekedi have come to an agreement and we should now help.'[27] If the Bangwato started Councils, he added, then the Balete might decide to copy them. But he advised the Bangwato that if they were to bring in this new system, they should do it properly. He said he had visited countries where the system worked well. Finally he told the assembly that he regarded the diKgosi as one in three and three in one, carrying on the work of the Bangwato in thought and deed.[28]

Allison closed the Kgotla, at Rasebolai's request. His speech was listened to in complete silence, as it was translated into Setswana. He appealed to the Tribe to make Seretse's decision a success. 'Any angry words and unpleasantness are an insult to him,' he said, 'because they are an insult to what he has done.'[29]

The Kgotla was 'absolutely quiet and respectful', reported Allison to headquarters.[30] The addresses had been long, but the vast crowd had listened intently to every word. Their only reaction, as each speaker ended his address, was a solemn shout of '*Pula*'. Seretse had been 'clearly the dominating personality at the Kgotla and he spoke forcefully and authoritatively'.[31] The meeting broke up in very good spirits and the 'Big Three' went across to Rasebolai's house for a short press conference. Allison noticed that respect for Rasebolai as the Kgotla came to an end was very obvious – for Rasebolai was seen to have brought back Seretse.[32]

'The people were happy to see me back,' wrote Seretse to John

Hatch, 'but the question of my renunciation of the chieftainship was, as you can expect, reluctantly accepted.' There was a fear, he explained, that if they insisted on installing him as Chief and leader of the Tribe, in the place of the Native Authority, 'your British Government would send me packing'.[33] But despite the disappointment of not being able to call Seretse their Kgosi, there was great happiness and a sense of real hope for the future. Now that Seretse was back, Peto Sekgoma told the press, negotiations with Anglo-American would soon reach a conclusion. 'We are hopeful', he said, 'that this will eventually bring about complete economic independence for the territory and remove for all time the threat of incorporation by the Union.' But in any case, that threat now appeared to have slipped away. When the *Star* asked Tshekedi, 'What about incorporation?' he simply answered, 'I think we can forget about that.'[34]

The 'Big Three' then travelled around the Bangwato Reserve. On 22 October a Kgotla at Sefhare was attended by about 1,800 people. Next day, there was an Assembly of between 500 and 600 people in Palapye. On the night before the Palapye Kgotla, Seretse had a nosebleed and a temperature; and at the meeting itself, he felt unwell. It was clear that the tour would have to be interrupted for a few days, to allow him time to recover. It was no wonder he felt weak, thought Wray, given the intense heat, the travelling and the general strain of his 'continuously good performances'.[35]

Everywhere the meetings were a great success. Only at Sebinas was there any departure from the usual pattern. Despite a warm speech of welcome, followed by two other speakers who made a point of praising Tshekedi for bringing Seretse back, one young man, speaking forcefully – and despite the protests of the other men – complained that he had heard enough about Tshekedi, who had oppressed them too much in the past. Another speaker said that while he welcomed the settlement, talk of gratitude to Tshekedi would only keep the dispute alive. But the Kgotla ended well. When Rasebolai asked if anybody wished to speak against the settlement, there was an almost unanimous murmur that there was no disagreement.[36]

When Seretse and Rasebolai went to Mahalapye, they stopped off to see the local official, Winstanley, and stayed for tea. When the housemaid heard that Seretse was there, she immediately rushed out to the veranda, 'and kneeling humbly and reverently before Seretse greeted him with deep emotion. He responded with exquisite courtesy and shook her proffered hand.' It was 'immediately obvious to me,' commented Winstanley, 'why the Bamangwato adored him.'[37]

Rasebolai and Seretse were getting on very well together. Wray was aware, though, that these first weeks back in Bechuanaland were a terrible strain for Seretse. He was exhausted – 'His right hand has been wrung by so many people that it is now rather sore.' He had been searching for a house for his family and eventually found a sprawling, iron-roofed bungalow in the middle of the village. He had originally thought that he should live outside Serowe, to avoid embarrassing Rasebolai, but they were getting on so well that this would clearly not be a problem. There was no electricity or gas in the house, but Seretse had a paraffin-operated refrigerator installed and there was a coal range; tapped water was pumped from a borehole.[38]

Seretse interrupted his tour of the Reserve when Ruth and the children arrived, three weeks after himself. The *Daily Mail* in London had made much of the difficulties facing Ruth, as she prepared to leave London:

> These are the two worlds of Ruth Khama. *She leaves* a typical London home with accepted European amenities: electricity, telephone, radio.
>
> *She goes* to a country of thatched huts. To a country without power. To a country without radio. To a country separated from London by thousands of miles . . . and thousands of years.[39]

But the lack of amenities did not bother Ruth. 'I am looking forward to returning to Bechuanaland which I regard as my home,' she told the *Daily Mirror*.[40] The only thing that worried her, she said, was education – both Tshekedi and Seretse had gone to Lovedale and Fort Hare, but she and Seretse were prohibited immigrants in South Africa. Then she explained her support for Seretse's renunciation of the chieftainship. In London, she said, Seretse could do nothing for his people; but in Bechuanaland, even as a private citizen, he could do a lot. And there was a lot that needed to be done, because the lives of the Bangwato had declined: 'Their sole source of income, cattle, has been allowed to run down . . . Well, now the Bamangwatos have two heads,

Tshekedi and Seretse, two of the wisest best-educated heads in Africa.'

She also felt there was 'a big part, for me, as a woman, to play'; with Seretse's help, she hoped to do something to improve women's lives. When she had lived in Serowe, she said, she had realized how backward the country was in terms of welfare and health – and that the women led 'a purdah-like existence'; she remembered that scores of women had come every day to talk about their troubles. 'Of course,' she added, 'I was the Chief's wife then. It may make a difference now. But I doubt it.' She was longing to return: the greeting of the Bangwato, she said, 'is already music in my ears . . . *Pula, Pula*, they say to you.'[41]

Preparations for Ruth's return with Jackie and Ian had been causing headaches for the CRO, because their plane would need to land in Salisbury. The family would offend against the colour bar that dominated Southern Rhodesia and they were hated by most of the white community in the country. What should they do, worried Sykes, a CRO official, if the plane carrying Ruth and her family arrived in Salisbury too late to fly on to Bechuanaland the same evening? 'I feel we can hardly expect two little children', he objected, 'to bounce about in the back of a car during an all night journey in the way that would have been tolerable for Seretse.'[42] He tried to make a reservation for Ruth and the children at the Meikles Hotel, the premier hotel in Salisbury, but the hotel refused. After long discussions, the Meikles reluctantly agreed – 'but only on our plea', reported Sykes in hot indignation, 'that children could not be stranded overnight'.[43] The management said that Mrs Khama would have to take her meals in the bedroom with the children; she might be glad to do this, thought Sykes protectively, to avoid 'ill-mannered stares in the dining-room'.[44] To make the family as comfortable as possible and to avoid any embarrassment, he reserved a sitting room for them, where meals could be served.[45]

Sykes and Miss Emery referred respectfully to Ruth as 'Mrs Khama' in their correspondence with each other. This was in marked contrast with the attitudes towards 'Ruth' of CRO officials in 1950, when she had been banished from Bechuanaland. The story of the Khamas was now being seen through a different lens. Alan Lennox-Boyd, the Colonial Secretary – who had advocated the permanent exclusion of Seretse in 1951 – now enclosed a note of good wishes for Mrs Khama with a letter to Lord Home. If appropriate, he said, he would be most grateful if the note could be passed on to Mrs Khama before she left London. 'I congratulate you so much on this decision,' he told Home.[46]

With her two children clinging tightly to her skirt, Ruth arrived at Salisbury airport at lunchtime on 31 October and was met by the District Officer of Mafikeng, who had been at Oxford with Seretse. The stay at the Meikles Hotel had been so carefully planned that it went smoothly, and early the next morning the family flew on to Bechuanaland in a chartered light plane. When they arrived at the Serowe airstrip, Seretse helped Ruth down over the plane's wing and then embraced Jackie and Ian, overjoyed to bring them home. Allison, in his role as District Commissioner, officially welcomed Ruth. But Mrs Allison was not present, nor were any other European women. When Miss Emery heard about this, she was cross – there was no need for an enormous reception committee, she thought, but 'it would have been a pleasant gesture, if one European lady, Mrs Allison, if possible could have been there'.[47] Clearly, the European community did not want Ruth back in Serowe.

But the Bangwato – and especially the women – were ecstatic at her return, with the two children. Hundreds of tribesmen and thousands of Bamangwato women and children, reported the *Rhodesia Herald*, 'were preparing to give Mrs Khama a rousing welcome'.[48] She was greeted as the Mother of the people – *Mohumagadi* – and was driven to her new home through knots of dancing women. When she arrived, reported a correspondent for the *Daily Telegraph*, who had flown to Bechuanaland to cover the Khamas' return, 'Bamangwato women besieged Mrs Khama in her new home at Serowe with shouts of welcome.'[49] Ruth and Seretse, holding the children and smiling broadly, stood on the veranda in front of a vast crowd, who were craning their necks to see them and stretching out their arms. Ruth was wearing an outfit of green cotton, with a floral motif, and a black sequin-trimmed velvet hat and black accessories, according to the Johannesburg *Star*. She had arrived quietly and without any fuss, 'with a measure of poise and dignity. She made it clear that she regards herself as a Bangwato subject.'[50] Speaking on behalf of Ruth in Setswana, Seretse told the cheering people how happy his wife was to have come home and to be with them. Later that morning, Tshekedi arrived at the house – and 'the family reunion', said the *Telegraph*, 'was complete.'[51]

The Nationalist Government of South Africa had been silent on the ending of Seretse's and Ruth's exile. But in large parts of the country, there was jubilation – it seemed to herald a real change in the racial politics of southern Africa. In the townships of Johannesburg, towards the end of 1956, people danced joyfully to a song by Miriam Makeba – *Pula Kgosi Seretse*. The Federation of South African Women – which just two months before had organized a massive march on the Union Buildings in Pretoria to protest against the extension of Passes to women – sent a letter to Ruth to welcome her back to southern Africa. 'We salute your courage', wrote Helen Joseph, the National Secretary, 'in opposing racial prejudice, your determination to choose your own way of life, to choose whom you marry.' They knew, she added,

of the difficulties that you have faced so courageously in the past, of the difficulties you will be called upon to face in the future, and we join with the other women of Africa in welcoming you, your husband and your children, back to the land of your choice, of your husband's birth.

She added that the National President of the Federation, Mrs Lilian Ngoyi, sent her personal greetings and recalled with pleasure getting to know Ruth in London.[52]

On the day after Ruth's return, she and Seretse strolled arm-in-arm through the town. They did some shopping and then drove round to the kgotla ground, where Seretse presented to his wife some of the African officials from the district. Then, with the children, they crossed the hill overlooking Serowe to the royal burial ground where Seretse's ancestors were interred. 'Every tribesman bowed low as the family passed', reported the Johannesburg *Star*, and 'every Bamangwato woman showed her respect. Some showed their joy by going through some motion connected with reaping the harvest.' On the long veranda of the Khama home, the reporter asked Ruth how it felt to be back in Serowe: 'She stared at the tight ring of Native huts spread out over the town, took a deep breath and said, "I'm so happy, ever so happy."'[53] So were the Bangwato. It was not long, according to the *Daily Herald*, before a song of local dancers, beginning with the words, 'Seretse and Ruth have come back to us', became popular all over the Reserve.[54]

25

The wind of change

'A great change has come over the Bamangwato Reserve,' wrote a correspondent for the Johannesburg *Star* in 1957. Since Seretse Khama had returned from exile with his English wife, he reported, 'the Bamangwato have settled down to a new and peaceful life. Gone are the conflicts in the Tribe, the refusal to cooperate with the authorities, and the tribal feuds, family against family.'[1] Gone, too, was the cloud of sorrow and grief that had cast a shadow over daily life in Serowe for six long years.

What had *not* gone were the seething resentments of the white community against Ruth. A few of them were loyal friends, but most lost no time in trying to make her life as miserable as possible. She was harassed by the police for trivial matters concerning her car, such as a badly positioned rear light. The police also tried to prosecute her under the liquor laws, when she bought alcohol from the hotel in Palapye. 'What was bugging [them] of course,' commented a sympathetic official, 'was that no doubt Seretse would enjoy some of the gin and being a "native" would be breaking the law.' When the Serowe tennis club committee learned that Seretse and Ruth planned to attend the annual dance the next day, with a party of four African friends, the event was quickly cancelled on the pretext of the extreme heat.[2]

But Ruth ignored these slights and settled into a happy domestic routine with her family. She also started the welfare work she had been longing to do for the people of Serowe, and launched the first club of the Council of Women, which provided a range of services for women, including crèches for the children of working mothers. With the help of the hospital where she had given birth to Jacqueline, she also organized classes in hygiene, baby care and nursing first aid, including how to make bandages from mealie bags. Spread around in her drawing room were catalogues and British women's magazines, from which she was collecting patterns for dressmaking, knitting and crochet classes. She was also arranging lessons to teach women how to grow their own vegetables, because a cabbage and many greens cost more than a day's wage; to demonstrate good methods, she had cultivated a flourishing vegetable patch in her own backyard.[3]

Sometimes Ruth wished the railway line was nearer, so that she could get fresh fruit and fish, to vary the daily meals of meat. She also missed her parents and sometimes drove all the way to Francistown to telephone her mother. But otherwise, she was content. The post came three times a week and letters of support came from all over the world, one of which was addressed to 'Ruth, Edge of Kalahari Desert'.

Together, Ruth and Seretse set up a cricket club, organizing non-racial matches in front of their house, as well as tennis and boxing clubs. They organized sports sessions and social functions such as dances, to raise funds for a community building. 'We can't rely on charity,' said Seretse – 'we've got to learn to help ourselves.'[4]

They were watched by the Bechuanaland Protectorate Special Branch, which filed regular reports to London.[5] They were also watched by South Africans who drove over the border to look at them, peering through car windows at the family. It was as though, said Seretse with distaste, 'we were some strange animals'.[6]

Seretse built a new house for his family high on a hill overlooking Serowe, with generated electricity and water pumped from a borehole; they moved in a year after their return. Then, in 1958, Ruth gave birth to twin boys: Tshekedi Stanford and Anthony Paul. In the past, twins had been regarded by the Bangwato people as an evil omen; but as they witnessed the joy of Seretse and Ruth, they welcomed the twins and joined in the celebrations.[7] Seretse's and Ruth's decision to name one of the twins after Tshekedi was a powerful way of demonstrating that the years of bitterness between nephew and uncle were firmly in the past. The other twin, Anthony, was named after Anthony Wedgwood Benn, who had done so much to help end the Khamas' exile and who by now had shortened his name to Tony Benn. Seretse was the godfather of Melissa, Benn's daughter.

'It's wonderful to be back,' said Seretse, 'and to feel I am doing something worthwhile.'[8] He was busy with his vast herds of cattle and carrying out experiments to improve farming in Bechuanaland.[9] But he was also becoming involved in politics. Before leaving the UK, at a press conference, he had described his hope 'to assist my people to develop a democratic system, to raise our standard of life, and to establish a happy and healthy nationhood'.[10] Now he put this into action.

Towards the end of 1957, he and Tshekedi took a leading role in the creation of a Bangwato Tribal Council, democratically elected in the Kgotla; Rasebolai was Chairman, Seretse was Vice-Chairman, and Tshekedi was Secretary. John Hatch, writing to Seretse from the UK, warned him that Tshekedi had 'an extremely tortuous mind, and one which continually harbours ulterior motives'. He was glad, he said, that uncle and nephew were cooperating together, but he was concerned that Seretse might be circumvented by his uncle's manoeuvres.[11] What Hatch did not understand was that both Seretse and Tshekedi genuinely wanted the best possible future for their nation – that although they had had their differences in the past, they had come together and reached a truce for the sake of their people.

As the designated Kgosi of the Bangwato, Seretse had been primarily concerned about the needs of his own people. But now he became involved in the politics of the Protectorate as a whole: he became a member of the African Advisory Council and the Joint Advisory Council, both advisory bodies to the Resident Commissioner, along with the European Advisory Council.[12]

Then the Bangwato suffered a great shock. Unexpectedly, Tshekedi fell gravely ill with kidney problems and was rushed to the UK, accompanied by his wife Ella, to consult specialists. Seretse flew to London to be with his uncle. When he arrived, Tshekedi – though struggling to stay conscious – greeted him with a joyful smile and said, 'I am glad you have come. Let's forget the past and start afresh.' Seretse had brought with him an agreement between the Bangwato and a mining company, so that Tshekedi could sign it as a witness. Tshekedi had missed the historic moment at which negotiations between the company and the Bangwato nation had been concluded

– negotiations in which he himself had taken such a crucial role. This was his very last signature.

Tshekedi moved closer to death. Seretse sat at his bedside, along with Ella, Tshekedi's sons and a stream of British friends and supporters, including W. A. W. Clark, David Astor, Michael Scott, Mary Benson (who was writing his biography) and members of the LMS.[13] The Earl of Home also visited: although Tshekedi was too weak to talk, he reached out to clasp Home's hand.[14] Finally, on 10 June 1959, at the age of only 54, Tshekedi died. In Bechuanaland, even those who had disagreed with him mourned the loss of this strong and powerful man, who had been at the centre of the Bangwato nation.

Tshekedi's death has been described as the end of an era, allowing Seretse, who now succeeded his uncle as Tribal Secretary, to develop his own path for the future of the Protectorate. Seretse's approach to politics was very different: he attracted support instead of creating conflict and antagonism.[15] He was a statesman who commanded respect and love – and not fear. Moreover, he was firmly committed to democracy, unlike his more autocratic uncle.

Seretse had very clear ideas about how the Protectorate could best meet the needs of its people and offer to the region the model of a non-racial state. As he said at his inaugural sitting on the Joint Advisory Council in 1958:

I think it is time that we ourselves in Bechuanaland, who neither belong to the Union of South Africa nor the Federation [of Rhodesia and Nyasaland], or any other part as far as I can see, except Great Britain, should try to formulate a policy of our own which is probably unique to us.

This policy, he explained, was one of 'even teaching those countries who profess to be more advanced than ourselves, that in as far as administration and race relationships [are concerned], they have more to learn from us than we from them'. He had been disturbed, he added,

to find that on the whole there is a tendency to look always over our shoulders. Perhaps I am wrong, if so I stand corrected. We want to see what is happening elsewhere instead of getting on with what we know is peculiar to us and to the country itself.

But, he urged,

We should get on and have no fear that we may incur someone's displeasure, as long as what we do is internationally accepted ... And if we are right I am afraid emotion must come into this; we should not bother very much with what anyone might say ... We have ample opportunity in this country to teach people how human beings can live together.[16]

The idea of teaching ways in which human beings could live together would have been a formidable challenge in any part of the world in the middle of the twentieth century. In southern Africa, racked by the sickness of racial segregation and white supremacy, it was a hugely ambitious plan – but all the more urgent.

Seretse and other prominent men from all over Bechuanaland called on the British Government to set up a multi-racial Legislative Assembly for the whole of the Protectorate, to which the Government agreed in 1960. Plans were developed for a Legislative Council that would rule Bechuanaland, subject to a British veto, with an Executive Council operating like a Cabinet. Although at least a third of the members would be nominated British officials, the remainder would be elected – ten African, ten white, and one Asian. Quite clearly, observed John Hatch, it was 'a constitution designed to lead gradually to eventual democratic representation'.[17] Elections were held in 1961, and because Seretse got twice as many votes as any other man, he was made a member of the Executive Council.

'Democratic development', said Seretse in a press interview that was reported by *Time*, 'is much better than being a Chief.' He was now starting to be seen not simply as the leader of the Bangwato, but the leader of the whole of the nation of Bechuanaland. He was 'obviously', added *Time*, 'the most powerful politician around.'[18]

One of Seretse's key concerns was the racial discrimination operating in the Protectorate. One of the most visible examples was the law prohibiting the sale of liquor to Africans; this was a relic of the days when Khama III and other diKgosi had called on Britain, as the protecting power, to enact this prohibition. It had now produced a situation where not only were Africans unable to purchase liquor, but hotels used this as a way of refusing customers on the grounds of race.[19] A Liquor Law was passed in 1961, abolishing all distinctions based on race in regard to the sale and consumption of liquor and replacing them with distinctions based on 'standards of civilisation'.

Then, in 1962, at the insistence of Seretse, a Select Committee on Racial Discrimination was appointed to examine ways of eliminating discriminatory practices. It produced a report recommending a number of measures: the unification of the legal system, with one set of courts for everyone; the same tax system for everybody; equal opportunities for employment; and the creation of a non-racial system of education. The report was met with hostility by many of the Europeans, especially the plan to open every school to all children, regardless of colour. They managed to water down the recommendations and suspend legislation.[20] Seretse was bitterly disappointed: clearly, the road to non-racialism would be uphill.

In 1962, Seretse formed a political party – the liberal-democratic Bechuanaland Democratic Party (BDP). Other founding leaders of the BDP included Ketumile Masire of the Bangwaketse, a former schoolteacher from Kanye and editor of *Naledi ya Batswana*, whom Seretse had met in 1960; like Seretse, he had studied at Tiger Kloof. The aim of the BDP was to build a non-racial society based on the principle of equal opportunities for all, and independence from Britain. 'Seretse Khama is a strong nationalist,' stated a report to the State Department in Washington, 'and his BDP policies call for early independence and a good positive program of economic and social development. They are campaigning earnestly.'[21] Equally earnest was the Opposition: the Bechuanaland People's Party (BPP), a nationalist organization led by Philip Matante, which had been formed before the BDP and which was actively supported by Ghana. Both parties called for independence from Britain. But unlike Matante, Seretse and Masire were more interested in finding pragmatic solutions to the problems of their country, than in the adoption of any movement or ideology.

Seretse and Masire complemented each other well: they came from two of the major nations of Bechuanaland, in the north and in the south; Seretse was royal, while Masire was a commoner; Seretse had natural authority, while Masire was a technocrat, with a great organizing ability and a sound knowledge of finance and economic affairs.[22]

They were a powerful team to bring the different regions of the Protectorate together into a nation.

In 1963, when Masire was going to the UK to attend a Commonwealth Parliamentary Course, Seretse sent a letter to Tony Benn in London, asking him to find someone to instruct Masire on party organization. He explained:

As you may have heard I lead a political party known as the Bechuanaland Democratic Party. We have been in existence for just over a year now . . . We have reason to believe that in a couple of years' time, Britain will grant us internal self government and with this in view, it is our wish to organise ourselves on a proper party basis.

Benn did all he could to help – 'We often think of you all and wonder how things are going. When are you coming back . . . to catch up with events in London? Your god-daughter is quite a big girl now and would love to see you again.'[23]

The British and US Governments were watching Seretse's growing political role – and his advocacy of a non-racial state – with approval and satisfaction. In 1961, G. Mennen Williams, the American Assistant Secretary of State for African affairs, reported to the Secretary of State in Washington that he had met Seretse Khama and been impressed by his intelligence and ability and by the 'constructive interest' of his wife in the future of Bechuanaland. While in the region, he added, he had had a frank and open discussion with Bernard Braine, the British Parliamentary Under-Secretary for Colonial Affairs, in which they had 'reviewed [the] African scene in general and High Commission Territories in particular'. Braine, he said, had 'developed [the] idea of making a Commission Territory a showpiece for multi-racial democracy in a critical area, to which I heartily subscribe'.[24] This was no different from Fenner Brockway's idea of creating a successful non-racial state, as a healthy alternative to South Africa (a far cry from Britain's policy just ten years earlier, of supporting South Africa at all costs). But the British and American Governments were less idealistic and more cynical than Brockway. Worried that the developing policy of apartheid would drive nationalists in the region into the arms of Communist groups and nations, they were hoping that Seretse – as a moderate, with close links to Western democracy –

would draw supporters away from radical groups such as the BPP, which was believed to have links with the USSR and China.[25]

The call for national sovereignty in Bechuanaland took place against a background of massive change in the British Empire. In 1945, when Seretse Khama had first sailed to the UK, the imperial motherland had over fifty formal dependencies in a colonial Empire that was scattered across the world. But in 1957, the year after Seretse's return from exile, the Gold Coast had become Ghana, the first British territory in Africa to achieve independence. 'Ghana's independence', declared Nkrumah, its first President, 'is meaningless unless it is linked with the total liberation of Africa.'[26] All over the continent, African nationalism was gaining ground, and many of the young African men who had been studying in the UK at the same time as Seretse had now returned home and were leading their countries to independence. The resolutions that had been passed with such passion and determination in 1945 at the Pan-African Congress in Manchester – by Nkrumah, Kenyatta, Banda and others – were at last coming to fruition.

In Britain, too, there was a growing sense of unease about the imperial role, especially in connection with Britain's handling in Kenya of the Mau Mau rebellion. In 1959, news emerged from Kenya that at the Hola 'rehabilitation' camp, eleven long-serving detainees had been beaten to death by guards and eighty-one had been injured. This caused an outcry in Parliament and was seen to discredit the Governor, Sir Evelyn Baring, especially when an inquiry revealed that he had presided over mass trials and death sentences, where emergency courts had sentenced men to capital punishment for very minor allegations. Baring did not resign and none of his senior officers was ever charged over these crimes. When Baring left Kenya at the end of his governorship in September 1959, he left under a shadow that became closely associated with the history of British Africa.[27] Another such shadow was the report of the Devlin Commission, which investigated the reasons for the imposition of Emergency Rule in Nyasaland (Malawi) and the brutality of the British Administration; it was heavily critical and accused the colonial Government of running a 'police state'.[28]

In any case, the Empire had been steadily in decline since the Second World War. This was highlighted by the humiliation of the UK over the Suez crisis. In early November 1956, only weeks after Seretse's and Ruth's return to Bechuanaland, Britain and France had responded to Nasser's nationalization of the Suez Canal by invading the region, on the pretext of separating Egyptian forces from an attacking Israeli army. But within a few days of the invasion, Britain was condemned by the UN and the USA and her troops were forced to leave Egypt. It emerged that Prime Minister Eden had lied to the House of Commons in denying prior knowledge of Israel's attack; he resigned in January 1957 and Harold Macmillan became Prime Minister. Ever afterwards, the Suez crisis was regarded as synonymous with the loss of British imperial power.

The waning of British rule in Africa was given a high profile in February 1960 by Macmillan. He went on an intensive six-week tour of Africa, which began with a visit to independent Ghana and covered 20,000 miles, ending in South Africa. On his way south, on 26 January, he stopped off in Francistown in Bechuanaland and attended a special meeting of the Joint Advisory Council in the airport building; there he met Seretse, as a member of the JAC, and also Ruth.[29] After this he flew on to Cape Town, where he gave a speech to the all-white South African Parliament, which – for the first time – gave a clear and highly publicized account of the difference between South African and British policy on the issue of race and the future of Africa. Drawing attention to the growing spirit of nationalism throughout the world, he discussed the impact of this development in Asia and, more recently, in Africa:

The wind of change is blowing through this continent, and whether we like it or not this growth of national consciousness is a political fact. We must all accept it as a fact and our national policies must take account of it.

Then he set out Britain's position:

We reject the idea of any inherent superiority of one race over another. Our policy therefore is non-racial. It offers a future in which . . . all play their full part as citizens . . . and in which feelings of race will be submerged in loyalty to new nations.[30]

Macmillan's speech was met with predictable dismay by Europeans all over Africa. But it was welcomed with enthusiasm by many people throughout the Empire and the world. As far away as Canada, the *Ottawa Journal* praised Macmillan's courage and concluded – rightly – that the speech 'may well find an honoured place in history books of the future'. In the UK, it was welcomed by many politicians on both the Left and the Right. But there was also hostility and right-wing Conservatives formed the Monday Club, to mark the 'Black Monday' on which the speech had been given.[31]

But they could not arrest the process of decolonization. After Ghana became independent in 1957, Nigeria followed in 1960. In the next year, it was the turn of Sierra Leone and Tanganyika, and then Uganda in 1962. Kenyatta, who was freed from prison in 1961, was sworn in as Prime Minister of a sovereign Kenya in 1963, inviting Seretse and Ruth to the Independence celebrations. Zanzibar also achieved independence in 1963, uniting with Tanganyika as Tanzania the following year. Northern Rhodesia and Nyasaland became independent as Zambia and Malawi, respectively, in 1964; the Gambia followed in 1965.

But the whites in Rhodesia, on the northern border of Bechuanaland, were not willing to give up their unfair advantages on the basis of colour. In November 1965, Ian Smith and the white community of Southern Rhodesia vowed they would not allow black rule in the country – which they now called Rhodesia – for 1,000 years. In an effort to ensure this, they made a Unilateral Declaration of Independence (UDI) from Britain; it was unilateral because Britain would not countenance an independent state in which the black majority did not have a fair share of power. Under white minority rule, only 220,000 whites held power, land and privileges at the expense of nearly 4 million blacks.

A British Government intelligence report observed that almost the entire white community of Bechuanaland, including British colonial officials, were vocally sympathetic to the Smith regime and applauded the declaration.[32] 'So Ian Smith has done it at last,' wrote Tony Read, an official in Molepolole, to his mother in November 1965:

Good on him, I say, although it's such a tragedy that such loyal & progressive people as the Rhodesians should be branded as traitors at the whim of communist-inspired bastards like Nkrumah & Kenyatta.[33]

The stated position of the British Government was by no means supported by all its officials working in the region.

Despite the hostility of the majority of whites in Bechuanaland, Seretse and other members of the Legislative Assembly argued that the time had come to move towards the full independence of the country. The Resident Commissioner held meetings with the Assembly in Lobatse in 1963, which led to a consensus – that there should be a national election, based on the principle of one man, one vote. Anxieties were felt by the diKgosi, who were afraid of losing power, and by Europeans, but the British Government backed the commitment to self-government.[34] It had also agreed to independence for Basutoland; one British official sourly commented that Seretse may have been pushing for sovereignty because he felt 'that he has to keep up with the Basuto Jones's'.[35]

It was agreed that the very first national election would be held on 1 March 1965, selecting members of the National Assembly to take the nation to independence the following year. It was also agreed that there would be a House of Chiefs, which would look at all proposals involving changes to traditional customs. Washington watched with interest. In 1963 it received a report from the region stating that in the view of the British High Commission, Bechuanaland was 'the best administered of the three Territories with Seretse Khama developing leadership potential (British obviously building him up).'[36]

For Bechuanaland to be independent, it needed to have a capital city within its own borders. The current anomaly was underlined by the fact that because Seretse was a prohibited immigrant in South Africa and could not go to Mafikeng, meetings of the Legislative Assembly had to take place in Lobatse. Plans were drawn up for the development of the village of Gaberones – which then became known as Gaborone – into a town, taking advantage of its proximity to the railway line and to a large water supply from a dam. 'For donkey's years,' observed the *Daily News* Africa Service, 'Gaberones has been an unambitious, sweltering one-horse dorp.'[37] But now it was set for a major expansion, to accommodate not only all the offices and homes in Mafikeng's Imperial Reserve, but also the institutions required by the capital city of an independent nation. Construction of the city began in February 1964, with the aim of being occupied by the

Government in time for the national election; it was completed in twelve months, enabling the Government to move out of Mafikeng earlier than was expected. The main credit for this, observed *The Times*, belonged to the people of Bechuanaland themselves – 'It has become the symbol of the country's belief in itself; of its ability to run its own affairs and of its future.'[38]

The three leading political parties began their campaigns for the election – the BDP, the BPP, and the Bechuanaland Independence Party, which was vigorously anti-white. On behalf of the Bechuanaland Democratic Party, Seretse travelled around the towns and the countryside, often accompanied by Ruth; together they smiled and gave the outstretched arm and clenched fist salute, as the crowds cheered. The new government, emphasized Seretse, would be elected on the basis of

each citizen casting one vote . . . irrespective of the citizen's standing in his community; in other words the Batswana, European, Asian and Bushman citizens of this country will have equal rights for electing the country's government . . .

May God help you to vote intelligently, and God bless Bechuanaland.[39]

On 1 March 1965, the first election in Bechuanaland took place. Even before six o'clock in the morning, people were streaming towards the polling stations.[40] Seretse and Ruth were among the first people to vote in Serowe. The heat was stifling, with the sun blazing down from a cloudless blue sky, but nothing could dent the determination of the voters – long queues formed of people of all ages, including women with babies on their backs and old men. They arrived on foot, on donkeys, on bicycles, on horses, on ox-wagons, on mules and on camels. One observer described election day in Mochudi:

the long slow-moving line of Mochudi voters, all in their best, the women in their blue aprons, flounced and corded, or in gay prints, some with umbrellas and some with babies, the men mostly in their best too, all clutching their registration cards, behaving as though they were going to church with no singing or shouting, but immense decorum.

In a sense, added the observer, it was a religious occasion. But afterwards, she saw 'one old woman doing a small happy dance, all by herself'.[41]

In his own district, Seretse received 5,904 votes, compared to just 53 and 39 received by his opponents. Overall, the Botswana Democratic Party won a resounding victory: 28 of the 31 seats, most of them by massive majorities. Seretse Khama had been chosen as leader of the nation – Kgosi by birth and now Prime Minister by the people's choice.[42] By political conviction he was modern, progressive and democratic, but he also had the advantage of being known everywhere as a man who had acted with supreme dignity in the face of exile by the British.[43] Ketumile Masire became Deputy Prime Minister.

A spokesman at the British embassy in Cape Town was quoted by the American embassy as saying that the Bechuanaland elections had 'turned out nicely' because the 'real chief (Seretse) had gone down into the market place'. The new Government, added the embassy, 'is the one we would have chosen ourselves'.[44]

As soon as the new Cabinet had been sworn in, preparations were started for full independence. One of the difficulties they faced was the expansionist aims of South Africa. Dr Hendrik Verwoerd, who had been the Prime Minister of South Africa since 1958, had withdrawn his country from the Commonwealth in 1961 and was now seeking to construct a series of satellites and buffers made up of South West Africa, the Bantustans, and the High Commission Territories. The idea that the High Commission Territories might form part of South Africa had been a consideration of British policy since 1910. But now that it was clear this was not going to happen – since Britain was backing their wish for self-determination – the Nationalists decided to woo public opinion in the High Commission Territories, especially among conservative diKgosi.[45] As part of this campaign, they reached out the hand of friendship to Seretse. After Seretse's election victory, Verwoerd announced that the South African Government had rescinded the 'prohibited immigrant' ban on him and his wife.[46]

Seretse had no intention of responding to Verwoerd's advances. But South Africa had to be managed very carefully: for although its policy of apartheid was roundly and robustly condemned by the African population of Bechuanaland, the Protectorate was dependent for its economic survival on its racist neighbour. In 1966, when Seretse was in London, he discussed the problem with Tony Benn. For his part, he said, 'he was being subjected to strong pressure from South Africa which wants to absorb the Protectorates into a new semi-independent Bantustan status'.[47]

Since Macmillan had given his 'wind of change' speech in March 1960, Verwoerd had been pressing ahead with the consolidation of apartheid, restricting African people in every aspect of their life. A few weeks after the speech, at Sharpeville, police had fired into a crowd protesting against the Pass Law; sixty-nine people were killed, including children, most of whom were shot in the back. The South African Government then declared a state of emergency and banned the ANC. After this, in the early 1960s, fugitives from the struggle for liberation from apartheid – including Mandela in 1962 – found a haven in Bechuanaland and an escape route to the north. Some refugees, like Joe Slovo, moved rapidly north to freedom; others, like Oliver Tambo, stayed there for a while before moving on to Zambia.[48]

The years leading up to the independence of Bechuanaland were exhausting for Seretse. He travelled all over the Protectorate and also to Europe and the US, seeking economic assistance to develop the country.[49] Many of the health problems that had plagued him over the years returned and although Ruth did her utmost to make him rest, Seretse drove himself hard. While in Washington in 1965, he had a medical check at a hospital where the examining physician told him he was a 'very sick man', with uncontrolled diabetes and anaemia. He urged immediate treatment, pointing out the risk of a diabetic coma. At the very least, he said, Seretse should be admitted to hospital in London before returning to Bechuanaland.[50] But despite the pressure of work and his suffering from ill health, Seretse never lost sight of his dream of his country's future – or even his sense of humour. During discussions of a suitable name for the new official residence of the President, names like State House and Presidential Palace were put forward – and Seretse asked, mischievously, 'What about the Woodpile?'[51]

Independence Day was set for 30 September 1966. To prepare for this, talks were held at Marlborough House in London in February 1966, to discuss the new constitution; these talks were attended by Seretse, Masire, Opposition Leader Philip Matante, Bathoen II, as representative of the House of Chiefs, and senior British officials from

Bechuanaland and the Colonial Office.[52] It was decided that the newly independent country would be called Botswana and the people would be known as Batswana; Botswana would remain within the Commonwealth, as the tenth African nation to choose to keep such a link with Britain. The talks were a resounding success, but at a cost for Seretse, who suffered an attack of diabetes and had to stay for a while in a London hospital before returning home.[53]

Shortly before Independence Day, Elizabeth II proclaimed Seretse as a Knight Commander of the Order of the British Empire. Only a decade and a half before, because of his marriage to Ruth, the leading men of the British Government had sought to keep secret a report stating that Seretse was a 'fit and proper person to be Chief', because they wanted to keep him out of any position of power. But now he became Sir Seretse Khama, and his wife became Lady Khama. 'The stone that was rejected had now become the head cornerstone!' observed Joe Appiah with amusement – Sir Seretse and Lady Khama 'had overcome the follies and prejudices of little men parading as gods'.[54]

26

Pula! Botswana 1966

The wind of change which blew the Republic of Botswana into being at midnight on 29 September 1966 was no simple gust – but a blizzard of biting, blinding sand from the Kalahari Desert. For six hours a gale had raged, with winds of up to 35 miles an hour. At the new airport just outside Gaborone, men rushed out to tie down the light aircraft parked in front of the single-storey reception building. There was a full moon, but it was almost hidden by the thick dust flying in swirls through the air.

Princess Marina of Kent had come to Gaborone on behalf of the Queen to hand over the reins of government. At Government House, where she was staying, her officials grew worried about the weather as it grew close to midnight, when the party of dignitaries would leave for the celebrations at the Independence Stadium. One of them suggested to Seretse the possibility of postponing the ceremony, to protect her from the storm. But Seretse was horrified. 'You cannot postpone independence!' he replied indignantly. The Princess was in complete agreement. She briskly pulled a headscarf over her tiara and set off for the stadium with the Queen's Commissioner.[1] In a gold lamé evening dress, she took her seat in the grandstand with the other dignitaries, in their morning coats and evening dresses, huddled under blankets.[2]

Guests from all over the world had arrived to share in the celebrations, including several British Government ministers. Many visitors experienced first-hand the difficulties of Botswana's dependence on South Africa, because the only straightforward route to Gaborone was via Jan Smuts Airport at Johannesburg, which some delegates, including those from Ethiopia, wanted to avoid. The best alternative was a long and circuitous journey: by aircraft to Lusaka, train to Livingstone, then by Bechuanaland National Airways from Livingstone, stopping overnight at Kasane and not arriving until the next day at Gaborone.[3] A compromise was organized: a waiting area and overnight accommodation were made available at the in-transit area of Jan Smuts, so that Botswana's guests would not have to enter South Africa officially.

In the stadium in Gaborone, 5,000 people were waiting for the moment when their country would become Botswana. Then Seretse arrived with Ruth, who was wearing a white dress with thin, black stripes, a white fur jacket and opera-length white gloves. The 8-year-old twins, Tshekedi and Anthony, wrestled under a blanket as they waited with 16-year-old Jacqueline and Ian, now 13.[4]

Nobody minded the dust as they waved banners and little flags in great excitement, singing and dancing. Bechuanaland was about to become the 38th independent state in Africa. The 39th would be Basutoland, which became Lesotho a few days after the Independence of Botswana; two years later, the last of the High Commission Territories – Swaziland – became independent. After this, Britain would no longer have any colonial responsibilities on the African continent, apart from Rhodesia.

In the hour leading up to midnight, the crowd was entertained by a march of the Royal Irish Fusiliers, dressed in kilts and carrying bagpipes. They were members of the force guarding Britain's Freedom Radio near Francistown, which was beamed to Rhodesia by the British Government as one strand of its various – but largely ineffective – measures to combat Ian Smith's UDI. Then a group of San performed dances celebrating a successful hunt; this was followed by dances and singing, including a prayer for rain.

The ceremony of transferring power from Britain to the people of Botswana was modelled on the formula that had quickly become established as, one by one, Britain's colonies had achieved their independence. In solemn silence and great dignity, Seretse arose; now 45 years old, the lanky figure of his younger years had become more sturdy and he looked very much a statesman. Then, ten minutes before midnight, a prayer was given and the lights of the stadium were put off. Seretse now stood in the arena, facing the grandstand, dressed simply in a dark suit; the Queen's Commissioner was on his right, wearing a starched white uniform and white helmet, plumed with ostrich feathers. In the darkness behind them, a detachment of police was drawn up in two lines, with fixed bayonets. The band played the opening bars of 'God Save the Queen' and the Union Jack – which had flown in Bechuanaland for eighty-one years – was finally lowered down a tall, thin pole.

Then a spotlight was focused on an adjoining white pole. In complete silence, the band started to play the new Botswana national anthem, *Fatshe leno la rona* – 'Blessed be this noble land'. Very slowly, the Botswana flag was run up. The flag has a thick strip of blue at the top, representing the sky; a thick strip of blue at the bottom, representing water; a black strip in the centre is bordered by two white strips, representing racial harmony. The motif of black and white stripes was taken from the zebra – an animal that, out of all the wild animals of the country, was not the totem of any particular section of the population. It was seen to represent the non-racial, inclusive, character of the new nation. Two zebras – with '*Pula*' inscribed underneath – appeared in the new coat of arms; it was also agreed that the inter-racial sporting teams which would go abroad to represent Botswana would be known as the 'Zebras'.[5]

Seretse stood rigidly to attention, by the flagpole, in front of his people. For a few moments, the flag remained stuck, caught in the gusts of sand and wind. Then, suddenly, it streamed out into the wind of the storm – to the jubilation of the crowd and shouts of '*Pula!*' At that moment, drops of rain were felt among the sand blowing through the air. After the searing drought, the rain had come – and many people could hardly believe their eyes. This was the start of several days of rain. The dam near Gaborone filled up to overflowing with badly needed water and the whole country was awash. At the airport, some children took their shoes off to wade through the wet, in order to reach their plane.[6] 'The weather gave its independence blessing with copious rains, after several years of drought,' reported the British High Commissioner to London.[7]

In Gaborone next day, at a ceremony in front of the newly built National Assembly building, Princess Marina formally handed over the Constitutional Instruments. The President took the oath of office, while Ruth stood proudly behind him, and Ketumile Masire was sworn in as Vice-President. This was followed by a series of celebrations: a combined church service, then a police parade and sporting events. Princess Marina opened a hospital named after her and visited a number of exhibitions and schools, where she was given a tumultuous welcome; she endeared herself to everyone by her lack of formality and her genuine interest in everything she saw.

The lowering of the British flag – and the raising of the Botswana flag – was repeated in towns and villages all over Botswana at midnight, so that everybody could participate. Everywhere, too, celebrations followed, such as dances, sports sessions and feasts of roast meat. Throughout the week, reported the *Mafeking Mail* – referring both to the weather and to the celebrations – 'the wind of change kept up a nice steady breeze'.[8]

One of the guests at the official celebrations, John Stonehouse, who had attended in his role as Under-Secretary of State for the Colonies, described them as 'Spartan'.[9] It was true that they were quieter and less lavish than the independence celebrations in Kenya or other former colonies. But it would have been more accurate to describe them as 'modest' – appropriate to the difficulties faced by an impoverished country. This style was adopted as a deliberate strategy by the new Government. Only the President travelled first class – the rest went by economy. This frequently caused confusion in host countries, as when Vice-President Masire and the Minister of Agriculture flew to Uganda in 1968. 'We flew by BOAC to Entebbe,' recorded an official who was travelling with them in economy class –

and just before we landed were instructed over the loudspeaker to remain seated when we landed because important Ugandan officials were coming on board. We did as instructed and I noticed much activity going on in the first class.

The official asked one of the stewards what was happening and was told they were looking for the dignitaries from Botswana – and he said they were sitting next to him. The Ugandans hauled them off the plane to a red carpet, and a lavish champagne reception in the VIP lounge. 'They were amazed', recorded the official, 'that Botswana Ministers should travel economy class.' In any case, he added, the reception did not last long, because neither Masire nor the Minister of Agriculture touched alcohol.[10] Even when he had become President, Seretse assumed none of the more pompous trappings that often accompany high office. He frequently strolled out of the office of the president to the nearby shops to buy a detective story, stopping for a chat about the latest books.[11]

In Francistown, the novelist Bessie Head – a refugee from South Africa who had adopted Botswana as her home – reflected on the changes brought by Independence:

'It is all right,' I thought. 'The whole world seems topsy-turvy but there is something here in the country that is good. Perhaps it is a weird kind of people who pull against the current; unprovokable; ever reasonable. Perhaps it is the rags and tatters of poverty that are worn with an upright posture and pathetic dignity. Whatever it is I say it is good because you feel it in your heart as peace.'[12]

Botswana had real advantages when it became independent, especially in relation to the unity of the people. Although there were eight principal nations, all of them spoke basically the same language, Setswana, and had a similar cultural background and system of government. In addition, the elected leaders of the country had a very clear idea of where their hopes lay for the country – transforming Botswana into an economically viable state, and creating a unified nation based on the ideals of non-racialism.

The Government demonstrated a firm commitment to democracy. Seretse made himself dispensable, unlike many other African leaders, such as Nkrumah in Ghana, who had proclaimed himself President for life in 1964, banning all opposition parties. 'Mr Khama, in discussing other African countries,' observed an American diplomat who visited Seretse for talks, 'commented that there were a considerable number of countries in Africa which possessed able rulers at the moment, but which appeared to have nobody other than one top man to hold the country together should the one man be removed from the scene.' In this regard, Seretse had told him, Bechuanaland was fortunate: '"If I were to go" (at which point Mrs Khama choked on her breakfast coffee) "Masire would immediately step into my place."

He said that both Mr Masire and B. C. Thema, the Minister of Education, were extremely able and popular.'[13] The new leaders were determined to learn from the failures of other African countries. As far as they were concerned, ideology was a luxury and they had to be pragmatic – what mattered was not something on the political Left or the Right, but what was good for Botswana.[14]

But economically, circumstances were far from propitious. 'Few Independence ceremonies,' noted one commentator, 'may have taken place under dustier, bleaker economic circumstances.'[15] Botswana was listed by the United Nations as one of the world's ten poorest nations and the least developed nation in Africa. 'Its problems are so great,' observed *The Times* on the day of independence, 'that its debut in the international world amounts to a striking act of faith that untrammelled self-rule is the supreme good.'[16] After several years of drought, two-thirds of the population were on famine relief from the World Food Programme, and 200,000 head of cattle were on emergency maize feeding.[17] Botswana's *Transitional Plan of Social and Economic Development*, which was dated on Independence Day, stated that:

Botswana is now experiencing the most calamitous drought in living memory. Its end is not in sight. No one yet knows how many cattle have died, but it is reliably estimated that the national herd has been reduced by over one-third and that the losses in some areas have exceeded 50 per cent. More particularly, a whole year's crop of calves has been lost.[18]

By 1964, two out of every three active male wage labourers were absent in South Africa at any given time, working in the mines and on farms. Not only did they earn very little to bring home, but their labour was contributing to the economic strength of South Africa and British-controlled business – not to their own country.[19] There was widespread ill health in Botswana, with people suffering from high infant death and maternal death, as well as a range of preventable diseases, including tuberculosis, malaria and tapeworm. Sanitation and water provision were hopelessly inadequate, as was medical care. There was no public health laboratory for routine medical investigation, so that even a test smear for malaria had to be sent to Johannesburg.[20]

A massive disadvantage for the new nation was the lack of people

qualified to work in the civil service and other professions; this problem had been caused by the shortage of educational facilities and the
unwillingness of whites in senior positions to train African juniors.[21]
At the most, there were fewer than thirty university graduates among
the black population.[22] As Margaret Nasha, who later became a
Government Minister, observed:

The situation with education and infrastructure illustrates the extent to which
the colonial government neglected the Bechuanaland Protectorate, as it was
then called. In the whole country there were very few secondary schools,
mostly run by missions. There were very few primary schools. There was
about twelve kilometres [seven and half miles] of tarred road ... Primary
health care and public health education were virtually nil.[23]

Seretse appealed to the Europeans in the civil service to stay on after
Independence, but most of them decided to leave.[24] A colonial official
in Molepolole was one of many who accepted the offer of 'compensation' and took his family back to the UK. 'Yes, considerations about
our future weigh heavily on all of us at the moment,' he wrote to his
mother, 'and it's inevitable that within a few minutes of a meeting
between two Government servants, one of them will ask, "Are you
going or staying?"'[25] He said he was worried about 'the uncertainty
which hangs over the whole African continent as far as the white man
is concerned'.[26]

But despite these – seemingly insuperable – obstacles, Botswana was
dramatically and remarkably transformed after Independence. In the
middle of 1966, Seretse introduced Food for Work programmes,
which aimed not simply at saving people from famine but also – in
the spirit of the self-help projects initiated by Khama III and Tshekedi
– at creating a spirit of service for the good of the country, especially
in water and soil conservation projects. These efforts were helped by
the return of rains in the months after Independence.

Then, just eight months after Independence, it was announced that
a major kimberlite 'pipe' had been discovered at Orapa. This became
the world's biggest diamond mine and two others were opened; Botswana was the largest producer in the world by the 1980s. It did not
squander this resource, however, but held steadily to its strategy of
restraint. It managed the discovery of diamonds so well that between

Independence and the start of the next century, Botswana had the fastest average economic growth rate in the world, at about 9 per cent each year. It channelled these resources into services for the people, which were developed throughout the country for the benefit of everybody, almost from scratch.

Botswana soon had a better level of education and literacy than anywhere else in sub-Saharan Africa, with the exception of some parts of South Africa. The same was true of health service provision.[27] Without qualification, Botswana was far better off as an independent nation than it had ever been under colonial rule.

Many people in Botswana thought that the nation had benefited from the fact that diamonds were not discovered until after Independence. 'In a way,' reflected Margaret Nasha, 'we may have been lucky. I've always said that if some of the country's rich mineral deposits had been discovered during the colonial period it would have led to bloodshed, people having to fight for Independence because there is something in their land the colonial Government wants to retain.' But the nation's poverty had saved them from foreign greed:

That's why other countries in Africa have had to fight so hard and lost so many lives for independence. On the other hand, the British government thought we had nothing worth fighting for, so it was through a process of negotiation that we made a peaceful transition to independence.

As I said, very little was done by the British during their period of rule in Botswana. They did not even build an administrative capital and were content to run the affairs of the country from South Africa.[28]

An additional challenge to Botswana in 1966 was that – with the sole exception of newly independent Zambia – it was smack in the middle of hostile, white-ruled, racist regimes: South Africa, Rhodesia and South West Africa. Even worse, it was dependent on South Africa for its survival. Because its main communication with the outside world was the railway running from Rhodesia to the Cape, every single mouthful of staple food consumed in Botswana during the drought, except meat, had to be imported on this railway.[29] Many experts had doubted whether Botswana could survive as a separate nation; at the very least, they expected it to become a puppet of South Africa and to function as a Bantustan. Even within Botswana's own boundaries, there were whites who opposed constitutional progress and tried to foment secessionist movements.[30] In effect, observed a report produced in Washington, Botswana was

an enclave in the 'White redoubt' of southern Africa, surrounded as it is by South Africa, Rhodesia and South West Africa. Its economy is wholly integrated with that of its white-governed neighbours. Therefore, the geographical and economic facts of life make it impossible for the territory to insulate itself from the crises affecting its neighbours.

'Our interest,' added the report, 'is in helping him [Seretse] to develop a more viable model of working multi-racialism in a part of the continent where the pattern is otherwise.'[31]

Seretse and his Government were determined to develop such a model, steering a tightrope political course. The nation quickly denounced apartheid and offered sanctuary to refugees from South Africa and Rhodesia, even though this led to reprisal raids. Although Botswana could not risk allowing its territory to be used as a base of attack against neighbouring governments, it made known its abhorrence of them and refused to establish formal diplomatic relations with either South Africa or Rhodesia. The apartheid regime, commented Mandela later in a speech to the people of Botswana, 'hoped that through kidnappings, bombings, armed raids and assassinations that violated the sovereignty and peace of your country, they would intimidate you. But they were wrong. They were deceiving themselves!'[32] In this respect Botswana differed sharply from Swaziland and Lesotho, which remained satellites of South Africa. It was easier for Botswana to avoid this, in so far as it had a tiny boundary with Zambia, offering a thread of contact with black Africa. But it was also an act of courage: in the words of John Hatch, 'Botswana was not in a position to act as a bastion against apartheid; but she repudiated the role of its servant.'[33]

Seretse's key task in foreign relations was to win respect from countries such as Zambia and Tanzania; in 1968 there was an exchange of presidential visits with President Kenneth Kaunda of Zambia, which developed into a strong friendship between the countries and other frontline states. Botswana came to be seen as a state with high principles, upholding liberal democracy and non-racialism. At the very least, wrote Julius Nyerere, the President of Tanzania, in

1980, so-called African experts had expected Botswana to become 'a puppet of South Africa's apartheid Government'. But, he said,

Time has proved that the pessimists left out of account two vital factors: the steadiness and determination of the people of Botswana; and the leadership of Seretse Khama and the Botswana Democratic Party.

Seretse was 'a true non-racialist', he added, who was completely honest and who 'brings honour to our continent'.[34]

Seretse was also the main architect of what became the Southern African Development Coordination Conference (SADCC) and Botswana was soon trusted throughout independent Africa. Nelson Mandela thought it was remarkable that in Botswana, 'men who had no previous experience whatsoever in government as it functions today should be able to run modern states with such success'.[35] After the liberation of South Africa from apartheid, at a rally in Gaborone, Mandela observed that, 'Botswana has a proud history as a successful democratic country and as a model of economic success. Democratic South Africa is eager for close relations with Botswana. We have a lot to learn from you.'[36]

As First Lady, Ruth was able to push ahead her plans for voluntary organizations. She was elected Founding President of the Botswana Red Cross Society and was instrumental in the establishment of many Red Cross centres; she was also a Founder and first President of the Botswana Council of Women, and the Child to Child Foundation. Wherever she went, she was greeted with love and called '*Mma Rona*' – 'Our Mother'. But her first loyalty was always to Seretse. 'The honest love they found in England,' observed a visiting American journalist, 'is still there, and has been deepened by Botswana's distance and silence.' When Seretse was tardy in arriving for dinner one night, he hurried to Ruth's side: '"I am so sorry," he said, like any late husband. Ruth smiled, gave him a wifely kiss, and said: "Never mind. I suppose it's got to happen in your business."' Their relationship, added the journalist, was easy and relaxed, and State House was very much a home.[37] Every evening, the family came together in the family room for a drink before dinner. Seretse never lost his unconditional kindness towards everyone. One day, Government staff suggested that he get rid of a retainer who waited at table, on the grounds that he was not very good at his job.[38] But Seretse kept the retainer on, because he knew that he was doing his best.

The Botswana Democratic Party was returned to power in 1969 with an increased majority; then the party was re-elected in the 1974 elections and again in 1979. This meant that Seretse was under constant pressure as leader of the nation. Ruth did everything she possibly could to support him in his gruelling schedule, though she never interfered in his work. Her support became increasingly essential as his health deteriorated. She carefully monitored his diet and his daily routine, in a determined effort to maximize his strength.[39]

But eventually, even Ruth could no longer keep Seretse alive. He became so ill that Ruth rushed him to London for specialist care, where he was diagnosed as suffering from the advanced stages of cancer of the abdomen. They were told that he would never recover. He and Ruth flew home so that he could take his last breath in Gaborone. There he died two weeks later at 4.45 in the morning of 13 July 1980. He was only 59 and had been president of Botswana for fourteen years.

The nation was numb with sorrow. A month of official mourning was declared, during which time flags flew at half-mast. Government held no official functions and the public were requested to keep private functions to small personal gatherings. Ketumile Masire, who succeeded as president, appealed to the people to face their loss with the dignity and calm that had been shown by their great President and to offer thanks: 'May God keep Sir Seretse Khama and we give thanks for the years we have been allowed to have him as our President.' Messages of condolence poured in from foreign Heads of State. 'To me, personally,' wrote President Kaunda of Zambia, 'Sir Seretse's death will mean the loss of a brother, wise counsellor and advisor. His steadying hand will be missed by all his brothers among the leaders of the Frontline States.' He was the kind of man, he added, who the strife-torn region of southern Africa could ill afford to lose.[40]

One of his many achievements in the region was a leading role in negotiations to bring about the Independence of Zimbabwe under majority rule, which he witnessed just three months before he died. He also experienced another great joy before his death: in 1979, he saw the installation of his son, Seretse Khama Ian, who had trained at the Royal Military Academy at Sandhurst in Britain, as Kgosi of the Bangwato people – Kgosi Khama IV.

The Memorial Service for Sir Seretse Khama was attended by 20,000 people and by many Heads of State, including Samora Machel of Mozambique, King Moshoeshoe II of Lesotho, Julius Nyerere of Tanzania, Dr Kaunda of Zambia, and the Reverend Canaan Banana of Zimbabwe. On the day after the service, Seretse was taken to the Khama burial ground in Serowe, at the top of the hill by the Kgotla, to be buried alongside the graves of the Great Khama III, his father Sekgoma II, and his uncle Tshekedi. All the way from the airstrip to the Kgotla, people lined the road, weeping, beside themselves with sorrow. The village was thronged by mourners and about twenty people fainted; women of all ages collapsed with grief and the atmosphere was melancholy. When the public were invited to see and pay their last respects to the late President, there was a stampede, causing some fractured limbs, because some people were afraid they would not get a chance to see him; as a result, the public were allowed to visit his coffin until six o'clock the following morning.[41]

Seretse's death was announced by the BBC World Service, at the top of its news bulletin. Sir John Redcliffe-Maud, who had been the British High Commissioner of South Africa at the time of Independence, sadly lamented the loss in an obituary for *The Times*:

However dangerous the prospect, either for his country or his own health, his courage, integrity and tolerance were as steadfast as his sense of humour – but it was Ruth who kept him alive and happy. Africa owes both of them a great debt of gratitude.[42]

Lady Khama was shattered.[43] She was now 56 and some people outside Botswana thought she would return to Britain. But the idea never crossed her mind:

I am completely happy here. I travel to Britain and Switzerland as part of my charity work for the Red Cross, but I have no desire to go anywhere else . . . My home is here. I have lived here for more than half my life. My children are here. When I came to this country I became a Motswana.[44]

She lived alone on her farm in Ruretse, enjoying her children and grandchildren. She also continued to work hard for the Botswana

Red Cross Society, regularly attending the General Assembly at the international headquarters of the Red Cross in Geneva, Switzerland. In 1982, Lady Khama became president of SOS Children's Villages, which was a project close to her heart. As Botswana started to suffer from the ravages of HIV/AIDS, making a growing number of children into orphans, she frequently visited the children at the SOS Children's Village in Tlokweng and did what she could to make them feel loved and cared for. She died twenty-two years after the loss of Seretse, at the age of 78, on 23 May 2002, on a night that saw the first rain in three months – even though it seldom rains in May. Her funeral in Serowe was attended by more than 10,000 mourners and she was buried in the hilltop cemetery reserved for the Khama family, next to her beloved husband.

Sir Seretse Khama has been internationally acknowledged as an outstanding statesman and one of the great successes of twentieth-century African politics. Whenever Nelson Mandela has saluted the heroes and giants of Africa, who ensured its liberation from the inhumanity of apartheid – such as Kwame Nkrumah of Ghana, Patrice Lumumba of Zaire, Amilcar Cabral of Guinea Bissau, Eduardo Mondlane and Samora Machel of Mozambique, W. E. B. Du Bois and Martin Luther King of the United States, Marcus Garvey of Jamaica, and Albert Luthuli and Oliver Tambo of South Africa – he has always included Seretse Khama of Botswana.[45] In 2000, he described him as 'that great son of Africa':

One of the great African patriots from this region, a man renowned for the manner in which he put the dignity and well-being of his people above all other considerations. The legacy of Sir Seretse Khama lives on in his country that continues to be a shining beacon of light and inspiration to the rest of us in Southern Africa.

'As we stand at the beginning of a new millennium,' continued Mandela, 'sincerely hoping that this will be the century of Africa and the developing world, the need to remain true to that legacy of Seretse Khama is as urgent as at any other time.'[46]

'I think we were lucky,' observed Sir Ketumile Masire, who followed Sir Seretse Khama as President, 'in that the combination of traditional respect for Seretse and his personality really made him the ideal person to have started this country on the course in which it is going.' His marriage to Ruth, and all that went with it, added Sir Ketumile, 'made Seretse the Mandela of Botswana'. He had been close to both men, he added, 'and it is remarkable how they were able to put the past behind them and act in exactly the opposite way in which a human being would usually act'.[47]

Seretse simply did not have the capacity to hate. Even though Tshekedi had been so cruel to him, he forgave him totally. He never said anything against the people who had mistreated him and he never allowed cruel words from anyone else about them.[48] He could have been soured by his years of persecution by the British Government – but he was not. 'I, myself,' he said in 1967 on a visit to Malawi, 'have never been very bitter at all, although at a certain stage I lived in exile, away from my country, in the United Kingdom for quite some time.' He went on:

Bitterness does not pay. Certain things have happened to all of us in the past and it is for us to forget those and to look to the future. It is not for our own benefit, but it is for the benefit of our children and children's children that we ourselves should put this world right.[49]

List of Abbreviations
used in Notes

ANC	African National Congress
BCA	Balliol College Archive
BECM	British Empire and Commonwealth Museum
BLCAS	Bodleian Library of Commonwealth and African Studies
BNARS	Botswana National Archives and Records Services
BP	Bechuanaland Protectorate
CAN:CER	Department of Foreign Affairs and International Trade (Canada)
CHUR	Churchill Archives Centre
CRO	Commonwealth Relations Office
CROUW	Central Records Office, University of the Witwatersrand
DUL	Durham University Library, Archives and Special Collections
HCO	High Commissioner's Office
HCT	High Commission Territory
ICwS	Institute of Commonwealth Studies, Archives and Special Collections
KIII	Khama III Memorial Museum
LHASC	Labour History Archive and Study Centre, People's History Museum
NAC	National Archives of Canada
NARA	National Archives and Records Administration of the USA RG Record Group

NASA	National Archives of South Africa
	BLO High Commission to London
	BVV External Affairs Department
	PM Prime Minister's Office
OIOC	Oriental and India Office Collections, British Library
RA	Royal Archives, Windsor Castle
SADCC	Southern African Development Coordination Conference
SADC	Southern African Development Community, Secretariat Library
SOAS	School of Oriental and African Studies, Archives and Manuscripts
	CWM Council for World Mission
	LMS London Missionary Society
	MCF Movement for Colonial Freedom
SUL (UK)	Sussex University Library Special Collections
SUL (US)	Syracuse University Library, Special Collections Research Center
TNA:PRO	The National Archives of the UK: Public Record Office
	CAB Cabinet Papers
	CO Colonial Office
	DO Dominions Office
	PREM Prime Minister's Office
WASU	West African Students Union
WCLUW	William Cullen Library, University of the Witwatersrand

Notes

I FROM AFRICA TO WARTORN BRITAIN

1. Margaret Bourke-White to Bill, n.d., SUL (US), MB-W, Box 25.
2. Speech by Sir Seretse Khama at State Banquet, Blantyre, first anniversary of the Republic of Malawi, 5 July 1967, BECM.
3. Sampson, *Mandela*, pp. 21–5; Mandela, *Long Walk to Freedom*, p. 44.
4. Parsons, Henderson and Tlou, *Seretse Khama*, p. 59.
5. Mandela to Masire, n.d. [July 1980], ANC, Oliver Tambo Papers.
6. Nkomo, *The Story of My Life*, p. 35.
7. Parsons, Henderson and Tlou, *Seretse Khama*, p. 59.
8. Sampson, *Mandela*, pp. 34–5.
9. Mandela, *Long Walk to Freedom*, pp. 105–6.
10. Information provided by Anna Sander, Lonsdale Curator of Archives and Manuscripts, Balliol College, Oxford.
11. Coupland to Buchanan, 25 October 1945, BNARS, S 169/15/1.
12. Keith, 'African Students in Great Britain,' pp. 65–6; Kirk-Greene, 'Doubly Elite', in Killingray (ed.), *Africans in Britain*, pp. 221–2.
13. Speech by Sir Seretse Khama at State Banquet, Blantyre, first anniversary of the Republic of Malawi, 5 July 1967, BECM.
14. Comment by Lancelot Gama, quoted in Callinicos, *Oliver Tambo*, pp. 108–9.
15. Muriel Sanderson to author, 28 July 2003.
16. Abrams, *The Population of Great Britain*, p. 21; Flint, 'Scandal at the Bristol Hotel', p. 75; Banton, *The Coloured Quarter*, pp. 66–8. Banton asserts the impossibility of knowing either the total number of 'coloured' people in Britain at the time, or how they were distributed through the country; the figure given here is therefore an estimate, based on figures estimated by Flint and by Banton.
17. Political and Economic Planning, *Colonial Students in Britain*, pp. 85–6.

18. Constantine, *Colour Bar*, pp. 25–6.

19. *Picture Post*, 2 July 1949.

20. Flint, 'Scandal at the Bristol Hotel', pp. 77–8.

21. ibid., p. 76.

22. Caryl Phillips, 'To Ricky with love', *Guardian Review*, 23 July 2005.

23. Morton and Ramsay, *Birth of Botswana*, pp. 102–9; Robins, *White Queen in Africa*, p. 21.

24. Bent, *Ten Thousand Men of Africa*, p. 99.

25. Muriel Sanderson to author, 28 July 2003.

26. Adi, *West Africans in Britain*, pp. 137–8; Anderson, *Histories of the Hanged*, pp. 36–7.

27. Gabolebye Dinti Marobele to Head, in Head, *Serowe*, pp. 97–8.

28. Zweiniger-Bargielowska, *Austerity in Britain*, pp. 214–15.

29. Seretse to Tshekedi, 5 December 1945, BNARS, S 169/15/1.

30. Parsons, Henderson and Tlou, *Seretse Khama*, p. 65.

31. ibid., p. 47.

32. Speech by Sir Seretse Khama at State Banquet, Blantyre, first anniversary of the Republic of Malawi, 5 July 1967, BECM.

33. J. E. C. Hill to Seretse Khama, 27 February 1976, BCA, dossier Khama S. (1945).

34. Lord Lindsay of Birker to A. Sillery, 3 May 1948, BCA, dossier Khama S. (1945).

35. Admission records for Seretse Khama, 1945–6, Inner Temple Archives.

36. Seretse to Tshekedi, 14 June 1946, BNARS, S 169/15/1.

37. Pilkington to Chirgwin, 15 July 1946, SOAS, CWM/LMS, AF/37.

38. Coupland to Buchanan, 25 July 1946, BNARS, S 169/15/1.

39. A. D. Lindsay, Master, Handshaking Notes on Seretse Khama, Hilary Term, 1947, BCA, Studies & Discipline 8.

40. Charles Njonjo to author, 12 March 2004.

41. Hon. Gladstone Mills, Foreword to Braithwaite, *Colonial West Indian Students in Britain*, p. viii.

42. Charles Njonjo to author, 12 March 2004.

43. ibid., 6 January 2005.

44. Stonehouse, *Prohibited Immigrant*, p. 14.

45. Speech by Dr Kamuzu Banda at State Banquet, Blantyre, first anniversary of the Republic of Malawi, 5 July 1967, BECM.

46. *Oxford Dictionary of National Biography*: Harry Nkumbula.

47. The Hon. Gerard Noel to author, 11 July 2005.

48. Keith, 'African Students in Great Britain,' pp. 65–6.

49. *The Times*, 14 July 1990.

50. Appiah, *Joe Appiah: The Autobiography of an African Patriot*, p. 150.

51. C. L. R. James, 'Africans and Afro-Caribbeans: A Personal View (1984)' in Procter (ed.), *Writing Black Britain*, pp. 61–2.

52. Keith, 'African Students in Great Britain,' p. 70.

53. Murray-Brown, *Kenyatta*, p. 218.

54. Olusanya, *The West African Students' Union*, p. 107.

55. Quoted in Adi, *West Africans in Britain*, p. 120.

56. Nwauwa, *Imperialism, Academe and Nationalism*, p. 171.

57. *Hansard*, 21 February 1946.

58. Padmore, *History of the Pan-African Congress*, 2nd edn, p. i.

59. Padmore, *Colonial . . . and Coloured Unity*, p. 29.

60. Quoted in Murray-Brown, *Kenyatta*, p. 220.

61. Quoted in Adi, *West Africans in Britain*, p. 128.

62. *The Autobiography of Kwame Nkrumah*, p. 47.

2 LOVE MATCH

1. Charles Njonjo to author, 12 March 2004.

2. Muriel Sanderson to author, 17 November 2004.

3. *Sunday Dispatch*, 2 April 1950.

4. *Ebony*, June 1951.

5. Braithwaite, *Colonial West Indian Students in Britain*, pp. 209–21.

6. *Ebony*, June 1951.

7. *Sunday Dispatch*, 9 April 1950.

8. Margaret Bourke-White to Bill, n.d., SUL (US), MB-W, Box 25.

9. Tshekedi to Burns, December 1947, quoted in Parsons, Henderson and Tlou, *Seretse Khama*, p. 67.

10. Dutfield, *A Marriage of Inconvenience*, p. 6.

11. Charles Njonjo to author, 12 March 2004.

12. *Today*, 27 February 1960.

13. *Ebony*, June 1951.

14. *Sunday Dispatch*, 9 April 1950.

15. Monks, *Eyewitness*, p. 274.

16. Charles Njonjo to author, 12 March 2004.

17. Seretse to Tshekedi, 12 September 1948, BNARS, S 5990/10.

18. Dutfield, *A Marriage of Inconvenience*, p. 8.

19. *Sunday Dispatch*, 16 April 1950.

20. Seretse to Tshekedi, 12 September 1948, BNARS, S 5990/10.

21. Gabolebye Dinti Marobele to Head, 1974, in Head, *Serowe*, pp. 97–8.

22. A. Sillery, 'Working Backwards,' n.d., BLCAS, Mss Afr r 207.

23. Copy of Baring to Douglas Buchanan, 22 September 1948, Annexure 'H', TNA:PRO, DO 119/1279.

24. Baring to Eric Machtig, 23 September 1948, TNA:PRO, CO 981/36.

25. Douglas Buchanan to John Buchanan, 23 September 1948, TNA:PRO, DO 119/1279.

26. Douglas Buchanan to Ronald Orchard, 24 September 1948, SOAS, CWM/LMS, AF/37.

27. Tshekedi to Seretse, 24 September 1948, TNA:PRO, DO 119/1279.

28. Quoted in Redfern, *Ruth and Seretse*, p. 35.

29. Pilkington to Tshekedi, 27 September 1948, TNA:PRO, DO 119/1279.

30. Eugenics Society, *Aims and Objects of the Eugenics Society*, p. 4.

31. Pilkington to Tshekedi, 27 September 1948, TNA:PRO, DO 119/1279.

32. Quoted in Smith, *When Jim Crow Met John Bull*, p. 70.

33. Njonjo to author, 13 January 2005; Mwangilwa, *Nkumbula*, p. 25.

34. Njonjo to author, 13 January, 2005.

35. Syers to Baring, 27 September 1948, TNA:PRO, DO 35/4113; Coupland to Syers, 29 September 1948, ibid.

36. Hayford, 'White Brides and Black Husbands,' p. 1009.

37. Sir Charles Arden-Clarke to Sir Thomas Lloyd, 2 January 1952, TNA:PRO, CO 967/175.

38. Winston James, 'Black Experience in Twentieth-Century Britain', in Morgan and Hawkins (eds), *Black Experience and the Empire*, pp. 369–70.

39. Quotation from interview with Sam King, in Phillips and Phillips, *Windrush*, p. 82.

40. Political and Economic Planning, *Colonial Students in Britain*, pp. 85–6.

41. Statement by Ruth's mother, quoted in Robins, *White Queen in Africa*, p. 54.

42. *Sunday Dispatch*, 16 April 1950.

43. *Saga Magazine*, June 1991.

44. Charles Njonjo to author, 13 January 2005.

45. *Today*, 27 February 1960.

46. *Saga Magazine*, June 1991.

47. *Today*, 27 February 1960.

48. Pilkington to Tshekedi, 27 September 1948, TNA:PRO, DO 119/1279.

49. Pilkington to Tshekedi, 27 September 1948, BNARS, S 169/15/1.

50. Pilkington to Tshekedi, 27 September 1948, TNA:PRO, DO 119/1279.

51. John Buchanan to Douglas Buchanan, 26 September 1948, ibid.

52. *Today*, 27 February 1960.

53. Charles Njonjo to author, 13 January 2005.

54. *Sunday Dispatch*, 16 April 1950.

55. *Today*, 27 February, 1960.

56. Quoted in Benson, *Tshekedi Khama*, p. 179.

57. Coupland to Syers, 5 October 1948, TNA:PRO, DO 35/4113.

58. Quoted in Benson, *Tshekedi Khama*, p. 178.

59. Tshekedi to District Commissioner, Serowe, 11 October 1948, TNA: PRO, DO 119/1279.

60. Quoted in Benson, *Tshekedi Khama*, p. 179.

61. Quoted in ibid.

3 THE BECHUANALAND PROTECTORATE

1. Mandela to Mary Benson, 1987, quoted in Sampson, *Mandela*, p. 161.

2. Movietone newsreel, 'African domain of Ruth Williams', 25 August 1949.

3. These figures are given as an estimate in Tshekedi Khama (ed.), *Bechuanaland. A General Survey*, p. 2.

4. Gasebalwe Seretse, *Tshekedi Khama*, pp. 114–16.

5. Chirenje, *Chief Kgama and His Times*, p. 6.

6. Gasebalwe Seretse, *Tshekedi Khama*, p. 106.

7. Figures for 1946, presented as an estimate in Tshekedi Khama (ed.), *Bechuanaland. A General Survey*, p. 2.

8. Billy Woodford to Head, in Head, *Serowe*, p. 104.

9. ibid., pp. 26–7.

10. Quoted in Parsons, *The Word of Khama*, pp. 8 and 6.

11. Photograph, Khama Family Papers.

12. Tlhoka-Ina to Head, in Head, *Serowe*, pp. 84–6.

13. Quoted in Head, *Serowe*, pp. 84–5.

14. Gasebalwe Seretse, *Tshekedi Khama*, pp. 112–14.

15. Head, *Serowe*, p. 80.

16. Seager, *The Shadow of a Great Rock*, p. 48.

17. Lenyeletse Seretse to Head, in Head, *Serowe*, p. 81.

18. Tlhoka-Ina to Head, in Head, *Serowe*, p. 86.

19. Fawcus and Tilbury, *Botswana*, pp. 39–40.

20. Bourke-White, *Portrait of Myself*, p. 316.

21. The Journal of Queen Victoria, RA, VIC/QVJ, 1895: 19 November.

22. Quoted in Parsons, *The Word of Khama*, p. 11.

23. Bourke-White, 'The White Queen', unpublished chapter from memoir, SUL (US), MB-W.

24. Fawcus and Tilbury, *Botswana*, pp. 39–42.

25. Estimated figure for 1968, given by Marit Kromberg in Head, *Serowe*, p. 115; no other figures are available.

26. *Ebony*, June 1951.

27. Goareng Mosinyi to author, 12 November 2004.

28. Fairlie, *No Time Like the Past*, p. 107.

29. ibid., p. 142.

30. Copies of briefs for Mr Braine' [1961], 'Racial Discrimination', BLCAS, Mss Afr s 1256 (11).

31. Gasebalwe Seretse, *Tshekedi Khama*, p. 19.

32. Benson, *Tshekedi Khama*, p. 97.

33. Movietone newsreel, 'Meet Kgosi Tshekedi in Exclusive Talk', 18 September 1933.

34. Morton and Ramsay, *The Birth of Botswana*, p. 59.

35. Constantine, *Colour Bar*, p. 183.

4 THE DECISION OF THE BANGWATO ASSEMBLY

1. Gerald Nettelton to Priestman, 1 November 1948, TNA:PRO, DO 35/4113.

2. Wylie, *A Little God*, p. 181.

3. Record of proceedings at Serowe, Harragin Enquiry, 16 November 1949, BNARS, S 599/11.

4. Note of meeting held at Serowe on 28 and 29 December 1948, TNA:PRO, CO 981/36.

5. Union Opdom, 6 January 1949, TNA:PRO, DO 35/4113, 120180.

6. Quoted in A. J. Haile to Ronald Orchard, 17 May 1949, SOAS, CWM/LMS, AF/37.

7. Haile to Orchard, ibid.

8. Lenyeletse Seretse to Head, in Head, *Serowe*, p. 82.

9. Seager, *The Shadow of a Great Rock*, p. 51.

10. Sillery to Harragin, 4 January 1949, BNARS, S/69/15/3.

11. Harragin to Cecil Syers, 25 April 1949, ibid.

12. *Daily Mail*, 7 January 1949.

13. *Today*, 12 March 1960.

14. Bourke-White, 'The White Queen', unpublished chapter from memoir, SUL (US), MB-W.

15. Betty Thornton to author, 5 August 2004.

16. *Sunday Dispatch*, 16 April 1950.

17. Gabolebye Dinti Marobele to Head, in Head, *Serowe*, p. 98.

18. Goareng Mosinyi to author, 12 November 2004; Gasebalwe Seretse, *Tshekedi Khama*, p. 29.

19. Sillery, 'Working Backwards', n.d., BLCAS, Mss Afr r 207.

20. Sillery to Tshekedi, 19 May 1949, Truman Library, Joseph Sweeney Papers, Box 2, File Bamangwato Tribal Dispute.

21. Laurenson to Sillery, 1 June 1949, BNARS, S/69/15/3.

22. Gasebalwe Seretse, *Tshekedi Khama*, pp. 97–8.

23. Vivien Ellenberger to Sillery, 22 June 1949, BNARS, S/69/15/3.

24. 'Memorandum on Security Measures Ngwato Tribal Dissension: 1949', signed by Acting Commissioner, BP Police, BNARS, S 170/1/1.

25. Gasebalwe Seretse, *Tshekedi Khama*, p. 29.

26. Wylie, *A Little God*, p. 184.

27. Fairlie, *No Time Like the Past*, pp. 138–9.

28. Hatch, *New from Africa*, pp. 80–81.

29. Fairlie, *No Time Like the Past*, p. 142.

30. Gasebalwe Seretse, *Tshekedi Khama*, pp. 91–2.

31. Ellenberger to Sillery, 20 June 1949, BNARS, S/69/15/3.

32. Record of Proceedings at Judicial Enquiry Re Seretse Khama, CRO [November 1949], vol. 14, TNA:PRO, DO 35/4123.

33. Record of Proceedings at Judicial Enquiry Re Seretse Khama, ibid., vol. 13.

34. Ellenberger to Sillery, 22 June 1949, BNARS, S/69/15/3.

35. Record of Proceedings at Judicial Enquiry Re Seretse Khama, CRO [November 1949], vol. 14, TNA:PRO, DO 35/4123.

36. Gasebalwe Seretse, *Tshekedi Khama*, pp. 138–9.

37. Record of Proceedings at Judicial Enquiry Re Seretse Khama, CRO [November 1949], vol. 14, TNA:PRO, DO 35/4123.

38. ibid.

39. ibid.

40. Quoted in Wylie, *A Little God*, p. 186.

41. Gasebalwe Seretse, *Tshekedi Khama*, p. 105.

42. Report by Ellenberger on Kgotla of 20–25 June 1949, 29 June 1949, BLCAS, Mss Afr s 1181(1), A.

43. *Daily Mail*, 24 June 1949.

44. Ellenberger to High Commissioner's Office, 23 June 1949, BNARS, S/69/15/3.

45. Dubbeld, *Seretse Khama*, p. 13.

46. Gasebalwe Seretse, *Tshekedi Khama*, p. 103.

47. Parsons, Henderson and Tlou, *Seretse Khama*, p. 49.

48. Gasebalwe Seretse, *Tshekedi Khama*, p. 92; emphasis added.

49. Record of Proceedings at Judicial Enquiry Re Seretse Khama, CRO [November 1949], vol. 14, TNA:PRO, DO 35/4123.

50. ibid.

51. Gasebalwe Seretse, *Tshekedi Khama*, p. 108.

52. Record of Proceedings at Judicial Enquiry Re Seretse Khama, CRO, [November 1949], vol. 10, TNA:PRO, DO 35/4123.

53. Harragin Report, 1 December 1949, TNA:PRO, PREM 8/1308.

54. Peto Sekgoma to Sullivan, 1 July 1947, BNARS, S 170/1/1.

55. Heads of the Bangwato Tribe to Sullivan, 18 July 1949, BNARS, S 170/1/4.

56. G. M. Kgosi to Philip Noel-Baker, 8 August 1949, TNA:PRO, DO 119/1280.

5 RUTH

1. *Today*, 12 March 1960.

2. Betty Thornton to author, 5 August 2004.

3. John and Esme Goode to author, 29 March 2004.

4. See press cuttings in SOAS, CWM/LMS AF/39.

5. *Sunday Dispatch*, 16 April 1950.

6. Robins, *White Queen in Africa*, p. 50.

7. Betty Thornton to author, 5 August 2004.

8. Keith to Tait, 13 July 1949, TNA:PRO, CO 981/36.

9. *Pretoria News*, 6 July 1949.

10. *Today*, 12 March 1960.

11. Betty Thornton to author, 5 August 2004.

12. *Sunday Dispatch*, 2 April 1950.

13. *Saga Magazine*, June 1991.

14. Nettelton to Ellenberger, 4 July 1949, BNARS, S/69/15/3.

15. Nettelton to Tait, quoted in Noel-Baker to Baring, 6 August 1949, TNA:PRO, DO 119/1284.

16. Minute by Tait, 13 July 1949, TNA:PRO, DO 35/4114.

17. Keith to Jeffries, 4 March 1949, TNA:PRO, CO 981/36.

18. John and Esme Goode to author, 29 March 2004.

19. Marwick, *The Home Front*, p. 23.

20. ibid., p. 28.

21. ibid., p. 157.

22. Monks, *Eyewitness*, p. 270.

23. John and Esme Goode to author, 29 March 2004.

24. Marwick, *The Home Front*, p. 138.

25. *Sunday Dispatch*, 2 April 1950.

26. ibid.

27. John and Esme Goode to author, 29 March 2004.

28. Dubbeld, *Seretse Khama*, p. 7.

29. S. V. Lawrenson to Nettelton, 16 November 1948, BNARS, S 169/15/1.

30. Wylie, *A Little God*, p. 201.

31. Note of meeting at Serowe, 16 August 1951, TNA:PRO, DO 119/1315.

32. Baboni, Mmakgama, Oratile and Milly to Earl of Athlone, 21 July 1926, reproduced in Daymond et al. (eds), *Women Writing Africa*, p. 181.

33. Oratile to Resident Magistrate, 31 September 1929, reproduced in ibid., p. 185.

34. Baboni, Mmakgama, Oratile and Milly to Earl of Athlone, 21 July 1926, reproduced in ibid., p. 181.

35. Oratile to Administration, 26 September 1926, reproduced in ibid., p. 184.

36. Baring to CRO, 14 July 1949, TNA:PRO, DO 35/4114.

37. Redfern, *Ruth and Seretse*, p. 12.

38. Chas. Olley to Huggins, 20 July 1949, TNA:PRO, DO 119/1284.

39. Huggins to Baring, 22 July 1949, ibid.

40. Sillery to Provincial Commissioner, Livingstone, 4 August 1949, BNARS, S 170/1/4.

41. Dutfield, *A Marriage of Inconvenience*, p. 114.

42. Muriel Sanderson to author, 10 November 2004.

43. *Saga Magazine*, June 1991.

44. Ruth Khama to Betty Thornton, 19 September 1949, Khama Family Papers.

45. Photograph in *Naledi ya Batswana*, 3 September 1949.

6 THE DARK SHADOW OF APARTHEID

1. W. A. W. Clark to Cecil Syers, 28 June 1949, TNA:PRO, CO 981/36.

2. Forsyth to Egeland, 29 June 1949, NASA, BLO 84, PS 2/5.

3. Noel-Baker to Baring, 2 July 1949, TNA:PRO, DO 35/4113.

4. Egeland to Forsyth, 30 June 1949, NASA, BLO 84, PS 2/5.

5. Noel-Baker to Baring, 2 July 1949, TNA:PRO, DO 35/4114.

6. Sillery to Baring, 5 July 1949, TNA:PRO, DO 119/1282.

7. Baring to Gerald Nettelton, 3 November 1948, TNA:PRO, DO 35/4113.

8. Handwritten note by Sillery, 7 July 1949, on typed minutes by V. Ellenberger, 5 July 1949, BNARS, S 170/1/1.

9. Liesching to Baring, 8 July 1949; draft initialled by Syers, 6 July 1949, and by Noel-Baker, 7 July 1949; TNA:PRO, DO 35/4114.

10. 'A Public Declaration made by Kgosi Regent Tshekedi Khama and the undersigned Headmen of the Tribe on the crisis that has arisen from the marriage of Seretse Khama to Ruth Williams' [1949], LHASC, Bechuanaland: General Correspondence and Documents.

11. D. Buchanan to J. Buchanan, 14 July 1949, SOAS, LMS CWM, AF/37.

12. Baring to Noel-Baker, 9 July 1949, TNA:PRO, DO 35/4114.

13. Baring to Liesching, 11 July 1949, TNA:PRO, DO 119/1283.

14. ibid.

15. Berridge, *South Africa, the Colonial Powers and 'African Defence'*, pp. 24–5.

16. Michael Dutfield's book, *A Marriage of Inconvenience. The Persecution of Seretse and Ruth Khama* (1990), argues that the supply of uranium was key to the British Government's decision to exile the Khamas – that it gave South Africa overwhelming and compelling leverage over the British Government. No doubt uranium was part of the overall picture, given the tensions of the developing Cold War. However, on the basis of careful scrutiny of the evidence that is now available, it is clear that the British Government would have taken exactly the same measures against Seretse, even if uranium had not played any role in relations between South Africa and Britain. The uranium theory has the attraction of being a 'smoking gun' and also diminishes the role of racist attitudes among British officials, but it is speculative and not proven. The racist attitudes behind the decision of exile, however, are fully documented in the evidence that is available.

17. Huggins to Baring, 7 July 1949, TNA:PRO, DO 35/4115.

18. Debate of Legislative Assembly, Southern Rhodesia, 7 July 1949, BNARS, S 599/11.

19. African Tribal Affairs Committee, 17 July 1949; TNA:PRO, DO 119/1280.

20. Kaunda, *Zambia Shall Be Free*, p. 34.

21. G. W. R. Lange, MP for Nkana, reported in *Bulawayo Chronicle*, 8 July 1949.

22. Baring to Noel-Baker, 11 July 1949, BNARS, S 170/1/3.

23. 'Stimson of BBC', [n.d., 1950?], Truman Library, Sweeney Papers, Box 2, File: Bamangwato Tribal Dispute.

24. Baring to Liesching, 11 July 1949, TNA:PRO, DO 119/1283.

25. Baring to Liesching, 12 July 1949, TNA:PRO, DO 35/4114.

26. Minute by Liesching, 14 July 1949, ibid.

27. Minute by Gordon Walker, 15 July 1949, ibid.

28. Noel-Baker to Creech Jones, 16 July 1949, TNA:PRO, CO 537/4714.

29. Noel-Baker to Baring, not sent [July 1950], TNA:PRO, DO 35/4114.

30. Minute by Noel-Baker to Liesching, 7 July 1949, ibid.

31. *Natal Mercury*, 23 July 1954.

32. Garner, *The Commonwealth Office*, p. 292.

33. Minute signed D. A., 12 July 1949, TNA:PRO, DO 35/4114.

34. Memorandum to Cabinet by Noel-Baker, 20 July 1949, TNA:PRO, PREM 8/1308, Part 1.

35. Noel-Baker to Baring (draft), attached to Memorandum to Cabinet by Noel-Baker, 20 July 1949, ibid.

36. Cabinet Conclusions, 21 July 1949, TNA:PRO, CAB 128.

37. Liesching to Baring, 21 July 1949, DUL, GRE/1/13/19.

38. *Natal Witness*, 2 July 1949.

39. *Cape Times*, 9 July 1949.

40. *Star*, 8 July 1949.

41. Phethu Kgari to Sullivan, n.d., attached with letter from Sullivan to Nettelton, 5 August 1949, BNARS, S 170/1/4.

42. Private Secretary to Commonwealth Secretary, to Private Secretary to High Commissioner for South Africa, with text of proposed announcement, 29 July 1949, NASA, PS 2/5.

43. Huggins to Clark, 29 July 1949, TNA:PRO, DO 119/1284.

44. Baring to Cecil Syers, 16 September 1949, ibid.

45. Seager, *The Shadow of a Great Rock*, p. 55.

7 OUR MOTHER – *MOHUMAGADI*

1. *Naledi ya Batswana*, 3 September 1949.

2. *Today*, 12 March 1960.

3. Sandy Grant to author, 11 November 2004.

4. Redfern, *Ruth and Seretse*, p. 11.

5. Anthony Sillery, 'Working Backwards', n.d., BLCAS, Mss Afr r. 207.

6. Dutfield, *A Marriage of Inconvenience*, p. 117.

7. *Ebony*, June 1951.

8. Dutfield, *A Marriage of Inconvenience*, p. 115.

9. *Today*, 12 March 1960.

10. *Saga Magazine*, June 1991.

11. ibid.

12. A. E. Seager to R. K. Orchard, 29 August 1949, SOAS, CWM/LMS, AF/37.

13. *Saga Magazine*, June 1991.

14. *Ebony*, June 1951.

15. 'Memorandum to Mr Paver', n.d. [1949], TNA:PRO, DO 119/1282.

16. Sillery to Baring, 13 September 1949, BNARS, S 170/1/4.

17. Ruth Khama to Betty Thornton, 19 September 1949, Khama Family Papers.

18. Margaret Bourke-White to Bill, n.d., SUL (US), MB-W, Box 25.

19. *Sunday Express*, April 1950.

20. Quoted in Dutfield, *A Marriage of Inconvenience*, pp. 118–19.

21. *Life*, 6 March 1950.

22. *Cape Times*, 8 July 1949.

23. *Life*, 6 March 1950.

24. M. Malau to *Naledi ya Batswana*, 27 August 1949.

25. Redfern, *Ruth and Seretse*, p. 63.

26. Ruth Khama, 'My Baby – and the Future', *Sunday Express*, April 1950.

27. *Today*, 12 March 1960.

28. Ruth Khama to Betty Thornton, 31 January 1950, Khama Family Papers.

29. *Daily Mail*, February 1950.

30. Bourke-White, 'The White Queen', unpublished chapter from memoir, SUL (US), MB-W Papers.

31. Ruth Khama to Betty Thornton, 19 September 1949, Khama Family Papers.

32. Bourke-White, 'The White Queen', unpublished chapter from memoir, SUL (US), MB-W Papers.

33. *Daily Mail*, 10 October 1956.

34. Redfern, *Ruth and Seretse*, pp. 64–5.

35. Constantine, *Colour Bar*, p. 183.

36. Redfern, *Ruth and Seretse*, pp. 15–6.

37. ibid., pp. 63–4.

38. Baring to Gordon Walker, 15 March 1950, TNA:PRO, CO 537/5928.

39. Alan Bradshaw to Hope Lovell, 1 April 1950, BNARS, MSS.6/5.

40. Doris Bradshaw to Kit and Harry, 3 July 1950, TNA:PRO, DO 119/1297.

41. Sillery to Baring, 13 September 1949, BNARS, S 170/3/1.

42. Sillery to Baring, 13 September 1949, BNARS, S 170/1/4.

43. *Sunday Express*, April 1950.

44. Baring to Cecil Syers, 16 September 1949, TNA:PRO, DO 119/1284.

45. Colin Legum, 'Tshekedi's desert refuge', 15 August 1951, BLCAS, Mss Afr s 1681.

46. Gabolebye Dinti Marobele to Head, in Head, *Serowe*, p. 98.

47. Monks, *Eyewitness*, p. 267.

48. Quoted by Monsarrat to Clark, 17 April 1950, TNA:PRO, DO 119/1293.

49. *Picture Post*, 29 April 1950.

50. Ruth Khama to Margaret Bourke-White, 10 January 1950, SUL (US), MB-W, Box 25.

51. 'Bourke-White', n.d., ibid.

52. Margaret Bourke-White to Bill, n.d., ibid.

53. Bourke-White, 'The White Queen', unpublished chapter from memoir, SUL (US), MB-W Papers.

54. Margaret Bourke-White to Bill, n.d., SUL (US), MB-W, Box 25.

55. ibid.

56. ibid.

57. Bourke-White, 'The White Queen', unpublished chapter from memoir, SUL (US), MB-W Papers.

58. Quoted in *The Recorder*, 3 September 1949.

59. H. Lewis to Commonwealth Relations Office, 17 April 1952, TNA:PRO, DO 35/4145.

60. Secretary, Dutch Reformed Church of Natal, to Baring, 1 September 1949, TNA:PRO, DO 119/1280.

61. Dutfield, *A Marriage of Inconvenience*, p. 120.

62. *Today*, 12 March 1960.

63. Naledi Khama to author, 13 November 2004.

64. Ruth Khama to Betty Thornton, 31 January 1950, Khama Family Papers.

65. *Life*, 28 April 1950.

66. Margaret Bourke-White to Bill, n.d., SUL (US), MB-W, Box 25.

8 THE HARRAGIN INQUIRY

1. *Today*, 12 March 1960; Harragin Report, 1 December 1949, TNA:PRO, PREM 8/1308, Part 1.

2. Monks, *Eyewitness*, p. 276.

3. Harragin to Clark, 15 August 1949, TNA:PRO, DO 119/1284.

4. Harragin to Holmes, 20 October 1949, BNARS, S 599/13.

5. See picture of Fraenkel in *Leader Magazine*, 11 March 1950.

6. Statement by Hudson, 19 July 1949, TNA:PRO, DO 35/4114.

7. Monks, *Eyewitness*, p. 303.

8. Baring to Sillery, 9 August 1949, TNA:PRO, DO 119/1284.

9. Sillery, 'Working Backwards', n.d., BLCAS, Mss Afr r 207.

10. Clark to Chief Secretary, 29 September 1949, TNA:PRO, DO 119/1285; emphasis added.

11. Baring to Sillery, 4 October 1949, ibid.; emphasis added.

12. Sillery to Baring, 18 October 1949, ibid.

13. Baring to Sillery, 21 October 1949, ibid.

14. Winship to Secretary of State, 1 November 1949, NARA, RG 59, Decimal Files (1945–9), Box 6192.

15. *Star*, 26 October 1949.

16. Speeches transcribed in document sent from Secretary for External Affairs, Cape Town, to Egeland, 27 March 1950, TNA:PRO, DO 35/4115.

17. Egeland to Forsyth, 13 October 1949, NASA, BLO 84, PS 2/5.

18. Attlee to Malan, 2 November 1949, TNA:PRO, PREM 11/1183.

19. *Daily Mirror*, 2 November 1949.

20. Record of Proceedings at Judicial Enquiry Re Seretse Khama, CRO, [November 1949], vols 1–14, TNA:PRO, DO 35/4123. All subsequent references to – and quotations from – the Inquiry draw on this source.

21. Haile to Orchard, 3 November 1949, SOAS, LMS, AF/38.

22. 'Protest' to Baring, Serowe, 2 November 1949, TNA:PRO, DO 119/1286.

23. Mandela, *Long Walk to Freedom*, pp. 154–5.

24. Sisulu, *Walter and Albertina Sisulu*, p. 104.

25. *Today*, 12 March 1960.

26. Dutfield, *A Marriage of Inconvenience*, p. 128.

27. Robins, *White Queen in Africa*, p. 41.

28. Pela, 'A tribal Chief gets married', *Common Sense*, June 1949, CROUW, M. D. J. Jeffreys Collection.

29. Gasebalwe Seretse, *Tshekedi Khama*, p. 32.

30. [Miss] Dykes to Holmes, 22 December 1949, BNARS, S 599/13.

31. *Today*, 12 March 1960.

9 'A FIT AND PROPER PERSON TO BE CHIEF'

1. Harragin Report, 1 December 1949, TNA:PRO, PREM 8/1308, Part 1.

2. Baring to Huggins, 7 December 1949, TNA:PRO, DO 119/1286; Benn, *Years of Hope*, p. 40.

3. Huggins to Clark, 12 December 1949, TNA:PRO, DO 119/1286.

4. Clark to Resident Commissioner, Maseru, 15 December 1949, ibid.

5. Brigadier C. E. R. Hirsch to Sillery, 20 December 1949, ibid.

6. Fraenkel to Nettelton, 22 December 1949, BNARS, S 529/2/2.

7. Minute to Baxter, 12 December 1949, TNA:PRO, DO 35/4118; emphasis added.

8. Note of a meeting at CRO, 16 December 1949, TNA:PRO, CO 537/4714.

9. Noel-Baker to Attlee, 21 December 1949, TNA:PRO, PREM 8/1308.

10. Memorandum by Noel-Baker on issue of Bechuanaland Succession, n.d. [21 December 1949], ibid.

11. Attlee to Noel-Baker, 21 December 1949, TNA:PRO, PREM 8/1308.

12. Mandela, *Long Walk to Freedom*, pp. 130–32.

13. Enclosure I, Seretse Khama [by Baring], 29 October 1949, TNA:PRO, DO 119/1286.

14. Memorandum [by Baring] on aspects of South African opinion, December 1949, ibid.

15. Quintin Whyte to Baring, 6 September 1949, ibid.

16. Huggins to Clark, 19 December 1949, ibid.

17. Clark to Huggins, 22 December 1949, ibid.

18. Gordon Walker to Attlee, 21 January 1950; Attlee to Gordon Walker, 22 January 1950, TNA:PRO, PREM 8/1308.

19. Lambert to Cohen, 28 January 1950, TNA:PRO, CO 537/5927.

20. Minute by Cohen, 30 January 1950, ibid.

21. Noel-Baker to Attlee, 1 February 1950, TNA:PRO PREM 8/1308, Part 1.

10 TRICKED BY THE BRITISH GOVERNMENT

1. Clark to Redman, 5 February 1950, TNA:PRO, DO 119/1288.

2. *Today*, 12 March 1960.

3. Clark to Sillery, 28 November 1949, TNA:PRO, DO 119/1286.

4. Doris Bradshaw to Hope Lovell, 6 February 1950, BNARS, MSS.6.

5. Bourke-White, 'The White Queen', unpublished chapter from memoir, SUL (US), MB-W Papers.

6. *Star*, 9 February 1950.

7. Sillery to Baring, n.d. [8 February 1950], TNA:PRO, DO 119/1288.

8. *Star*, 9 February 1950.

9. Doris Bradshaw to Hope Lovell, 9 February 1950, BNARS, MSS.6.

10. Sillery to Baring, n.d. [8 February 1950], TNA:PRO, DO 119/1288.

11. ibid.

12. *Star*, 9 February 1950.

13. Bourke-White, 'The White Queen', unpublished chapter from memoir, SUL (US), MB-W Papers.

14. Movietone newsreel, 'Seretse Khama Comes to England Alone', 20 February 1950.

15. Sillery to Baring, 13 February 1950, TNA:PRO, DO 119/1288.

16. *Ebony*, June 1951.

17. S. G. Seretse and O. Ratshose to Noel-Baker, 15 February 1950, TNA:PRO, DO 119/1288.

18. Bourke-White, 'The White Queen', unpublished chapter from memoir, SUL (US), MB-W Papers.

19. ibid.

20. 'Bourke-White', n.d., SUL (US), MB-W, Box 25.

21. Pathe newsreel, 'Seretse Khama Comes in from Africa', 20 February 1950; see also 'Seretse Khama Comes to England Alone,' Movietone newsreel, 20 February 1950.

22. Baxter to Liesching, 14 February 1950, TNA:PRO, DO 121/57.

23. Baxter to Liesching, 11 February 1950, TNA:PRO, DO 35/4119.

24. Liesching to Noel-Baker, in Noel-Baker to Baring, 15 February 1950, TNA:PRO, DO 119/1288.

25. Note of Mr Keith's report of his conversations with Seretse on 14 February, 15 February 1950, TNA:PRO, DO 35/4119.

26. Note of a meeting at the CRO, Thursday 16 February, TNA:PRO, DO 119/1288.

27. Note of a conversation between Seretse and Keith, 17 February 1950, TNA:PRO, PREM 8/1308.

28. *Sunday Express*, 19 February 1950.

29. Liesching to Gordon Walker and Addison, 28 February 1950, TNA:PRO, PREM 8/1308.

30. Attlee's draft autobiography, quoted in Pearce (ed.), *Patrick Gordon Walker*, pp. 17–18.

31. Pearce, Introduction to *Patrick Gordon Walker*, p. 20.

32. Gann and Gelfand, *Huggins of Rhodesia*, p. 217.

33. Photograph in ibid., opp. p. 209.

34. Liesching to Gordon Walker and Addison, 28 February 1950, TNA:PRO, PREM 8/1308.

35. Cabinet Conclusions, 3 March 1950, TNA:PRO, CAB 128.

36. ibid.

37. A. Johnston to Norman Brook, 6 March 1950, TNA:PRO, CAB 21/3167.

38. *Ebony*, June 1951.

39. ibid.

40. Movietone newsreel, 'Seretse Khama Talks to Movietone', 13 March 1950.

41. Monks, *Eyewitness*, p. 280.

42. *Today*, 12 March 1960.

43. *Ebony*, June 1951.

44. Quoted in Mockford, *Seretse Khama and the Bamangwato*, p. 5.

45. *Life*, 28 April 1950.

11 THE HUMILIATION OF SIR EVELYN BARING

1. Diary entry for 2 April 1950, Pearce (ed.), *Patrick Gordon Walker*, p. 188.

2. Gordon Walker to Attlee, 7 March 1950, with additional note by Attlee, 7 March 1950, TNA:PRO, PREM 8/1308.

3. *Hansard*, 8 March 1950.

4. Egeland to Malan, 8 March 1950, NASA, PM, vol. 1/4/21, 1/15.

5. Brockway, *Towards Tomorrow*, p. 161.

6. Brockway, *Outside the Right*, p. 76.

7. *The Times*, 9 March 1950.

8. *Hansard*, 8 March 1950.

9. Brockway, *Outside the Right*, p. 76.

10. *Hansard*, 8 March 1950.

11. Monks, *Eyewitness*, p. 280.

12. *Ebony*, June 1951.

13. Baring to Liesching, 8 March 1950, TNA:PRO,CO 537/5927.

14. Gordon Walker to Baring, 10 March 1950, TNA:PRO, PREM 8/1308 Part 1.

15. Baring to Gordon Walker, 10 March 1950, TNA:PRO, CO 537/5928.

16. 'Stimson of BBC (after 1 hr talk with Clark of High Commission Office)', n.d. [March 1950], Truman Library, Sweeney Papers, Box 2, File: Bamangwato Tribal Dispute.

17. 'Native Chiefs Ignore High Commissioner', Movietone newsreel, 30 March 1950.

18. Doris Bradshaw to Kit and Harry, 3 July 1950, TNA:PRO, DO 119/1297.

19. 'Stimson of BBC (after 1 hr talk with Clark of High Commission Office)', n.d. [March 1950], Truman Library, Sweeney Papers, Box 2, File: Bamangwato Tribal Dispute.

20. Redfern, *Ruth and Seretse*, p. 123.

21. Monks, *Eyewitness*, pp. 280–81.

22. *The Times*, 13 March 1950.

23. Sillery, 'Working Backwards', n.d., BLCAS, Rhodes House, Mss Afr r 207.

24. *Cape Times*, 11 March 1950.

25. Goareng Mosinyi to author, 12 November 2004.

26. Monks, *Eyewitness*, p. 281.

27. Fairlie, *No Time Like the Past*, p. 146; Monks, *Eyewitness*, p. 281.

28. Doris Bradshaw to Kit and Harry, 3 July 1950, TNA:PRO, DO 119/1297.

29. Redfern, *Ruth and Seretse*, p. 125.

30. Monks, *Eyewitness*, p. 281.

31. Baring to CRO, 15 March 1950, TNA:PRO, CO 537/5928.

32. Uniform described by Douglas-Home, *Evelyn Baring*, pp. 120–21.

33. Nicholas Monsarrat, *Life is a Four-Letter Word*, vol. II, *Breaking Out*, pp. 271–3.

34. Monks, *Eyewitness*, p. 282.

35. Movietone newsreel, 'Native Chiefs Ignore High Commissioner', 30 March 1950.

36. 'Memorandum of Conversation', between Clark, Connelly and Sweeney (US Embassy), 9 March 1950, Truman Library, Sweeney Papers, Box 2, File: Bamangwato Tribal Dispute.

37. *The Times*, 14 March 1950.

38. Fairlie, *No Time Like the Past*, p. 147.

39. *The Times*, 14 March 1950.

40. Report of press conference enclosed with letter to Clark from Resident Commissioner's Office, 14 March 1950, TNA:PRO, DO 119/1290.

41. Redfern, *Ruth and Seretse*, p. 127.

42. Monsarrat to Clark, 17 April 1950, TNA:PRO, DO 119/1293.

43. Liesching to Baring, 14 March 1950, TNA:PRO, DO 119/1291.

44. Charles Douglas-Home, *Evelyn Baring*, p. 191.

45. Gordon Walker to Liesching, 13 March 1950, TNA:PRO, DO 121/57.

46. Baring to Gordon Walker, 15 March 1950, TNA:PRO, DO 119/1290.

47. *The Times*, 14 March 1950.

48. Fairlie, *No Time Like the Past*, p. 147.

49. Seager, *The Shadow of a Great Rock*, p. 63.

50. Redfern, *Ruth and Seretse*, p. 130.

51. X. Y. Z. Kgobera to *Naledi ya Batswana*, sent 17 March 1950, not published, TNA:PRO, DO 119/1292.

52. See Kuper, *Passive Resistance in South Africa*; Menon, *Passive Resistance in South Africa*; Itzkin, *Gandhi's Johannesburg. Birthplace of Satyagraha*.

53. Doris Bradshaw to Hope Lovell, 1 April 1950, ibid.

54. ibid.

55. Baring to CRO, 15 March 1950, TNA:PRO, CO 537/5928.

56. Doris Bradshaw to Kit and Harry, 3 July 1950, TNA:PRO, DO 119/1297.

57. *Daily Mail*, 17 March 1950.

58. Doris Bradshaw to Hope Lovell, 1 April 1950, BNARS, MSS.6/5.

59. Alan Bradshaw to Hope Lovell, 1 April 1950, ibid.

60. Baring to CRO, 15 March 1950, TNA:PRO, CO 537/5928.

61. Clark to Baxter, 3 July 1950, TNA:PRO, DO, 35/4124.

62. Reported in Thompson to Baring, 15 April 1950, TNA:PRO, DO 119/1293.

12 COVER-UP

1. *Ebony*, June 1951.

2. The Committee comprised representatives from the African League, the East African Students Union, the British African Institute of Culture, the Gold Coast Union, the Sierra Leone Study Group, the Caribbean Labour Congress, the Coordinating Council for Colonial Student Affairs, the Council for Overseas Indians, the Sudan Association, the League of Coloured Peoples, the Coloured Workers Association and the West Indian Students Union. List from South Africa House, 22 March 1950, NASA, BLO PS 2/5A.

3. Howat, *Learie Constantine*, p. 151.

4. Adi, *West Africans in Britain*, p. 129.

5. ibid., p. 158; List from South Africa House, 22 March 1950, NASA, BLO PS 2/5A.

6. *The Times*, 10 March 1950.

7. *The Times*, 13 March 1950.

8. Constantine, *Colour Bar*, p. 185.

9. *The Times*, 20 March 1950.

10. Mulumba, Secretary-General African League, to 'Friends' [March 1950], TNA:PRO, CO 537/5926.

11. Note of meeting between Griffiths, Gordon Walker and Seretse Khama Fighting Committee, 17 March 1950, TNA:PRO, DO 35/4125.

12. US Attaché Tibbetts to US Department of State, 20 March 1950, NARA, RG 59, Decimal File, Box 4897.

13. Minute in Colonial Office, initials unclear, 9 March 1950, TNA:PRO, CO 323/1912/10.

14. Record of conversation between Secretary of State and Krishna Menon, 15 March 1950, TNA:PRO, DO 35/4120.

15. *The Times*, 13 March 1950.

16. Reuters, 28 March 1950, NASA, BLO PS 2/5A.

17. Resolution of the West Indian Political Forum, 13 March 1950, ibid.

18. Joseph D. Sweeney to Secretary of State, March 1950, Truman Library, Sweeney Papers, Box 2, File: Bamangwato Tribal Dispute.

19. Baring to Liesching, 27 May 1950, NASA, PM, vol. 1/4/21, 1/15.

20. Williams to Gordon Walker, 28 March 1950, TNA:PRO, DO 35/4125.

21. Horne, *Black and Red*, p. 184.

22. L. Finnegan to Williams, n.d., TNA:PRO, DO 35/4125.

23. Copied from Sillery to Baring, 16 March 1950, TNA:PRO, DO 119/1290.

24. Mahabane to Attlee, n.d. [March 1950]; Naicker to Attlee, 11 March 1950, TNA:PRO, DO 119/1301.

25. State Information Office, Cape Town, Political Survey, 13 March 1950, NASA, BLO PS 2/5A.

26. Walter Carey to *The Times*, 11 March 1950.

27. Neilson to Attlee, n.d. [March 1950], TNA:PRO, DO 119/1301.

28. HC to CRO, 28 April 1950, TNA:PRO, CO 537/5926; UK Information Office to CRO, 29 April 1950, TNA:PRO, CO 323/1912/10.

29. Paver to Baring, 6 April 1950, TNA:PRO, DO 119/1292; Paver to Baring, 24 April 1950, TNA:PRO, DO 119/1293.

30. *The Times*, 9 March 1950.

31. Tibbetts to US Department of State, 20 March 1950, NARA, RG 59, Decimal File, Box 4897.

32. H. G. Apsimon et al. to *The Times*, 13 March 1950.

33. Diary entry for 2 April 1950, *Patrick Gordon Walker. Political Diaries 1932–1971*, p. 189.

34. Egeland to Malan, 13 March 1950, NASA, BLO 84, PS 2/5.

35. ibid.

36. Diary entry for 18 April 1950, in Pottle (ed.), *Daring to Hope. The Diaries and Letters of Violet Bonham Carter*, p. 88.

37. Churchill to Smuts, 15 March 1950, CHUR 02/101.

38. Smuts to Churchill, 16 March 1950, ibid.

39. Smuts to Churchill, 16 March 1950, ibid.

40. Diary entry for 2 April 1950, *Patrick Gordon Walker. Political Diaries 1932–1971*, pp. 188–9.

41. *The Times*, 16 March 1950.

42. Isobel Cripps to Gordon Walker, 13 March 1950, TNA:PRO, DO 121/57.

43. Gordon Walker to Isobel Cripps, 14 March 1950, ibid.

44. Baring to Gordon Walker, 15 March 1950, TNA:PRO, DO 119/1290.

45. Cabinet Meeting (1950) 11th, Conclusions, TNA:PRO, CO 537/5928.

46. Appiah, *Joe Appiah*, p. 182.

47. Note of meeting between Griffiths, Gordon Walker and Seretse Khama Fighting Committee, 17 March 1950, TNA:PRO, DO 35/4125.

48. Baring to Gordon Walker, 20 March 1950, TNA:PRO, CO, 537/5928.

49. CRO, 'Bechuanaland Protectorate. Succession to the Chieftainship of the Bamangwato Tribe', March 1950, HMSO, Cmd. 7193.

50. Circular from CRO, 22 March 1950, TNA:PRO, DO 35/4120.

51. Annan to Gordon Walker, 30 March 1950, TNA:PRO, DO 35/4125.

52. Archbishop of Canterbury to Attlee, 21 April 1950, TNA:PRO, DO 35/4217.

53. Tibbetts to US Department of State, 29 March 1950, NARA, RG 59, Decimal File, Box 4897.

54. Akinola Maja, Chairman, and Mbonu Ojike, Secretary, to Colonial Secretary, 11 April 1950, TNA:PRO, CO 847/45/3.

55. Acting General Secretary, United Gold Coast Convention, to Secretary of State, 3 May 1950, ibid.

56. Harewood to Blackburne, 25 March 1950, TNA:PRO, CO 323/1912/10.

57. Huggins to Secretary of State for the Colonies, 1 April 1950, TNA:PRO, CO 847/45/3.

58. Oliver Franks to Ernest Bevin, 28 April 1950, ibid.

59. Council on African Affairs to Trygve Lie, 27 May 1950, NASA, BVV 98/82.

60. Seretse Khama to *The Times*, 24 March 1950.

61. *Report of the House of Assembly*, Cape Town, 24 March 1950.

62. Minute by Liesching, 25 March 1950, TNA:PRO, DO 119/1291.

63. Gordon Walker to Attlee, 28 March 1950, TNA:PRO, DO 35/4115.

64. Egeland to Malan, 24 March 1950, NASA, BLO 84, PS 2/5.

65. CRO to HCO, 25 March 1950, TNA:PRO, PREM 8/1308 Part 1.

66. Egeland to Malan, 28 March 1950, NASA, PM, vol. 1/4/21, 1/15.

67. Gordon Walker to Attlee, 28 March 1950, TNA:PRO, DO 35/4115.

68. Egeland to Malan, 28 March 1950, NASA, PM, vol. 1/4/21, 1/15.

69. *Hansard*, 28 March 1950.

70. Diary entry 2 April 1950, *Patrick Gordon Walker. Political Diaries 1932–1971*, p.189.

71. *Hansard*, 28 March 1950.

72. Quoted in Jackson, *Rebels and Whips*, p. 90.

73. Egeland to Forsyth, 28 March 1950, NASA, PM, vol. 1/4/21, 1/15.

74. Egeland to Malan, 30 March 1950, NASA, BLO 84, PS 2/5.

13 IN AFRICA, BUT KEPT APART

1. *The Times*, 29 March 1950.

2. Movietone newsreel, 'Seretse Khama Back in Bechuanaland', 10 April 1949.

3. HCO to CRO, 3 April 1950, TNA:PRO, DO, 35/4120.

4. *Daily Graphic*, 1 April 1950.

5. Photograph in *Cape Argus*, 1 April 1950.

6. *Daily Graphic*, 1 April 1950.

7. Movietone newsreel, 'Seretse Khama Back in Bechuanaland', 10 April 1949.

8. HCO to CRO, 3 April 1950, TNA:PRO, DO, 35/4120.

9. Monks, *Eyewitness*, p. 283.

10. Baring to CRO, 3 April 1950, TNA:PRO, CO, 537/5928.

11. Reported in Dutfield, *A Marriage of Inconvenience*, p. 190.

12. Baring to Resident Commissioner, 3 April 1950, TNA:PRO, DO 119/1292.

13. MacKenzie to Nettelton, 17 April 1950, TNA:PRO, DO 119/1293.

14. Monsarrat to Clark, 19 April 1950, ibid.

15. Monsarrat to Clark, 17 April 1950, ibid.

16. HCO to CRO, 13 April 1950, TNA:PRO, DO 35/4120.

17. Haile to Orchard, 17 April 1950, SOAS, LMS, AF/37.

18. Baring to Gordon Walker, 31 March 1950, TNA:PRO, DO 119/1291.

19. Sillery to Baring, 14 March 1950, TNA:PRO, DO 119/1290.

20. Fairlie, *No Time Like the Past*, p. 145.

21. Moikangoa to Seretse, 10 April 1950, TNA:PRO, DO 119/1293.

22. Clark to Baring, 13 April 1950, TNA:PRO, DO 119/1292.

23. Gibson to Baxter, 12 April 1950, TNA:PRO, DO 35/4120.

24. HCO to CRO, 2 May 1950, TNA:PRO, CO 537/5926.

25. Report by Freedman, 20 April 1950, TNA:PRO, DO 119/1293.

26. Nettelton to Clark, 22 April 1950, ibid.

27. HCO to CRO, 12 April, 1950, TNA:PRO, PREM 8/1308, Part 1.

28. HCO to CRO, 14 April 1950, ibid.

29. Baring to CRO, 15 April 1950, TNA:PRO, DO 35/4121.

30. Fenner Brockway to Hope Lovell, 24 April 1950, BNARS, MSS.6/5.
31. *Today*, 12 March 1960.
32. *Sunday Express*, 2 April 1950.
33. HCO to CRO, 13 April, 1950, TNA:PRO, DO 35/4120.
34. Nettelton to Baring, 1 April 1950, TNA:PRO, DO 119/1292.
35. *Ebony*, June 1951.
36. HCO to CRO, 2 May 1950, TNA:PRO, CO 537/5926.
37. *The Times*, 17 April 1950.
38. Monsarrat, *Life is a Four-Letter Word*. Vol. II, *Breaking Out*, pp. 274–5.
39. *Ebony*, June 1951.
40. *The Times*, 17 April 1950.
41. Resident Commissioner, Mafikeng, to High Commissioner, Cape Town, 8 April 1950, TNA:PRO, DO 119/1292.
42. HCO to CRO, 2 May 1950, TNA:PRO, CO 537/5926.
43. ibid.
44. Tlou and Campbell, *History of Botswana*, p.307.
45. *The Times*, 17 April 1950.
46. *Today*, 12 March 1960.
47. Monsarrat to MacKenzie, 19 April 1950, TNA:PRO, DO 119/1293.
48. HCO to CRO, 2 May 1950, TNA:PRO, CO 537/5926.
49. *Today*, 12 March 1960.
50. HCO to CRO, 2 May 1950, TNA:PRO, CO 537/5926.
51. Monsarrat to Clark, 19 April 1950, TNA:PRO, DO 119/1293.
52. Fairlie, *No Time Like the Past*, pp. 147–8.
53. *Daily Mail*, 3 October 1956.
54. Dutfield, *A Marriage of Inconvenience*, p. 200.
55. *Today*, 12 March 1960.
56. Dutfield, *A Marriage of Inconvenience*, p. 201.
57. *Life*, 12 June 1950.
58. Naledi Khama to author, 13 November 2004.
59. Minute by Clark, 11 January 1949, TNA:PRO, DO 119/1279.
60. *Life*, 12 June 1950.
61. Monks, *Eyewitness*, pp.284, 279.

14 TOGETHER IN LOBATSE

1. *Today*, 12 March 1960.
2. Monks, *Eyewitness*, p. 284.
3. Baring to Gordon Walker, 24 July 1950, TNA:PRO, DO 119/1296.

4. Report to DC at Lobatse by Mr H. Palphramand, 24 July 1950, signed R. B. M. Sullivan [24 July 1950], ibid.

5. Sullivan to Ellenberger, 24 July 1950, ibid.

6. Quoted in Benson, *Tshekedi Khama*, p. 204.

7. Press cutting, July 1950 (no further information given), Truman Library, Sweeney Papers, Box 5.

8. HCO to CRO, 21 June 1950, TNA:PRO, DO 35/4121.

9. Quoted in Benson, *Tshekedi Khama*, p. 203.

10. See ibid, p. 203 ff.

11. Resident Commissioner to Clark, 21 June 1950, TNA:PRO, DO 119/1295.

12. HCO to CRO, 21 June 1950, ibid.

13. MacKenzie to Nettleton, 10 July 1950, TNA:PRO, DO 119/1296.

14. Minute by Liesching, 19 July 1950, TNA:PRO, DO 35/4121; *Hansard*, 20 July 1950.

15. Fraenkel and Gerricke to Ellenberger, 21 June 1950, TNA:PRO, DO 119/1295.

16. Meeting at Mahalapye between Fraenkel and Elders, 3 June 1950, ibid.

17. Meeting at Shoshong between Fraenkel and Elders, 3 June 1950, ibid.

18. Diary entry for 2 April 1950, *Patrick Gordon Walker. Political Diaries 1932–1971*, pp. 188–9.

19. Baring to Gordon Walker, 22 June 1950, TNA:PRO, DO 119/1295.

20. Gordon Walker to Baring, 19 May 1950, TNA:PRO, DO 35/4121.

21. Note of meeting, 19 June 1950, TNA:PRO, DO 121/57.

22. Resident Commissioner to Clark, 21 June 1950, TNA:PRO, DO 119/1295.

23. 'Results of leaving Seretse in the Protectorate but outside the Reserve', n.d. [1950], TNA:PRO, DO 119/1294.

24. 'Memorandum by Sir Evelyn Baring (June 1950). IV – Mrs Khama', TNA:PRO, DO 121/59.

25. Attlee, *As It Happened*, p. 178.

26. Brook to Prime Minister, 28 June 1950, TNA:PRO, PREM 8/1308, Part 1.

27. Hartley Shawcross to Kenneth Roberts-Wray, 23 June 1950, TNA:PRO, DO 119/1296.

28. Minutes by Baxter, Liesching and Gordon Walker, 29 June 1950, TNA:PRO, DO 35/4121.

15 INTO EXILE

1. Copy of Savingram telephoned at 9.50 a.m. on 29 July 1950, TNA:PRO, DO 119/1296.

2. Births and Deaths Registration Proclamation for Jacqueline Khama, 15 July 1950, ibid.

3. Ellenberger to Dashwood, 24 July 1950, ibid.

4. Chief Secretary, Pretoria, to Government Secretary, Mafikeng, 27 July 1950, ibid.

5. Forwarded from Baring to Gordon Walker, 29 July 1950, ibid.

6. Sillery, 'Working Backwards', n.d., BLCAS, Mss Afr r 207.

7. Clark to Liesching, 3 August 1950, TNA:PRO, PREM 8/1308 Part 1.

8. Report by Clark to CRO, 3 August 1950, TNA:PRO, CO 537/5926.

9. Clark to Liesching, 3 August 1950, TNA:PRO, PREM 8/1308 Part 1.

10. Monks, *Eyewitness*, p. 284.

11. MacKenzie to Ellenberger, 3 August 1950, TNA:PRO, DO 119/1297.

12. Baring to Huggins, 21 July 1950, TNA:PRO, DO 119/1296.

13. Baring to Lady Baring, 20 August 1950, quoted in Douglas-Home, *Evelyn Baring*, p. 193; HCO to CRO, 24 August 1950, TNA:PRO, DO 35/4122.

14. Seretse Khama and Tshekedi Khama, 'Aide-Memoire', Lobatse, 16 August 1950, KIII, TKP 52.

15. *Ebony*, June 1951.

16. Seretse and Tshekedi to Baring, 16 August 1950, TNA:PRO, DO 119/1297.

17. Fairlie to Nettelton, 14 July 1950, TNA:PRO, DO 119/1296.

18. Seretse and Tshekedi to Baring, 16 August 1950, TNA:PRO, DO 119/1297.

19. Report by Clark to CRO, 19 August 1950, TNA:PRO, DO 35/4132.

20. Johannesburg, *Star*, 18 August 1950.

21. *Rand Daily Mail*, 16 August 1950.

22. Report by Clark to CRO, 19 August 1950, TNA:PRO, DO 35/4132.

23. ibid.

24. Tshekedi Khama and Seretse Khama to Sir Evelyn Baring, 16 August 1950, KIII, TKP 52.

25. Press cutting, 17 August 1950 (title of source excised), Sweeney Papers, Truman Library.

26. *Rand Daily Mail*, 18 August 1950.

27. ibid.

28. Report by Clark to CRO, 19 August 1950, TNA:PRO, DO 35/4132.

29. ibid.

30. Baring to Gordon Walker, 24 August 1950, TNA:PRO, DO 119/1297.

31. Seretse Khama, Farewell speech, 17 August 1950, KIII, TKP 52.

32. *Rhodesia Herald*, 17 August 1950.

33. Report by Clark to CRO, 19 August 1950, TNA:PRO, DO 35/4132.

34. *Rand Daily Mail*, 18 August 1950.

35. Report by Clark to CRO, 19 August 1950, TNA:PRO, DO 35/4132.

36. HCO to CRO, 9 August 1950, TNA:PRO, CO 537/5926.

37. Report by Clark to CRO, 19 August 1950, TNA:PRO, DO 35/4132.

38. Photograph and report, *Rand Daily Mail*, 18 August 1950.

39. Monks, *Eyewitness*, p. 284.

40. ibid., p. 283.

41. Photograph in *Rand Daily Mail*, 18 August 1950.

42. Press cutting, 17 August 1950 (title of source excised), Truman Library, Sweeney Papers, Box 5.

43. Johannesburg *Star*, 18 August 1950.

44. Press cutting, 17 August 1950 (title of source excised), Truman Library, Sweeney Papers, Box 5.

45. *Rand Daily Mail*, 18 August 1950.

46. Monsarrat, *Life is a Four-Letter Word*, vol. II, *Breaking Out*, pp. 276–7.

47. ibid., pp. 277–8.

48. Baring to Lady Baring, 20 August 1950, quoted in Douglas-Home, *Evelyn Baring*, p. 193.

49. MacKenzie to Ellenberger, 21 August 1950, TNA:PRO, DO 119/1298.

50. Message from meeting of headmen conveyed by Mr Fraenkel, n.d. [August 1950], ibid.

16 LIVING IN LONDON

1. Pathe newsreel, 'People in the News', 24 August 1950.

2. Movietone newsreel, 'Seretse Here', 24 August 1950.

3. Robins, *White Queen in Africa*, p. 54.

4. Naledi Khama to author, 13 November 2004.

5. Baxter to Gwatkin, 4 September 1950, TNA:PRO, DO 119/1298.

6. C. D. Heriot, Report on The Baker's Daughter, 17 August 1950, TNA: PRO, DO 119/1298.

7. Muriel Sanderson to author, 17 November 2004.

8. Tibbetts to State Department, Washington, 2 October 1950, NARA, RG 59, Decimal Files [1950–54], Box 3571.

9. *Today*, 12 March 1960.

10. Naledi Khama to author, 13 November 2004.

11. Commentary in Phillips and Phillips, *Windrush*, pp. 100–103.

12. Pathe newsreel, 'Farewell dance for West Indies XI', 28 September 1950.

13. 'Note of a visit to Mr and Mrs Khama on 14th November 1950', TNA:PRO, DO 35/4131.

14. Norton to Scott, 27 November 1950, BLCAS, Anti-Slavery Society Papers, File 12.

15. Baxter to Syers, Liesching, Ogmore, 8 February 1951, TNA:PRO, DO 35/4131.

16. 'Note of a visit to Mr and Mrs Khama on 14th November 1950', ibid.

17. Muriel Sanderson to author, 17 November 2004.

18. 'Note of a visit to Mr and Mrs Khama on 14th November 1950', TNA:PRO, DO 35/4131.

19. Muriel Sanderson to author, 10 November 2004.

20. 'Note of a visit to Mr and Mrs Khama on 14th November 1950', TNA:PRO, DO 35/4131.

21. Note by Gordon Walker, 16 November 1950, ibid.

22. Stonehouse, *Prohibited Immigrant*, pp. 25–6.

23. Freud, *Freud Ego*, pp. 95–6.

24. Clement Freud to author, 30 June 2005 and 4 July 2005.

25. Lee, *My Life with Nye*, p. 167.

26. Foot, *Aneurin Bevan*, p. 414.

27. Movietone newsreel, 'Seretse Khama's Xmas Party', December 1951.

28. John and Esme Goode to author, 29 March 2004.

29. Brockway, *Towards Tomorrow*, p. 162.

30. Clark to Baxter, 9 February 1951, TNA:PRO, DO 35/4131.

31. Lewis, 'Note of a meeting with Seretse and Ruth Khama on 31st January 1951', 2 February 1951, TNA:PRO, DO 35/4131.

32. Clark to Baxter, 9 February 1951, ibid.

33. Freud, *Freud Ego*, p. 101.

34. Fawcus and Tilbury, *Botswana*, p. 56.

35. Bankole, *Kwame Nkrumah from Cradle to Grave*, p. 104.

36. Naledi Khama to author, 18 June 2003.

37. *Daily Mail*, 3 October 1956.

38. Stonehouse, *Prohibited Immigrant*, p. 26.

39. *Ebony*, June 1951.

17 SIX THOUSAND MILES AWAY FROM HOME

1. Baring to Syers, 27 September 1950, TNA:PRO, DO 35/4131.
2. Seretse to Tshekedi, 17 October 1950, TNA:PRO, DO 119/1308.
3. Morton and Ramsay, *The Birth of Botswana*, p. 128.
4. Gasebalwe Seretse, *Tshekedi Khama*, pp. 125–6.
5. *Rand Daily Mail*, 13 November 1950.
6. Liesching to Baring, 27 October 1950, TNA:PRO, DO 35/4131.
7. *Rand Daily Mail*, 13 November 1950.
8. Fletcher to Scott, 15 November 1950, BLCAS, Mss Afr s 1681, Box 226, File 7.
9. Fletcher to Scott, 19 November 1950, ibid.
10. Secretary of State's discussions, 13 December 1950, TNA:PRO, DO 35/4131.
11. Gordon Walker to Liesching, 16 December 1950, ibid.
12. Hatch, *New from Africa*, p. 77.
13. Fairlie, *No Time Like the Past*, p. 150.
14. Germond to Col. Beetham, 27 December 1950, BNARS, S535/12/1.
15. *Daily Express*, 31 January 1951.
16. Redfern, *Ruth and Seretse*, p. 144.
17. Beetham to Allison, 22 December 1950, BNARS, S535/12/1.
18. Germond to Beetham, 29 December 1950, ibid.
19. Seager, *The Shadow of a Great Rock*, p. 63.
20. Redfern, *Ruth and Seretse*, p. 144.
21. Seager, *The Shadow of a Great Rock*, p. 63.
22. Redfern, *Ruth and Seretse*, p. 144.
23. ibid., p. 145.
24. Statement by Bangwato to Gordon Walker, Serowe, 1 February 1951, BNARS, S535/12/3.
25. *Daily Express*, February 1951.
26. Notes for Secretary of State's Speech at Serowe, 1 February 1951, TNA:PRO, DO 35/4131.
27. Cabinet Report, CP (51) 109, 16 April 1951.
28. Gordon Walker to Liesching, 3 February 1951, TNA:PRO, CO 537/7222.
29. Comment by Mary Benson, in response to review by Paul Landau of Dutfield, *A Marriage of Inconvenience*, in *Southern African Review of Books*, No. 17, January/February 1991.
30. Tshekedi Khama to *The Times*, 8 June 1951.

31. Tibbetts to State Department, Washington [June 1951], NARA, RG 59, Dept of State, Decimal Files [1950–54], 845E. 411/6–1251.

32. *Picture Post*, 7 July 1951.

33. His initial suggestion was to send three MPs, but the Conservative and Liberal Parties refused to send any of their members. Labour, with a majority of only five, could not afford to send three MPs. He came up with the alternative of sending three men of public standing.

34. Secretary to Astor, to Benson, 21 March 1951, BLCAS, Rhodes House, Mss Afr s 1681, Box 226, File 6.

35. Seretse to Scott, n.d. [March 1951], ibid.

36. For a full account of this episode, see Michael Crowder, 'Professor Macmillan Goes on Safari: The British Government Observer Team and the Crisis over the Seretse Khama Marriage, 1951', in Macmillan and Marks (eds), *Africa and Empire*, pp. 254–328.

37. Notes from diary of Legum, 7 August 1951, BLCAS, Mss Afr s 1681, Box 226, File 6.

38. Bullock to Gordon Walker, 15 August 1951, TNA:PRO, DO 35/4135.

39. *Rand Daily Mail*, 17 August 1951.

40. Memorandum by Bangwato women to UK visitors, Serowe, 16 August 1951, BNARS, S 529/4.

41. Report by Bullock and Macmillan, published in White Paper, Cmd 8423: 'Bechaunaland Protectorate: Report of Observers', 6 December 1951.

42. Bamangwato Women's Association (signed by the Secretary, Lets M. Matseka, the Chairlady, K. Gochani, and Committee Member Ottotten Leakwe) to the Native Authority, Serowe, 19 October 1951, TNA:PRO, DO 119/1304.

43. G. M. Kgosi to Churchill, 23 July 1951, ibid.

18 BANISHED FOREVER

1. Liesching, aide-memoire on Bamangwato affairs, 24 November 1951, TNA:PRO, DO 119/1320.

2. Le Rougetel to Liesching, 22 October 1951, TNA:PRO, DO 119/1317.

3. Constantine, *Colour Bar*, p. 186.

4. HCO to CRO, 22 June 1951, TNA:PRO, DO 119/1311.

5. High Commissioner to CRO, 23 June 1951, TNA:PRO, PREM 8/1308 Part 2.

6. David Anderson, *Histories of the Hanged*, p. 3.

7. Benson, *Tshekedi Khama*, p. 252.

8. Minute by Lambert, 13 November 1951, TNA:PRO, CO 1015/358.

9. Cabinet meeting 22 November 1951, TNA:PRO, PREM 11/1182, 120180.

10. *Hansard*, 6 December 1951.

11. Quoted in Michael Crowder, 'Professor Macmillan Goes on Safari: The British Government Observer Team and the Crisis over the Seretse Khama Marriage, 1951', in Macmillan and Marks (eds), *Africa and Empire*, p. 276.

12. *Hansard*, 6 December 1951.

13. Statement by Chief Seretse Khama, 6 December 1951, TNA:PRO, DO 119/1320.

14. Cabinet meeting, 19 December 1951, TNA:PRO, PREM 11/1182, 120180.

15. Clark to Baxter, 13 February 1953, TNA:PRO, DO 35/4279.

16. Lloyd to Foot, 18 January 1952, TNA:PRO, CO 537/7776.

17. Foot to Lloyd, 28 January 1952, ibid.

18. Memorandum by Commonwealth Secretary, 13 March 1952, TNA:PRO, PREM 11/1182.

19. Salisbury to Prime Minister, 18 March 1952, ibid.

20. Record of conversation, 24 March 1952, TNA:PRO, DO 121/151.

21. Ismay, *Memoirs*, p. 462.

22. Record of interview with Mr and Mrs Khama, 26 March 1952, TNA:PRO, DO 119/1327.

23. *Rand Daily Mail*, 2 October 1956.

24. *Rand Daily Mail*, 28 March 1952.

25. *Daily Mail*, 2 October 1956.

26. *Cape Times*, 28 March 1952.

27. O. K. Maokisa, 'The British Govt Decision Grieves the Bamangwato', translation of article in *Naledi ya Batswana*, 19 April 1952, TNA:PRO, DO 119/1328.

28. HCO to CRO, 29 March 1952, TNA:PRO, CO 1015/359.

29. Goareng Mosinyi to author, 12 November 2004.

30. HCO to CRO, 31 March 1952, TNA:PRO, DO 35/4143.

31. Consolidated Security Report for the Week Ending 26 March 1952, by B. R. Sands, Intelligence Officer, TNA:PRO, DO 119/1327.

32. *Time*, 7 April 1952.

33. *Hansard*, 27 March 1952, also for subsequent references to the debate.

34. Tony Benn to author, 2 February 2005.

35. *Hansard*, 27 March 1952.

36. Salisbury to Welensky, 21 February 1965, BLCAS, Welensky Papers, 770/4.

37. *Hansard*, 27 March 1952.

38. ibid.

39. *Hansard*, 31 March 1952.

40. Miss X to Sir, Commonwealth Relations Office, n.d. [1952], TNA:PRO, DO 35/4145.

41. Messel to Eden, [2 April 1952], TNA:PRO, FO 371/96649.

42. Statement by CRO, 'Seretse Khama', 9 May 1952, attached to Robinson to Ottawa, 16 May 1952, NAC, 10283-B-40/99/99.

43. The letter was signed by Dr J. S. Moroka, president-general, Walter Sisulu, secretary-general, and Dr S. M. Molema, treasurer. Telegram Mafikeng to CRO, 1 April 1952, TNA:PRO, CO 1015/359.

44. J. H. Le Rougetel to Lord Salisbury, 23 April 1952, TNA:PRO, DO 119/1328.

45. Naledi Khama to author, 13 November 2004.

46. Redfern, *Ruth and Seretse*, p. 216.

47. Appiah, *Joe Appiah*, p. 185. Appiah is drawing on Ruth 1:16: 'Where you go I will go, and where you stay I will stay. Your people will be my people and your God my God.'

19 ENVOYS FOR JUSTICE

1. Head, *Serowe*, p. 77; Seager, *The Shadow of a Great Rock*, p. 72.

2. Hatch, *New from Africa*, p. 68.

3. Beetham to Bent, 13 December 1951, TNA:PRO, DO 119/1320.

4. Intelligence Report for the period ending 10 March 1952, DO 119/1326.

5. Intelligence Report for week ending 19 February 1952, DO 119/1324.

6. Text of address by Resident Commissioner, Serowe, in High Commissioner, Cape Town, to CRO, 9 March 1952, TNA:PRO, CO 1015/359.

7. Intelligence Report for the period including 28 March, DO 119/1326.

8. Seager, *The Shadow of a Great Rock*, p. 67.

9. ibid., p. 69.

10. South African Press Association–Reuters, 10 April 1952, TNA:PRO, DO 119/1307.

11. Movietone newsreel, 'Bamangwato Chiefs Arrive in London', 14 April 1952.

12. Pathe News, 'In support of Seretse', 14 April 1952.

13. Redfern, *Ruth and Seretse*, p. 195.

14. ibid.

15. *The Times*, 12 April 1952.

16. *Hansard*, 27 March 1952.

17. *The Times*, 31 March 1952.

18. Redfern, *Ruth and Seretse*, p. 196.

19. *East Africa and Rhodesia*, 24 April 1952; *Daily Mail*, 16 April 1952.

20. Colin Turnbull to Greenidge, 18 April 1952, BLCAS, Mss Br Emp s.22.

21. *East Africa and Rhodesia*, 24 April 1952; *Daily Mail*, 16 April 1952.

22. Report on Seretse Khama Meeting, 15 April 1952, TNA:PRO, DO 35/4139.

23. Clark to Baxter, 6 April 1952, ibid.

24. Report on Seretse Khama Meeting, 15 April 1952, ibid.

25. Clark to Baxter, 8 April 1952, TNA:PRO, DO 35/4143.

26. Bickford to Baxter, 18 April 1952, ibid.

27. Baxter to Bickford, 19 April 1952, ibid.

28. Notes for the Secretary of State's meeting with the Bamangwato Delegation on Monday 21 April, ibid.

29. Clark to Baxter, 18 April 1952, ibid.

30. Baxter to Clark, 19 April 1952, ibid.

31. Record of meeting between the Commonwealth Secretary and the Bamangwato Delegation, 21 April 1952, ibid.

32. Redfern, *Ruth and Seretse*, p. 199.

33. Memorandum presented by the Bamangwato Tribal Delegation to the Secretary of State, 21 April 1952, TNA:PRO, DO 35/4143; Clark to HCO, 22 April 1952, ibid.

34. *The Times*, 24 April 1952.

35. *Hansard*, 24 April 1952.

36. *The Times*, 30 April 1952.

37. ibid.

38. ibid.

39. K. Kgamane, P. Sekgoma, K. Baitswe, M. M. Mathangwane, Gaothobogwe Leposo, M. Mpotokwane to Salisbury, 5 May 1952, TNA:PRO, DO 35/4143.

40. *Manchester Guardian*, 12 May 1952.

41. Collins, *Partners in Protest*, p. 186.

42. *Birmingham Post*, 12 May 1952.

43. ibid.

44. Note by Joyce, 23 May 1952, TNA:PRO, DO 35/4469.

45. *Ebony*, June 1951.

46. 'Telephone message from Mafeking. Intelligence. Bamangwato Reserve' from High Commissioner, Cape Town, to Secretary of State, 2 May 1952, TNA:PRO, DO 119/1328.

47. Goareng Mosinyi to author, 12 November 2004.

20 SORROW IN SEROWE

1. 'Received by Telephone – 11 a.m., 21 May 1952', Resident Commissioner, Mafikeng, to Chief Secretary, Cape Town, TNA:PRO, DO 119/1329.

2. 'Telephone message from Mafeking received 12.10 p.m., 23 May 1952', report sent in telegram from High Commissioner, Cape Town, to Secretary of State, London, ibid.

3. HCO to CRO, 12 June 1952, TNA:PRO, CO 1015/359.

4. Neil Parsons to author, November 2004; Goareng Mosinyi to author, November 2004.

5. Peter Sebina, 'From My Note Book', 6 June 1952, KIII, TKP 58.

6. HCO to CRO, 9 June 1952, TNA:PRO, CO 1015/359.

7. *Rand Daily Mail*, 27 May 1952; *Time*, 16 June 1952.

8. Report by Fraenkel, 12 June 1952, SUL (UK), Benn Levy Papers, 6/9.

9. High Commissioner to CRO, 30 May 1952, TNA:PRO, PREM 11/1182.

10. Seager, *The Shadow of a Great Rock*, p. 75.

11. HCO to CRO, 7 June 1952, TNA:PRO, CO 1015/359.

12. Parsons, 'The Serowe Kgotla riot of 1952'; Fraenkel to Brockway, 2 June 1952, repeated in CRO to HCO, 16 June 1952, TNA:PRO, CO 1015/359; HCO to CRO, 8 June 1952, ibid.

13. Parsons, 'The Serowe Kgotla riot of 1952'.

14. Peter Sebina, 'From My Note Book', 6 June 1952, KIII, TKP 58.

15. 'Telephone messages, report sent in telegram from High Commissioner, Cape Town, to Secretary of State, London, TNA:PRO, DO 119/1329.

16. HCO to CRO, 2 June 1952, TNA:PRO, PREM 11/1182.

17. Seager, *The Shadow of a Great Rock*, pp. 76–7.

18. HCO to CRO, 3 June 1952, TNA:PRO, CO 1015/359; *The Times*, 5 June 1952.

19. *The Times*, 3 June 1952; HCO to CRO, 8 June 1952, TNA:PRO, CO 1015/359.

20. *The Times*, 5 June 1952.

21. HCO to CRO, 9 June 1952, TNA:PRO, CO 1015/359.

22. Clark to National Council for Civil Liberties, 2 September 1952, TNA: PRO, DO 35/4310.

23. Report by Fraenkel, 12 June 1952, SUL (UK), Benn Levy Papers, 6/9; Fraenkel to Brockway, 10 June 1952, repeated in CRO to HCO, 16 June 1952, TNA:PRO, CO 1015/359; Intelligence Report for June 1952, TNA: PRO, DO 119/1324.

24. HCO to CRO, 9 June 1952, TNA:PRO, CO 1015/359.

25. HCO to CRO, 6 June 1952, ibid.

26. *Hansard*, 10 June 1952.

27. Quoted in Macmillan, *Tides of Fortune*, p. 391.

28. *Hansard*, 10 June 1952.

29. HCO to CRO, 12 June 1952, TNA:PRO, CO 1015/359.

30. *Daily Worker*, 19 August 1952.

31. Clark to National Council for Civil Liberties, 2 September 1952, TNA: PRO, DO 35/4310.

32. *Manchester Guardian*, 20 August 1952.

33. *Daily Worker*, 19 August 1952.

34. Statement by Vieyra, repeated in Keaboka and others v. the Queen, 18 December 1952, TNA:PRO, DO 35/4501.

35. Goareng Mosinyi to author, 12 November 2004.

36. Judgement by Harold Willan, Lobatse, 9 September 1952, TNA:PRO, DO 35/4501.

37. Report on Kgotla held at Mahalapye on 11 July 1952 by Assistant District Officer, TNA:PRO, DO 119/1311.

38. Head, *Serowe: Village of the Rainwind*, p. xxii.

39. High Commissioner to Secretary of State, 20 April 1953, TNA:PRO, DO 119/1337.

40. Raditladi to *Naledi ya Batswana*, 2 August 1952.

41. *Cape Times*, 5 April 1952.

42. Beetham to Chief Secretary, 6 August 1952, TNA:PRO, DO 119/1311.

43. High Commissioner to Secretary of State, 7 August 1952, ibid.

44. Secretary of State to High Commissioner, Pretoria, 13 August 1952, TNA:PRO, DO 119/1332.

45. Daymond et al. (eds), *Women Writing Africa*, p. 180.

46. Morton and Ramsay, *The Birth of Botswana*, pp. 117–18.

47. Secretary of State to High Commissioner, Pretoria, 13 August 1952, TNA:PRO, DO 119/1332.

48. ibid.

49. Bent, *Ten Thousand Men of Africa*, p. 91.

50. Thomas Tlou and Alec Campbell, *History of Botswana*, p. 308.

51. Winstanley, *Under Two Flags in Africa*, p. 57.

52. Benson, *A Far Cry*, p. 101.

53. Winstanley, *Under Two Flags in Africa*, p. 57.

54. Printed letter by E. B. Beetham, circulated to Bangwato, 11 September 1952, TNA:PRO, DO 119/1332.

55. Seager, *The Shadow of a Great Rock*, p. 82.

56. Report of meeting at Sefhare Kgotla, 29 September 1952, TNA:PRO, DO 119/1333.

57. Johannesburg *Star*, 10 November 1952.

58. Reports from Serowe, 10 and 11 November 1952, TNA:PRO, DO 119/1334.

59. ibid.

60. Johannesburg *Star*, 12 November 1952.

61. Reports from Serowe, 10 and 11 November 1952, TNA:PRO, DO 119/1334.

62. Seager, *The Shadow of a Great Rock*, p. 84.

63. *The Times*, 9 March 1953.

21 A WATERSHED IN OPINION

1. Huddleston, 'The Birth of a Struggle', in Henderson, *Man of Christian Action*, pp. 47–8.

2. W. H. Ingrams, 'Memorandum. Europeans and Race Relations', 27 April 1951, TNA:PRO, CO 537/7787.

3. Exchange of minutes between 13 June 1951 and 6 May 1953, ibid.; Jeffries to Archbishop of Canterbury, 9 February 1953, ibid.

4. Mungai Lenneiye to author, 19 September 2005.

5. See David Anderson, *Histories of the Hanged*; also Douglas-Home, *Evelyn Baring*.

6. *Guardian*, 20 May 1952.

7. He was being watched by MI5: see TNA:PRO, KV2/1921 for MI5 file.

8. Brockway and Grimond to Maude, 25 August 1952, SUL (UK), Benn Levy Papers, 6/8.

9. Fenner Brockway, article in FACT (Liberal Party publication), January 1953.

10. Bickford to Baxter, 22 September 1952, TNA:PRO, DO 35/4469.

11. Telegram from Secretary of State, London, to High Commissioner, Cape Town, 24 March 1954, TNA:PRO, DO 119/1340.

12. Note by Joyce, 23 May 1952, TNA:PRO, DO 35/4469.

13. Carr to Seretse, 2 October 1952, SUL (UK), Benn Levy Papers, 6/8.

14. Open letter, Council for the Defence of Seretse Khama to Friends in the Bechuanaland Protectorate, 14 May 1953, SUL (UK), Benn Levy Papers, 6/9.

15. *The World*, 18 February 1956.

16. *Yorkshire Post*, n.d., cutting in TNA:PRO, DO 119/1333.

17. Naledi Khama to author, 13 November 2004.

18. See Cockett, *David Astor and the Observer*, chapter 6, 'Africa'.
19. Quoted in Memorandum of the Council for the Defence of Seretse Khama, September 1953, SUL (UK), Benn Levy Papers, 6/9.
20. Quoted in ibid.
21. Quoted in ibid.
22. *Daily Herald*, 11 March 1953.
23. Quoted in Booker to Clark, 10 March 1953, TNA:PRO, DO 35/4279.
24. *Daily Mail*, 2 October 1956.
25. *Today*, 12 March 1960.
26. Brockway, *Outside the Right*, p. 76.
27. *ibid.*, p. 148.
28. Charles Njonjo to author, 12 March 2004.
29. *Daily Mail*, 10 October 1956.
30. *Evening Standard*, 31 October 1955.
31. *Today*, 12 March 1960.
32. Sisulu, *Water and Albertina Sisulu*, p. 134.
33. Appiah, *Joe Appiah*, p. 213.
34. ibid., pp. 219–20.
35. ibid., p. 224.
36. ibid., p. 225.
37. *Oxford Dictionary of National Biography*: Edward Mutesa II.
38. Constantine, *Colour Bar*, p. 188.
39. Stonehouse, *Prohibited Immigrant*, p. 103.
40. Mutibwa, *Uganda since Independence*, p. 15.
41. Liesching to Le Rougetel, 13 March 1953, TNA:PRO, DO 119/1336.
42. MacKenzie to Turnbull, 17 April 1953, TNA:PRO, DO 119/1337.
43. Batho to Bamangwato, 2 April 1953, KIII, TKP 58.
44. Signatories c/o K. M. Ketshabile to Seretse Khama Campaign Committee, 13 April 1953, TNA:PRO, DO 119/1338.
45. Report of the Council for the Defence of Seretse Khama, n.d., SUL (UK), Benn Levy Papers 6/9.
46. *The Times*, 7 May 1953.
47. Fraenkel to Rathcreedan, 24 June 1953, SUL (UK), Benn Levy Papers, 6/9.
48. Seager, *The Shadow of a Great Rock*, p. 87.
49. Notes for Secretary by Clark, 28 April 1953, TNA:PRO, DO 35/4278.
50. *Hansard*, 13 May 1953.
51. *The Times*, 14 May 1953.

22 THE CAMPAIGN INTENSIFIES

1. Quoted in Sampson, *Mandela*, p. 99.

2. See Anderson, *Histories of the Hanged*.

3. Elkins, *Britain's Gulag*, p. 209.

4. Kimathi to Dr Mabuyo Mugwanji, 23 May 1954, in Maina Wa Kinyatti (ed.), *Kenya's Freedom Struggle. The Dedan Kimathi Papers*, p. 20.

5. Wedgwood Benn to Benn Levy, n.d. [1954], SUL (UK), Benn Levy Papers, 6/9.

6. Open letter from Brockway, 17 December 1954, SOAS, MCF, Box 11.

7. Owen, 'Critics of Empire in Britain', pp. 204–5; see also Howe, *Anti-Colonialism in British Politics*.

8. Wedgwood Benn to Benn Levy, n.d. [1954], SUL (UK), Benn Levy Papers, 6/9.

9. Handlist, by Andrew B. Strachan, SOAS, Archives of Movement for Colonial Freedom, October 1984, p. 1.

10. See SOAS, MCF Box 84 for further details on the structure and activities of the MCF.

11. District Secretary, National Union of General and Municipal Workers, to Hatch, 5 February 1955, LHASC, Hatch Papers.

12. Meeting between Parliamentary Under-Secretary and Seretse Khama, 17 May 1954, TNA:PRO, DO 119/1341.

13. Redfern, *Ruth and Seretse*, p. 217.

14. K. M. Ketshabile to Monica Whately, n.d. [June 1953], TNA:PRO, DO 35/4278.

15. Telephone message from MacKenzie at 10.30 a.m., 4 June 1953, TNA:PRO, DO 119/1338.

16. Fraenkel to Rathcreedan, 24 June 1953, SUL (UK), Benn Levy Papers, 6/9.

17. Telephone message from MacKenzie at 10.30 a.m., 4 June 1953, TNA:PRO, DO 119/1338.

18. Ketshabile to Whately, n.d. [June 1953], TNA:PRO, DO 35/4278.

19. Bechuanaland Protectorate Police, Serowe, Consolidated Intelligence Report for Week ending 21.6.54, TNA:PRO, DO 119/1341.

20. Winstanley, *Under Two Flags in Africa*, p. 52.

21. Grievances of the members of the Bamangwato Tribe, n.d. [1954], TNA:PRO, DO 119/1342.

22. Thomas V. Scrivenor to High Commissioner, 31 October 1955, TNA:PRO, DO 119/1344.

23. Peto Sekgoma to Officer Commanding BP Police, 28 November 1955, ibid.

24. Brockway to Dodds-Parker, 14 December 1955, ibid.

25. Robinson to DC, Serowe, 3 January 1956, ibid.

26. Notes by Scrivenor, 5 January 1956 and [illegible], 7 August 1956, ibid.

27. Sekoko and Sebina to Hatch, n.d., LHASC, Hatch Papers.

28. Hatch, *New from Africa*, p. 67.

29. *Daily Mail*, 27 September 1956.

30. Hatch, *New from Africa*, p. 86.

31. ibid., pp. 78–9.

32. *Manchester Guardian*, 11 July 1955.

33. *Die Transvaler*, 21 July 1955 (translation).

34. Kavuma, *Crisis in Buganda 1953–55*, p. 102.

35. Swinton to Lennox-Boyd, 17 September 1954, TNA:PRO, DO 35/4368.

36. Quoted in Thorpe, *Alec Douglas-Home*, p. 301.

37. Dickie, *The Uncommon Commoner*, p. 112.

38. Discussion between Secretary of State and the Labour Party Delegation, 9 August 1955, TNA:PRO, CAB 21/3167.

39. Redfern, *Ruth and Seretse*, pp. 214–15.

40. *Manchester Guardian*, 14 October 1955.

41. *Star*, 13 October 1955.

42. Home to Eden, 29 November 1955, TNA:PRO, PREM 11/1182.

43. ibid.

44. Eden to Home, 29 November 1955, ibid.

45. Walker, *Women and Resistance in South Africa*, p. 168.

46. Stewart, *Lilian Ngoyi*, pp. 21–2.

47. Helen Joseph to Ruth Khama, 29 October 1956, WCLUW, FSAW.

48. *The World*, 18 February 1956.

23 THE ENDING OF EXILE

1. Tshekedi to Creech Jones, 22 November 1955, KIII, TKP 58.

2. *Hansard*, 14 June 1956.

3. John Hatch, 'Minerals, Economic Development and the High Commission Territories', June 1956, BLCAS, Mss Brit Emp s 332, Box 19.

4. Instructions to Counsel, S. J. Markowitz, by Kgosi Mokgosi, 22 September 1953, KIII, TKP 58.

5. Annual Report: Ngwato District 1954, TNA:PRO, DO 119/1342.

6. *Hansard*, 14 June 1956.

7. Tshekedi to Astor, 29 March 1956, KIII, TKP 58.

8. Page to Noble, 5 June 1956, TNA:PRO, DO 35/4297.

9. Sharp, *Bechuanaland*.

10. *Hansard*, 1 August 1956.

11. ibid.

12. Fowler to Laithwaite, 14 August 1956, TNA:PRO, DO 35/4300.

13. Muriel Sanderson to author, 17 November 2004.

14. Seretse and Tshekedi to Home, 15 August 1956, TNA:PRO, DO35/4300.

15. Home to Liesching, 15 August 1956, ibid.

16. Mandela, *Long Walk to Freedom*, pp. 222–3.

17. Huddleston to *Observer*, 13 September 1953.

18. Mandela, *Nelson Mandela Speeches 1990*, p. 71.

19. Quintin Whyte to L. M. Thompson, 3 December 1954, LHASC, Hatch Papers.

20. Lewin to Hatch, 12 November 1954, ibid.

21. *Hansard*, 13 April 1954.

22. Mandela, *Nelson Mandela Speeches 1990*, p. 71.

23. Address by Strijdom, 25 June 1956, TNA:PRO, DO 35/4239.

24. Home to HCO, 26 June 1956, ibid.

25. On 21 August, 28 August, 6 September and 7 September 1956.

26. Liesching to Home, 18 August 1956, TNA:PRO, DO 35/4300.

27. Home to Eden, 7 September 1956, TNA:PRO, PREM 11/1182.

28. Eden to Home, 7 September 1956, ibid.

29. Garner to Laithwaite, 13 September 1956, British Library, OIOC, MSS Eur/F 138/160.

30. Home to Liesching, 14 September 1956, TNA:PRO, DO 35/4300.

31. Liesching to Home, 24 August 1956, ibid.

32. *Today*, 12 March 1960.

33. Press release, 26 September 1956, TNA:PRO, DO 35/4301.

34. *The Times*, 27 September 1956.

35. Thorpe, *Alec Douglas-Home*, p. 19.

36. *Afro-American*, October 1956.

37. *Rand Daily Mail* 27 September 1956.

38. *Daily Telegraph*, 27 September 1956.

39. Telegram from Secretary of State, London, to High Commissioner, Cape Town, 8 March 1954, TNA:PRO, DO 119/1340.

40. Naledi Khama to author, 13 November 2004.

41. *Daily Mail*, 10 October 1956.

42. ibid.

43. Pathe Gazette, 'People in the News – Seretse Khama Returns to His Country', n.d. [October 1956].

44. Liesching to Home, 10 September 1956, TNA:PRO, DO 35/4300.

45. Wedgwood Benn to *Observer*, 7 October 1956.

46. Winstanley, *Under Two Flags in Africa*, p. 74.

47. Announcement by Resident Commissioner, 26 September 1956, NAC, 10283-B-40.

48. CRO to HCO, 18 September 1956, TNA:PRO, DO 35/4301.

49. *Manchester Guardian*, 27 September 1956.

50. *Rand Daily Mail* 27 September 1956.

51. *Die Transvaler*, 27 September 1956.

52. Under-Secretary for External Affairs to Secretary for External Affairs, 9 December 1955, CAN:CER, vol. 22–737, DEA/12354–40.

53. *Rhodesia Herald*, 28 September 1956.

54. Wray to CRO, 13 October 1956, TNA:PRO, DO 35/4304.

55. *Rand Daily Mail*, 27 September 1956.

24 'BEFORE THEIR EYES IT RAINED'

1. *Life*, 19 November 1956.

2. *Today*, 12 March 1960.

3. See picture in *Life*, 19 November 1956.

4. *Daily Mail*, 3 October 1956.

5. *Life*, 19 November 1956; *Rand Daily Mail*, 11 October 1956.

6. *The Times*, 11 October 1956; Wray to CRO, 13 October 1956, TNA:PRO, DO 35/4304.

7. *Bulawayo Chronicle*, 11 October 1956.

8. *Rand Daily Mail*, 11 October 1956; Wray to CRO, 11 October 1956, TNA:PRO, DO 35/4304.

9. Wray to CRO, 13 October 1956, ibid.

10. *Star*, 15 October 1956.

11. *Sunday Times*, [Sunday, 14] October 1956.

12. Wray to CRO, 12 October 1956, TNA:PRO, DO 35/4304.

13. Winstanley, *Under Two Flags in Africa*, p. 75.

14. *Bulawayo Chronicle*, 12 October 1956.

15. Wray to CRO, 13 October 1956, TNA:PRO, DO 35/4304.

16. *Life*, vol. 41, 19 November 1956.

17. *Ebony*, May, 1966.

18. HCO to CRO, 18 October 1956, TNA:PRO, DO 35/4304.

19. Allison to Fawcus, 19 October 1956, ibid.

20. HCO to CRO, 18 October 1956, ibid.

21. *Scotsman*, 19 October 1956.

22. Allison to Fawcus, 19 October 1956, TNA:PRO, DO 35/4304.

23. HCO to CRO, 18 October 1956, ibid.

24. Johannesburg *Star*, 18 October 1956.

25. HCO to CRO, 18 October 1956, TNA:PRO, DO 35/4304; Johannesburg *Star*, 18 October 1956.

26. Allison to Fawcus, 19 October 1956, TNA:PRO, DO 35/4304.

27. Reuters, 19 October 1956, ibid.

28. Allison to Fawcus, 19 October 1956, ibid.

29. Reuters, 19 October 1956, ibid.

30. Allison to Fawcus, 19 October 1956, ibid.

31. HCO to CRO, 18 October 1956, ibid.

32. Allison to Fawcus, 19 October 1956, ibid.

33. Seretse to Hatch, 8 February 1957, LHASC, Hatch Papers.

34. Johannesburg *Star*, 5 November 1956.

35. Wray to CRO, 1 November 1956, TNA:PRO, DO 35/4304.

36. ibid.

37. Winstanley, *Under Two Flags in Africa*, p. 76.

38. Wray to CRO, 1 November 1956, TNA:PRO, DO 35/4304.

39. *Daily Mail*, 3 October 1956.

40. *Daily Mirror*, 10 October 1952.

41. *Daily Mail*, 3 October 1956.

42. Sykes to Redman, 15 October 1956, TNA:PRO, DO 35/4304.

43. Sykes to High Commissioner, 23 October 1956, ibid.

44. Sykes to Emery, 19 October 1956, ibid.

45. Sykes to High Commissioner, 25 October 1956, ibid.

46. Lennox-Boyd to Mrs Khama, 14 October 1956; Lennox-Boyd to Home, 10 October 1956, TNA:PRO, DO 35/4301.

47. Minute by Emery, 9 November 1956, TNA:PRO, DO 35/4303.

48. *Rand Daily Mail*, 1 November 1956; *Rhodesia Herald*, 1 November 1956.

49. *Daily Telegraph*, 2 November 1956.

50. Johannesburg *Star*, 3 November 1956.

51. *Daily Telegraph*, 2 November 1956.

52. Helen Joseph to Ruth Khama, 29 October 1956, WCLUW, FSAW

53. Johannesburg *Star*, 3 November 1956.

54. *Daily Herald*, 2 May 1957.

25 THE WIND OF CHANGE

1. *Star*, 10 July 1957.

2. Winstanley, *Under Two Flags in Africa*, pp. 77–8; Extract, Tergos No. 2, February 1957, TNA:PRO, DO 35/4306.

3. *Daily Mail*, 15 July 1957; *Daily Herald*, 2 May 1957.

4. *Daily Herald*, 2 May 1957.

5. See TNA:PRO, DO/4306, 7175, 7308.

6. Quoted in Robins, *White Queen*, p. 56.

7. ibid.

8. *Daily Mail*, 15 July 1957.

9. Bessie Head to Randolphe Vigne, 10 February 1967, in *A Gesture of Belonging*, p. 49.

10. Pathe Gazette, 'People in the News – Seretse Khama Returns to His Country,' n.d. [October 1956].

11. Hatch to Seretse, 4 March 1957, LHASC, Hatch Papers.

12. This chapter has drawn heavily on Dubbeld, *Seretse Khama*, chapters 5–7, and on Gabatshwane, *Seretse Khama and Botswana*, ch. 2.

13. Benson, *Tshekedi Khama*, pp. 302–5.

14. Dickie, *The Uncommon Commoner*, p. 111.

15. Fawcus and Tilbury, *Botswana*, pp. 55–6.

16. Joint Advisory Council 7th session, April 1958, 87, quoted in J. Ramsay, 'Twentieth-Century Antecedents of Decolonising Nationalism in Botswana', in Edge and Lekorwe, *Botswana*, p. 103.

17. Hatch, *A History of Postwar Africa*, p. 234.

18. *Time*, 30 June 1961.

19. Fawcus and Tilbury, *Botswana*, p. 78.

20. Bechuanaland Government, 'Agreement to suspend application of Race Relations Legislation', press statement, 19 March 1964, LHASC, Bech: Gen Correspondence and Documents 1956–67.

21. American Consulate Mbabane to Secretary of State Washington, 21 November 1964, NARA, RG 59, Central Foreign Policy Files [1964–66], Box 1912, File: Pol. 19 Bech.

22. Fawcus and Tilbury, *Botswana*, pp. 90–91.

23. Seretse Khama to Tony Benn, 8 April 1963; Benn to Seretse, 26 April 1963, LHASC, Bech: Gen Correspondence and Documents 1956–67.

24. Report by Bartlett and Williams to Secretary of State, 21 August 1961, NARA, Rg 59. Records of G. Mennen Williams, Box 22, File: Basutoland Trip, August 1961.

25. Lord Harlech to Gordon Walker, 16 November 1964, TNA:PRO, DO 216/34.

26. Quoted in Hatch, *Africa – the Rebirth of Self-rule*, p. 56.

27. *The Times*, 8 July 1978.

28. See Darwin, *The End of the British Empire*, p. 20.

29. *The Times*, 27 January 1960.

30. Quoted in Fisher, *Harold Macmillan*, p. 236.

31. Horne, *Macmillan 1957–86*, pp. 194–5; Fisher, *Harold Macmillan*, p. 237.

32. Bechuanaland Protectorate, Central Intelligence Committee, 1965, TNA: PRO, CO 1048/461.

33. Read to Mrs Read, 14 November 1965, BLCAS, Mss Afr s 1613.

34. Fawcus and Tilbury, *Botswana*, p. 135.

35. Monson to Osborne, 24 August 1964, TNA:PRO, CO 1048/484.

36. Report from US diplomat to Secretary of State, 5 September 1963, NARA, RG 59, Central Foreign Policy File 1963, Box 3824, File. Pol – Bech.

37. Durban, *Daily News*, 16 January 1965.

38. *The Times*, 30 September 1966.

39. Election message by Seretse Khama, Serowe, January 1965, in Khama, *From the Frontline*, p. 10.

40. Winstanley, *Under Two Flags in Africa*, p. 229.

41. Mitchison, *Return to the Fairy Hill*, pp. 214–15.

42. Gabatshwane, *Seretse Khama and Botswana*, p. 81.

43. Fawcus and Tilbury, *Botswana*, p. 89.

44. American Embassy, Cape Town, to Department of State, Washington, NARA, RG 59, Central Foreign Policy Files, [1964–66], Box 1912, File: Pol 19 Bech.

45. Stephenson to Home, 'Bantustans and their political relationship to the High Commission Territories', 24 September 1963, TNA:PRO, DO 216/18.

46. American Embassy, Cape Town, to Department of State, 23 March 1965, NARA, RG 59, Sub-Numeric Files [1964–66], Box 1911, File: Pol 12 Bech.

47. Benn, *Out of the Wilderness*, p. 452.

48. Winstanley, *Under Two Flags in Africa*, p. 185.

49. US Department of State, Memorandum of Conversation, 3 August 1964, NARA, RG 59, Central Foreign Policy Files [1964–66], Box 1912, File: Political Affairs and Relations Bech.

50. Department of State to American Consul, Mbabane, 5 November 1965, NARA, RG 59, Sub-Numeric Files [1964–66], Box 1911, File: Pol – Bech.

51. Cooke, *One White Man in Black Africa*, p. 240.

52. 'Note for meeting between Dr Seretse Khama and Mr Masire with the Prime Minister', 19 February 1966, TNA:PRO, PREM 13/711.

53. Dubbeld, *Seretse Khama*, p. 45.

54. Appiah, *Joe Appiah*, p. 185.

26 *PULA!* BOTSWANA 1966

1. Muriel Sanderson to author, 17 November 2004.

2. Stonehouse, *Death of an Idealist*, p. 63.

3. Foreign Office to Addis Ababa, 12 August 1966, TNA:PRO, FO 371/188143.

4. Robins, *White Queen in Africa*, p. 180.

5. ibid., pp. 166–7.

6. ibid., pp. 179–83; Alan and Juni Tilbury to author, 24 April 2005.

7. J. S. Gandee, British High Commissioner in Botswana, to Secretary of State for Commonwealth Affairs, 'Botswana: The First Year', 13 November 1967, TNA:PRO, FCO 31/19.

8. *Mafeking Mail*, 7 October 1966.

9. Stonehouse, *Death of an Idealist*, p. 63.

10. Winstanley, *Under Two Flags in Africa*, p. 247.

11. Muriel Sanderson to author, 17 November 2004.

12. Bessie Head, 'Chibuku beer and Independence', *New African*, November 1966.

13. American Consul Mbabane to Department of State Washington, 27 January 1966, NARA, RG 59, Sub-Numeric Files [1964–66], Box 1911, File: Pol 2 Bech.

14. Sir Ketumile Masire to author, 19 November 2004.

15. Dahl, *Botswana's First Independence Decade*, p. 2.

16. *The Times*, 30 September 1966.

17. 'Note for meeting between Dr Seretse Khama and Mr Masire with the Prime Minister', 19 February 1966, TNA:PRO, PREM 13/711.

18. Quoted in Dahl, *Botswana's First Independence Decade*, p. 1.

19. Morton and Ramsay (eds), *The Birth of Botswana*, p. 187.

20. B. O. Wilkin, Medical Officer of Health, 'Malaria in the Bechuanaland Protectorate', 1955–1961, BLCAS, Rhodes House Mss Afr s 1378, Wilkin Box 3/2.

21. Clark to Department of State, 4 June 1963, NARA, RG 59, Sub-Numeric Files, 1963, Box 3824, File: Pol – Bech.

22. American Embassy Pretoria to Secretary of State Washington, 8 July

1964, NARA, RG 59, Sub-Numeric Files [1964–66], Box 1911, File: Pol 15–5 Bech.

23. Interview with Margaret Nasha, August 1983, in Qunta (ed.), *Women in Southern Africa*, pp. 199–200.

24. Anthony Read to Mrs Read, 1 November 1966, BLCAS, Mss Afr s 1613.

25. Anthony Read to Mrs Read, 14 March 1966, ibid.

26. Anthony Read to Mrs Read, 8 April 1966, ibid.

27. The World Bank, *World Development Report 2000/2001. Attacking Poverty*, Oxford, Oxford University Press, 2000.

28. Interview with Margaret Nasha, August 1983, in Qunta, (ed.), *Women in Southern Africa*, pp. 199–200.

29. 'Note for meeting between Dr Seretse Khama and Mr Masire with the Prime Minister', 19 February 1966, TNA:PRO, PREM 13/711.

30. Morton and Ramsay (eds), *The Birth of Botswana*, p. 192.

31. Memorandum from Ulric Haynes of the National Security Council Staff to the President's Special Assistant for National Security Affairs (Bundy), 2 November 1965, CAN:CER, *Foreign Relations 1964–1968*, vol. XXIV, pp. 692–3.

32. Speech by Nelson Mandela at Serowe Kgotla, 6 September 1995, ANC Documents: see http://www.anc.org.za/ancdocs/index.html

33. Hatch, *Africa Emergent*, p. 132.

34. Foreword by Nyerere, February 1980, in Seretse Khama, *From the Frontline*, pp. ix–xiv.

35. Mandela to Masire, n.d. [July 1980], ANC, Oliver Tambo Papers.

36. Speech by Nelson Mandela at Serowe Kgotla, 6 September 1995, ANC Documents.

37. Quoted in Robins, *White Queen*, p. 62.

38. John and Esme Goode to author, 29 March 2004.

39. ibid.

40. *Botswana Daily News*, 26 July 1980.

41. ibid., 14 July 1980, 16 July 1980, 17 July 1980, 26 July 1980; *Daily News* Special: 'In Memory Sir Seretse Khama', 10 July 1981.

42. *The Times*, 16 July 1980.

43. John and Esme Goode to author, 29 March 2004.

44. *Saga Magazine*, June 1991.

45. 'African Unity', statement at meeting of the OAU, Tunis, 13–15 June 1994, in Asmal, Chidester and James (eds), *Nelson Mandela in his Own Words*, pp. 533–4.

46. Speech by Mr Nelson Mandela on the occasion of the award of the

Sir Seretse Khama Southern African Development Community medal, in Windhoek, Namibia, 6 August 2000, SADC Library.

47. Sir Ketumile Masire to author, 19 November 2004.

48. ibid.

49. Speech by Sir Seretse Khama at State Banquet, Blantyre, 5 July 1967, in set of speeches made during the First Anniversary of the Republic of Malawi, p. 10, BECM.

List of Archive Repositories

BOTSWANA

Botswana National Archives and Records Services (BNARS)
Gaborone
Khama Family Papers
Held privately by the Khama Family
Khama III Memorial Museum (KIII)
Serowe
SADC (Southern African Development Community) Secretariat Library
Gaborone

CANADA

Department of Foreign Affairs and International Trade (CAN:CER)
Ottawa.
National Archives Canada (NAC)
Ottawa

SOUTH AFRICA

African National Congress Archieves (ANC)
University of Fort Hare Library
Alice
Central Records Office, University of the Witwatersrand (CROUW)
Johannesburg
National Archives of South Africa (NASA)
Pretoria

The Nelson Mandela Centre of Memory and Commemoration Project
Johannesburg
William Cullen Library, University of the Witwatersrand (WCLUW)
Johannesburg

UNITED KINGDOM

Balliol College, Archives and Manuscripts
Oxford University
Bodleian Library of Commonwealth and African Studies (BLCAS), Rhodes
House
Oxford University
Bodleian Library, Department of Special Collections and Western Manuscripts
Oxford University
British Empire and Commonwealth Museum (BECM)
Bristol
British Library, Oriental and India Office Collections (OIOC)
London
Churchill Archives Centre (CHUR)
Churchill College, Cambridge
Durham University Library, Archives and Special Collections (DUL)
Durham
The Inner Temple Archives
Inner Temple, London
Institute of Commonwealth Studies, Archives and Special Collections (ICwS)
School of Advanced Study, University of London
Labour History Archive and Study Centre, People's History Museum
(LHASC)
Manchester
The National Archives of the UK (TNA): Public Record Office (PRO)
Kew, London
Royal Archives (RA)
Windsor Castle
School of Oriental and African Studies, Archives and Manuscripts (SOAS)
University of London
Sussex University Library Special Collections (SUL UK)
Brighton

USA

Harry S. Truman Library (Truman Library)
Independence, Missouri
National Archives and Records Administration of the United States of America (NARA)
Washington, DC
The New York Public Library, The Schomburg Center for Research in Black Culture
New York, NY
Syracuse University Library, Special Collections Research Center (SUL US)
Syracuse, NY

Select Bibliography

Abrams, Mark, *The Population of Great Britain. Current Trends and Future Problems* (London, George Allen & Unwin, 1945).

Adi, Hakim, *West Africans in Britain 1900–1960* (London, Lawrence & Wishart, 1998).

Ajayi, J. F. Ade and Peel, J. D. Y., *People and Empires in African History. Essays in Memory of Michael Crowder* (Harlow, Longman, 1992).

Akinsemoyin, Kunle, 'Tragedy of Mixed Marriages', *West African Review* (October 1949): 1125.

Anderson, David, *Histories of the Hanged. Britain's Dirty War in Kenya and the End of the Empire* (London, Weidenfeld & Nicolson, 2005).

Appiah, Joseph, *Joe Appiah: The Autobiography of an African Patriot* (New York, Praeger, 1990).

Attlee, Clement R., *As It Happened* (London, William Heinemann, 1954).

Bagnall, Sheila, *Sheila Bagnall's Letters from Botswana*, ed. Sandy Grant (Odi, Botswana, Leitlho Publications, 2001).

Banton, M. P., *The Coloured Quarter: Negro Immigrants in an English City* (London, Jonathan Cape, 1955).

Benn, Tony, *Conflicts of Interest. Diaries 1977–80*, ed. Ruth Winstone (London, Hutchinson, 1990).

——, *Years of Hope: Diaries, Letters and Papers 1940–1962* (London, Arrow, 1994).

Benson, Mary, *Tshekedi Khama* (London, Faber & Faber, 1960).

——, *Nelson Mandela. The Man and the Movement* (1986; rpt London, Penguin, 1994).

——, *A Far Cry. The Making of a South African* (1989; rpt Harmondsworth, Penguin, 1990).

Bent, R. A. R., *Ten Thousand Men of Africa. The Story of the Bechuanaland Pioneers and Gunners 1941–1946*, with a Foreword by Sir Evelyn Baring (London, HMSO, 1952).

Benton, Jill, *Naomi Mitchison. A Century of Experiment in Life and Letters* (London, Pandora, 1990).

Berridge, G. R., *South Africa, the Colonial Powers and 'African Defence'. The Rise and Fall of the White Entente, 1948–60* (London, St Martins Press, 1992).

Boahen, A. Adu, *African Perspectives on Colonialism* (Baltimore, MD, Johns Hopkins University Press, 1987).

Borstelmann, Thomas, *Apartheid's Reluctant Uncle. The United States and Southern Africa in the Early Cold War* (Oxford, Oxford University Press, 1993).

Botswana. The Story of Mineworkers in an Independent African Country. Workers of the World Series Number 1. International Labour Research and Information Group (University of Cape Town, Cape Town, 1984).

Bourke-White, Margaret, *Portrait of Myself* (London, Collins, 1964).

Braithwaite, Lloyd, *Colonial West Indian Students in Britain* (Kingston, Jamaica, University of the West Indies Press 2001).

Brockway, Fenner, *African Journeys* (London, Victor Gollancz, 1955).

——, *Outside the Right* (London, George Allen & Unwin, 1963).

——, *Towards Tomorrow* (London, Rupert Hart-Davis, 1977).

——, *98 Not Out* (London, Quartet Books, 1986).

Burns, Sir Alan, *Colour Prejudice* (London, Allen & Unwin, 1948).

Burridge, Trevor, *Clement Attlee. A Political Biography* (London, Jonathan Cape, 1985).

Burt, Robert A., 'Colour Prejudice in Great Britain', Senior Thesis for BA at Princeton University, 22 April 1960.

Burya, Gabriel Lohodedoo, *Nelson Mandela and the Wind of Change* (Zaria, Nigeria, Ahmadu Bello University Press, 1993).

Callinicos, Luli, *Oliver Tambo. Beyond the Engeli Mountains* (Claremont, South Africa, David Philip, 2004).

Carter, Gwendolen M., *The Politics of Inequality. South Africa since 1948* (London, Thames & Hudson, 1958).

Chabal, Patrick, *Power in Africa* (London, Macmillan, 1992).

Chirenje, J. Mutero, *Chief Kgama and his Times, c. 1835–1923. The Story of a Southern African Ruler* (London, Rex Collings, 1978).

Cockett, Richard, *David Astor and the Observer* (London, André Deutsch, 1991).

Cocks, Michael, *Labour and the Benn Factor* (London, Macdonald, 1989).

Colclough, Christopher and McCarthy, Stephen, *The Political Economy of Botswana – a Study of Growth and Distribution* (Oxford, Oxford University Press, 1980).

Collins, Canon L. John, *Faith Under Fire* (London, Leslie Frewin, 1966).

Collins, Diana, *Partners in Protest. Life with Canon Collins* (London, Victor Gollancz, 1992).

Constantine, Learie, *Colour Bar* (London, Stanley Paul & Co., 1954).

——, Lord (ed.), *Living in Britain* (London, Virtue & Company, 1970).

Cooke, John, *One White Man in Black Africa. From Kilimanjaro to the Kalahari 1951–1991* (Thornhill, Tynron Press, 1991).

Crowder, Michael, *The Flogging of Phineas McIntosh: A Tale of Colonial Folly and Injustice, Bechuanaland 1933* (New Haven, Conn., Yale University Press, 1988).

Dachs, Anthony J., *Khama of Botswana* (London, Heinemann, 1971).

Dahl, Hans-Erik, *Botswana's First Independence Decade 1966–1976. A Survey.* (Bergen, University of Bergen, 1978).

Dale, Richard, *Botswana's Search for Autonomy in Southern Africa* (Westport, Conn., Greenwood Press, 1995).

Darwin, John, *The End of the British Empire. The Historical Debate* (London, Basil Blackwell, 1991).

Davidson, Basil, *Report on Southern Africa* (London, Jonathan Cape, 1952).

——, *The Black Man's Burden* (London, J. Currey, 1992).

Daymond, Margaret J. et al. (eds), *Women Writing Africa*, vol. 1, *The Southern Region*, Women Writing Africa Project (New York, Feminist Press at the City University of New York, 2003).

Dickie, John, *The Uncommon Commoner. A Study of Sir Alec Douglas-Home* (London, Pall Mall Press, 1964).

Donoughue, Bernard and Jones, G. W., *Herbert Morrison. Portrait of a Politician* (1973; rpt London, Phoenix Press, 2001).

Douglas-Home, Charles, *Evelyn Baring: The Last Proconsul* (London, Collins, 1978).

Drachler, Jacob (ed.), *African Heritage. An Anthology of Black African Personality and Culture* (London, Collier Books, 1964).

Dubbeld, G., *Seretse Khama* (Cape Town, Longman, Maskew Miller, 1992) (for schoolchildren).

Dutfield, M., *A Marriage of Inconvenience. The Persecution of Seretse and Ruth Khama* (London, Unwin Hyman, 1990).

Edge, W. A., and Lekorwe, M. H. (eds), *Botswana: Politics and Society* (Pretoria, J. L. van Schaik, 1998).

Egeland, Leif, *Bridges of Understanding. A Personal Record in Teaching, Law, Politics and Diplomacy* (Cape Town and Pretoria, Human & Rousseau, 1977).

Elkins, Caroline, *Britain's Gulag. The Brutal End of Empire in Kenya* (London, Jonathan Cape, 2005).

Empire Club of Canada Speeches 1958–1959, The, (Toronto, Empire Club Foundation, 1959).

Eugenics Society, *Aims and Objects of the Eugenics Society* (London, 1944).

Evans, Harold, *Downing Street Diary. The Macmillan Years 1957–1963* (London, Hodder & Stoughton, 1981).

Fairlie, Michael, *No Time Like the Past* (Edinburgh, Pentland Press, 1992).

Fawcus, Peter and Tilbury, Alan, *Botswana. The Road to Independence* (Gaborone, Pula Press, 2000).

Feit, Edward, *African Opposition in South Africa. The Failure of Passive Resistance* (Stanford, CA, Hoover Institution on War, Revolution and Peace, 1967).

Ferguson, Niall, *Empire. How Britain Made the Modern World* (London, Penguin, 2003).

First, Ruth, *Black Gold. The Mozambican Miner, Proletarian and Peasant* (Sussex, Harvester Press, 1983).

Fisher, Nigel, *Harold Macmillan* (London, Weidenfeld & Nicolson, 1982).

Flint, John, 'Scandal at the Bristol Hotel: Some Thoughts on Racial Discrimination in Britain and West Africa and its Relationship to the Planning of Decolonisation, 1939–47', *Journal of Imperial and Commonwealth History*, XII (1) (October, 1983): 74–93.

Foot, Michael, *Aneurin Bevan. Volume Two: 1945–1960* (London, Davis-Poynter, 1973).

[Fort Hare], *A Short Pictorial History of the University College of Fort Hare 1916–1959* (Alice, Lovedale Press, 1961).

Frank, Lawrence Peter, 'Khama and Jonathan: A Study of Authority and Leadership in Southern Africa', PhD thesis, Columbia University, 1974.

——, 'Khama and Jonathan: Leadership Strategies in Contemporary Southern Africa', *Journal of Developing Areas*, 15 (January 1981): 173–98.

Freud, Clement, *Freud Ego* (London, BBC, 2001).

Gabatshwane, S. M., *Introduction to the Bechuanaland Protectorate History and Administration* (Kanye, 1957).

——, *Seretse Khama and Botswana* (Kanye, Bechuanaland Press, pub. by J. G. Mmusi and S. M. Gabatshwane, 1966).

Gaitskell, Hugh, *Diary of Hugh Gaitskell*, ed. Philip M. Williams (London, Jonathan Cape, 1983).

Gann, L. H., and Gelfand, M., *Huggins of Rhodesia. The Man and His Country* (London, George Allen & Unwin, 1964).

Gann, L. H., and Duignan, Peter (eds), *Colonialism in Africa 1870–1960*.

Vol. 2: *The History and Politics of Colonialism 1914–1960* (Cambridge, Cambridge University Press, 1970).

Garner, Joe, *The Commonwealth Office 1925–68* (London, Heinemann, 1978).

Gelfand, Michael and Ritchken, Joseph, *The Rt Hon Godfrey Martin Huggins, First Viscount Malvern of Rhodesia and Bexley. His Life and Work* (*Central African Journal of Medicine*, Salisbury, Rhodesia (n.d.)).

Gish, Steven, *Alfred B. Xuma. African, American, South African* (Houndmills, Macmillan, 2000).

Goldsworthy, David, *Colonial Issues in British Politics 1945–1961. From 'Colonial Development' to 'Wind of Change'* (Oxford, Clarendon Press, 1971).

Gordon Walker, Patrick, *The Commonwealth* (London, Martin, Secker & Warburg, 1962).

——, *Patrick Gordon Walker. Political Diaries 1932–1971*, ed. Robert Pearce (London, Historians Press, 1991).

Gowing, Margaret, *Reflections on Atomic Energy History* (The Rede Lecture 1978) (Cambridge, Cambridge University Press, 1978).

——, *The Origins of Britain's Status as a Nuclear Power* (lecture delivered at St Antony's College, Oxford, 4 November 1987) (Oxford Project for Peace Studies, 1988).

Grant, Sandy, *Mochudi around the Time of Independence* (Mochudi, Phuthadikobo Museum, 2002).

Hailey, William Malcolm, Lord, *Native Administration in the British African Territories*, part V (London, Commonwealth Relations Office, 1953).

——, *An African Survey* (London, Oxford University Press, 1956).

Hall, Richard, *The High Price of Principles. Kaunda and the White South* (London, Hodder & Stoughton, 1969).

Halpern, Jack, *South Africa's Hostages: Basutoland, Bechuanaland and Swaziland* (Harmondsworth, Penguin, 1965).

Hatch, John, *New from Africa* (London, Dennis Dobson, 1956).

——, *A History of Postwar Africa* (London, Andre Deutsch, 1965).

——, *Africa – The Rebirth of Self-rule* (London, Oxford University Press, 1971).

——, *Africa Emergent* (London, Secker & Warburg, 1974).

Hayford, J. E. S., 'White Brides and Black Husbands', *West African Review* (September 1949): 1009.

Head, Bessie, *A Question of Power* (London, Davis–Poynter, 1973).

——, *Serowe: Village of the Rainwind* (London, Heinemann, 1981).

——, A Gesture of Belonging. Letters from Bessie Head 1965–1979, ed. Randolph Vigne (Portsmouth, NH, Heinemann, 1991).

Henderson, Ian (ed), Man of Christian Action. Canon John Collins – the Man and his Work (Guildford and London, Lutterworth Press, 1976).

Hennessy, Peter, Never Again. Britain 1945–51 (London, Jonathan Cape, 1992).

Holland, R. F., European Decolonization 1918–1981: An Introductory Survey (London, Macmillan, 1985).

——, The Pursuit of Greatness. Britain and the World Role, 1900–1970 (London, Fontana Press, 1991).

Home, Alec Douglas-Home, Lord, The Way the Wind Blows, An Autobiography (London, Collins, 1976).

Hooker, James R., Black Revolutionary. George Padmore's Path from Communism to Pan-Africanism (London, Pall Mall Press, 1967).

Horne, Alistair, Macmillan 1957–1986, Volume II of the Official Biography (London, Macmillan, 1989).

Horne, Gerald, Black and Red, W. E. B. Du Bois and the Afro-American Response to the Cold War, 1944–63 (Albany, State University of New York Press, 1986).

Houghton, D. Hobart, The Tomlinson Report. A Summary of the Findings and Recommendations in the Tomlinson Report (Johannesburg, South African Institute of Race Relations, 1956).

Howat, Gerald, Learie Constantine (London, George Allen & Unwin, 1975).

Howe, Stephen, Anti-Colonialism in British Politics: the Left and the End of Empire (Oxford, Oxford University Press, 1993).

Huddleston, Trevor, Naught for Your Comfort (London, Collins, 1956).

Hyam, Ronald, 'The Political Consequences of Seretse Khama: Britain, the Bangwato and South Africa', Historical Journal 29(4) (1986): 921–47.

——, and Henshaw, Peter, The Lion and the Springbok: Britain and South Africa since the Boer War (Cambridge, Cambridge University Press, 2003).

Ismay, Hastings Lionel, Lord, The Memoirs of General the Lord Ismay (London, Heineman, 1960).

Itzkin, Eric, Gandhi's Johannesburg. Birthplace of Satyagraha (Johannesburg, Witwatersrand University Press in association with Museum Africa, 2000).

Jackson, Ashley, Botswana 1939–1944. An African Country at War (Oxford, Clarendon Press, 1999).

Jackson, Robert J., Rebels and Whips. An Analysis of Dissension, Discipline and Cohesion in British Political Parties (London, Macmillan, 1968).

Juckes, Tim J., *Opposition in South Africa. The Leadership of Z. K. Matthews, Nelson Mandela, and Stephen Biko* (London, Praeger, 1995).

Kaunda, Kenneth D., *Zambia Shall Be Free. An Autobiography* (London, Heinemann, 1962).

Kavuma, Paulo, *Crisis in Buganda 1953–55. The Story of the Exile and Return of the Kabaka, Mutesa II* (London, Rex Collings, 1979).

Keith, J. L., 'African Students in Great Britain', *African Affairs* (April 1946): 65–72.

Keitseng, Fish, *Comrade Fish: Memories of a Motswana in the ANC Underground*, compiled by Barry Morton and Jeff Ramsay (Gaborone, Pula Press, 1999).

Kennedy, Raymond, 'Colonial Crisis and the Future', in Ralph Linton (ed.), *The Science of Man in the World Crisis* (New York, Columbia University Press, 1945).

Kerr, Alexander, *Fort Hare 1915–48. The Evolution of an African College* (London, C. Hurst and Co., 1968).

Khama, Seretse, *From the Frontline. Speeches of Sir Seretse Khama*, with a foreword by President Julius Nyerere, ed. Gwendolen M. Carter and E. Philip Morgan (London, Rex Collings, 1980).

Khama, Tshekedi, *Bechuanaland and South Africa* (London, Africa Bureau, 1955).

Khama, Tshekedi (ed.), *Bechuanaland. A General Survey* (Johannesburg, South African Institute for Race Relations, 1957).

Killingray, David (ed.), *Africans in Britain* (London, Frank Cass, 1994).

Kirk-Greene, Anthony, 'Doubly Elite: African Rhodes Scholars', in David Killingray (ed.), *Africans in Britain* (London, Frank Cass, 1994).

Kuper, Hilda, *Sobhuza II. Ngwenyama and King of Swaziland* (London, Duckworth, 1978).

Kuper, Leo, *Passive Resistance in South Africa* (London, Jonathan Cape, 1956).

Lake, Anthony, *The 'Tar Baby' Option: American Policy Toward Southern Rhodesia* (New York, Columbia University Press, 1976).

Lamb, Richard, *The Macmillan Years, 1957–1963. The Emerging Truth* (London, John Murray, 1995).

Lee, Jennie, *My Life with Nye* (London, Jonathan Cape, 1980).

Legum, Colin, *Southern Africa. The Secret Diplomacy of Détente: South Africa at the Cross Roads* (London, Rex Collings, 1975).

Lewis, John, *Lord Hailsham. A Life* (London, Jonathan Cape, 1997).

Lewis, W. Arthur, Scott, Michael, Wright, Martin and Legum, Colin, *Attitude to Africa* (Harmondsworth, Penguin, 1951).

Luckhardt, Ken, and Wall, Brenda, *Organize or Starve! The History of the South African Congress of Trade Unions* (London, Lawrence & Wishart, 1980).

Luthuli, Albert, *Let My People Go* (1962; rpt Glasgow, Fontana Books, 1987).

McClintock, Anne, *Imperial Leather. Race, Gender and Sexuality in the Colonial Contest* (London, Routledge, 1995).

Mace, Rodney, *Trafalgar Square. Emblem of Empire* (London, Lawrence & Wishart, 1976).

MacKenzie, John M., *Propaganda and Empire. The Manipulation of British Public Opinion 1880–1960* (Manchester, Manchester University Press, 1984).

Macmillan, Harold, *Tides of Fortune 1945–55* (London, Macmillan, 1969).

Macmillan, Hugh and Marks, Shula (eds), *Africa and Empire. W. M. Macmillan, Historian and Social Critic* (London, Temple Smith/Institute of Commonwealth Studies, 1989).

Majeke, Nosipho, *The Role of the Missionaries in Conquest* (Johannesburg, Society of Young Africa, 1952).

Mandela, Nelson, *Nelson Mandela Speeches 1990. 'Intensify the Struggle to Abolish Apartheid'*, ed. Greg McCarton (New York, Pathfinder Press, 1990).

——, *Long Walk to Freedom* (London, Abacus, 1994).

——, *Nelson Mandela in His Own Words, from Freedom to the Future. Tributes and Speeches*, ed. Kader Asmal, David Chidester and Wilmot James (London, Little, Brown, 2003).

Marks, Shula and Trapido, Stanley (eds), *The Politics of Race, Class and Nationalism in Twentieth-Century South Africa* (London, Longman, 1987).

Marwick, Arthur, *The Home Front. The British and the Second World War* (London, Thames & Hudson, 1976).

Matthews, Frieda, *Remembrances* (Cape Town, Mayibuye Books, 1995).

Matthews, Z. K., *Freedom for My People. The Autobiography of Z. K. Matthews: Southern Africa 1901 to 1968*, ed. with a memoir by Monica Wilson (London, Rex Collings in association with David Philip, Cape Town, 1981).

Maylam, P., *Rhodes, the Tswana, and the British: Colonialism, Collaboration, and Conflict in the Bechuanaland Protectorate, 1885–1899* (Westport, Conn., Greenwood Press, 1980).

Meer, Fatima, *Higher than Hope. A Biography of Nelson Mandela* (1988; rpt. Harmondsworth, Penguin, 1990).

Menon, K. N., *Passive Resistance in South Africa* (New Delhi, K. N. Menon, 1952).

Mitchison, Naomi, *Return to the Fairy Hill* (London, Heinemann, 1966).

Mockford, Julian, *Seretse Khama and the Bamangwato* (London, Staples Press, 1950).

Monks, Noel, *Eyewitness* (London, Frederick Muller, n.d. [1956]).

Monsarrat, Nicholas, *Life is a Four-Letter Word*. Volume II: *Breaking Out* (London, Cassell, 1970).

Morgan, Kenneth O., *Labour in Power 1945–51* (Oxford, Clarendon Press, 1984).

Morgan, Philip D. and Hawkins, Sean (eds), *Black Experience and the Empire*, Oxford History of the British Empire Companion Series (Oxford, Oxford University Press, 2004).

Morton, Fred and Ramsay, Jeff, *The Birth of Botswana* (Botswana, Longman, 1987).

—— and ——, *The Making of a President. Sir Ketumile Masire's Early Years* (Gaborone, Pula Press, 1994).

Moss, Norman, *The Politics of Uranium* (London, André Deutsch, 1981).

Mpho, Motsamai, *The Autobiography of Motsamai Mpho*, written by Wayne Edge (Gaborone, Lepopo Publications, 1996).

Munger, Edwin, *Bechuanaland: Pan-African Outpost or Bantu Homeland?* (London, Oxford University Press, 1965).

Murray-Brown, Jeremy, *Kenyatta* (London, Fontana/Collins, 1972).

Mutibwa, Phares, *Uganda since Independence. A Story of Unfulfilled Hopes* (London, Hurst & Co., 1992).

Mwangilwa, Goodwin B., *Harry Mwaanga Nkumbula: a Biography of the Old Lion of Zambia* (Lusaka, Multimedia Publications, 1982).

Nasson, Bill, *Britannia's Empire. Making a British World* (Stroud, Tempus Publishing, 2004).

Nkomo, Joshua, *Nkomo. The Story of My Life* (London, Methuen, 1983).

Nkrumah, Kwame, *The Autobiography of Kwame Nkrumah* (Edinburgh, Thomas Nelson & Sons, 1959).

Nwauwa, Apollos O., *Imperialism, Academe and Nationalism. Britain and University Education for Africans 1860–1960* (London, Frank Cass, 1997).

Olusanya, G. O., *The West African Students' Union and the Politics of Decolonization 1925–1958* (Ibadan, Daystar Press, 1982).

Owen, Nicholas, 'Critics of Empire in Britain', in Judith M. Brown and W. M. Roger Louis (eds), *The Oxford History of the British Empire. The Twentieth Century* (Oxford, Oxford University Press, 1999).

——, *Time to Declare* (London, Penguin, 1991).

Padmore, George (ed.), *Colonial and . . . Coloured Unity. A Programme of Action. History of the Pan-African Congress* (Manchester, Pan-African Federation, 1947; 2nd edition, with additional material, London, Hammersmith Books, 1963).

Parson, Jack, *Botswana. Liberal Democracy and the Labour Reserve in Southern Africa* (London, Gower, 1984).

Parsons, Neil, 'The Serowe Kgotla Riot of 1952: Popular Opposition to Tshekedi Khama and Colonial Rule in Botswana', *Societies of Southern Africa in the 19th and 20th Centuries* (London, Institute of Commonwealth Studies), 16 (1991): 24–36.

——, 'The Idea of Democracy and the Emergence of an Educated Elite in Botswana, 1931–1960', in *Botswana – Education, Culture and Politics*, Proceedings of a conference held in the Centre of African Studies, University of Edinburgh, 15–16 December 1988 (Centre of African Studies, University of Edinburgh/National Institute of Development, Research and Documentation, University of Botswana, n.d.).

——, *King Khama, Emperor Joe and the Great White Queen: Victorian Britain through African eyes* (Chicago, University of Chicago Press, 1998).

Parsons, Neil, Henderson, Willie and Tlou, Thomas, *Seretse Khama 1921–1980* (Botswana Society 1995; rpt Braamfontein, South Africa, 1997).

Parsons, Q. N. [Neil], *The Word of Khama* (Lusaka, Historical Association of Zambia, 1972).

——, *The High Commission Territories, 1909–1964. A Bibliography* (Kwaluseni, University of Botswana, Lesotho and Swaziland, 1976).

Pela, W. S., 'A Tribal Chief Gets Married', *Common Sense* (Johannesburg, June 1949).

Peters, Pauline E., *Dividing the Commons. Politics, Policy and Culture in Botswana* (Charlottesville and London, University Press of Virginia, 1994).

Phillips, Caryl, *A New World Order. Selected Essays* (London, Secker & Warburg, 2001).

Phillips, Mike and Phillips, Trevor, *Windrush. The Irresistible Rise of Multiracial Britain* (1998; rpt London, HarperCollins, 1999).

Picard, Louis A., *The Evolution of Modern Botswana* (London, Rex Collings, 1985).

Pilkington, Roger, *Males and Females* (London, Delisle, 1948).

——, *Biology, Man and God* (London, Lutterworth Press, 1951).

Plaatje, Solomon T., *Sechuana Proverbs with Literal Translations and their European Equivalents* (London, Kegan Paul, Trench, Trubner & Co, 1916).

Political and Economic Planning, *Colonial Students in Britain* (London, PEP, June 1955).

Pottle, Mark (ed.), *Daring to Hope. The Diaries and Letters of Violet Bonham Carter 1946–1969* (London, Weidenfeld & Nicolson, 2000).

Prain, Sir Ronald, *Reflections on an Era. Fifty Years of Mining in Changing Africa* (Letchworth, Metal Bulletin Books Ltd, 1981).

Procter, James, *Writing Black Britain 1948–1998. An Interdisciplinary Anthology* (Manchester, Manchester University Press, 2000).

Qunta, Christine N. (ed.), *Women in Southern Africa* (Johannesburg, Skotaville Publishers, 1987).

Rathbone, Richard, *Nkrumah and the Chiefs. The Politics of Chieftaincy in Ghana 1951–60* (Oxford, James Currey, 2000).

Redfern, John, *Ruth and Seretse. 'A Very Disreputable Transaction'* (London, Victor Gollancz, 1955).

Rey, Charles, *Monarch of All I Survey. Bechuanaland Diaries 1929–37*, eds Neil Parsons and Michael Crowder (London, James Currey, 1988).

Richmond, Anthony H., *The Colour Problem. A Study of Racial Relations* (Harmondsworth, Penguin Books, 1955).

Rider, Clare, 'The "Unfortunate Marriage" of Sereste Khama', *The Inner Temple Yearbook 2002/2003* (London, Inner Temple, 2003).

Robins, Eric, *White Queen in Africa* (London, Robert Hale, 1967).

Rosenthal, Jane, *Dora Tamana* (Series: *They Fought for Freedom*) (Cape Town, Longman, 1995).

Russell, Margo and Russell, Martin, *Afrikaners of the Kalahari, White Minority in a Black State* (Cambridge, Cambridge University Press, 1979).

Saayman, Willem A., *A Man with a Shadow. The Life and Times of Professor Z. K. Matthews* (Pretoria, University of South Africa Press, 1996).

Sadiq Ali, Shanti, *Gandhi and South Africa* (Delhi, Hind Pocket Books, 1994).

Samatar, Abdi Ismail, *An African Miracle. State and Class Leadership and Colonial Legacy in Botswana Development* (Portsmouth, NH, Heinemann, 1999).

Sampson, Anthony, *Mandela. The Authorized Biography* (London, HarperCollins, 1999).

Schapera, Isaac, *A Handbook of Tswana Law and Custom* (London, Oxford University Press for the International Institute of African Languages and Culture, 1938; 2nd edition 1955, rpt. 1977).

——, *Married Life in an African Tribe* (London, Faber & Faber, 1940).

——, *Migrant Labour and Tribal Life: A Study of Conditions in the Bechuanaland Protectorate* (London, Oxford University Press, 1947).

——, *Rainmaking Rites in Tswana Tribes* (Cambridge, African Studies Centre, 1971).

——, *Tribal Innovators: Tswana Chiefs and Social Change 1795–1940* (London, Athlone Press, 1970).

——, *The Tswana* (1953; rpt London, Kegan Paul International, 1991).

Schire, Robert (ed.), *South Africa. Public Policy Perspectives* (Cape Town, Juta & Co. Ltd., 1982).

Scott, James C., *Weapons of the Weak. Everyday Forms of Peasant Resistance* (New Haven, Conn., Yale University Press, 1985).

Scott, Michael, *A Time to Speak* (London, Faber & Faber, 1958).

Seager, Alan, *The Shadow of a Great Rock* (Flintshire, I*D Books, 2004).

Segal, Ronald, *Into Exile* (London, Jonathan Cape, 1963).

Seretse, Gasebalwe, *Tshekedi Khama: The Master Whose Dogs Barked At (A Critical Look at Ngwato Politics)* (Gaborone, Gasebalwe Seretse, 2004).

Sharp, Gene, *Bechuanaland. What Seretse's Exile Means*, with a Foreword by Seretse Khama (London, Movement for Colonial Freedom and Peace News, n.d. [1956]).

Sillery, A., *Sechele. The Story of an African Chief* (Oxford, George Ronald, 1954).

——, *Founding a Protectorate* (The Hague, Mouton, 1965).

——, *Botswana: a Short Political History* (London, Methuen, 1974).

Sisulu, Elinor, *Walter and Albertina Sisulu. In Our Lifetime* (2002; rpt London, Abacus, 2003).

Smith, Alison and Bull, Mary (eds), *Margery Perham and British Rule in Africa* (London, Frank Cass, 1991).

Smith, Graham, *When Jim Crow Met John Bull. Black American Soldiers in World War II Britain* (London, I. B. Tauris, 1987).

South African Institute of Race Relations, *Bechuanaland. A General Survey* (Johannesburg, 1957).

Stedman, Stephen John (ed.), *Botswana. The Political Economy of Democratic Development* (Boulder and London, Lynne Rienner Publishers, 1993).

Stewart, Dianne, *Lilian Ngoyi* (Series: *They Fought for Freedom*) (Cape Town, Longman, 1996).

Stonehouse, John, *Prohibited Immigrant* (London, Bodley Head, 1960).

——, *Death of an Idealist* (London, W. H. Allen, 1975).

Thompson, Leonard, *The Political Mythology of Apartheid* (New Haven, Conn., Yale University Press, 1985).

Thorpe, D. R., *Alec Douglas-Home* (London, Sinclair-Stevenson, 1996).

Timothy, Bankole, *Kwame Nkrumah from Cradle to Grave* (Dorchester, Gavin Press, 1981).

Tlou, Thomas and Campbell, Alec, *History of Botswana* (Gaborone, Macmillan Botswana, 1984).

Tyler, Humphrey, *Life in the Time of Sharpeville* (Cape Town, Kwela Books, 1995).

Volz, Stephen, *Chief of a Heathen Town. Kgosi Sechele and the Arrival of Christianity among the Tswana* (African Studies Program, University of Wisconsin, Madison, 2001).

wa Kinyatti, Maina (ed.), *Kenya's Freedom Struggle. The Dedan Kimathi Papers*. Foreword by Ngugi wa Thiong'o (London, Zed Books, 1987).

Walker, Cherryl, *Women and Resistance in South Africa* (London, Onyx Press, 1982).

Wild, Percy Turner, *Bwana Polish (Under Three Flags)* (Braunton, Merlin Books Ltd, 1993).

Wingate, Ronald, *Lord Ismay: a Biography* (London: Hutchinson, 1970).

Winks, Robin W. (ed.), *The Oxford History of the British Empire*, vol. V, *Historiography* (Oxford, Oxford University Press, 1999).

Winstanley, George, *Under Two Flags in Africa. Recollections of a British Administrator in Bechuanaland and Botswana 1954–1972* (Kelvedon, Colchester, Blackwater Books, 2000).

Woods, Eric (Timber), *From Flying Boats to Flying Jets. Flying in the Formative Years of BOAC 1946–1972* (Shrewsbury, Airlife Publishing, 1997).

The World Bank, *World Development Report 2000/2001* (Oxford, Oxford University Press, 2000).

Wylie, Diana, *A Little God. The Twilight of Patriarchy in a Southern African Chiefdom* (Hanover, Wesleyan University Press, 1990).

Young, Robert J. C., *Colonial Desire. Hybridity in Theory, Culture and Race* (London, Routledge, 1995).

Zaffiro, James J., *From Police Network to Station of the Nation: A Political History of Broadcasting in Botswana 1927–1991* (Gaborone, Botswana Society, 1991).

Zweiniger-Bargielowska, Ina, *Austerity in Britain. Rationing, Controls, and Consumption, 1939–1955* (Oxford, Oxford University Press, 2000).

Index